THE SOCIAL WORK INTERVIEW

Fourth Edition

THE SOCIAL WORK INTERVIEW

A Guide for Human Service Professionals

Alfred Kadushin
Goldie Kadushin

Fourth Edition

Columbia University Press   New York

Columbia University Press
Publishers Since 1893
New York   Chichester, West Sussex
Copyright © 1997 Columbia University Press
All rights reserved

Library of Congress Cataloging-in-Publication Data
Kadushin, Alfred.
    The social work interview: a guide for human service
professionals / Alfred Kadushin, Goldie Kadushin. — 4th ed.
        p.   cm.
    Includes bibliographical references and index.
    ISBN 0-231-09658-5. — ISBN 0-231-09659-3 (pbk.)
    1. Interviewing. 2. Social service. I. Kadushin, Goldie.
II. Title.
HV43.K26   1997
        361.3'22—dc20   96-38296
  ∞   CIP

Printed in the United States of America

c 10 9 8 7 6 5 4 3 2
p 10 9 8 7 6

Contents

Introduction   xiii

I. **General Orientation and
Basic Concepts of Interviewing and Communication**   I

  1. **The Interview in Social Work**   3

    Defining the Interview and Distinguishing an Interview
        from a Conversation   4
    Defining the Social Work Interview   II
    Purposes of Social Work Interviews   14
      Information-Gathering or Social Study Interviews   15
      Assessment, Decision-Making Interviews   16
      Therapeutic Interviews   16
    Universal Aspects of Interviews   17
    Common Features of Social Work Interviews   18
    Alternatives to and Limitations of the Interview   19
      Limitations   19
      Structured Interviews   20
      Computers   21
    Summary: Chapter I   22
    Suggested Readings   24

  2. **The Interview as Communication**   27

    Defining *Communication* and Its Essential Elements   27
    Metacommunication   29

Sequential Steps in the Process of Communication   30
    Encoding by the Interviewer   30
    Transmitting   31
    Decoding by the Interviewee   31
    Encoding by Interviewee   33
Understanding the Message   36
    Words and Meanings   39
    Jargon and Miscommunication   40
    Immediacy and Concreteness in Communication   41
Feedback   43
Summary: Chapter 2   46
Suggested Readings   46

3. **Listening: A Basic Communication Skill**   49

Hearing Versus Listening   49
Conditions for Good Listening   50
Relating Listening to the Interview   51
Social Listening Versus Interview Listening   52
The Value of Knowledge for Listening   56
Guidelines for Listening   57
Summary: Chapter 3   60
Suggested Readings   61

II. **Sequential Phases in the Interview Process
and Associated Techniques**   63

4. **Introductory Phase**   65

Interviewee's Background—What the Interviewee Brings   66
Interviewer's Background—What the Interviewer Brings   67
Deciding to Become a Social Work Interviewee   69
The Path to the Agency—Selecting and Locating an Agency   69
    Approaching the Interview   71
    Scheduling   72
    Reception   73
    Waiting   74
Interviewers' Preparation   75
    Setting   75
    Homework   76
    Direction or Outline   77
    Role Image   79
Nonagency Settings   80
    Interviewee's Home   81

Institutions and Hospitals   85
The Start of the Interview   88
    Preinterview Amenities: Meeting, Greeting, and Seating   88
    The Opening Question   92
    Clarifying the Purpose   93
    Inducting the Interviewee   95
Summary: Chapter 4   96
Suggested Readings   98

5. **Beginning the Interview:
First Phase Objective—Establishing a Relationship**   99

Defining the Relationship   99
Significance of a Positive Relationship   100
Empirical Confirmation of Relationship's Significance   101
Developing a Positive Relationship   103
    Acceptance   104
    Empathic Understanding   108
    Genuineness and Authenticity   111
    Interviewee Self-Determination   113
    Confidentiality   118
    Respect for Clients' Individuality   122
    Interest, Warmth, Trust, Respect   124
Relationships as an Interactional Event   127
Inner Attitudes and Expressed Behaviors   128
Transition from Opening Phase to the Body of the Interview   132
Summary: Chapter 5   133
Suggested Readings   133

6. **Problem Exploration Phase**   135

The Meaning and Sequence of Techniques   135
Attending Behaviors and Minimal Encouragements
    (Expressions of Attention and Interest)   137
Paraphrasing   141
Reflection   144
    Reflection of Content   144
    Reflection of Feeling   145
Summarizing   150
Transitions   152
    Types of Transitions   154
    Making Transitions   155
    Transitional Interruptions   156

Transition Caveats   157
Interviewee-Initiated Transitions   160
Reaching for Feelings   163
  Identifying and Calling Attention to Feelings   163
  Sanctioning Feelings   165
  Using Euphemisms and Indirection   167
  Discouraging Expression of Feelings   168
Summary: Chapter 6   169
Suggested Readings   170

7. **Developmental Phase:**
   Problem-Solving Interventions   173

   Clarification   173
   Interpretation   175
   Confrontation   183
   Self-Disclosure   190
     Objectives of Self-Disclosure   192
     Dangers and Disadvantages   194
   Sharing Information   200

8. **Developmental Phase:**
   More Problem-Solving Interventions   205

   Support and Reassurance   205
   Advice   208
   Silence   213
     Interviewees' Use of Silence   214
     Interviewers' Use of Silence   215
     Ending the Silence   216
   Humor   218
     Caveats Regarding Use of Humor   225
   Figures of Speech   228
   Environmental Modification   228
   Empirical Studies of Interventions Used   229
   Summary: Chapters 7 and 8   232
   Suggested Readings   234

9. **Developmental Phase:**
   Questions and Questioning Techniques   235

   General Classifications: Open and Closed Questions   237
     Advantages of Open-Ended Questions   238

Disadvantages of Open-Ended Questions   239
Closed Questions   241
Other Dimensions   243
Probing Questions   244
Formulation and Phrasing: Some Common Errors   248
The Leading or Suggestive Question   248
The Yes or No Question   252
The Double Question   254
The Garbled Question   255
The "Why" Question   256
Additional Guidelines for Formulating Questions   258
Interviewers' Preparation for Asking Questions   265
Summary: Chapter 9   268

10. **Termination, Recording, and Evaluation**   271

Termination Techniques   272
Summary and Postinterview Conversation   276
Review and Evaluation   279
Note Taking   280
Recording   282
Summary: Chapter 10   283
Suggested Readings   284

III.   **Some Special Problems in Interviewing**   285

11. **Nonverbal Communication**   287

Sources of Nonverbal Communication   289
Chronomics   289
Artifactual Communication   291
Smell   294
Touch   295
Paralinguistics   298
Proxemics   300
Body Language—Kinesics   302
Significance of Nonverbal Communication
for Interviewing   309
Process Considerations   314
Problems in Inferring Meanings   315
Summary: Chapter 11   317
Suggested Readings   319

12. **Cross-Cultural Interviewing**   321

Selective Examples of Cross-Cultural Interviews   322
Race   323
White Interviewer, African-American Interviewee   323
African-American Interviewer, White Interviewee   326
The Aged Client   327
Sexual Orientation   331
Individualizing the Cross-Cultural Client   336
Should Interviewer and Interviewee Be Matched?   337
Research on Matching   339
Defining the Culturally Sensitive Interviewer   345
The Use of Interpreters   348
Interpreting for the Deaf   350
Summary: Chapter 12   351
Suggested Readings   352

13. **Some Problematic Interviews:**
The Involuntary Adult Client and the Sexually Abused Child   355

Involuntary Interviewees   355
Interviewing in Intrafamily Child Sexual Abuse   368
Basic Attitudinal Approach to the Interview   369
General Guidelines   372
Summary: Chapter 13   384
Suggested Readings   385

IV.   **The Essence of the Good Interviewer**   387

14. **The Competent Interviewer**   389

Personality Attributes   389
Need for Knowledge   391
Resolving Antithetical Demands   394
Interviewees' Perceptions of the Good Interviewer   395
Interviewees' Contribution to Interviewer Competence   397
Distinguishing More and Less Competent Interviewers   398
Summary: Chapter 14   403
L'Envoi—   404

Appendix: Transcribed Interview and Critique   407
References   425
Index   447

Introduction

Many people in many different professions conduct interviews. Social workers are only one such group. But for social workers interviewing is a preeminently important activity. In fact, carrying out most of their responsibilities depends on interviewing. Social work interviews differ from those of other professional groups in some crucial ways, reflecting what is unique about social work. This book describes the general art of interviewing as adapted and used by social workers in a social agency setting. Both experienced and inexperienced practitioners, struggling with the recurrent problems of interviewing and seeking specific guidelines and answers, may profit from an explicit examination of the interview. We hope this book will stimulate self-assessment.

A major part of the book is concerned with the techniques of social work interviewing. *Technique* has a bad sound—cold, mechanical, inhuman, manipulative: applicable to things but not to people. The word deserves to be rescued, its image refurbished. Techniques are devices whose application enables us to accomplish our purposes, to carry out our professional responsibilities. They are clear formulations of what we should do in a given situation to offer our service effectively and efficiently.

Technical skill is not antithetical to spontaneity. In fact, it permits a higher form of spontaneity. The skilled interviewer can deliberately violate the techniques as the occasion demands and apply techniques with greater discrimination. Awareness and command of technical knowledge have another advantage. To be technically skilled is to be prepared; to be prepared is to experience less anxiety; less anxiety increases the interviewer's freedom to respond fully to the interviewee.

Competent artistry requires mastery of technology.. The French have a saying: "It is necessary to know geometry to build a cathedral; building a cathedral is, however, an act of faith"—and, we would add, an artistic creation. But neither the act of faith nor the art would be possible without the knowledge of geometry.

Another objection to concern with technique derives from the sentiment that technique is unimportant, a poor second to the feeling the social worker has for the client. If the worker's attitude is right, everything will be right; if it is wrong, no technical expertise can rescue the interview from failure. The viewpoint is expressed well in a Chinese maxim: "When the right person uses the wrong means, the wrong means work in the right way; when the wrong person uses the right means, the right means work in the wrong way." But what, then, is the power of the right people using the right means in the right way? Surely they accomplish more and do it more efficiently than the right people using the wrong means even if they do work in the right way.

Many might say that if they had to choose between feeling and technique they would choose feeling. Perhaps so, but if we have to choose between these qualifications, we have already done the client an injustice. We should be able to offer the client an interviewer who is both attitudinally correct and technically proficient. The best interviewer combines the appropriate feeling and attitude with skilled interviewing techniques. The emphasis should be on the geometry, the technical knowledge that gives substance to our faith and enables us to implement our goodwill.

The greater measure of truth lies, as is so often the case, not with "either-or" but "both." If technique without feeling is ineffectual, feeling without technique is inefficient. If technical competence without compassion is sterile, compassion without competence is an exercise in futility.

A good relationship is a necessary but not sufficient condition for good interviewing. Good technique permits optimum use of a relationship. A good technician working in the context of a modest relationship is apt to achieve a better outcome than a technically inept interviewer in an excellent relationship. The emotional response of the interviewer may be unfailingly correct. Yet feeling does not automatically translate into effective interview behavior. And clients respond more to behavior than to feelings. Only as feelings are manifested in behavior—verbal, nonverbal, open, or covert—do they have an effect on the client.

Teaching good interviewing technique is a matter of guiding the student to learn how to manifest the appropriate feelings behaviorally by applying the correct techniques, because correct techniques are the behavioral translation of the helpful attitude.

But can a book teach social work interviewing techniques? Of course not. "Knowing about" is clearly different from "knowing how." Ultimately, we learn interviewing only through doing. But even though *to know* is a far cry from *to do,* it is still an advance over not knowing what action is desirable. A book on interviewing is like a manual on courtship. No manual can tell lovers how to achieve their aims. But such books "can suggest some of the issues and tactics which are worth thinking about, consideration of which can make victory somewhat more likely" (Dexter 1970:24).

Clearly, someone can know all about the techniques of interviewing and yet be unable to apply them effectively. Some gifted practitioners also perform brilliantly without being able to say what they do or how they do it, often achieving success while breaking all the technical prescriptions. Further, the contention that good interviewers are born, not made, has some truth to it. Some intuitively gifted people seem to have a natural competence in the art of good personal relationships, of which interviewing is only a special example. But both those with a natural aptitude and those who interview well without knowing exactly what it is they are doing can profit from a conscious examination of their art. Whatever the limits of our natural capacities, learning may extend them.

We must recognize in the objections a desire to protect the existential magic of the good interview. Some fear that dispassionate didactic analysis destroys the creative spontaneity of the intuitively gifted clinician. Yet our support of schools of social work and our conduct of in-service training courses confirm the profession's confidence that interviewing can be taught. Generations of student social workers have encountered the problems that confuse and frustrate student workers today. Some solutions have evolved and are part of practice wisdom and the professional knowledge base. There is no reason that beginning interviewers should not be provided with the cumulative experience of others as a basis for their own practice. What we attempt here is to describe and codify some helpful responses that the discipline of social work has developed in dealing with recurrent situations and difficulties that workers encounter in field interviews.

Although the book has social work as its setting and context, the content is relevant and applicable to human service interviewing generally. Practitioners and students of different human service affiliations and in different human service settings will, we think, find the content both familiar and useful.

Within the human service family people conduct interviews in vastly different ways. Their methods vary in terms of the objectives—intake interview, social study–case history interview, diagnostic assessment, mental status interview, intervention treatment interview. Some interviews are distinguished by the particular problems of a specialized client population—child abuse interviews, substance abuse interviews, eating disorder interviews. Interviews vary in terms of the theoretical identification of the interviewer. Some interviewers are oriented toward psychoanalysis, others toward behavior modification or Gestalt, and so on.

But however diverse these varieties of interviews are in terms of specifics and details, all human service interviews—whatever the purpose, whatever the specific client population, whatever the target pathology, whatever the theoretical orientation of the interviewer—have a great deal in common.

The intent of the book is to focus on the common factors that we can identify and explore. *All* interviews follow a similar sequence. And *all* human service interviewers use similar techniques—attending, reflecting, paraphrasing, questioning, clarifying, summarizing, confronting, and interpreting—with varying degrees of emphasis and in different combinations. And *all* human service interviews require a positive relationship between interviewer and interviewee as a prerequisite for success.

By translating common interview elements and characteristics in terms of a specific occupational setting—in this instance the social work context—readers interested in and identified with social work are not burdened with the task of translating general interviewing dicta to their field. Because its examples come from the world of social work, this book provides the translation. Social work readers will immediately recognize the applicability of the techniques described here and will be familiar with the content.

This is the fourth edition of a book first published in 1972; a second edition was published in 1983 and a third edition in 1990. What justifies a fourth edition of *The Social Work Interview* at this time?

Since the third edition considerable research has been published that bears on its content—research on interviewing in multicultural contexts and on interviewing the sexually abused child, the involuntary client, and the use of a variety of technical interviewing skills. A fourth edition seemed necessary to bring the content up to date.

In preparing the fourth edition we sent questionnaires to instructors who were using the text, soliciting suggestions for changes. We have incorporated many of them and offer our heartfelt and sincere thanks to those faculty members who responded.

We need to include here an appeal to our readers' compassion, understanding, and common sense regarding the stylistic dilemma all authors face regarding the use of gender pronouns. In selecting case examples we have made a good-faith effort to give equal time to each gender as interviewer and interviewee.

The fourth edition is a collaborative effort. The senior author was a member of the School of Social Work faculty, University of Wisconsin, from 1950 to 1992 and has taught in Holland, Israel, and Australia. He is now a professor emeritus. He was responsible for the first three editions. The junior author is a social worker who has taught social work since 1990 at West Virginia University and at the School of Social Welfare of the University of Wisconsin at Milwaukee. Directly or indirectly, the social work interview has been a part of her teaching responsibilities.

Our collaboration led to a reorganization of the book for greater coherence and clarity, a wider review of the relevant literature, and greater clinical emphasis. The content derives from the experience of both authors in teaching interviewing and engaging in research that involves interviewing clients as well as observing client-worker interviews.

Our sincere and grateful thanks to Carol Grogan, who uncomplainingly typed and retyped much of the new content with commendable efficiency, proficiency, and accuracy. And our sincere thanks to Polly Kummel, whose skillful editing made this a cleaner, clearer, and leaner book.

PART ONE

General Orientation and Basic Concepts of Interviewing and Communication

ONE

The Interview in Social Work

Although social work involves a great deal more than interviewing, social workers spend more time in interviewing than in any other single activity. It is the most important and most frequently used social work skill. This is most clearly true for the direct service worker. But the group worker and community organizer also frequently participate in interviewing.

The human service literature describes the interview as "the most pervasive basic social work skill," as a "fundamental social work activity," and as "a primary social work tool-in-trade." The interview is the context through which social workers offer and implement most human services. The interview is the primary instrument they use to obtain an understanding of clients and their situation and for helping clients deal with their problem.

Baldock and Prior (1981) note that "the client interview, which lies at the heart of the social work process, is an event which is not merely the context of but the basic resource for social work practice" (pp. 19–20). Interviewing skills are the central skills on which all components of the social work process depend. Nonetheless the interview does not belong to social work alone. The purpose of this chapter is to describe how the social work interview is different from interviews in other disciplines. First, however, we must define the interview and make a distinction between it and another activity with which it is frequently confused—the conversation.

Defining the Interview and
Distinguishing an Interview from a Conversation

The simplest definition of an interview is that it is a conversation with a deliberate purpose that the participants accept. An interview resembles a conversation in many ways. Both involve verbal and nonverbal communication between people during which they exchange ideas, attitudes, and feelings. Both are usually face-to-face interactions, aside from the telephone interview or conversation. As in a conversation participants in the interview influence each other. A good interview, like a good conversation, gives pleasure to both participants.

Because we were conversing long before we started interviewing, we expect to bring to the interview habits of conversational interaction to which we have long become habituated. There is value, then, in recognizing the factors that differentiate the interview from the conversation because those differences alert us to the special kind of communication that interviewing represents and require us to modify our habitual patterns of conversational interaction.

The crucial characteristic that distinguishes an interview from a conversation is that the interview is designed to achieve a conscious purpose.

The purpose might be to help a mother decide to place her child in day care, a family decide about nursing home care for an elderly relative, parents to learn about and accept more effective discipline techniques, or to assist recovered alcoholics to reestablish in the community. The purpose of the interview may even be to establish a purpose—for example, the protective service worker sent by the agency to visit a family and explore with the mother how the agency can be of help. The purpose may be to resolve differences in perception and find some *mutually* acceptable purpose. Adolescents on probation may see their contact with the correctional social worker as purely a formality, whereas the social worker perceives it as an opportunity to help clients with some specific problem. In another interview the worker may encourage the client to define the reason for the contact. But this too is a purpose. If the interaction has no purpose, it may be conversation, but it is not yet an interview.

From this critical characteristic of the interview flows a series of consequences for the way participants relate to each other and for the way the interaction is structured.

1. Because the interview has a definite purpose, *the interviewer selects the content to facilitate its achievement.* The interviewer excludes any content,

however interesting, that will not contribute to the purpose of the interview. On the other hand, a conversation may include diffuse content. The orientation of the conversation is associational; it has is no central theme. The content of an interview is likely to have unity, a progression, and thematic continuity. Focused interaction is one characteristic of the interview because the communication is related to some common purpose.

Unlike a conversation the interview is a bounded setting. The participants in an interview limit what they give their attention to, what they notice, and what they include in their interaction. A conversation, on the other hand, covers everything but concentrates on nothing.

The interviewer focuses the content and controls the process to achieve the purpose of the interview.

2. If the participants are to achieve the purpose, *one person has to take responsibility for directing the interaction so that it moves toward the goal.* A differential allocation of tasks is necessary. One person is designated as interviewer and charged with responsibility for the process, and someone else is designated as interviewee. The role relationships are structured. A conversation has no comparable terms that allocate status and role behavior to each participant. Participants in a conversation have mutual responsibility for its course.

We will discuss the tasks of the interviewer in greater detail later. At this point let us note that, at the least, anybody who accepts the title of interviewer needs to know something about the process of interviewing in order to keep the interview moving toward the objective. An interviewer needs to know enough about the relevant content to be able to recognize what is extraneous and what is pertinent.

Conducting an interview requires some technical knowledge of interviewing procedure, how to start it, how to keep it on course, how to end it, and what content to cover. The experienced interviewer has such knowledge and skill. Consequently, the interviewer has to be responsible for conducting the interview.

3. *The differences in the roles of interviewer and interviewee imply a relationship that is not reciprocal.*

Because the interviewer is responsible for achieving specific tasks, the person in that role has certain prerogatives. In a conversation the participants have an opportunity to ask similar kinds of questions and are equally entitled to introduce a topic. But the interviewer has greater prerogative to introduce content and can ask the kinds of questions that the interviewee is not entitled to ask.

Interviewers act in a manner that encourages the interviewee to reveal a great deal of personal detail while interviewers reveal little. Interviewees reveal a wide segment of their life, interviewers only their professional self. If the interviewer asks, "How is your wife?," the interviewee is not expected to reciprocate by at some point by asking, "And how is your husband?" Such reciprocation, the expected form in a conversation, is not helpful in resolving the client's problem.

But this nonreciprocal relationship follows from the design of the encounter, which is to serve principally the interests of the client. The professional obligation of the interviewer is to perform clearly defined services for the client. The purpose of the interview is unidirectional. In an interview two people are working on the problem of one.

4. Although the behavior of all parties to a conversation may be spontaneous and unplanned, *the actions of the interviewer must be planned, deliberate, and consciously selected to further the purpose of the interview;* this is part of the prescribed role behavior. Unlike a conversation, an interview is a program of planned and organized communication. This pattern is predetermined by the positions people occupy in the interview, by the formal structure of reciprocal roles and expectations.

Because the interviewers are responsible for directing the interview so that it achieves its purpose, they have to select the interventions they want to make. Further, unlike participants in a conversation, interviewers have to be cognizant of any feelings and attitudes they have toward the interviewee that may impede or distort the achievement of purpose. Because interviewers are responsible for consciously guiding the interview to achieve its purpose, they are obliged to plan the interview to whatever extent possible. Conversely, no one ever consciously prepares for engaging in a conversation.

5. No one is obliged to initiate or continue a conversation. The *professional is, however, obliged to accept the client's request for an interview.* And because the purpose of the contact to meet the needs of the client, interviewers have an obligation to maintain contact until the purpose is achieved or until it is clear that the purpose cannot be achieved.

Whatever their feelings about the interview, interviewers cannot terminate it for personal reasons without being open to a charge of dereliction of responsibility. Withdrawing from a conversation if it is not enjoyable carries no professional or social penalty.

6. An *interview requires exclusive attention to the interaction.* The interviewer's commitment to participate in the interview is intense. A conversa-

tion, however, can be peripheral to other activities such as eating, gardening, and the like. We have a greater obligation to concentrate on listening during an interview. We listen differently and with a sharper focus.

Most conversations follow a predictable script. Experienced conversationalists have learned many scripts and can converse in a routine manner without much deliberate thought. An interview requires concentrated specific attention to the interaction between the participants.

7. Because it has a purpose, *the interview is usually a formally arranged meeting.* The participants establish a definite time, place, and duration for the interview. Unlike a conversation, an interview moves purposefully to accomplish its objectives within a given period of time. The formal structure and the time schedule specifically allotted to an interview seek to guarantee no interruption. Time allocation is asymmetrical in the interview, with the interviewee allotted maximum time without competition from the interviewer.

People engaged in a conversation expect a balance of presentation and to participate actively. An interview has a deliberately skewed balance, the interviewer talking less, the interviewee talking more. Interviewers refrain from taking their turn when the conversational ritual calls for this, because the emphasis is on permitting the interviewee the greatest opportunity to speak.

8. *We choose conversational partners; we are assigned interviewees.* Communications defined as conversations are an end in themselves. People engage in them because the interaction provides satisfaction. For this reason we usually choose to converse with those with whom we have a great deal in common. *Homophyly,* or likeness, between conversational participants increases the probability of obtaining satisfaction. Interview participants usually differ in terms of background, experience, and lifestyle. The young, white, upper middle-income, college-educated female may never have occasion to converse with an older, lower-income, grade-school-educated Asian male. However, such disparate people participate in interviews daily. We *choose* those with whom we are likely to hold a conversation; we *are assigned* those with whom we are likely to conduct an interview. Heterogeneity of participants is a much more likely condition in an interview. Homophyly is not a characteristic of interview participants.

9. *The interview modifies or violates the rules of conduct that characterize conversations.* In the interview we move from being regulated by the social norms of interpersonal communication to professional norms. Professional

norms supersede or modify social norms in dictating the behavior of interviewers—what they should and should not do.

Because an interview has a purpose other than amusement, the parties do not avoid unpleasant facts and feelings. In fact, an interviewer has a specific obligation to introduce unpleasant facts and feelings if this will be of help. In a conversation the usual tacit agreement is to avoid the unpleasant. Participants in a conversation expect their partner to interact with tact and caution, to refrain from introducing anything that might be embarrassing, anxiety provoking, controversial, or unduly intimate. Many of the conversational norms that govern what subject matter is appropriate and permissible are suspended, modified, or mitigated in an interview.

The interview, unlike the conversation, puts a premium on making explicit what the participants often recognize but leave unstated. The interviewer needs to penetrate the private thoughts and feelings of the interviewee. The interviewer asks questions that are not ordinarily asked and makes comments not frequently made in conversation. To highlight this difference we might say that interviewing in social work is the skill of facilitating disclosure of personal information for professional purposes.

The interaction in an interview may become a matter for discussion. If an interview is proceeding haltingly, the interviewer might say, "You seem reluctant to talk about this," an intervention rarely used in a conversation. The interviewee needs the protection of guarantees of confidentiality and anonymity, safeguards ordinarily unnecessary in a conversation.

Ethnomethodologists have studied the minute details of commonplace events such as face-to-face conversation. They note that just as we have learned a language and complex rules of grammar without being aware of how or when we learned them, we have learned complex rules of social conduct. We have become habituated to conventional behavior for talking to each other. But some of these ways do not apply in the interview. The interviewer has to learn a slightly different language of conduct.

Etiquette is suspended once the formal interview starts. The interviewer can raise indelicate, indiscreet questions, can challenge the interviewee's statements, and elicit and discuss strong feelings. In conversations we tolerate each others' myths and collaborate in performances that validate the self we present, however fabricated that self is. Such tolerance is counterproductive in an interview.

After interviewing a voluble articulate client who took charge of the interview and talked nonstop, the worker commented,

I didn't know how to politely break into her talking. Is there any polite way of doing this? Perhaps one has to learn to be impolite if the task of the interview demands it. Over the years I had learned the opposite—being polite. I paid for it here in having to listen, it seemed endlessly, to a lot of irrelevant detail. I guess I deserved it if I was too weak to interrupt.

The interviewer who has to obtain considerable personal information that transcends the etiquette barrier may feel a sense of discomfort. This is suggested by the interviewer who says,

> The interviewer is required to be *two* things to all people. First he must be a *diplomat:* warm, sympathetic, sensitive to the respondent—just the sort of person who in ordinary social life does not go about asking embarrassing questions because, through sensitivity and tact, he knows how to avoid them. But at the same time, he must be something of a *boor:* no sympathetic understanding of the respondent will prevent him from elbowing his way right in with questions that might embarrass or discomfort the other person.
>
> (Converse and Schuman 1974:31)

10. *Patterns of speech distinguish a conversation from an interview.* Hesitations, fractured sentences, circumlocutions, ambiguities, and repetitions are characteristic of ordinary conversational speech. Interviewing speech seeks to be more formal, precise, structured, explicit, and organized—at least on the part of the interviewer.

One interviewer says she knows she is interviewing when she greets an interviewee with "How are you?" In conversation she is more likely to say "How ya doing?"—the more formal greeting being more appropriate for an interview.

Sociability is the principal descriptive attribute of a conversation; professionalism is the principal defining characteristic of the interview. Conversations are oriented around sociability; interviews are task- and goal-oriented.

11. *A final difference between an interview and a conversation relates to the interviewer's obligation regarding accountability.* The interviewer has to remember and record what went on during the interview in order to make subsequent use of the material in helping the interviewee. Participants in a conversation do not have such obligations.

These characteristics define the interview and distinguish it from a conversation. In summary (see box 1.1), then, an interview differs from a conversation in that it involves interpersonal interaction for a conscious and mutually accepted purpose. The interview involves a more formal structure, a clearly defined allocation of roles, a different set of norms regulating the process of interaction, and a clearly designated time and place.

Box 1.1 Differences Between Conversation and a Helping Interview

CONVERSATION	INTERVIEW
1. No deliberate, conscious plan, purpose, or objective.	1. Deliberately defined, planned purpose or objective; task oriented.
2. No clear delineation or differential roles and obligations.	2. Clearly defined role differentiation: interviewer-interviewee.
3. No formal setting as to time, place, duration, and frequency.	3. Specifically selected place, time, duration, and frequency.
4. Interaction follows social expectations and norms.	4. Rules of professional interaction supersede social etiquette in regard to form and acceptable content.
5. Speech patterns are informal, characterized by fractured sentences, hesitancies, repetitions, and circumlocutions.	5. Speech patterns tend to be formal, structured, and organized.
6. Communication flow is balanced, bidirectional, and reciprocal.	6. Balance of speech flow is unidirectional from interviewee to interviewer; focus is unidirectional in favor of interviewee.
7. Participants have no obligation to initiate or continue conversation.	7. Interviewer has professional obligation to initiate contact and continue until purpose is achieved.
8. Participants are equal in authority and power.	8. Allocation of authority and power is unequal in favor of the interviewer.
9. Participants most often are culturally alike.	9. Participants often are culturally dissimilar.
10. Participants have no subsequent accountability for the conversation.	10. Interviewer has subsequent accountability to interviewee.

The interview may involve more than two people, as in a family interview or a cotherapy interview. In every instance, however, it involves only two clearly defined *parties*—one or more people interviewing one or more people. An interview can, and does, take place on the street if clients meet their worker during a crisis. Interviews take place in tenement hallways, in supermarkets, and on buses as workers accompany clients to the hospital, employment office, or day care center. What starts as a conversation may turn into an interview.

The characteristics that distinguish an interview from a conversation are common to all interviews. And a wide variety of people—social workers, journalists, public opinion pollsters, doctors, lawyers, clergy, and so on— conduct interviews for a wide variety of purposes. What distinguishes the social work interview?

Defining the Social Work Interview

Social work interviews are concerned with social work content, are scheduled to achieve social work purposes, and take place primarily in social work settings. To say this is to recognize immediately the difficulty in making such distinctions. If society designated social work as a profession having clear and exclusive concern with certain areas of activity, the statement would have unambiguous meaning. As it is, we must concede that the content of social work overlaps with that of other human service professions— psychiatry, psychology, educational counseling, the ministry, and others. Despite the overlap, despite the blurred boundaries between related disciplines, social work does have an area of principal concern that is distinctive—its concern with people in the enactment of their social roles and in their relation to social institutions. All attempts at defining social work point to the relationship between people and their social environment.

Social service is defined by the United Nations as an "organized activity that aims at helping to achieve a mutual adjustment of *individuals and their social environment*" (emphasis added; United Nations 1963:105). The Model Statute Social Workers' Licensing Act defines social work as "the professional activity of helping individuals, groups, or communities enhance or restore their capacity for *social functioning* and creating societal conditions favorable to this goal" (emphasis added; National Association of Social Workers [NASW] 1967:7).

Two special issues of *Social Work* (September 1977 and January 1981), the principal journal of the NASW, report the proceedings of two national conferences explicitly concerned with defining the nature of social work. Although the presentations differ in in various details, both emphasize the distinctive and differentiating concern of social work with "social functioning," "social problems," "social needs," "social roles," "social policy," "social institutions," and "social well being."

The inclusion of the word *social* in the professional title reflects social workers' primary concern with social problems and the interaction of clients and social institutions. More specifically, however, different agencies perform different functions relating to different social problems.

The social worker in the mental health center or the psychiatric hospital is concerned with the social antecedents, concomitants, and consequences of mental disabilities; the social worker in the health care setting is concerned with the social antecedents, concomitants, and consequences of physical illness; family and child welfare agencies are concerned with the social aspects of marital disruption and parent-child relationships; the social worker in the correctional setting is concerned with the social aspects of a disordered relationship to the legal institutions of society; and income maintenance agencies are concerned with the social aspects of a disordered relationship to the economic institutions of society.

Each agency, then, by focusing on some particular aspect of social functioning, some recurrent significant social problem area, defines the content most relevant for interviews.

At whatever level in the process the social worker intervenes, whether at the community level in trying to effect change in the social environment or at the direct service level in trying to effect change in the individual, family or group situation, the concern is, again, primarily with *social* phenomena. The function and focus of the profession thus determine in a general way the distinctive content of social work interviews.

At a hospital three different people—a doctor, a lawyer, and a social worker—may interview a woman who was injured in an auto accident and who is the mother of four young children. All three may use the same general principles and procedures to ensure an effective interview. In each instance the interview would have a purpose, but the purpose would be different. Consequently, the content of the medical interview might be to uncover significant details of the woman's physical functioning so as to plan appropriate treatment. The lawyer's purpose might be to find out more about the nature of the accident in preparation for a lawsuit. The social worker's purpose would be to find out about the disruptive effects of the injury on the woman's significant social roles—as wife, mother, and employee. The purpose might be to determine how to ensure adequate care for the dependent children, the effects of the injury on the marital relationship, the effects of her loss of income on the family, and the effects of her injury on her relationships with friends.

Because the problems people bring to the social worker are often diffuse and ambiguously defined, the social worker cannot focus the interview as sharply as a doctor or a lawyer might. Listening to social work interviews shows that they tend to be longer and more discursive than interviews by doctors, for example (Baldock and Prior 1981).

We should note some other characteristics of social work interviews. The concern of the social work interview is with the unique entity—the unique individual, the unique group, the unique community. *Casework* refers to a particular instance and is not a term reserved to social work. The term *case book* in law or in business management illustrates the generality of the word *case*.

The concern with the unique instance gives the social work interview a character that distinguishes it from the public opinion interview, for instance. The public opinion interviewer approaches a respondent is as one of a number of comparable persons. The interviewer's interest is not in the response of this particular person per se but in the particular person as a member of a group. Hence the effort to standardize the interview and to do everything possible to discourage the development of anything unusual, or special, in any particular interview. The interviewer controls the interviewee's participation and confines it so far as possible to a set series of questions.

The antithesis is true of most social work interviews. Social workers try to maximize clients' participation, to encourage the development of the interview so that it follows the clients' preferences, to minimize standardization and maximize individuality of content. Social workers have no set interview agenda and attempt to keep their control of the interview to a minimum. Of course some social work interviews do require the worker to cover uniform content, even though this requirement may not be spelled out on a specific form. A social study at a mental hospital requires coverage of psychosocial development, school history, marital history, work history, symptoms of developmental difficulties, and so forth. An adoption interview typically requires coverage of motivation, reaction to infertility, child preference, experience with children, and marital interaction. An interview to determine eligibility for public assistance has to cover family composition, need, resources, and the situation precipitating the application. An assessment for discharge planning in an acute care hospital might require coverage of the patient's social support system, insurance and financial resources, physical arrangement of the patient's living quarters, any formal resources already in place, and the patient's ideas about an appropriate plan. But every effort is made to individualize content elicited.

The social work interview generally takes place with troubled people or people in trouble. What they discuss is private and highly emotional. Social work interviews are characterized by a great concern with personal interaction, considerable emphasis on feelings and attitudes, and less concern for objective factual data.

Social work interviews are also apt to be diffuse and concerned with a wide segment of the client's life. Although the areas covered by different agencies are somewhat delineated, agencies tend to state their functions rather broadly. The tendency is for workers to feel that they need to know much about the client that in a strict sense might be regarded as extraneous to the agency's functions. The more the worker explores the client's personal world, the greater the likelihood of affective interaction and of emotional involvement.

The social work interview also is diffuse because of the imprecision of technical procedures for helping. The more precise a profession's technology, the more definite its solutions, the more likely it is to circumscribe its area for exploration and intervention. If we could specify what we needed to know to do precise things for and with the client in effecting change, our interview would be less diffuse.

To recapitulate, the social work interview, whatever its auspices, differs from other kinds of interviews in that it is concerned with problems relating to how clients deal with their social environment. Compared with many other kinds of interviews, the social work interview is apt to be diffuse, not standardized, interviewee controlled, with no set agenda, focused on affective material, and concerned with the interpersonal interaction of participants. As a consequence social work interviewers have a difficult assignment. They generally cannot determine in advance much of what they have to do in the interview; they must respond to the situation as it develops. Interviewers have to have considerable discretion to do almost anything they think might be advisable, under highly individualized circumstances, to achieve the purpose of the interview. The content, the sequence in which it is introduced and how it is introduced, and the interpersonal context in which it is explored—all these matters of strategy and tactics in interview management are the responsibility of the interviewer.

Purposes of Social Work Interviews

The purposes of the social work interview follow from the functions of social work. We can describe the general purposes of most social work interviews as informational (to make a social study), assessment (to arrive at an understanding), and therapeutic (to effect change). These are discrete categories only for the purpose of analysis; the same interview can, and often does, serve more than one purpose. For example, the psychiatric social worker in a child guidance clinic may interview a father to obtain detailed information about a child referred for service and at the same time seek therapeutically to support the father in the parent-child relationship.

Considering the questions the interviewer raises in order to obtain information forces many clients to review those questions explicitly, which makes them therapeutically more aware of their feelings. The reverse can also be true of course. An interview whose primary purpose is therapeutic may reveal information previously withheld.

The structure and conduct of interviews reflect the differences in their primary purposes. An interview focused on social study is distinguishable from an interview conducted for assessment, and both are further distinguishable from an interview whose purpose is primarily therapeutic.

Information-Gathering or Social Study Interviews

The purpose of information-gathering interviews is to obtain a focused account of the individual, group, or community in terms of social functioning. The point of departure is the socially stressful situation for which the client might seek or is seeking the agency's help.

The social study interview is a selective gathering of a client's life history as it relates to social functioning. The information enables the worker to understand the client in relation to the social problem. *Knowledge* of clients and their situation is a necessary prerequisite to an *understanding* of clients in their situation. And understanding is a necessary prerequisite for effectively intervention to bring about change. Hence the information to be gathered includes that which helps the interviewer understand the situation and that which is relevant to the kind of help the agency can provide. We do not seek to learn all there is to know about the client but only what we need to know so that we can help effectively. The information we seek includes both objective facts and subjective feelings and attitudes.

In a series of contacts with the client such information gathering is cumulative; every interview elicits some new, previously unshared, information. Early interviews are likely to be devoted to explicitly obtaining information. In later interviews social study information is typically incidental to achieving some other purpose.

In some instances a social study interview is the specific charge to the interviewer. The psychiatric social worker in a guidance clinic or psychiatric hospital is sometimes asked to do a social study to present at a staff conference to determine the next step for the client. A worker in a neighborhood service center may be asked to interview people in the community to determine what social problems cause them the most concern.

Assessment, Decision-Making Interviews

Another type of interview is geared toward appraisal and determining eligibility for a service. These interviews facilitate specific administrative decisions. The child welfare worker, for example, interviews foster care or adoptive applicants to determine whether the agency should place a child with them. Although such interviews are highly individualized, they are conducted so that the worker can assess particular characteristics of the interviewee deemed essential for eligibility for a particular service or to justify some decision. A child who is to be accepted for counseling at a child guidance clinic must display some capacity to establish a relationship and some ability to verbalize; a couple that seeks marital counseling at a family service agency must show some motivation to change; an abusive parent must be judged likely to repeat the assault to justify removing a child from the home.

Whatever the social policy criteria that affect the decision—whether the agency offers services at a preventive rather than a rehabilitative level, whether it works with the disabled who can make limited use of help but who need it most or with those who need less help but make the most effective use of service, whether an agency focuses on changing the system in social institutions or changing symptoms in individual clients—an agency will require an assessment interview of some kind so that it can to make decisions regarding applicants. Because the agency has defined its requirements and criteria before the interview occurs, the interviewer generally has an outline of the content that such interviews may cover.

The purpose of the appraisal interview is to obtain selective information for making some decision. The decision involves an assessment process in the mind of the worker—a process of applying theoretical generalization to the data obtained and organizing the data for valid inferences. The assessment process leads to an evaluation—a decision on what the agency will do.

Studies of social work decision making suggest that social workers do look for definite but limited information in assessment interviews and that they frequently base their decisions on such information (Golan 1969).

Therapeutic Interviews

The purpose of the therapeutic interview is to effect change in clients, their social situation, or both. The goal is more effective social functioning on the part of the client as a result of therapy. Such interviews involve the use of special remedial measures to effect changes in the client's feelings, attitudes, and behavior in response to the social situation. These interviews can also involve efforts to change the social situation in order to reduce social pressures on the client. Because therapeutic interviews are the most highly individualized and idiosyncratic, outlining them in advance is more difficult.

The interview might be the instrument through which change is effected. In this situation the interviewer works with the interviewee in attempting to change feelings, attitudes, or behavior. The interview is psychotherapeutic, that is, the interviewer uses psychological principles and procedures in an effort to exercise a deliberate, controlled influence on the psychic functioning of interviewees, with their consent and in their behalf. The purpose of such interviews is helping and healing through communication in a therapeutic relationship.

The school-based social worker interviews children to help them adjust to the classroom setting. The medical social worker interviews a convalescent mother to improve her attitude toward the homemaker assigned to help the family. The gerontological social worker interviews aged clients to intensify their motivation to use senior citizen facilities in the community.

Interviews may have a therapeutic purpose, but the person for whom the change is sought need not be present. These include interviews with people important in the client's life, where the social worker acts as a broker or advocate for the client. The social worker may interview people in strategic positions in an attempt to influence them in behalf of the client. The purpose is to change the balance of forces in the social environment in the client's favor. The school social worker may interview teachers in order to influence them to show more accepting understanding of a child. The social worker at the neighborhood service center may interview a worker at the housing authority or at the local department of public welfare to obtain for the client full entitlement to housing rights or to assistance. Or a social worker may accompany an inarticulate client to an employment interview. In each instance the scheduled interview has a definite and, in these cases, therapeutic purpose in behalf of the client.

This book's primary focus is on social work interviews conducted with agency clients as the interviewees. We are less concerned with interviews conducted by social workers for administrative, supervisory, consultative, research purposes or with interviews by social workers in private practice.

Universal Aspects of Interviews

The ultimate objective of the different kinds of interviews is to help clients deal more effectively and less dysfunctionally with a problematic social situation. Each purpose of interviews is part of the overall process. The steps taken to achieve the objective of helping the client involve treatment (specific interventions with therapeutic intent) based on understanding (data assessment) derived from the facts (social study data gathering).

There are, then, many different kinds of social work interviews. And each kind can be conducted in different ways—as a dyad (interviewer-interviewee), as a group interview (one interviewer–multiple interviewees), as a interview (multiple interviewers–one interviewee). And interviews for the same purpose may be conducted in different ways, depending on the theoretical preference of the interviewer. The social worker oriented toward ego psychology as an explanatory framework will emphasize different content than will a behavior modification–oriented social worker or an existential social worker.

Common Features of Social Work Interviews

Although the theoretical approaches to human service helping are many and various (psychoanalytic, behavior modification, cognitive, rational emotive, Gestalt, Rogerian, etc.), all use some universally applicable procedures and techniques in their interviews. For instance, all approaches use questions, summaries, transitions, reflection, silence, and so forth. These basic techniques are part of the repertoire of all helping professionals, no matter their theoretical identification or agency affiliation.

And these universally applicable techniques become potent and effective when used in the context of a positive relationship. What the many helping theories have in common is that they call for a positive worker-client relationship and use basic interviewing techniques. We are therefore not concerned here with the details of the different therapeutic orientations. Our concern is with the universal aspects of the interview used by all human service helpers of any theoretical persuasion in any agency.

We have described different social work interviews that have distinctively different principal purposes. However, each kind of interview covers the steps in the social work problem-solving process, the gathering of information about the client and the client's social situation (social study, data gathering) in order to understand the situation (data assessment) so that we might intervene effectively (therapy, change). (The the repetition here is deliberate.).

Unlike the journalist's interview, the interview with a television commentator, or public opinion interview, a social work interview is generally one in a series of interviews. Each interview is generally part of a more inclusive process leading to the objective of the interviewee's contact with the agency.

Each interview in a sequence is designed to achieve some limited purpose, contributing in some measure to attaining the goal of the contact. Each interview is a chapter in the novel.

And in *some* measure *every* social work interview follows each step or stage in this helping process. Each and every interview mirrors and replicates in microcosm the total process implemented over time. Whenever we meet a client (individual, family, group, community), we first have to become acquainted or reacquainted and obtain some information about the situation so that we can understand what help we might sensibly offer now.

Consequently, studying the social work interview in general helps us understand the individual interview in particular.

Alternatives to and Limitations of the Interview

The interview is the principal technique through which social workers achieve their purposes. But it is not the only way to achieve them. Social workers also obtain information about the client from documents, records of previous agency contacts, and from medical examinations and psychological tests.

And social workers help clients by providing concrete services—money, homemakers, a foster home, day care, and the like—in addition to whatever help they can offer through personal contact during the interview. Such procedures supplement rather than substitute for the interview, which remains the principal instrument for human service helping.

Limitations

The interview does have limitations. A series of studies has compared information on family functioning obtained through interviews with information obtained through direct observation (Weller and Luchterhand 1969). Other studies have compared information about child development obtained retrospectively through interviews with the records compiled on the same child during childhood (Yarrow, Campbell, and Burton 1964). Each study has found discrepancies between the interview data and the observed or documentary material. The studies establish some general limitations of the interview as a technique for obtaining information on child development and family functioning. However, observation has its own limitations, which the interview is designed to surmount.

Observation presents social workers with a sample of behavior; they still have to infer its meaning. The worker observes a mother, for example, who has come to the day care center at the end of the day to pick up her child. She shouts at her child when he is slow in putting on his boots and overcoat. Is her action displaced hostility toward her boss, with whom she has had an argument earlier in the day? Is it anxiety about getting home late and, in a shaky marriage, risking another argument with her husband? Is it shame that her child is not as capable as other children? Is it impatience because of physical fatigue? Does the child's slowness reactivate anxiety that as a working mother she is failing her child? The one behavior has many potential meanings. An interview with the mother can help the worker understand which interpretation best explains her outburst. Observation without interviewing yields dubious inferences.

On the other hand, the data we obtain in the interview when interviewees relate their experience are not the experience itself. Data are a retrospective verbal reconstruction of what happened. The verbal account presented within the interview is a symbolic surrogate for the actual events. As a result we really cannot know with any confidence the nature of that objective reality. We only can know the interviewee's subjective perception and interpretation of that reality and then only to the extent that the interviewee is willing to share the details with us. The only approach the interviewer can take is to accept what the person says as the interviewee's *subjective reality.*

We need to recognize that the relationship between verbal reports and actual behavior is somewhat tenuous (Deutscher 1966; Socor 1989). Thus some slippage is likely to exist between the interviewee's verbal description of the events and the actual event. This is one shortcoming of the interview.

Structured Interviews

The typical human service interview is relatively unstructured. Social workers turned to structured interviews because of some recurrent dissatisfactions with unstructured clinical interviews. These interviews presented such problems as "poor reliability of data derived from the interview because of many sources of variability. Examples were differences in phrasing of questions, changes in interview procedure by the same interviewer at different times, the interaction of differing interview styles and patient characteristics, the use of clinical judgments in unspecified ways and informal methods of recording information" (Young et al. 1987:614). Unstructured interviews raised questions about the accuracy and completeness of the information obtained.

In response to these problems social workers have formulated structured interview formats for use with particular populations regarding specific problems. Such formats provide interviewers with exactly what they must cover. Structured formats are designed to reduce information variance and provide systematically organized data for diagnostic assessment. The data that need to be obtained in the structured interview schedule generally incorporate the criteria for assessment given in the fourth edition of the *Diagnostic and Statistical Manual of Mental Disorders (DSM-IV)* (American Psychiatric Association 1994). Hodges (1993) has reviewed a variety of such interview schedules designed for use with children and adolescents. Agencies also use structured interviews in determining entitlement to various social services. Standardized structuring of data assures that the interviewer has obtained the information. An additional advantage of structured interview schedules is that they permit scoring by a computer. However, structured interviews have the disadvantage of limited interviewer discretion in responding to unanticipated events. The structured interview does not encourage spontaneous clinical intuition. In fact, studies show that the professionals often prefer the unstructured interview, the typical social work interview, to well-designed, structured clinical interviews such as the Structured Clinical Interview for DSM III (SCID) (Segal, Hersen, and Van Hesselt 1994:316).

Computers

Because of growing interest we must briefly address computer-assisted interviewing (Ferriter 1993). In this situation a computer interviewers the client. Computer programs of structured interviews are available for a variety of human service problems. These programs are becoming more sophisticated in asking follow-up questions, omitting questions that are inappropriate based on previous answers, and offering sophisticated options. The computer interview efficiently elicits routine standard information. Sophisticated computer programs can permit flexibility and limited individualizing of the client-computer interaction. The computer has the advantage of never getting tired or bored. It never displays nonverbal messages that might imply rejection, inattention, or impatience. It never forgets to ask a question and it always asks it the same way. It invariably and accurately records the interviewee's response and has a perfect memory. It never displays a suggestion of superior status vis-à-vis the interviewee. It provides the ultimate in privacy and is consequently less embarrassing for interviewees in sharing sins and shortcomings.

On the other hand, computers are impersonal and inhuman. They do not permit the nuanced flexibility of the human interviewer who can spontaneously follow an unanticipated turn in the interview. They cannot respond to the variety of meanings that a word or phrase or intonation might communicate. The human interviewer can perceive and respond to many channels of communication. The computer is responsive to cognitions; the human interviewer also responds to feelings. The computer's perception is narrowly confined to messages conveyed by words. The human interviewer can explore broad areas of general concern. The more effective computer interview programs tend to be narrowly and sharply focused around a specific area of concern—suicide risk, drug abuse, sexual dysfunction, and the like. More comprehensive computer programs are difficult to design to provide for a broad range of responses. Computers need to be constantly reprogrammed to include new developments in research and practice. Computers cannot use nonverbal cues that make for more refined understanding.

Despite its shortcomings, the computer does offer significant competition to the human interviewer. Interviewees are accepting of the computer and respond positively to the experience. Interviewees disclose intimate sensitive material to the computer as readily as they do to the human interviewer. Computers efficiently elicit the clinically relevant information. For example, some computer programs automate the diagnostic interview schedules associated with DSM-IV. Such interviews have demonstrated a level of reliability and validity comparable to results from human clinical interviews (Millstein 1987). Computers are less capable of providing the personal interactions required for effective treatment.

Computers have proved their ability to augment and parallel the work of the human interviewer. Given their limitations, however, they are unlikely to replace the human interviewer. The interview, despite its shortcomings, is the most flexible and responsive way to obtain peoples' life stories, their thinking, attitudes, and emotional states. We can obtain information not only about people's experiences but their interpretation of and responses to such experiences. In an interview workers can adapt their approach to any lead offered by the interviewee, thus individualizing the interaction.

Through words, which are vicarious actions, the worker can experience with the client various situations in the past, present, and future. The interview is bound by neither time or space. Furthermore, through the interview the worker has access to the client's feelings and attitudes, the subjective meaning of the objective situation.

Despite definite shortcomings and deficiencies, the advantages, versatility, and flexibility of interviewing have made the clinical interview the procedure of choice for social work interaction with the client.

Summary: Chapter 1

Social workers spend more time interviewing than in any other single activity. Interviewing skills are the primary skills on which all other aspects of social work depend.

We can define the interview as a conversation with a deliberate purpose that is accepted by the participants. However, several characteristics distinguish an interview from an conversation. Whereas conversations contain diffuse content, interviews focus on specific content. Conversations involve no structured role relationships; a differential allocation of roles and tasks is characteristic of the interview. Conversations are reciprocal; interviews are not—interviews focus on meeting the needs of the interviewee. Conversations are spontaneous and unplanned; interviews are planned to achieve some purpose. Conversations occur naturally, but interviews are formally arranged. Although no one is obligated to initiate or continue a conversation, the interviewer is obligated to accept a request for an interview and continue the interaction until the interview is concluded. Conversations are based on tact and etiquette, but interviews are regulated by professional norms that sanction the uncovering of unpleasant facts and feelings. Compared to conversational speech, the interviewer's speech is formal and structured. Conversations require only casual attention, but an interview requires concentrated specific attention to the interaction. Participants are not accountable for what occurs during a conversation, whereas the interviewer has an obligation regarding accountability. Interviews, but not conversations, frequently occur between people who differ in regard to background, experience, and lifestyle.

The social work interview differs from other types of interviews in that it is concerned with problems in social functioning. The social work interview is more likely than other kinds of interviews to be discursive, diffuse—not standardized—and focused on affective content. Because social work interviewers cannot determine much of their strategy in advance, responding to the situation as it unfolds, they must have considerable professional skill to decide when and how to introduce content and determine the interpersonal context in which to explore content.

The general purpose of most social work interviews is informational (to complete a social study), evaluative (to arrive at an assessment), and therapeutic (to effect change). However, each different kind of interview covers the steps in the social work problem-solving process: data gathering, assessment, and intervention. Each interview in a sequence is designed to achieve some limited purpose that cumulatively achieves the purpose of the contact. Each and every interview mirrors and replicates in microcosm the helping process, from data gathering to intervention. Consequently, studying the social work interview in general helps us understand the individual interview in particular.

The clinical interview, the type of social work interview most frequently used, has limitations. The data obtained in clinical interviews represent a retrospective and subjective interpretation of reality. Some discrepancy is likely to exist between the interviewee's verbal account of events and the actual event. Alternatives to the clinical interview include the structured interview and the computer-assisted interview. However, the clinical interview remains the most flexible and responsive method for obtaining people's life stories, thinking, attitudes, and emotional states.

Suggested Readings

Social Work Texts

A number of other books published within the last fifteen years are concerned in whole or in part with the social work interview.

Alfred Benjamin. *The Helping Interview*, 4th ed. Boston: Houghton Mifflin, 1987. (290 pp.)
  A warmly written account of the details of the helping interview—the spirit as well as the specifics of practice. Although concerned with the helping interview generally, the book includes the social work interview, and much of the content is applicable.

Laura Epstein. *Talking and Listening: A Guide to the Helping Interview.* St. Louis: Times Mirror/Mosby, 1985. (305 pp.)
  Written by a professor at the University of Chicago School of Social Service Administration, the book is a good overview of the essential elements of the interview with a social service perspective.

Annette Garrett. *Interviewing: Its Principles and Methods*, 4th ed. Revised by S. Donner and P. Sessions Milwaukee: Families International. 1995. (305 pp.)
  First published in 1942, this book is a classic in social work. The author was associate director of Smith College School for Social Work from 1934 until her death in 1957. The book was revised by Elinor Zaki and Margaret Margold for the second edition, published in 1972, and the third in 1982. It contains a clear statement of the attitudes and understandings required for a good interview and an exposition of some basic techniques. This is followed by illustrative excerpts from social work interviews.

Margaret Schubert. *Interviewing in Social Work Practice: An Introduction*, rev. ed. Alexandria, Va.: Council on Social Work Education, 1994. (118 pp.)
  By a professor of social work, this is a tightly written account of some essentials of the social work interview, the recurrent problems, and the solutions developed through practice wisdom.

Lawrence Shulman. *The Skills of Helping Individuals Groups and Families*, 3d ed. Itasca, Ill.: Peacock Press, 1992. (740 pp.)
  Skills related to interviewing are explicated throughout the text.

From Counseling and Psychology

A number of books are written for the counselor or psychologist, but social workers will find much of the content useful.

Ivey Allen. *Intentional Interviewing and Counseling.* Monterey, Calif.: Brooks/Cole, 1988. (346 pp.)
 A step-by-step text addressed to the broad spectrum of professionals with responsibility for using the interview to help people with personal problems. The book describes microcounseling principles and then introduces and explains selective interviewing skills, which readers then practice by completing the assigned program.

William Cormier and L. Sherilyn Cormier. *Interviewing Strategies for Helpers: A Guide to Assessment, Treatment, and Education,* 3d ed. Monterey, Calif.: Brooks/Cole, 1991. (640 pp.)
 Organized around three major foci in personal helping —assessment, treatment, and evaluation—the book details the interventions necessary to implement these processes. The layout is interesting, with boxed summaries of key points and exercises designed to involve the reader.

Barbara F. Okun. *Effective Helping, Interviewing, and Counseling Techniques,* 4th ed. Monterey, Calif.: Brooks/Cole, 1992. (320 pp.)

General Interviewing

A number of books that describe, discuss, and analyze the interview address primarily professionals in fields other than social work and human service. Nonetheless they are potentially helpful and useful to the social worker interested in learning more about interviewing.
 These two books are by authors whose area of concern is the public opinion interview:

Raymond L. Gordon. *Basic Interviewing Skills.* Itasca, Ill.: F. E. Peacock, 1992. (236 pp.)
 Although Gordon's principal interest has been public opinion interviewing, this book has a more general focus on the nuts and bolts of interviewing in human service.

Charles J. Stewart and William B. Cash. *Interviewing Principles and Practice,* 6th ed. Dubuque, Iowa: W. C. Brown and Benchmark, 1994. (320 pp.)
 A general text directed to a diverse audience, the first half is devoted to general principles of interviewing.

Rob Millar, Valerie Crute, and Owen Hargie. *Professional Interviewing.* New York: Routledge, 1992. (205 pp.)
 A social interactional perspective on interviewing directed at professionals for whom interviewing is a regular responsibility. Although this book cites social work only occasionally, much of its content is translatable to the social work interview.

From the Health Professions

Because doctors and nurses are regularly involved in interviewing patients, many books on interviewing are directed at that audience. Once again, social work practitioners, particularly those involved in health settings, may want to take a look.

Lewis Bernstein, Rosalyn Bernstein, and Richard Dana. *Interviewing the Patient: A Guide for Health Professionals*, 4th ed. New York: Appleton-Century-Crofts, 1985. (240 pp.)

Allen J. Enlow and Scott N. Swisher. *Interviewing and Patient Care*, 3d ed. New York: Oxford University Press, 1985. (229 pp.)

Shawn Christopher. *Psychiatric Interviewing: The Art of Understanding*. Philadelphia: W. B. Saunders, 1988. (569 pp.)

Christopher's book is written with a sensitivity to what all human service helpers need to know about interviewing.

Peter G. Northhouse and Laurel Northhouse. *Health Communication Strategies for Health Professionals*, 2d ed. Norwalk, Conn.: Appleton and Lange, 1992. (286 pp.)

Sandra Sundeen et al. *Nurse Client Interaction: Implementing the Nursing Process*, 4th ed. St. Louis: C. V. Mosby, 1994. (406 pp.)

TWO

The Interview as Communication

Communication is the sharing of thoughts, feelings, attitudes, and ideas through the exchange of verbal and nonverbal symbols. We share our private thoughts and feelings with others through communication. The word derives from *communicare*, the Latin verb that means to 'make common.'

Defining *Communication* and Its Essential Elements

An interview is a special form of communication. Although the social work interview is a particular type of communication situation, its characteristics include many aspects of the general process of communication. Consequently, understanding the general process of communication contributes to a better understanding of the social work interview. That is why we are introducing this material before we discuss the specifics of the social work interview.

The interview involves two people, each of whom possesses a receiving system, a processing system, and a transmitting system. The receiving system consists of the five senses, the receptors. Communication primarily involves two receptors—the eyes and the ears. Having received the incoming signal, we process it; this involves making sense of the message received. The processing consists of recalling stored information, relating other information relevant to the message, thinking about the message, evaluating the message, and translating it so that the message is coherent within the receiver's frame of reference. As receivers we select certain items from the incoming message, ignore others, and rearrange what we hear into interpretable patterns. We then formulate a message in response. "Effector organs"—the voice, mouth, hands, eyes, and so on—transmit selected words and nonverbal gestures so that the other party in the interview can receive them; the second party in turn processes the message in order to formulate a response.

Communication once initiated is a circular reciprocally interacting process. The receiver-decoder of the message becomes the encoder of the next message. Each unit is a consequence of the unit that preceded it and an antecedent of the unit that follows. Participants in the communicative act are both senders and receivers.

A message is not a message until it is received and decoded. A communication loop is not complete until the person to whom the message is addressed begins to respond. As someone once said, "I never know what I said until I hear the response to it."

While receiving, processing, and responding to messages that originate externally, the interview participant is also receiving, processing, and responding to messages that originate internally. We are constantly engaged in checking how we feel physically and emotionally. The brain acts as a communication center, processing all the messages, interpreting them, and formulating an appropriate response.

Encoding and decoding are possible only if interviewer and interviewee are speaking the same language. They are using, in effect, a shared common code, a particular society's consensual sign system. But as Alfred North Whitehead, the English philosopher, once said, "Spoken language is merely a series of squeaks." The mind has to translate the squeaks so that they make sense. If the recipient is to receive the message with the meaning that the sender intended when encoding it, sender and receiver have to define the words they use in the same way.

The signals are meaningless sound until we decipher the sounds by attributing meanings to them. The meanings, not in the words themselves, are in the mind. .

Perception and comprehension of the message are not solely the result of actual signals transmitted, seen, and heard but are constructed from the signals and sifted through prior experience, knowledge, biases, and attitudes.

Good communication exists when one person encodes the thought and transmits it freely and with fidelity and the message decoded by the hearer is a faithful reproduction of the original message and when the meanings of the symbols transmitted and received correspond exactly. When this happens, we come closest to approximating the derivation of the word communication, namely, to make common. As Nunnally and

Moy (1989) note, good communication is the achievement of shared meaning.

The serial nature of communication makes it a hazardous undertaking. Each cycle of interaction—encoding, sending, receiving, processing, decoding—follows from the previous cycle so that difficulty encountered in any one cycle adversely affects communication in the subsequent cycles. And although it is interactional, going from interviewer to interviewee to interviewer, and so on, it is also dynamic; it builds. If we could photograph it, the interaction would look like a spiral or helix rather than a circle.

Communication is also irreversible. What we have said cannot be unsaid. Unlike the written word, which can be erased or edited, the spoken word is irretrievable. If your foot slips, you can regain your balance; if your tongue slips, you cannot recall your words.

Messages achieve part of their meaning from the context in which we send them. The same question in different settings evokes different aspects of the client's situation. The question "How are things going?" in a public assistance setting relates to budget and finances; in a child guidance clinic, it would relate to the child referred for service; in the marital counseling agency it would refer to the marriage.

Every communication encapsulates a content message and a relationship message. It says something about how the participants feel about each other and the difference in their status and power. Every communication evokes feelings as well as cognition. A communication, then, involves an exchange of feelings as well as ideas.

To recapitulate, communication is an interactional cycle of coding, sending, receiving, processing, and decoding verbal and nonverbal symbols that have no intrinsic meaning. We achieve maximum communication when the message we send is decoded exactly as we encoded it. However, physical, social, and psychological barriers in both encoding and decoding make fidelity in communication difficult. Communication is dynamic, transactional, irreversible, contextual, and multidimensional.

Metacommunication

Metacommunication further complicates the process of communication. Metacommunications are messages instructing us how to interpret the communication: "I only said that to get your goat"; "Don't take it seriously"; "It's between us"; and "I'm only kidding." Metacommunication provides the frame of reference within which to interpret the content of messages.

Nonverbal images, smiles, and hand gestures that accompany the words are metacommunications that modify, cancel, mitigate, or reinforce the meanings given to the words (see chapter 11). Vocalizations—pauses, inflections, amplitude, tone accompanying the words—also are significant components of the message that shape its meaning. These accompaniments instruct us how the words are meant to be interpreted.

Depending on the metacommunication—the message explaining the message—the same words can be a question, a paraphrase, an order, a request, or a neutral descriptive statement. "So you went with them to have a drink" can be a paraphrase if said in one way, a reprimand if said in another. Effective communication requires that we attend not just to what the words mean but what the speaker means and the context of the communication.

Sequential Steps in the Process of Communication

Let us follow the communication process, noting the more frequent problems encountered at significant points.

Encoding by the Interviewer

The process starts with the interviewer, who is responsible for initiating and guiding the interview.

Interviewers have the problem of selecting what to say from among a number of things that they might say and then deciding how to say it. Determining what to say requires that the interviewer answer such questions as "What am I trying to achieve at this point in the interview?" and "What can I say that would best further this objective and maintain or enhance the positive relationship?" How to say something requires answers to such questions as "How can I say what needs to be said verbally and nonverbally so that, given the interviewee's culture, vocabulary, and competence, this person is likely to clearly understand?"; "How can I say it to ensure that I maintain a positive relationship with the client?"; and "How can I say it so that it's appropriate to the context and ties in with the last message from the client?"

At this point in the process interviewers need to be aware of their feelings toward the client that might lead to a message that is rejecting, seducing, or confrontational. Feelings about the subject matter being discussed (incest, illness, poverty, childlessness, and the like) are additional determinants of what the interviewer chooses to say and how to encode it.

In this internal dialogue sorting out the alternatives in content and feeling about the message being considered is the necessary precursor to the next step—actually encoding the message. The interviewer needs to translate the thought into the verbal and visual symbols that will carry the message.

Communication involves converting private thoughts into public utterances. In encoding the message interviewers have to have at their command a sufficiently elaborate vocabulary to select the precise symbols and nuances to communicate their intended meaning. Workers need a vocabulary rich enough to convey the meaning of their thoughts and varied enough to adapt to the vocabulary of different clients.

The next step involves externalizing the inner dialogue by actually articulating the words that will carry the message. Events and experiences cannot be communicated as such. They have to be translated into words that carry a symbolic representation of the experience. The message as transmitted is the thought or idea encoded in the overt behavior of words and gestures. (Multiple channels are available for communication, but for the sake of simplicity we shall at this point discuss primarily the verbal channel of communication, leaving for chapter 11 a discussion of nonverbal communication.)

Transmitting

Having encoded the message in words most likely to ensure its undistorted reception, we still face the mechanical problem of transmission and reception. The setting for the interview might be noisy. The message to be transmitted may have to compete with the rumble of traffic, cross-talk from other interviews, the hum of fans and air conditioning, and the sounds of radio or television.

Noise in the external channel of communication is anything that obscures or distorts the signals transmitted between the interviewer and the interviewee. Clear transmission of a message in a quiet context, adequately protected from competing noises, is apt to be more the exception than the rule. Furthermore, effective communication requires the ability to speak clearly and loudly enough to understandably transmit the words embodying the message. A hoarse voice or a speech defect, a stutter, a serious lisp, or a difficult accent may reduce the fidelity of the transmission.

Decoding by the Interviewee

The eyes and ears of the receiver then receive for decoding the aural and visual symbols that carry the communication. Good reception requires that the interviewee have no hearing or sight impairment. It also requires that the interviewee be motivated to pay attention, that is, the interviewee be listening to and looking at the interviewer. Having heard and seen the communication stimuli, the interviewee has the problem of decoding the symbols. Listening is a component in the communication cycle of particular significance for interviewing.

Suppose that the receiver's ears hear exactly what the speaker has said. Communication has not yet taken place. The message is only one variable determining the information as received. Interviewees, at whom the message is directed, have a set of mental filters that guard against receiving messages that make them feel uncomfortable or that threaten their favorable perception of themselves, their psychic peace and quiet. Their ears may hear what was said, but they never permit the message to reach their mind.

Barriers to effective communication We have noted that physical impairments of speech, hearing, and vision are barriers to effective communication. There are psychological barriers as well.

Decoding, like encoding, is a selective process. The interviewee defends against admitting to conscious recognition communications that might increase anxiety, guilt, or shame or lower self-esteem. The interviewee receives the aural and visual symbols, has heard and seen them, but does not recognize them. Some people screen parts of the message for rejection or distortion. As one client said, "I don't hear and see things as they are. I see and hear as I am."

Selective perception permits us to hear only what we allow ourselves to hear and in the way we allow ourselves to hear it. It has been said that there is no "immaculate perception." What we hear, we convert so that it relates with minimum conflict to our experience, values, ideas, and preconceptions.

Each defense mechanism is a different kind of distortion of the message heard. In *projection* we hear the message not in terms of what was said but in terms of what we would have said in this situation; in *displacement* we attribute to one person the message from another; in *repression* we are deaf to the message being sent; in *reaction formation* we hear the opposite of the message transmitted. These mental processes protect us from hearing what would be inconvenient, hurtful, or frightening.

Selective perception is rapid and automatic so that we are not consciously aware of what communication we failed to receive. This is partly a result of the multiplicity and complexity of the communicative stimuli coming toward us and against which we need to defend for fear of an overload. But it is also partly a result of selectively permitting reception of what we can emotionally afford to hear and what communication we regard as relevant to the objectives of the interview.

Encoding by Interviewee

Having decoded the message, the interviewee-receiver now becomes the interviewee-transmitter, formulating and encoding a message in reply. At this point the interviewee faces the same problem the interviewer faced—what to say and how to say it. The interviewee now needs to sort through a number of psychological barriers.

Even before we put a thought into words for transmission, we pass it through a series of internal screens. We will not speak a thought that, if transmitted, is likely to lead to our being rejected by the person receiving the message. We also will not encode a thought that, if spoken, would make us more aware of what we are ashamed of, leading to a risk of self-rejection. Screens of psychological resistance and psychic repression block communication of anxiety-provoking thoughts. *Resistance* is conscious suppression of thoughts that seek expression. *Repression* indicates that barriers to the expression of some thoughts exist below the level of conscious awareness. People screen out these thoughts without recognizing that they exist or that they are censoring them.

Interviewees may be willing but unable to communicate some of the necessary information, attitudes, and feelings about their situation. People forget some facts and feelings and they become difficult to recall; some have been repressed so that they are beyond recall. Freudian slips are, of course, examples of thoughts that have eluded the screens and filters and achieved expression.

Other filters inhibit the encoding of thoughts that violate the etiquette of the communication situation. Swearing and openly hostile remarks get blocked out at this point. The interviewee is less likely to be open about thoughts and behaviors that are considered socially undesirable. This postinterview comment illustrates self-censorship—suppression of socially and personally unacceptable comments:

A 46-year-old woman has discussed a problem of residential care for her mother with a medical social worker.

When I first came, I thought I would say how I felt my mother was very difficult to live with, and I want an old-age home for her for my own comfort as well as because it might be good for her. But how can you say that, that you really don't like your mother when she is old? How can you tell that and not think people will feel you're lousy? Even when I say it to myself—that my mother annoys me, that she can be a pain—I think, "What kind of a daughter am I?"

Readiness to share and the location of the boundaries between public and private information vary among individuals and among groups. Individuals are more or less reticent; different groups in the community regard information about sex life, financial situation, and marital interaction as more or less private.

Being willing to share is a function of confidence that such involvement will result in some benefit for us. We accept the doctor's request to undress because we feel some assurance that to do so will help us with our pain. But if we lacked such motivation, would we be willing to undress? Why should we share our secrets if we will achieve nothing useful in exchange? We give interviewers access to only as much of ourselves as they need to know in order to help, and we do so only because we feel some assurance that as a result they are willing, ready, and able to assist us.

A feeling of social distance between client and worker represents a barrier. Clients have sometimes felt it hopeless to expect the worker to understand them. In the interviewee's perception the parties to the interview live in two different worlds.

Male, 18, probation interview.

So then they sent me to the school counselor, but he never took speed or cocaine—he never even tried pot—so I figured how can you talk to him? He wouldn't know how it was, and I didn't know how to tell him. I couldn't talk to him.

Discretion in the face of power is a barrier to free communication. Frequently, the interviewer controls access to some resource that the interviewee wants and needs—medical care, adoptive children, money. Frequently, the interviewer also can apply punishing legal sanctions—in probation and parole, protective service, or public assistance. Interviewees have to censor their communication so that they increase the possibility of getting what they want and prevent the application of negative sanctions.

We fashion and respond to communication not only to defend ourselves against threats to personal integrity, self-esteem, individuality, autonomy, and adequacy but also to present a positive, flattering, and acceptable image of ourselves. In selecting a message for communication we seek to induce others to perceive us positively.

We use language in communication to influence, persuade, cajole, demand, or excuse.

Physical contexts determine our communication choices. An interview in the privacy of an office might permit us to say some things that we

Figure 2.1 Diagram of a Single Cycle of Interview Communication

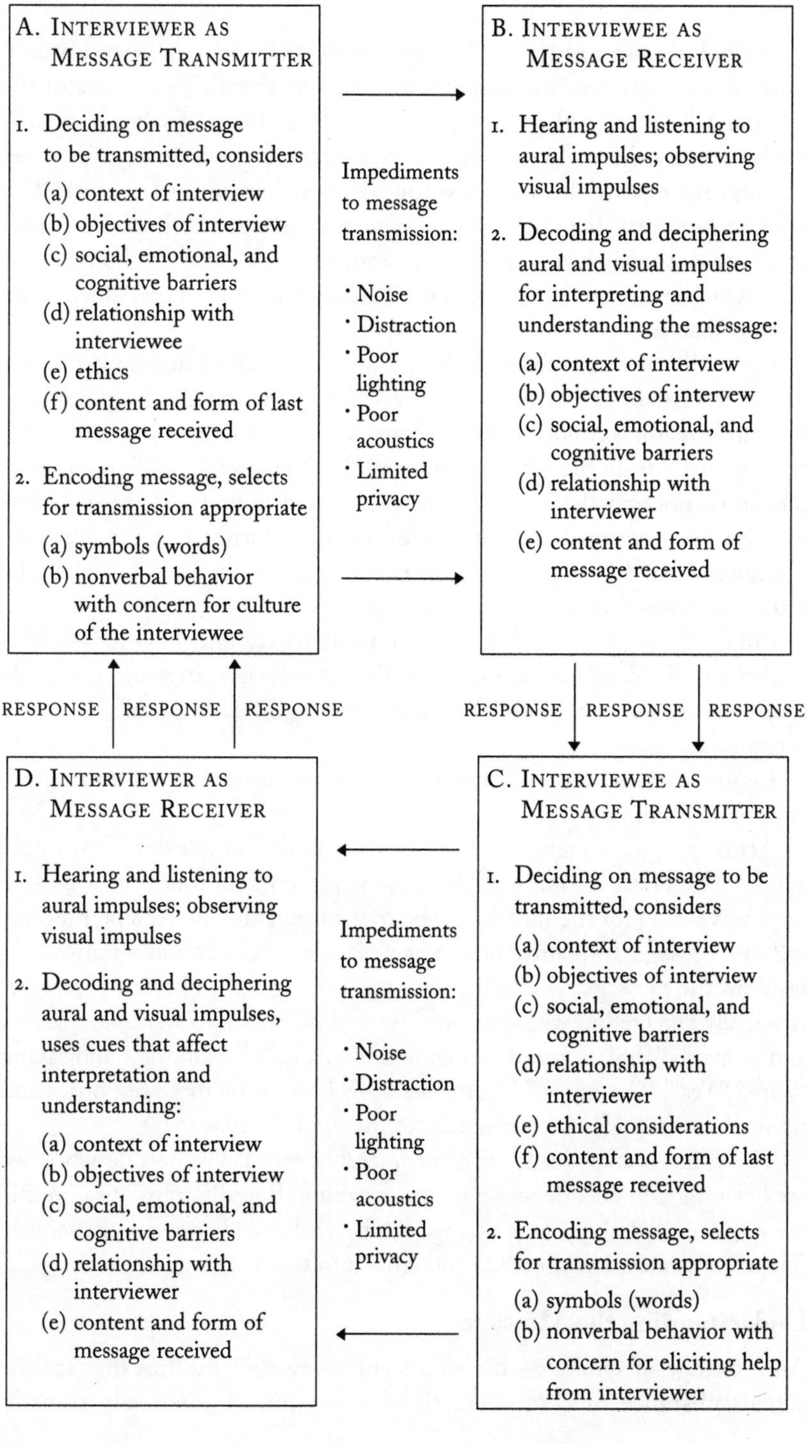

A. INTERVIEWER AS MESSAGE TRANSMITTER

1. Deciding on message to be transmitted, considers
   (a) context of interview
   (b) objectives of interview
   (c) social, emotional, and cognitive barriers
   (d) relationship with interviewee
   (e) ethics
   (f) content and form of last message received

2. Encoding message, selects for transmission appropriate
   (a) symbols (words)
   (b) nonverbal behavior with concern for culture of the interviewee

Impediments to message transmission:

· Noise
· Distraction
· Poor lighting
· Poor acoustics
· Limited privacy

B. INTERVIEWEE AS MESSAGE RECEIVER

1. Hearing and listening to aural impulses; observing visual impulses

2. Decoding and deciphering aural and visual impulses for interpreting and understanding the message:
   (a) context of interview
   (b) objectives of intervew
   (c) social, emotional, and cognitive barriers
   (d) relationship with interviewer
   (e) content and form of message received

RESPONSE | RESPONSE | RESPONSE   RESPONSE | RESPONSE | RESPONSE

D. INTERVIEWER AS MESSAGE RECEIVER

1. Hearing and listening to aural impulses; observing visual impulses

2. Decoding and deciphering aural and visual impulses, uses cues that affect interpretation and understanding:
   (a) context of interview
   (b) objectives of interview
   (c) social, emotional, and cognitive barriers
   (d) relationship with interviewer
   (e) content and form of message received

Impediments to message transmission:

· Noise
· Distraction
· Poor lighting
· Poor acoustics
· Limited privacy

C. INTERVIEWEE AS MESSAGE TRANSMITTER

1. Deciding on message to be transmitted, considers
   (a) context of interview
   (b) objectives of interview
   (c) social, emotional, and cognitive barriers
   (d) relationship with interviewer
   (e) ethical considerations
   (f) content and form of last message received

2. Encoding message, selects for transmission appropriate
   (a) symbols (words)
   (b) nonverbal behavior with concern for eliciting help from interviewer

might not choose not to say during a home visit or in an open hospital ward. But communication contexts are also emotional. The nature of the relationship between the participants is a determinant of what a client is likely to freely share. A comfortable, pleasant, safe relationship stimulates sharing. A negative, hurtful, rejecting relationship inhibits sharing. The relationship both shapes the interaction and is shaped by it. What is said and how it is said either enhance or diminish the quality of the relationship, which in turn enhances or diminishes the quantity of personal information shared.

Generally, any thought or feeling that we consider expressing aloud is part of a series of exchanges. Deciding whether the thought is appropriate for transmission is conditioned to a considerable extent by the communications received from the other participant(s) in the interview. Thus communication is not only the product of what each person brings to the interview but also a consequence of what each experiences during it. A thought suppressed early in the interview may be encoded and communicated when the interviewee has decided it is safe to share it.

Finally, having decided what they want to say and how to say it in response to the decoded message from the interviewer, interviewees encode their message for transmission to the interviewer. The communication cycle is complete.

Figure 2.1 is a diagram of one cycle of the interviewer-interviewee communication.

Actually, figure 2.1 tends to do an injustice to the complexity of the interaction. The chart is simplistic because it presents an image of a passive receiver waiting for the message to be transmitted and, on receipt, processing the message. In reality the receiver plays a role in how the transmitter fashions the message. While the message is being transmitted, the receiver is actively engaged in what has been termed *back-channel responses*—verbal and nonverbal emissions—smiling, nodding, and "uh-huming," and saying "Sure," "Yes," "Of course." Interviewers are affected by these responses and refine their messages from moment to moment (Krause 1987).

The process takes place with considerable speed. We decode while we are listening and encode while we are speaking. Rapidly translating multiple visual and aural symbols that we receive and decode, we simultaneously formulate a response, encoding thoughts into words and gestures.

Understanding the Message

An exchange of symbols—the words and nonverbal gestures that are the actual substance of communication—does not automatically transfer meaning. The symbols activate and evoke meanings. The meanings evoked depend the subjective perception of the person receiving them.

The verbal symbols that are encoded, transmitted, received, and decoded have no intrinsic meaning. The participants in the communication give meaning to the symbols.

Cantril (1956) uses three umpires to illustrate the percept that communication is not complete until the receiver has translated the message. Speaking of calling pitches, the first umpire says, "Some are balls and some are strikes and I call them as they is." The second umpire says, "Some are balls and some are strikes and I call them as I see them." The third umpire says, "Some are balls, some are strikes, and they ain't nothing 'til I call them."

The dictum "no communication without interpretation" implies that the message we ultimately receive is not the same as the message that was sent. We classify, catalogue, and interpret incoming messages by relating them to past experiences and learning. Then we organize the material we have selectively received so we can search for its meaning.

During an interview the interviewer invests a considerable amount of energy in processing communication. After workers decode what they have heard but before they respond, they attempt to make sense of it. This is the assessment process in microcosm. How does this particular item of communication fit into the series of messages previously received? What does the client mean? How am I to understand this? These introspective comments by a worker in a public assistance agency illustrate the process:

Up until now we were discussing how hard it is to feed the kids adequately on the AFDC budget. The last remark was about the fact that she hadn't gotten a new dress in two years. What is she trying to tell me? That she, too, is deprived? That I should have some pity for her? That she is trying hard to be a good mother, putting the kids' needs first? That I ought to try to do something to help her and not only be concerned about the kids? That she missed, and wanted, some guy hanging around? What makes her say this at this point in the interview? I also tried to decide at this point how concerned she was with this, because I was not sure whether to shift the interview to focus directly at this point on her concern about a new dress or table it and bring it up later while I continued to focus on the problem of feeding the kids on the budget. I decided that she was upset, but not all that upset about it that it couldn't hold and, although I didn't clearly understand what prompted the remark at this point, I decided to acknowledge the remark, indicate we would come back to it later, but continue, for the time, to discuss the problem of feeding the kids.

The next interview and the interviewer's introspective comments demonstrate the problems that interviewers face as they process what they hear:

Interviewee: female, 54, protective service.

MRS. L.: Yes he is, I'm telling you. He's very hard to understand. If I knew to this day . . . that he was mean to his first wife in [names a city] here, he lived here . . . I'd've never married the man. [*Pause.*] His folks are . . . oh, *wonderful* people, they're . . . they love me, and they love the kids, but I never hear from them. Because they're real old. They're, uh. . . . They, uhm. . . . They stopped sending Christmas cards after, uh . . . I was divorced from him. . . . They didn't send no more Christmas cards. . . . They, uh, ask about me, they ask about my stepson—they ask, they all ask *about* me, and that's all right. They ask about us, and I ask about *them*. We get, I get along with the two sons that I kept in touch with, even Sid came and seen me, and he was jealous of his own son come and visit me. His son come and stayed . . . when he was goin' away to Chicago, he came and visited me. . . . And just 'cause he stayed here till noon . . . to have dinner with me, he was very jealous. He thought I had intercourse with his own son. [*Pause.*] His imagination, you know, I mean sort of. . . . And then when I visited, we used to be down to his own father. . . . He thought I'd have intercourse with his own dad, imagine. . . . His imagination, that was all in his head. . . . Because he, that's all what *he* always wanted all the time I lived with him. Constantly. And that's what he wanted.

The interviewer comments,

This is the type of response which confused me most. I just did not and do not understand this "free association" of topics and lines of thought. Similarly, I do not understand what function this seemingly aimless talk played for Mrs. L. Was it to ward off questions or comments which she feared? Was it preferable to any silence? Was the tension of the interview bringing it about, or does she always speak in such a manner? Was it a desperate attempt to show she was "good" and worthy of my care, that it was everyone else who did "bad" things? Was she not even perceiving me or was she checking out my reactions while she talked? All these various alternatives were going through my mind and suggesting alternative modes of action. I did not know whether she was crying out for some external ordering from me or whether she feared that as of yet and needed to be accepted in her wandering, dissociated ways before she would be able to accept direction or direct herself.

Words and Meanings

We need to be reminded that English has about six hundred thousand words and that the five hundred most commonly used words have fourteen thousand dictionary definitions. Each word has a general meaning, the dictionary meaning we all recognize. But each word also has a special meaning, which we give to a word based on our own background.

Words evoke a subjective world of idiosyncratic associated images. Socialization and experience provide everyone with a unique schemata, a cognitive map that is the blueprint for perceiving, understanding, and dealing with the world. Schema are the templates that we apply to infer meanings from the symbols communicated. Because no two schema are the same, no two people translate one communication identically. Living in private worlds, we systematically personalize the meanings we give to words, giving them individual thoughtprints.

"It must have been hard for you" may reduce to tears a young girl who feels lonely, rejected, and misunderstood. A 25-year-old male who prides himself on his masculinity and his ability to cope with difficulties will react to the same message with anger. The message is the same; the reaction is different because the perception of its meaning is different.

Given the differences in socialization and living experience, words like *rape, domestic violence,* and *glass ceiling* do not convey the same cognitive and affective meanings to the average man as they do to the average woman. Thus income level, gender, and ethnicity shape the meanings of the words we use.

Middle-income language is different from lower-income language. Komarovsky notes differences in word connotation between blue-collar respondents and college-educated interviewers in a study of blue-collar marriages.

> The word "*quarrel*" carried the connotations of such a major and violent conflict that we had to use "spat," "disagreement," and other terms to convey a variety of marital clashes. To "confide" often meant to seek advice rather than share for its own sake. "Talk" to a few implied a long discussion (telling each other news isn't talking). "Intelligent" and "smart" were the terms used, not "bright"; "unfair," not "unjust." What kinds of things make you pleased or satisfied with yourself, we asked. "When I get my work done," "When I get a bargain," and similar responses were given by some. But to a large proportion of the men and women the phrase "pleased with yourself" implied the unfavorable connotations of being "stuck on yourself." These tended to answer the question in the manner of one confessing moral defects.
>
> (1967:19–20)

Tannen (1990) has detailed the differences in male and female use of language.

Because the interviewee's frame of reference, perceptual set, and personal constructs may be different from those of the interviewer, some distortion in message reception takes place as the interviewee interprets the words used by the interviewer.

We, as interviewers, err in assuming that because we know what we intend to say, our partner in the interaction has understood our meaning. Interviewees, in giving meaning to the words received, do not understand that they do not understand.

Jargon and Miscommunication

Another source of potential misunderstanding derives from jargon—the professional language of the social work interviewer. Professional education provides the interviewer with special connotative meaning to many ordinary words.

Worker and client may nominally speak the same language but actually not understand one another. *Eligibility* sounds one way and has one meaning to the worker; it sounds quite different to and evokes a different set of responses in the client. We say *home study* and *court record* and *therapy* without knowing how these unfamiliar words sound to the client.

From habit we toss off acronyms that are baffling to interviewees— AFDC, OASDI (Old Age, Survivors, and Disability Insurance), SSI (Supplemental Security Income), and so on. We use terms such as *support network, generic approach, self-actualization, treatment milieu,* and *systems intervention,* which make sense to us but are likely to bewilder interviewees.

Although we might expect the social work interviewer and interviewee to give different meanings to technical terms, this can also be true for everyday phrases. For instance, hospital workers note that doctors and patients interpret the phrase "going home from the hospital soon" quite differently. The doctors inferred *soon* to mean two to four days. Many patients interpreted it as *tomorrow.*

Words that seem obvious to the interviewer may not be so obvious to the interviewee. Following a discussion of an unmarried woman's reaction to the recent birth of her child and that of her parents, who were pressing for adoption, the social worker summarizes:

INTERVIEWER: You seem to be really happy about being a new mother, but there still seems to be some residuals of unresolved conflict between yourself and your parents.

INTERVIEWEE [*After a short pause.*]: I don't get you.

A medical social worker asks the interviewee if the family has any history of cardiac arrest. The interviewee responds with some vehemence that nobody in the family has ever been arrested.

A middle-aged man referred to a family service agency for marital counseling is talking about his difficulty in being on time for appointments. The worker tries to determine whether tardiness is a general problem:

INTERVIEWER: Do you have other kinds of difficulties in this area?

INTERVIEWEE: No, not in this area, but I did have the same trouble when I lived in Cincinnati.

Immediacy and Concreteness in Communication

Subtleties in the use of language may change the meaning of the message without our being fully aware of the significance of the choices we are making.

Choice of wording can permit us to depersonalize a message. "Doing this is foolish" is less personal than "I am foolish for doing this."

Choice of wording can shift the locus of attribution of the problem, as in "I was overcome by guilt" as against "I felt guilty." In the first instance the interviewee is acted upon; in the second the interviewee is the actor.

Subtle variations in word choice may be cues to differences in underlying attitudes. In talking about a child's achievements a mother might say, "It wasn't bad," or she might say, "It was good." In discussing an abusive incident a father might say, "I am not at all happy about what happened" or "I am unhappy about what happened." The choice of phrasing reflects different degrees of ambivalence. In discussing marital conflict the interviewee who says, "People often fight" or "One often fights" is saying something different from the interviewee who accepts greater ownership by saying, "We fight"—or, even more immediate, "I fight."

Words that sound concrete, specific, and definite on second thought are not. This is particularly true of words describing emotions. What does the interviewee mean by being *worried* or *depressed* or *independent* or *responsible*? The words are slippery and until more clearly defined in behavioral or situational terms may evoke different images in the minds of the interviewee and interviewer.

Concreteness and immediacy, then, require moving from the general to the specific, from the past to the present, from the impersonal to the personal, and from the indefinite to the definite and precise.

Box 2.1 summarizes barriers to effective communication.

Box 2.1 Barriers to Effective Communication

INTERNAL VARIABLES IN TRANSMITTING

Emotional-Psychological-Social Barriers

• Message screening to avoid rejection, anger, anxiety, shame, seduction
• Message screening to enhance acceptance, positive image, influence
• Screening to control prejudiced (racist, sexist, homophobic) speech
• Speech inapropriate to context and client, jargon, vocabulary

Cognitive Barriers

• Language competence, vocabulary adequacy, expressiveness
• Knowledge/information regarding content
• Conceptual grasp of relevant ideas

Physical Barriers

• Speech impediments: stuttering, lisp
• Fatigue, burn-out

EXTERNAL CHANNEL VARIABLES

• Noise, vibrations, competing stimuli
• Distractions (phones, interruptions)
• Poor lighting
• Poor acoustics
• Limited privacy

INTERNAL VARIABLES IN RECEIVING

Emotional-Psychological-Social Barriers

• Screening incoming message to avoid anxiety, guilt, shame, inadequacy, rejection
• Screening incoming message to enhance self-esteem, favorable self-image
• Screening taboos, socially unacceptable terms and ideas
• Distorting the message in response to expectations of biases

Cognitive Barriers

• Vocabulary adequacy
• Ability to grasp relevant information, ideas
• Experience—frame of reference of receiver different from transmitter

Physical Barriers

• Hearing problems
• Vision problems
• Fatigue

Feedback

Given the various barriers to clear undistorted communication, misunderstandings as a result of miscommunication are a frequent problem. Thus feedback is important.

The message encoder needs feedback to determine whether the message sent was the message received; the decoder needs feedback to determine whether the message received was the message sent.

Because communication goes on at so many different levels, through so many different channels, and is so easily distorted, feedback is a necessity. Often we do not realize that we do not understand. As sociologist William F. Whyte says, "The great enemy of communication is the illusion of it." Achieving good communication requires, then, a presumption of ignorance—the frequent acceptance that although we think we know what the interviewee said, we may not really know. The corrective for presumptive ignorance is feedback. We check our understanding of the message by asking for confirmation.

Once the message is encoded and sent, the sender loses control over it. What is done to it—how it is received or ignored or misinterpreted or distorted—is beyond the sender's power to change. Just as the receiver never knows what the message, as formulated by the sender, actually was, the sender never knows how the message was actually received. The receiver hears only the words and sees only the nonverbal cues that stand for the message sent; the sender sees and hears only the behavioral and verbal responses that stand for the message received. The sender may try again in response to feedback about how the message is received, if the sender recognizes that the message was unsuccessful. We are often tempted to say, "I know that you believe you understand what you think I said, but I am not sure you realize that what you heard is not what I meant."

Because the meaning expressed is not always the meaning communicated, the interviewer must encourage the client to offer feedback. If the interviewee lacks the courage or does not feel entitled to offer feedback, the client loses the opportunity to correct a miscommunication.

A worker asks a client about whether any "repercussions" followed her decision to stay home from work to care for a sick child. The client looks puzzled and asks, "What do you mean?" The worker then translates *repercussions* and comments, "Fortunately, the client was willing to display her ignorance. Had she wanted to impress me, or had she been an adult embarrassed because she didn't understand the terminology used, she may have given an inaccurate and/or very general response."

We get feedback not only from others—in their nod of recognition, in their happy smiles or puzzled grimaces, in their responses that indicate we have hit the target—but from ourselves. We listen to the way we say what we mean to say and evaluate the success with which we have said it. If it sounds unclear to us, or muddled, or ambiguous, we pat it into shape with an explanatory phrase here or a clarifying sentence there. And because language is inexact, we make ourselves understood by a series of repetitive statements, successive approximations of our meaning.

Communication involves not only an external dialogue between worker and client but also a series of internal monologues—clients with themselves, workers with themselves. They are talking and listening to themselves while talking and listening to each other. Both the external dialogue and the internal feedback monologues go on at different levels of more or less explicit communication. Content is both overt and manifest, and latent and covert. There are the words directly spoken and the less obvious indirect meanings of what was said.

The following is a section of a social work interview with both manifest and latent content presented, the material having been obtained from the participants after the interview.

Interviewer is male, 32, white social worker.

Interviewee is female, 30, African American lower middle income, seeking assistance from the homemaker unit of a family services bureau.

(Manifest comment is in roman, *latent comment in parentheses and italics.)*

Manifest Content	Latent Content
WORKER: Could you tell me something about what brings you to the agency?	*(Hope she won't think we're racist if we turn down her request, whatever it is. Hope it's something simple we can handle.)*
CLIENT: The social worker at the hospital . . . I have to go for an operation, and there is not going to be anybody to care for the kids because my husband works all day, and the kids have to have somebody look after them, and she said I might have a homemaker to look after the kids while I am away.	*(Honky, always a honky. Can't I ever get to talk to a black worker? Is he going to think I really need this or is he going to give me all that "uh" "uh" and get my black ass out of here? What will the kids do then? I've really got to sell this.)*

WORKER: What kind of an operation is it you're scheduled for? How long will you be in the hospital?

(How necessary is this and for how long? We have only a few homemakers, and if we tie up one for a long time we will be in a bind.)

CLIENT: I have this trouble with my gall bladder all the time, all the time. It gets worse, and the doctor said I need this operation. It will be worse for me and the kids the longer I put it off.

(Does he believe me? Does he think I am making it worse than it really is? How the hell do I know how long it's going to take?)

WORKER: Could you tell me who your doctor is and when we can contact the doctor to discuss your situation?

(You can't expect the patient to know the medical details. If we have to plan for this, we should find out the situation from the person who knows it best—the doctor.)

CLIENT: Sure, sure. Dr. _____ is the one I see when I go to the clinic. He knows all about it. Why do you have to talk to him?

(What does he want to know this for? Is he going to check what I tell him? I wonder if Dr. _____ will back me up on this. He gets sore if a lot of people ask him questions.)

WORKER: That's a good question. It's not that we don't believe you or that we want to check up on you, but we find that the person asked to have the operation, in this case yourself, doesn't often know the medical details we need for planning. For instance, if we were going to put a homemaker in the home—and at this point we are just talking about it—we would have to know for how long and what you could do after you came home from the hospital on convalescence and how much the homemaker would have to do.

(Suspicious? Worried about our talking to the doctor? Afraid he might tell us something she would not want us to know? Or is it that she really doesn't know what purpose would be served in contacting the doctor? Have to be careful about making it clear what we have in mind.)

CLIENT: Well, I really need a homemaker if I am going for the operation. The kids can't care for themselves. They are too young.

(Why do they always have to make it so complicated? He hasn't even asked me about how old the kids are and how many of them there are. Right away they want to speak to someone else. Speak to me. I know more about this than anybody else does.)

Summary: Chapter 2

Communication is the sharing of thoughts, feelings, attitudes, and ideas through the exchange of verbal and nonverbal symbols. Effective communication requires that we attend not just to what the words mean but to what the speaker means.

The interview process begins with the interviewer, who has the problem of selecting what to say from a number of possibilities and then deciding how to say it. Once the massage is encoded, the interviewer transmits it. Barriers to effective communication at this point in the interview include noise in the interview channel and problems enunciating clearly. The interviewee then decodes the message. Impediments to communication during decoding include the tendency for people to defend against, and not consciously acknowledge, communications that increase anxiety, guilt, and shame or that lower self-esteem. Once the message is decoded, the interviewee encodes a message in reply. At this point the interviewee may filter the communication to make it more socially desirable. The interviewee unconsciously screens out thoughts (represses). Status differences may discourage clients who believe that the worker will not be able to understand them. Interviewees may also censor communication if the interviewer controls access to a resource they need.

An exchange of symbols does not automatically transfer meaning. The meanings that are evoked are dependent on the subjective perception of the person receiving the symbols. The interviewer invests a considerable amount of energy in attempting to assess the meaning of the client's communication. Because the interviewee's frame of reference may be different from that of the interviewer, some distortion occurs when the interviewee interprets the words used by the interviewer. Given the various barriers to clear undistorted communication, misunderstandings often are the result of miscommunication. Thus obtaining feedback from the client is important: it confirms that the message we intended to send was actually received.

SUGGESTED READINGS

Communication

Whole libraries have been devoted to interpersonal communication. The following are highly selective and limited examples of this literature. The books cover the essential concepts that help in understanding interpersonal communication and offer leads to additional reading.

Bobby R. Patton and Kim Giffin. *Interpersonal Communication: Basic Text and Readings*, 3d ed. New York: Harper and Row, 1980. (499 pp.)

A good, solid, readable basic text in interpersonal communication. Selected from among dozens of such texts because it seems to provide the essentials briefly and clearly.

William W. Wilmot. *Dyadic Communication*, 3d ed. New York: Random House, 1987. (290 pp.)

Because the interview is primarily an example of dyadic communication, this adaptation of principles and concepts of two-way communication is especially useful.

Elam Nunnally and Caryl Moy. *Communication Basics for Human Service Professionals*. Newbury Park, Calif.: Sage, 1989. (170 pp.)

A basic text discussing communication in the context of human services settings.

Owen Hargie, Christine Saunders, and David Dickson. *Social Skills in Interpersonal Communication*, 3d ed. New York: Rutledge, 1994. (369 pp.)

A well-written, up-to-date overview of communication skills with particular focus on concerns of professionals.

THREE

Listening: A Basic Communication Skill

One significant step in the communication cycle is listening. The interviewer must spend a considerable amount of time and effort listening to the interviewee. Nelson-Jones (1988) notes that for the human service worker "the capacity to be a good and understanding listener is perhaps the most fundamental skill of all" (p. 17).

Researchers have found that interviewers who spend less than two-thirds of an interview listening and more than one-third talking are more active than they should be. A common error of inexperienced interviewers is to talk too much and to listen too little. Overactive talking makes for underactive listening. Listening is deceptively simple; effective listening is difficult, an active rather than a passive technique. Good listening requires carefully following what is said overtly as well as the undertones. It requires being expectantly attentive and receptive. It requires a relaxed alertness that the interviewer uses to reach out mentally to bring in what the interviewee is saying. To listen effectively we must be silent. Because the listener is quiet, we tend to think of listening as a passive function. The apparent passivity of the listener is accentuated by the overt activity of the talker. Actually, good listening requires a considerable amount of internal activity. The Japanese ideograph for *listen* is composed of the character for *ear* nested in the character for *gate*. In listening we move beyond the interviewees' gate and into their world.

Hearing Versus Listening

Hearing and listening, while related, are in fact two different processes. Hearing is a physiological act—the apprehension of sound. It is a necessary antecedent to listening. Listening is more difficult than hearing because hearing is a natural biological act and listening is a learned activity. Whereas hearing primarily involves reception, listening primarily involves perception. Hearing happens automatically; we have to make listening happen. We hear with our ears; we listen with our brains. Listening is a cerebral act— understanding the sound that has been heard by deriving meaning from it. Unlike hearing, listening requires deliberate attention to sound. Just as you can look without seeing, you can hear without listening.

Listening is the dynamic process of attaching meaning to what we hear, making sense of the raw verbal-vocal symbols. It is a purposive and selective process in which the hearer screens, gives attention to, recognizes, comprehends, and interprets sounds communicated by a speaker.

From all the words uttered by someone speaking to us, all of which we hear, we select a limited number on which to focus our awareness. Until we actually attend to the communication, we have only heard but have not as yet listened. We then engage in a process of ascribing meaning to the limited number of sentences we listen to and go on to interpret their meaning. Listening involves the cognitive structuring of the message we select for attention.

The distinction between hearing and listening derives from the ability to hear without understanding. Listening involves providing the understanding; the mind provides the meaning to the sound. We can hear a foreign language, but if we do not know the language, we cannot listen and derive meaning.

Because listening, unlike hearing, is not an automatic process, we have to make a conscious, deliberate, and continuing commitment to listen. It almost requires that we occasionally command ourselves to listen.

Listening involves attention not only to the words per se but to the vocalizations accompanying the words. This permits us to distinguish a command from a request or a question. We discuss the vocal nonverbal aspects of interview communication more fully in chapter 11.

Conditions for Good Listening

Although listening is distinct from hearing, it depends on good hearing. If you cannot hear the sounds, you cannot process them. Any distractions or impediments to good hearing impede listening. A quiet room with a minimum of competing sounds is a prerequisite for good listening. Frequently, the interviewer has to accept a poor hearing-listening situation as a given—

poor acoustics, interviewees who have speech defects or a difficult accent, or who talk at an inaudible level or in rapid, jerky tempo.

Interviewees who slur their words because they have been drinking or taking drugs or who speak in a low voice present problems for hearing and listening. These difficulties mean the interviewer has to expend more energy merely to hear what is said, which results in fatigue and a desire for relief from the work of listening.

Gently and courteously telling interviewees they are inaudible is a helpful communication and one that clients may accept without resentment because it reflects the worker's sincere interest in trying to listen. The interviewer is responsible for helping interviewees present their situation in a way that helps the worker listen effectively.

Admittedly, some interviewees make listening more difficult. They talk in a monotone. They put little drama into their presentation. They are repetitive and discuss their problem in the least imaginative, most uninteresting manner. They use long pauses and frequently interject "you know" or "eh, eh." Messages that lack coherence and discernible structure also present a problem for the listener. Some interviewees are easier to listen to. But the obligation to listen to the presentation of the least interesting interviewee is as great as the obligation to listen to the most interesting.

Relating Listening to the Interview

Listening is basic to a good interview. Unless interviewers listen carefully to what clients are saying, interviewers cannot follow, reflect, or paraphrase accurately, summarize correctly, or offer appropriate feedback to clients. Listening is not only basic to implementing the instrumental aspects of interviewing; it is also related to the interview's expressive aspects. Listening requires effective attending and shows respect and concern for the interviewee. Careful listening demonstrates that the interviewee is worthy of the full attention of the interviewer.

Interviewers use feedback to determine the success of their listening; interviewees accept feedback as reflecting an understanding of their message. (Feedback interventions such as paraphrase and reflecting are discussed in greater detail in chpater 6.)

Researching clients' reactions to interviewers' interventions, Nugent found that active listening consistently tends to evoke for interviewees a feeling of being understood (1992:25).

Interviewers also need to present an attitude of listening to visually communicate that they are listening. Interviewees need such confirmation. An attending stance, eye contact, a forward lean, and a physically attentive orientation show that the worker is listening. More to the point are the interviewer's accurate reflecting, correct paraphrasing, and appropriate summarizing, all of which show that the interviewer has listened.

Although careful to use body language to signify listing, the good listener is equally careful to refrain from any signs of inattention. Furtive glances at the clock, idle doodling on a notepad, sorting material on the desk, and glancing out the window to check the weather all suggest wandering attention.

In order to listen workers must control their desire to speak, assume ignorance of what the speaker is likely to say, and intensify a desire to learn what the speaker wants to say. As Schulman says, the good listener "develops large eyes, big ears, and a small mouth" (1974:121). Courteous considerate listening involves devoting your undistracted uninterrupted attention and interest to the verbal and nonverbal messages with the intent to understand their meaning.

Because listening is a process that requires considerable expenditure of mental and emotional effort, fatigue reduces the ability to listen. Fatigue decreases the attention span, makes concentration more difficult, and attenuates the motivation to listen. Listening is apt to be less efficient toward the end of a long interview. This argues for interviews of reasonable length—not much more than one hour without a break.

Listening requires a mind that is not burdened with personal preoccupations and a body that does not call attention to itself. A pain in the joints, a persistent itch, or digestive discomfort pulls attention away from what is being said. However, too much comfort is also the enemy of listening. We drift off into a hazy daze if we are warmly, wonderfully comfortable.

Social Listening Versus Interview Listening

Typical day-to-day social interaction encourages the development of poor listening habits. Social interaction involves a considerable amount of hearing but only a limited amount of listening. Very often we courteously feign listening but pay only peripheral attention to what we hear. We know from experience that to listen to everything we hear is a regrettable waste of time involving a considerable effort for the return provided. We have learned not to listen because many people to whom we have only a limited obligation to listen say much that is irrelevant. Much of what we hear is ritualistic noise, and we practice pretending to listen. For good reasons and in self-protection we have, as a consequence of long experience in commonplace social interaction, developed listening habits that are bad for good interviewing. In learning to listen most effectively in the interview you will find helpful to consciously identify your habituated patterns of listening and to determine what you need to change.

In contrast to the polite civil inattention with which we generally listen to others, the interview requires that we listen with our ears, our eyes, our brains, and our hearts.

Many people engaged in social conversation tend to be redundant, which further encourages dysfunctional listening habits. Because people repeat themselves, we do not pay a high price for failing to listen the first time around. We have learned that we will catch anything important the second or third time around.

In everyday social situations listening usually involves interacting with somebody we know—spouse, children, friends, coworkers. Our knowledge of patterns of past interaction helps us to listen and make sense of what they are saying. We can anticipate with some validity some things they are likely to say. We can correctly fill in gaps. This makes for listening with diminished concentration. And we once again tend to develop lazy listening habits. Interviews with strangers, often the case in social work, requires greater effort. We have no history of patterns of interaction on which to draw in understanding the communication. Listening in the interview requires more attention because we do not know the person. We have fewer prior assumptions and preconceptions to guide us (Schlesinger 1994).

In social situations we often listen defensively. We busy ourselves with preparing our rebuttal to ideas, attitudes, and values being expressed that are in opposition to our own and that consequently threaten us. Preparing our counterpresentation interferes with full and effective listening. We are devoting a considerable amount of energy to formulating an answer rather than to listening. Consequently, we often listen inattentively, impatiently awaiting the opportunity to have our turn to talk.

Without realizing it we frequently tend to interrupt each other in social conversations rather than hear each other out. We think we get the point, we are impatient to respond, and we start talking before the other person has finished. We resent our partner's continuing to talk while we are interrupting. Interrupting is antithetical to listening. During an interview, however, interviewees expect that the interviewer will not finish listening before they finish talking.

Sometimes we do not listen because we cannot afford to listen. To listen with a willingness to understand may risk internal conflict and dissonance as our cherished beliefs are challenged and perhaps contradicted. Or we may learn things that make us feel inadequate or inferior or call attention to a problem we are trying to suppress. We often listen with our fears, not our ears, which distorts or screens out what has been said.

A social worker in corrections was checking the tape of an interview with the wife of a prisoner in a state penitentiary.

> As I listened to the tape I was chagrined to find that a whole section of the interview had drifted out of my mind. Mrs. N. talked about the sadness she felt on separating from her husband after a recent visit. She went on to talk about the emptiness of the house and the effect of his absence on the family. I recalled none of this. Apparently the word *separation* triggered for me my own feelings about my impending divorce, and I kind of turned myself off at this point or tuned her out.

This is an example of how reactions may be triggered by stimuli of which we are not consciously aware but which have significant ego involvement for us. Perceptual discrimination, screening what gets listened to, occurs in terms of both feelings and information. True listening implies a readiness to consider that which challenges our preconceptions. It involves a willingness to lower the psychic barriers that might impede our undistorted perception of what the interviewee is saying.

Interview listening requires a different approach from social listening. Interviewers need to feel comfortable and unthreatened by anything the interviewee says in order to devote all their energy to listening freely. Although interviewers recognize that what is being said may be contrary to their own values and attitudes, workers are not called on to defend their values and attitudes in the interview.

The nature of spoken communication presents a special hazard that seduces the interviewer into an easy nonlistening mode. The hazard is the great discrepancy between the number of words normally spoken in one minute and the number of words that the brain can absorb in that time. Thinking speed is much faster than talking speed.

The average rate of spoken speech is about 125 words per minute. We can read and understand an average of three hundred to five hundred words per minute. There is, then, a considerable amount of dead time in spoken communication, during which the listener's mind can easily become distracted. Listeners start talking to themselves to take up the slack. Listening to the internal monologue may occur simultaneously with listening to the external dialogue. More often, however, it goes on at the expense of listening to the external dialogue. The interviewer becomes lost in some private reverie—planning, musing, dreaming.

Client, female, 68, upper middle income, medical social work interview.

MRS. M.: So because of the experience on the trip, Arnie has a better appreciation of how inconveniently crowded it might be with another person living in their relatively small house.

WORKER: Arnie?

MRS. M.: Yes—Arnie, Arnold, my daughter's husband. I told you this before.

The worker's introspective comment on this:

I felt ashamed about this. I was caught woolgathering. Mrs. M. had been telling me about a trip her daughter's family had taken recently out West. It didn't seem particularly consequential to the problem for which she was referred [helping her accept a post-hospital living situation with her daughter], and so I began to think about my coming vacation and a trip we were planning. I just monitored the cadence of what Mrs. M. was saying but really was not listening. I was thinking about what needed checking on the car and some of the reservations that needed to be made yet. Somewhere along the line, Mrs. M. must have switched from the trip to the reactions of the family, living crowded together in motel rooms. Somehow I must have become aware that the content was becoming more relevant, but I surfaced slowly from my own trip plans, and when she said Arnie, for the moment I couldn't place the name. She generally refers to him as "my daughter's husband." When she had to explain who he was, she must have sensed I had not been listening, because she was irritated and annoyed. Not so good.

The supposition is that if you are not talking, you must be listening. Actually, the interviewer may not be talking and not be listening, either—at least not to the interviewee.

This male psychiatric social worker's analysis of his pattern of listening is instructive:

I have become aware that I carry over to the interview some defensive listening patterns I have developed in general social interaction. It is a way of faking listening while permitting yourself the opportunity of enjoying your own private thinking. You look expectantly directly at the person, nod occasionally, or say, "Yes, yes," smile when he smiles, and laugh along with him—at what, you don't know because you haven't been listening. To protect my relationship with the speaker, I half-listen or listen sporadically. Every once in a while I'll really listen to check if I know what, in general, he is talking about. This is in case he should ask me a question. I listen for questions by the inflection. If the tone changes and I catch a rising inflection, I know I am being asked something. In social encounters, this gives me a lot of time for myself, and saves me from having to listen to an awful lot of BS. But I tend to slip into this pattern in the interview when the client bores me with repetition or with inconsequential detail. It bothers me because, unless I keep listening, how do I really know it's repetitive stuff or inconsequential?

The great possibilities for distraction from listening require considerable self-discipline from the would-be listener. Rather than becoming preoccupied in the time between the slowly spoken words, the good interviewer exploits this time in the service of more effective listening. The listener remains focused on the interviewee but uses the time to move rapidly back and forth along the path of the interview, testing, connecting, and questioning:

> How does what I am hearing now relate to what I heard before? How does it modify what I heard before? How does it conflict with it, support it, make it more understandable? What can I anticipate hearing next? What do I miss hearing that needs asking about? What is she trying to tell me? What other meanings can the message have? What are her motives in telling me this? How can I use what she is saying in order to be helpful to her? What does she want of me?

The Value of Knowledge for Listening

We hear much more than we listen to. We could not conceivably listen to all that we hear—all the sounds that bombard our ears and make for the physiological changes we define as hearing. Nor would it be functionally efficient. We are inevitably selective. From the variety of sounds that we hear we pay attention to relatively few for recognition, cognition, and understanding. Someone once described the average listener as a narrow-necked bottle over which the speaker tosses water. Some goes in, but much more goes by. If interviewers felt compelled to listen to everything that was said, they would be overwhelmed with stimuli. The ear, like the eye, receives more than the mind can efficiently process.

The criteria for selectivity in the interview situation is different from the criteria for selectivity in the social situation. Our professional knowledge of the social problem of concern to the interviewee and its potential solutions permit us to select what is relevant and consequential.

Because listening involves the cerebral process of ascribing meanings to the sounds heard, the more workers know about the social problems the client is describing, the more likely it is that they can listen effectively.

Being knowledgeable about the problems of old age, or single parenthood, or physical disability permits the worker to make mental connections that make listening less difficult. Interviewers find that they understand the client's situation better because of the background knowledge they bring to listening. This is rewarding and sustains the worker's motivation to continue to pay the close attention required for effective listening.

The disciplined concentrated attention required for effective listening is much more difficult to sustain when we cannot understand what is being said because we lack the requisite background knowledge. Most of us could listen attentively for only a short time to an interviewee talking about experimental procedures in subatomic physics.

General knowledge of the content also guides selectivity in listening. Having some expertise about a particular social situation for which the agency offers service permits us to assess what is of importance and significance in what the client is saying and what we can let go by because it's not particularly relevant.

Listening leads to understanding, but understanding facilitates listening. If the interviewer has some ideas that give meaning to what the interviewee is saying, the interviewer knows what to listen for. Listening is directed, guided, and selective rather than diffuse and scattered, which risks information overload. However, knowledge of the content presents its own problems. We may be so sure of the nature of the problem that we fill in the blanks and fail to listen. On the whole, however, knowledge derived from social work practice, literature, research, and theory permits easier and more effective listening.

Focused listening involves sifting the consequential from unessential information, the relevant from the irrelevant, and knowing the difference requires background knowledge.

Guidelines for Listening

At this point it may be helpful to consider some broad general guidelines for effective listening.

1. Clarity about the purpose of the interview is essential. A clear idea of the purpose of the interview is an important filter for selectivity in listening. Workers who know the objective of the encounter are in a good position to focus on certain things the client is saying. A clear conception of purpose acts as a magnifying glass, amplifying these points. Purpose structures attention.

2. The worker should listen for recurrent dominant themes rather than focus on detail. Listening to the essence of interviewees' communication

with an "ever-hovering attention" means listening to what interviewees mean rather than what they say.

Workers should formulate these dominant themes slowly in the course of the interview rather than decide upon them early. Although interviewers actively organize the material they listen to, they hold the developing configuration lightly, provisionally.

3. Effective interviewers suspend closure, holding everything they listen to tentatively and subject to revision because of what the client might say next. This is true not only for immediate interactions but during the longer course in the interview. Making up your mind about interviewees and their problem early in the interview is a decision that in itself filters out subsequent listening. Workers can fall into the trap of tending to listen to those things that confirm the early assessments and fail to listen to those communications that contradict that conclusion. It takes a deliberate effort to listen to the unexpected.

A middle-aged blue-collar worker was referred by a high-school teacher to a local family planning service when his 14-year-old daughter Ruth was found to be pregnant. The female social worker said,

> The way he talked early in the interview . . . I guess my stereotype of blue-collar workers' attitudes leads me to think of him as conservative in his thinking. Everything he said and his whole approach to problems seem to confirm it for me. He was a living twin of Archie Bunker of *All in the Family*. Consequently, I strongly anticipated that he would be against abortion. So when it came to discussing it, I actually heard him say in response to my question that he was against it. I was beginning to present, for consideration, some of the reasons which might make it an option in this instance when he interrupted. He said emphatically: "You didn't listen. I didn't say I was against an abortion for Ruth. I said I was in favor of it."

Here adherence to the stereotype raised expectations that distorted what the worker heard.

Interviewers' belief systems comprise expectations that predispose them to "hear" certain responses. If an interviewer hears an interviewee describe a preference for neatness and orderliness, the psychoanalytically oriented interviewer, associating certain personality traits with the anal character, is all set to expect the interviewee to say things that suggest a frugal and stubborn personality. We think in categories and expect a person to behave in some consistent manner, according to the pigeonhole we have assigned. As a result we think we know more about the interviewee than we actually do. If a man is a police officer, we expect that he will behave and speak as a police officer. We attribute to individuals the attributes of the groups with which we perceive them to be affiliated.

The stronger, more persistent, and more inflexible the stereotype that workers bring to the interview, the more certain they are that they know what the interviewee will say and the less inclined they are to actively and flexibly listen. Being aware of the stereotypes is one step in achieving more effective listening. Being ready to revise the stereotypes is another giant step. It is said that the human mind is like a parachute—it functions better when it is open.

Undistorted listening requires some recognition of the stereotypes, pre-conceptions, and mind-sets we bring to the interview. Clients cannot be expected to discard their stereotypes, preconceptions, or mind-sets. All that we can expect is that interviewers be aware of their preconceptions and treat them with sufficient suspicion to modify them in response to the individual interviewee. Stereotypes that are not subject to change, sometimes called "hardening of the categories," means that the interview runs a high risk of distorted listening.

4. Good listening requires an assumption and acceptance of ignorance. If workers knew what the interviewee was going to say, they would not have to listen. If workers make assumptions about what interviewees will say, rather than listening to what they are actually saying, interviewers will find themselves interrupting to finish clients' thoughts for them.

A 47-year-old man has been sharing his paranoid thoughts with a psychiatric social worker.

MR. A.: These things I've told you . . .

WORKER [*Interrupting*]: Strictly between you and me, confidential.

MR. A. [*Continuing*]: . . . are the way I think most of the time, and I hope you don't misinterpret me.

Our expectations increase the possibility that we will distort the communication we receive. Thus we ask for what we expect to hear—whether the person said it or not.

A medical social worker reports the embarrassing effects of expectations:

I had been seeing Mrs. M. after her hip replacement operation, and she had been recovering beautifully without any pain, about which I had frequently asked her. This time, as usual, I asked whether she was in any pain and she said, "Yes. It now is painful." Expecting the usual "no pain" answer, I said brightly, "That's good. Glad to hear it." Only after hearing myself say it did I catch myself and apologize. It was very embarrassing.

Here's another instructive example of failure to listen. A worker who had been trying to get in touch with a client was told, on calling, that the client was not available: "He died last week." On automatic listening the worker said, "Okay, I'll try calling back later." For more common errors in listening, see box 3.1.

Box 3.1 Common Errors in Listening

---

1. Persistence of dysfunctional listening habits developed in everyday social conversation.
2. Formulating a response while giving peripheral attention to incoming communication.
3. Listening for what you hope to hear.
4. Listening for what you expect to hear; biased listening.
5. Failure to listen to what you fear to hear.
6. Listening with too much attention to detail, neglecting patterns.
7. Inattentive listening resulting from boredom or fatigue.
8. Inattentive listening resulting from internal emotional distractions or daydreaming.
9. Inattentive listening resulting from disinterest in the client's message; lack of listening motivation.
10. Listening without sufficient knowledge or clear idea of your purpose so that you cannot direct your attention to what is most relevant.

Summary: Chapter 3

One significant step in the communication cycle involves the process of listening. Hearing and listening, while related, are in fact two different processes. Hearing is a physiological act that is automatic and involves the reception of sound. Hearing is an antecedent to listening. Listening is a cerebral act—that of understanding the sound heard and deriving meaning from it. Just as you can look without seeing, you can hear without listening. Although listening is distinct from hearing, it depends on good hearing. If you cannot hear the sounds, you cannot process them.

Listening is basic to a good interview. Unless interviewers listen carefully to what the client is saying, they cannot follow, reflect, or paraphrase accurately, summarize correctly, or offer appropriate feedback. Active listening consistently evokes for the interviewee a feeling of being understood. Fatigue and personal preoccupations may interfere with the ability to listen effectively.

The type of listening required by daily social interaction is different than the type of listening required in the interview situation. Social listening is based on the assumption that much of what we hear is redundant, that we can anticipate what people we already know will say, that it is permissible to interrupt or listen inattentively because we are impatient for our opportunity to talk. By contrast, interviewers are required to listen with their ears, eyes, brain, and heart. Because the parties frequently have no history of interaction, the interviewer cannot anticipate what the client will say or what it means. Although we may defend ourselves and screen out threatening content in social situations, interviewers need to lower their psychic barriers, which might distort their perceptions of what the interviewee is saying.

Because we speak and understand speech at two different speeds—we speak much more slowly than we absorb information—spoken communication includes a considerable amount of dead time during which a listener's mind can easily become distracted. The good listener remains focused on the what the interviewee is saying but uses this spare time to think about the interview interaction.

Knowledge of the client's social problem facilitates listening because it helps the interviewer select relevant information and understand the client's situation. Listening is also facilitated by being clear about the purpose of the interview, listening for dominant themes rather than details, and listening with an open mind.

SUGGESTED READINGS

Listening

Judi Brownell. *Building Active Listening Skills.* Englewood Cliffs, N.J.: Prentice-Hall, 1986. (309 pp.)

An overview of listening with a focus on developing listening skills.

Andrew Wolvin and Carolyn G. Coakley. *Listening,* 4th ed. Dubuque, Iowa: William C. Brown, 1995. (416 pp.)

An analysis of listening behavior. One section is devoted to therapeutic listening.

D. Borisoff and M. Purdy, eds. *Listening in Everyday Life.* Lanham, Md.: University Press of America, 1991. (338 pp.)

A series of articles on listening; much of the content is applicable to the social work interview.

PART TWO

Sequential Phases in the Interview Process and Associated Techniques

FOUR

Introductory Phase

Now that we have distinguished an interview from a conversation, described the distinctive nature of the social work interview, and discussed the interview as a special example of communication, we are ready to discuss the dynamics of the social work interview.

Each interview in a sequence is part of a process that over time achieves the goal of the contact between agency and client. And each interview has a beginning, a middle, and an end. The interview process is the consciously dynamic movement through successive stages to accomplish the purposes of the interview.

The problem-solving steps in social work—study, diagnosis, and treatment (or data collection, data assessment, and intervention)—are not clearly demarcated. Similarly, in a given interview the introductory activities are not sharply differentiated from those of the development phase, which in turn are not clearly demarcated from those of the termination phase. Process is somewhat like a symphony. Although at any particular time one phase or theme may be dominant, we hear the other steps, muted, in the background. For the purpose of more explicit analysis, we will artificially separate the steps and discuss each in turn.

This part of the book, chapters 4 through 10, is concerned with analyzing the steps in the interview from beginning to termination. The interview begins before the two participants meet, in their thoughts, feelings, and attitudes as they move toward the actual encounter. And such feelings, thoughts, and attitudes are the result of their lives before the interview. This determines what the participants bring to the interview, which to some extent determines how they will behave in the interview.

Interviewee's Background— What the Interviewee Brings

The interviewee brings reference group affiliations, primary group affiliations, and biopsychosocial history and current functioning to the interview.* Clients are members of a gender, age, racial, occupational, socioeconomic, religious, and ethnic groups. A client is identified, for example, as male, 25, white, bricklayer, lower middle income, Catholic, born in Italy. Or as female, 45, black, homemaker, lower income, Baptist, of American birth. Each identifying label tells us something, within limits, of the likely behavior, feelings, and attitudes of the client. Affiliation with each significant reference group affects some aspect of the client's behavior in the interview. But the client is more intimately a member of several primary groups—a family, a particular peer group on the job, a particular congregation, a friendship group.

All the primary group contacts modify in some way the behavior, feelings, and attitudes dictated by membership in a particular reference group. For example, lower-income adolescent males may be struggling for emancipation from the family. Your client, John, is most intimately associated with a peer group of adolescents who are not yet manifesting this kind of rebellion and seem comfortable in their dependent ties to their families.

Further, John has a particular physiology. He is tall or short, fat or thin, active or lethargic, healthy or somewhat ill. And he has had a particular psychosocial history. He grew up at a particular time, in a particular place, in a particular family, with a particular set of parents, and his life in growing up in these circumstances is unique—never before experienced in just this way by anyone and never again to be experienced in just this way by someone else.

All this background accompanies clients into the interview situation, shaping the way they think and feel and behave. Not every role, not every group membership, has potency for determining the interviewee's reaction. Behaviors associated with those roles that relate to the purpose of the interview are of greatest influence. The middle-aged woman talking to the medical social worker will exhibit in the interview those group and individual

---

*The reference group is that large identifiable social aggregate with whom the person identifies and is identified. The person's behavior is patterned in accord with its norms and perspectives. The primary group is of people who see each other frequently.

attitudes that are related to illness, medical treatment, and temporary institutional living. The relevant social role is that of a patient in a hospital, and all the beliefs and feelings of her reference groups about being a patient, as well as those that derive from her personal history, will be activated in the interview. Beliefs and feelings about her other significant social roles—wife, mother, daughter, employee, and the like—are less relevant to this interview situation.

Interviewer's Background—
What the Interviewer Brings

The worker also brings to the interview a configuration of determinants. The worker too has reference group affiliations—male or female, young or old, of some color, ethnicity, and religion. But trained in graduate school, undergraduate school, or an in-service program to enact a professional role, social work interviewers do not allow these identities to determine their interview behavior. The whole point of such training is to replace the behavior generally anticipated from, let us say, a white, young, middle-income Protestant with the professional behavior expected of a social worker. If interviewers consistently succeed in doing this, we say they are acting professionally in the interview. They have developed a professional identity that reflects the ways of the occupational subculture. The principal reference group affiliation that they bring to the interview is that of the profession.

Identifying with the profession as a reference group calls for behavior in accordance with certain professional values and ethics as codified in the Social Work Code of Ethics.

The profession is a remote and ambiguous entity; the pressure of the agency is immediate and visible: agency-directed requirements become a determinant of interviewers' behavior. For instance, some agencies emphasize deficiencies in the social situation as the primary factors contributing to the client's problems; other agencies emphasize the client's personal deficiencies as contributing factors. Social workers in these agencies therefore focus on different content and direct their interviews toward different solutions. Billingsly (1964) finds clear differences in the orientation of social workers in a family service agency and those with a child protective agency. Both groups regard themselves as social workers. But the agencies, dealing with different groups of clients, dictate different adaptations of the professional way to serve clients. Billingsly concludes that "the agencies exert a major and differential influence" on workers' role orientation and role performance (1964:187).

Individual interviewers further adapt the framework provided by the profession, as modified by the agency, in terms of their idiosyncratic biopsychosocial developmental history.

But again, the professional requirement is that the worker make every effort to ensure that these considerations are excluded from the interview. Ideally, workers are aware of those needs that derive from their psychosocial history and control their manifestations.

The aim and hope of professional education and in-service training are to reduce the idiosyncratic components in the interviewer's behavior. Instead of responding as a middle-aged, middle-income, white female with a unique developmental history, employed in a particular agency and a member of a particular peer group, the worker responds as a professional in terms of some standardized, presumably technically correct, precepts. All social work interviewers following a uniform theory and uniform professional precepts should then respond to the same interview situation in a similar manner, as dictated by professional socialization.

In reality that aim is only partially achieved. A study of tape-recorded interviews by experienced professional social workers shows that although they show some uniformity in their interview behavior, they also show considerable diversity (Mullen 1969). This result is to be expected even where a uniform theory—a set of clear and explicit generalizations—is available to guide the worker in most situations. The problem for the social worker is compounded because many significant situations that recur in the field do not have an applicable generalization. Workers then have to fall back on responding in terms of their personal background and makeup.

Despite these qualifiers, however, the goal of socializing the recruit is to develop some uniformities in thinking, feeling, and behavior that reflect the profession's expectations for anyone occupying the status of social work interviewer in a particular agency.

What happens in any one interview is the result of what the interviewee brings to the encounter, what the interviewer brings, and the interaction between the particular pair of participants at this point in time in the history of their contact with each other. The interaction is "reciprocally contingent," each person responding to the other's behavior, each a partial cause of the other's behavior.

This suggests a reevaluation of the relative importance of the factors that affect the interview. Despite the initial importance of background factors, reference and primary group affiliation, life history of individual participants, professional training, and theoretical orientation, once the interview begins the most potent factor determining the behavior of one participant is the behavior of the other. The start of the interview activates a new set of variables specific to this particular encounter.

Deciding to Become a Social Work Interviewee

Before interviewer and interviewee actually meet, the prospective interviewee has to make a series of decisions. The client's decision to contact the agency is often the result of a series of complex interrelated decisions that may affect the client's initial behavior in the interview.

Prospective clients first have to recognize that they have a problem that they cannot resolve on their own. A client may choose an informal nonprofessional source of help, such as a friend or relative or the local bartender. Some people have neither friends nor relatives in whom they can or would like to confide or find that their friends and relatives have neither the competence nor the resources to help them. At this point prospective clients have to make another decision—whether to turn to the more formal professional channels. Then they must choose from among the numerous professional resources available. The interpersonal problems that social agencies address are dealt with even more often by family doctors and local clergy. Or the prospective interviewee might choose to consult an individual—a psychologist, counselor, psychiatrist, or social worker—instead of an agency. At this point our interviewee has decided a problem exists, that informal sources of help are either not available or ineffectual, and has selected a social agency among the more formal sources of help available.

The Path to the Agency—
Selecting and Locating an Agency

Thus the prospective client who contacts the agency to schedule an interview has made a decision that is the result of a series of other decisions. And, having decided to consult an agency, the prospective interviewee has to select from the agencies listed and locate the agency.

Prospective clients often face frustration in trying to find the agency's listing in the telephone directory, in being shunted on the telephone from one person to another, and in having to repeat their request to a number of different people. This recurrent difficulty is confirmed by the findings of Kahn and his colleagues:

> A group of well-educated volunteers, competent in the use of the telephone and with easy access to it, tested the information system for us by calling agencies in a designated order, making standard, set inquiries. Many inquiries required a number of phone calls and much persistence before help was given. Many other inquiries led to a dead end. In fact, one-third of all

attempts ended without conclusive answers or offers to help. The average request required 3.5 telephone calls and considerable time, thus reflecting agencies' specialized functions and rather narrow conceptions of their responsibilities. Agencies rendering one specific type of service often seem to know nothing about other fields of service, even related fields. In fact, even within a given field an agency may know little about services other than its own.

(1966:48)

An irritating experience in scheduling an interview might cause the prospective client to develop a negative attitude that contaminates the beginning of the actual interview.

Clients may come to the interview after a number of false tries because of uncertainty about which agency offers the service they require. A process of sorting goes on between clients with particular needs and agencies with particular services. The agency's name—Family and Children's Services, Society for Prevention of Cruelty to Children, Family Planning Services—does some of the sorting. Some sorting results from agencies' auspices—Catholic Social Service Bureau, Jewish Child Care Association. Some agencies are eliminated because they are part of a social service department in a particular hospital or school. People make mistakes, of course. Sometimes the agency's title or auspices or location does not clearly communicate who it serves and the services it offers. When this happens, the referral procedure is a second screening device to direct the applicant to the proper agency.

The agency's image with respect to ethnicity and gender also acts as an inducement or disincentive. If an agency's auspices and staffing are congruent with a client's sensitive identification with race or gender, the client may be more inclined to use the service. The differences in utilization rates of mental health services by various ethnic groups suggests this (Sue, Zane, and Young 1994:786–87). Efforts to develop adoption agencies under African American (Kadushin and Martin 1988:595) or feminist auspices (Schwartz, Gottesman, and Perlmutter 1988) reflect this phenomenon.

In some instances the interviewee does not make the first contact. Rather the agency represented by the interviewer makes contact with the client. "Outreach programs" are examples of such efforts.

For another group of clients, coming to an agency is more clearly an involuntary action. A court may order abusive or neglectful parents to obtain agency service; courts also require delinquents to maintain contact with an agency. These people have been sent to the agency by others in the community; they did not make the decision on their own.

An interview scheduled after the prospective client has made the sequential decisions described earlier is apt to be different from the interview that begins after a client has reached only some, or none, of these decisions. The latter may appear for the interview as requested, but if they have not decided that they have a problem and want the interviewer's help, establishing a mutually acceptable purpose for the interview will be difficult.

Prospective clients forced by limited options to consult the agency are apt initially to be more resentful than clients who feel they made a choice.

In each instance, then, the events preceding the interview affect it in some measure.

Approaching the Interview

Prospective clients prepare for the interview by rehearsing it mentally. They also talk to other clients, finding out about the agency's procedures and learning what the social workers are like, what to say, what to avoid saying, and how to present their story. People living in neighborhoods where a high percentage of the people have had agency contacts are privy to a wealth of gossip about many of the social service agencies.

Special hazards accompany interviewing when prospective interviewees are in close contact with former and current interviewees. An active informal communications network is available to people in prisons, hospitals, schools, and institutions of every kind. And they often share information about the interview habits of the social work staff. Interviewees also bring expectations that relate to the professional identification of the human service interviewer. Clients' stereotypes of human service professionals tend to suggest that they expect psychiatrists to have greater experience, education, and knowledge than social workers, but clients expect social workers to be warmer and more caring (Koeske 1993).

The physical accessibility of the agency is also a determinant of the client's attitude. Many clients and their fretful children have to come long distances on public transportation to centrally located agency offices. Thus some prospective clients begin the interview physically exhausted and emotionally enervated. Some agencies have responded by decentralizing their operations, opening district offices close to the client group, often in storefront locations in the immediate neighborhood.

The location of the agency, its physical appearance, and its state of repair (or more often disrepair) say something to the client about the community's attitude toward the service and the client group. Particularly for public welfare agencies, the building often suggests that the service has low priority among community concerns and implies that the agency's client group need not be given any great consideration. This is disheartening to the interviewee and reinforces the supplicant attitude that many clients bring to the agency. If the agency is in an older rundown neighborhood, its location may make some clients anxious and uneasy, particularly if they have late appointments that mean they leave the agency at night. The availability or lack of parking facilities may lessen or increase clients' feelings of frustration.

In interviews many clients of a family service agency commented on the agency's physical environment—mostly negatively (Maluccio 1979). They remarked on the location and physical appearance of the agency, the size and condition of the waiting room and offices, and the lack of parking. Clients pointed out that the building looked run down and that the offices were old, too small, and looked cold. One client said, "I liked the location because of my job—but the building was something else. They should do something about it—fix it up a little bit—you know, it made me feel worse about myself because I couldn't afford anything better" (Maluccio 1979:164).

Scheduling

Agency time schedules affect the beginning of the interview. Clients who can be accommodated at their convenience are less apt to be resentful and hurried than clients who have to take time off from a job, perhaps losing pay. The availability of an evening or Saturday morning interview, although an imposition on the staff, may pay dividends.

Interviewers should start and end an interview promptly (although without undue rigidity) because doing so shows respect to interviewees and permits both parties to know clearly the time allotted for the work they have to do.

Scheduling should allow for some interviews to run over the allotted time. It should also allow for a break for the interviewer between sessions. A break between interviews allows time for clearing the mind, changing the mental scenery, making the transition. It permits the reverberations of the last interview to die away and provides the interviewer with an opportunity to prepare emotionally for the next interview. Thus a loose schedule is far preferable to a tightly scheduled program. Interviewers may conduct fewer interviews, but those they complete will be better.

Respect for time means respect for the interviewer's time as well as the interviewee's. An interviewer probably ought to resist the temptation to yield readily to a client's sudden demand for an emergency appointment or to the intrusion of an aggressive client who wants an appointment at will. Both situations require courtesy and firmness as well as an explanation. Conducting an interview when the interviewer is preoccupied and distracted with other scheduled obligations would not be giving the interviewee a good hearing. Of course unavoidable emergencies do arise, but workers need not masochistically put a client's need ahead of every other consideration.

Reception

Many interviewees have had an unnerving experience within the agency before they reach the interviewer's desk, and interviewers often are unaware of this.

The first contact of the interviewee with the agency is not with the interviewer but with the office receptionist.

Receptionists or secretaries actually conduct an informal and unscheduled initial interview. They usually obtain some essential identifying data to find out what the client wants and whether the client is at the right place. This generally involves a series of questions.

Hall studied the reception procedures in several social agencies in great detail. The person at the reception desk acts as a gatekeeper and regulates traffic flowing in the direction of the interviewer's room. The receptionist makes many discretionary decisions "at the point of initial contact between the agency and its clients" (1974:21). The receptionist acts as a buffer between the interviewee and interviewer, keeping the interviewee from intruding until the interviewer is ready, and as an advocate for clients, getting workers to see a particular client.

Hall notes the lack of privacy and the violation of confidentiality, which are routine in many agencies during such preinterview "interviews":

> Time and time again as I sat in a variety of waiting rooms I saw obvious distress on the part of visiting clients who were obliged to describe their problems in a room containing other people. The receptionists, accustomed to tales of misery and deprivation, were accustomed to most of the stories they were told and failed to see the lack of privacy as a problem. This was obvious from their attitude toward visitors and the way in which the clients were asked to "speak up" when they had obviously been trying to retain an element of intimacy between themselves and the receptionist.
>
> (1974:120)

A social work student, describing her experience in applying for service at a social agency, said,

We walked in the door and found ourselves standing in a hallway. The receptionist was located on the other side of the corridor wall in a secretarial pool
of about eight women and spoke to us through a hole in the wall. Having to
explain why you are there in the middle of a reception room and an opening
in the wall was very embarrassing. Fortunately there was no one there when
we showed up.

(Walden, Singer, and Thomat 1974:283)

Such experiences cannot help but affect the beginning of the formal scheduled interview with the social worker. An attractive comfortable waiting
room with easy access to lavatories and with a friendly and understanding
receptionist may help to get the interview off to a good beginning.

Waiting

Of more immediate concern is the client's experience while waiting for the
interview to begin. In public welfare and child welfare agencies clients wait
for long periods in noisy unattractive reception rooms, sitting uncomfortably on crowded hard benches. Even a half-hour delay may seem inter-
minable to anxious people uncertain whether they will be granted the help
they badly need.

Everyone finds waiting to be an indignity. When you wait, others are
controlling you, and all you can do is remain passive and available until the
other person is ready. Waiting arouses feelings of competition and resentment against whoever or whatever is occupying the other person. It evokes
feelings of anxiety about being abandoned. Will "they" remember that you
are there waiting?

Because the reaction to waiting is primarily negative, lessening the waiting time ensures a better start for the interview. Administrative problems,
shortage of staff, and constant heavy intake may make delays inevitable and,
beyond a certain point, irreducible.

Letting the interviewee know just how long the wait may be is an elementary courtesy. If the wait is unavoidably prolonged beyond the time
estimated, the receptionist should give the interviewee periodic reassur-
ances that the interview will occur, however belatedly.

When interviewer and interviewee finally meet, dissipating the frustration and resentment generated by the period of waiting takes time and
effort. Interviewers may be successful in communicating a genuine feeling
of respect. Nevertheless their job is made more difficult by the need to
counteract the disrespect inherent in the agency's procedures that result in
people having to wait.

If clients have waited a long time, interviewers may find it helpful to recognize explicitly at the beginning of the interview clients' annoyance at
having been kept waiting, to openly acknowledge that clients might have
some strong feelings about this, and invite them to discuss their reactions.
An interviewer says, "I began by noting that I knew she had been waiting a
long time and that she might be feeling annoyed."

All these considerations—the steps in deciding to seek help from a social
agency, selecting and finding an agency, its state of repair, experiences
around scheduling, reception, and waiting—all affect the start of the interview to some degree. Thus for the interviewee the interview begins before
it actually starts.

Interviewers' Preparation

The interview also begins before it starts for the interviewer. Interviewers
prepare in advance in a general way for all interviewees they will encounter
in the office.

Setting

One aspect of preparation is the physical setting for the interview; it
should optimize the likelihood of undistorted communication and minimize the possibility of distraction. A comfortable but unobtrusive setting
suggests that you are treating the interviewee like a respected acquaintance. Because an interview is not a social visit, however, the setting must
also suggest a businesslike purposefulness. A quiet office with privacy is
ideal. Chairs for all participants should be comfortable enough that people are not conscious of physical inconvenience (which would be distracting) and yet not so comfortable that they are lulled into lassitude. The temperature should be comfortable.

The office light should be sufficient to allow participants to clearly see
any nonverbal communication but not so bright that it hurts the eyes.
Although privacy is desirable, isolation may not be, particularly when one
participant is male and the other female. The intrusion of telephone calls is
an inevitable hazard unless the interviewer gives the office staff explicit
instructions to hold all calls.

Excesses in temperature or noise provoke irritation, which negatively
affects the interviewee's initial perception of the interviewer. Remember, you never get a second chance to make first impressions.

Fortunately, the human capacity to adapt to a less than ideal environment
permits the conduct of effective interviews under all sorts of adverse conditions. Still, it is best to reduce environmental irritants as much as possible.

If clients are likely to be accompanied by children, the agency should make a playroom and toys available; otherwise, the interview may be constantly interrupted by the child or disrupted by the mother's anxiety about what the child is getting into.

The physical distance separating the participants should not be so great as to preclude the interviewer's reaching over and touching the interviewee if this should prove desirable. Distance might also make for difficulty in seeing subtle changes of expression. Nor should the interview room present physical barriers to nonverbal communication. A desk between the interviewer and the interviewee means that half the interviewee's body is not observable. The desk masks any gestures of the lower part of the body—tapping feet, clamping knees together, clasping hands tensely in the lap. However, some people need the limited protection from the interviewer's observation that the table or desk affords. These people become anxious if they are too exposed and accessible to observation.

A desk or a table is helpful in other ways as well. You can lean on it and rest your hands on it. It is a convenience for ashtrays and purses that people otherwise have to hold in their hands or juggle on their lap.

A definite block of time cleared for the interview allows the interviewer to appear unhurried. A reasonably uncluttered desk helps confirm the impression that in effect the worker has cleared all other assignments to devote time and energy exclusively to the client.

The setting of the interview should provide psychological privacy as well as physical privacy. A closed room may ensure physical privacy, but thin walls that leak sound deny the interviewee the assurance of psychological privacy.

Privacy of sight is also important. If people can see interviewees, even though they cannot hear them, interviewees may be inhibited from displaying strong emotions such as crying.

Although such situations are infrequent, interviewers need to take elementary precautions if an interviewee could become violent. The interviewer needs to know about agency security arrangements and whom to contact in case of an emergency. If you expect trouble, notify a responsible person in the agency in advance, and keep the door of the interview room ajar.

Homework

Preparation for the interview involves more than concern with scheduling and with the physical setting. It involves the personal and professional preparation of the interviewer for the experience. It involves a review of whatever material about the interviewee is available. The agency may have a voluminous record of previous contacts or only the face sheet obtained by the receptionist. In any case, no one appreciates being asked questions that the agency already has answers to. Ignorance of essential data already acquired communicates a lack of interest. If the interviewer knows as a result of such preparation that the client is married and has three children of such and such ages, the interviewee's confidence in the interviewer increases.

A walk-in agency that schedules interviews without prior arrangements makes for a different start to the interview. The interviewer has little opportunity for preparation and no prior information for guidance.

Preparation may involve doing some homework. Interviewers need to know what information they need to obtain from the client, the purpose the information would serve if they obtain it, and how they can use it to help the client. They need to be aware of the premises that guide selection of information. This preparation gives interviewers a cognitive map of the area in which they will be traveling and a sense of coherence for the interview. An interview without some such guidelines is apt to be disorganized.

The problem may be a parent's concern about a child's bed-wetting. If the interviewer has not recently conducted interviews concerned with enuresis, the interviewer might do well to read some recent literature on the cause and management of the problem. If a medical social worker is scheduled to see a patient who has had a serious heart attack, reviewing the literature on the psychosocial consequences of crises may be helpful.

Preparation involves getting specific information that you might need, the addresses and telephone numbers of places to which you might refer the interviewee, the forms you might need, and be reasonably confident of knowing how to fill them out. Preparation also involves a review of the requirements and technicalities regarding procedures that you might be discussing—applying for vocational rehabilitation, making a job referral, getting into a retirement home, and so forth.

Direction or Outline

Interviewers' preparation must involve a clear idea of what they hope to accomplish. They need to make the purpose of the interview explicit mentally before they can communicate their perception of it to the interviewee. Thus interviewers must give some thought to what the interviewee's purpose might be and how to make the worker's purpose and the interviewee's purpose, if they are likely to differ, more congruent.

Preparation involves specifying the interview's purpose and translating goals into specific items that need to be covered. Interviewers need to ask how, in general, the purpose can be achieved, what questions they need to ask, what content they need to cover, and the best sequence in which to introduce such content.

An interview outline prepared in advance is an organizing device, a memory jogger. Beginners whose minds may go blank at some point in the interview may find an outline particularly helpful. Consider this young worker's experience:

Interviewer is female, 22, mental retardation unit.

The purpose of the interview was to get a clear picture of the reaction of the family to learning that Bobby was seriously retarded and not likely to change much. But that's a global sort of thing. I needed to know about reactions that related to specific aspects of their lives. I tried to list these in my mind as I drove out to the house—changes in Mrs. L.'s relationship to the other children, her changed perception of herself as a woman, the change in relationship between the siblings, changes in the marital relationship, changes in the family's goals now that finances had to be allocated differently, changes in family routines and allocation of roles and tasks in the family. I wondered what their reaction was to learning about the retardation. Did they feel mad, sad, guilty, frustrated, inadequate? Were they relieved at least to know definitely what the situation was? What was their feeling about Bobby—ready to abandon him, so sorry for him that they wanted to make restitution by breaking their backs for him, sore at him for spoiling things? These were some of the things I thought about, some of the things I might ask about in the interview.

Of course interviewers should apply their outline lightly and flexibly in the actual interview, modifying it in response to what the interviewee does. Planning dictates the general outline. Tactical decisions involve the fine-tuning of strategy during the interview in response to what actually happens. This does not, however, diminish the importance of advance preparation. The difference between planning an interview and inflexible adherence to a routine is important.

Developing an interview guide requires some decision about how much to cover during a specific time period. Just as beginning teachers try to teach all they know in the first period, beginning interviewers are apt to plan to cover too much. Whatever the ultimate goal of a series of contacts, each interview must have a proximate and immediate purpose that is clearly defined and limited enough to be achievable within the time set aside.

Preparation requires developing an awareness of what we confidently, but unwarrantedly, presume to be true about the interviewee. Interviewers sometimes do not ask some questions or cover some essential areas because they presume to know the answers. Because we know many things about sick people, or delinquents, or older citizens, or unmarried mothers, we think we know them about this particular sick person or older citizen. As Mark Twain said, "It isn't what we don't know that gets us into trouble, it is what we know which is not so."

Interviewers' preparation involves some effort at anticipatory empathy, an effort by interviewers to imagine they are coming to the agency for help. What does it feel like to be in such a position? What might clients be thinking about? What kind of interviewer would I like to meet if I had that problem? What kind of help would I hope was available? We often say that the interviewer should start where the client is. Following this precept requires considerable thought about where the client is or might be.

Thus preparation involves a resolution of some of the anxieties that every interviewer brings to every interview: Will I like the interviewee? Will this person like me? Will I be able to help this client? Will I be able to understand this client? Will I be able to handle the demands this client might make? Will I conduct a good interview? What areas are likely to present the greatest difficulty for interview management? What kinds of feelings is the interview likely to arouse in me that may cause difficulty?

Role Image

Preparation involves something more subtle as well—an effort during the interview to delineate who we are. Interviewers respond to the different images of what they think is their appropriate role in response to their image of the client. Public assistance workers may see themselves as the guardian of public funds. Or they may see themselves as representing the community's conscience in aiding the needy. The correctional social worker may see the delinquent as tough, bad, ruthless, and lacking in control or as a deprived pathetic child, a victim of a stressful home life. Interviewers may see themselves as the all-forgiving parent-confessor, as a crusader correcting social injustices, as a professional helper neutrally assessing what is feasible, as a rescue worker snatching the child or dependent adult from disaster, as society's avenger seeing that the deviant is brought into line, or as an impartial judge.

Clients also perceive the social work interviewer in a variety of ways—as a bleeding heart to be conned, a lover to be seduced, an ally against a hostile world and personal enemies, a source of influence with access to establishment resources, an antagonist to be outwitted or placated, an authority figure representing society's sanctions. The setting and auspices with which clients identify interviewers tend to define the clients' selective image of workers. The school social worker is apt to be regarded as a teacher; the social worker in the court setting tends to be perceived as authoritarian, the medical social worker in the hospital as a comforter, the child welfare worker as identified with children.

And we all have an image of ourselves. Indeed we have a variety of images, each of which we regard as more or less appropriate for some specific situation. Preparation for an interview requires some self-knowledge of who we think we are and whom we think we represent in this particular situation.

It is also easy to exaggerate the ultimate significance of preparation for conducting an interview. Being prepared is not as good as not being prepared is bad, because not being prepared suggests to interviewees they are of no importance. Once the interview actually begins, the nature of the interaction takes precedence, and even the most astute preparation effort may not anticipate what spontaneously unfolds.

Every interview is likely to be difficult. The interviewer is asked to be a member of the cast in a play being written while it is being performed. Conducting an interview has been compared to learning to play the violin in public while composing the music. Preparation involves tentatively writing some lines in advance.

Adequate preparation increases the interviewer's confidence, diminishes anxiety, and ensures a more positive start to the interaction. Because preparation resolves many routine problems in advance, the interviewer's mind is free to deal more adequately with unanticipated problems. If they are at ease, interviewers are less likely to stimulate anxiety in the interviewee.

Nonagency Settings

The social agency office is only one of a number of places where the social work interview may take place. Each setting has a different effect on the beginning of the interview, and each presents its special hazards. Social work interviews may take place, for example, in the home of the client, in hospital wards, on street corners, or in institutions.

The location varies with the agency. Social workers associated with mental health centers and clinics are likely to do most of their interviewing in the agency office. Social workers in public welfare and child welfare agencies are likely to do much more of their interviewing in the client's home.

In some instances a home visit for an interview may be a necessity rather than an option. Some interviewees are incapacitated and homebound. Some interviewees, despite repeated scheduling of office interviews, fail to come in and the worker needs to make contact in the client's home. Protective services require home visits. In this situation the interviewee is an involuntary client, and the worker who can see the living conditions to which the child is exposed is in a better position to assess potential risk of harm to the child.

In some situations neither the client's home nor the worker's office is the most desirable place for an interview. For a battered woman or a sexually abused adolescent the home setting may evoke hurtful experiences. The office may be too formal. In these instances the school or a restaurant— more neutral contexts—may be preferable.

A social agency office is a strange and unfamiliar setting to most people, who never or rarely have been inside one. Schools and parks are more familiar. Consequently, if the situation requires the worker to ensure that the setting does not intensify already heightened anxiety, neutral settings may be the better choice for an interview.

Office interviews have the advantage of allowing the interviewer to provide features that are desirable for interviewing. Always using the same place for interviewing affords the worker continuity and familiarity with the setting. And offices have the technology that facilitates the work of the interview—telephones, forms, record data, and the like.

Interviewee's Home

Conducting an interview in the interviewee's home has its own advantages. Home visits further our diagnostic understanding of clients and their situation. As a consequence the interviewer is in a better position to respond empathically to what the client says. The worker has an opportunity to observe the family's interaction in the natural setting that shapes the client's daily life, and the way in which clients arrange their homes is an expression of their individuality. Verbal descriptions are often misleading, and home visits have frequently led to changes in diagnostic thinking as the worker sees the home situation as it actually is.

Home visits give the worker the opportunity "to supplement what people say, by seeing what they do" (Overton and Tinker 1959:56; see also Hancock and Pelton 1989). Using our noses on home visits, we can learn something about the cooking, hygiene, and smoking or drinking habits of the client. We can visually assess opportunities or lack of opportunities for privacy. On home visits people are likely to dress more informally and be less formal in their interaction. Home interviews lessen the need to ask some questions to obtain information. Observation answers the unasked questions (Norris-Shortle and Cohen 1987).

One principal tenet of the home-based family treatment program, developed in response to the family preservation programs in child welfare, is treating the family in the home rather than the office. This has revived the idea of interviewing the family in the home rather than in the office. Writing in support of basing action on the home visit, Leonard Woods (1988) illustrates their advantage by presenting examples of the greater understanding the interviewer obtains from direct involvement in the client's daily routine.

According to Woods, the home visit offers the interviewer more opportunities for actually entering the life of the interviewee as a participant and consequently being perceived as less of a stranger. Holding a crying baby, opening a stuck window, moving a heavy box, and having coffee together are the kinds of events that involve the worker during home visits.

Clients may be gratified by a home visit, because it suggests the interviewer is sufficiently interested to make an inconvenient trip. However, the additional working time that travel requires of the worker is a disadvantage of home interviews.

In scheduling an appointment for a home visit the worker must keep the client's home routines in mind. Visits early in the morning and late in the afternoon are inconvenient because they interfere with meal preparation. Many older people have favorite radio or TV programs and therefore resent having visitors at certain hours. Every home visit involves some disruption of the family routine.

Respect for the interviewee requires that the worker be on time for a home interview. This might necessitate checking how to get there, knowing the route to take by auto, bus, or subway, and starting out early enough to arrive on time. Social workers tend to schedule a series of home interviews when out in the field. Delays and interviews that run over frequently make adherence to the schedule difficult. The worker may have to call in order to let a client know that the worker is likely to be late. Sometimes the client may have forgotten about the interview or may have needed to leave the house unexpectedly. In such instances workers should leave a note saying that they have made the visit.

In making a home visit workers should recognize that in some deteriorated urban areas house numbers may be missing. Having found the building, finding the proper apartment may be difficult if no names are on mailboxes and no numbers grace apartment doors.

Older people are often fearful about opening doors to strangers. Interviewers should be prepared to show credentials that certify their affiliation with the agency they represent.

Child protective service agencies generally provide the worker with photo identification to be shown to the interviewee when the worker appears at the home to investigate a report of child abuse or neglect. If a worker's request to enter the home is refused, the worker inquires about another more convenient time. If the worker's request for an interview is categorically refused, the worker can legitimately ask for police assistance, because the interview is mandatory.

The home visit may be somewhat threatening to the social worker. The interviewee, as host for the interview, gains a measure of control. The interviewee is in familiar friendly territory; the interviewer is in an unfamiliar setting. The interviewee controls seating arrangements and interruptions and can temporarily move out of the interview psychologically, or physically, by making some household excuse for moving around.

The interviewee can exercise a measure of self-protection by using "arranged distractions"—letting a radio or TV blare at full volume, giving a warm welcome to neighbors who drop in, or vigorously rattling pots and dishes while washing them during the interview. Because the setting is the interviewee's home, the interviewee has to take the initiative to turn down the radio or TV, although the interviewer can request this. Of course interviewers can, somewhat more subtly, gradually lower their voices until the interviewee is prompted to turn down the radio in order to hear. Visitors often persistent in intruding. Interviewers, having listened to visitors' comments, must be equally persistent in directing all their responses to the client.

Pets can be a problem. Dogs that bark throughout the interview or who keep jumping on the interviewer make concentration difficult. Trying to communicate the message of liking dogs (even though that may not be true) while fending them off is difficult. The interviewer may politely request that the dog be sent to another room so the interviewer can be as helpful as possible to the interviewee.

An interviewer making a home visit may have to accommodate to a degree of disorganization that might be routine for the interviewee but beyond anything in the interviewer's normal experience. One interviewer said,

> From my standpoint, the interview took place in total chaos. There was the radio, a record player—both on. The respondent's small son, her daughter's little girl, her husband and son (both embarking on what seemed like some rather dedicated drinking) were all there. A neighbor came in to use the phone, and there were two incoming phone calls. Chaos seemed an everyday occurrence and my respondent knew how to deal with it.
>
> (Converse and Schuman 1974:3)

During the home interview a parents may not be entirely free of competing role responsibilities as parent, spouse, and homemaker. These multiple roles may lessen their concentration on the interview while they engage in some household task that demands attention.

Invitations to a cup of coffee or a meal, which social workers handle without difficulty in their personal lives, pose a problem for them as professionals. In accepting these simple gestures of goodwill does the worker risk converting an interview into a purely social occasion? What effect will it have on the interaction? Clients have been known to use food as a tactic for ingratiation, a weapon in obligating the worker, and a digression from the difficult concerns of the interview.

A correctional social worker visiting a female probationer.

BARBARA, *a client*: Could I give you a cup of coffee? God, I gotta have one!

WORKER: Well, uh. [*Pause.*] Yes, maybe I will have a cup.

The worker commented afterward,

> My first response to Barbara's question was the feeling that I had been caught off guard. For a brief second I was trying to recall the so-called professional do's and don'ts. None came to mind! I then thought about the actual situation I was in and how the results of my response would add or detract from our already well-established relationship. I felt that Barbara and I had established a strong relationship, and yet I knew she needed constant reassurance of acceptance. I sensed that my not accepting the coffee would seem as if I were not accepting her. I really did not want coffee because I had just had a cup at the office. However, *in this situation*, want it or not, professional or not, I felt it was best to accept.

The home visit, like the family therapy session, poses the risk of having to respond to family conflict while it is being enacted. A public assistance social worker visits a 27-year-old woman who is receiving AFDC and about whom complaints of child neglect and abuse have been lodged:

MRS. W. [*To her 3-year-old daughter who is saying, "Want a cookie."*]: What? No, you don't need another cookie. [*The child repeats her request.*] I said no; you just had one. [*In the background the child again says, "Cookie."*] No! [*Again, "Cookie."*] Don't open! [*Child is saying, "Open."*] I said no. [*Child still saying, "Open."*] No. [*Child again says, "Open."*] What did I say? [*Child says, "Mom." Mother takes object from child and the child cries.*] There's your bedroom in there, young lady. [*The mother says this angrily, then pauses. The child is crying hard, so mother gets up and takes child's arm.*] Now pick up this stuff. [*Much noise, crying, and scolding in the background.*] You stay in there and play, unless you can behave yourself. [*The child is whining.*] Do you want to go to bed? [*Harshly.*] All right, in there and go to bed, because I'm not gonna listen to it. [*Mother takes the child by the hand and takes her into the bedroom; the child is crying.*] Stay there too. [*Mother closes the bedroom door and leaves the child, crying at the top of her lungs, in the room. Long pause.*]

The worker comments,

> The problem for me at this point in the interview was deciding what to do about the whole incident to which I had been a witness and about which I was developing some strong feelings. It was clear that Mrs. W. was harsh and rejecting and at the same time unhappy about the situation. Choking a little bit on it, I swallowed my growing dislike for Mrs. W., made a conscious deliberate effort to separate the person and the behavior, and decided to respond to Mrs. W.'s unhappiness. When she came back into the room, after the long pause during which we both tried to pull ourselves together, I said something about it's being tough to be both a father and a mother to the children.

A home visit is sometimes regarded as regressive, because it may compound clients' inability to mobilize themselves to come for an office interview. Social workers regard a client's accepting the opportunity to come to the office as a sign of responsibility and motivation.

Some interviewers feel uncomfortable about home visits because they suggest spying on the client. The sense of intrusion is greater if the worker drops in without previously making arrangements by telephone or letter. Home visits, initiated without advance preparation, may start with a greater measure of anxiety, suspicion, and resistance on the part of the interviewee. These initial responses are transitory in many instances, however.

The increasing dangerousness of some urban area locations, where some clients live, suggests that workers should let the agency know when and where they have scheduled home visits and when they expect to return.

Institutions and Hospitals

Interviews also take place in hospitals, institutions, and in the case of the life space interview in a variety of other settings. The life space interview permits the clinical exploitation of life events as these events take place. Such interviews take place wherever the significant event occurs—in a cottage, at the waterfront, on the street corner.

> When S., a thirteen-year-old youngster, was adamant in refusing to return to her group and marched up and down the institution's "campus," it was her [case-worker] who joined her in the march. The material handled during this time was not at all dissimilar to the content of their interviews; the child's feeling that she was too sick to be helped, that her rejection by the family was devastating and motivated these overwhelming feelings of hopelessness. When she marched past the gate, she said she could not control herself and not even the worker could control her. On the ensuing three-mile hike through neighboring towns and the final return to the grounds of the institution, the child received not only the demonstration of the worker's ability to control her, which diminished her feelings of anxiety, but also some insight into her current concern about her mother's illness and its relationship to the incident.
>
> (R. Shulman 1954:322)

In arranging for an interview in a hospital or prison the interviewer needs to know something about institutional routines. An interview arranged for a certain time may cause the interviewee miss a meal or some regularly scheduled activity in which the interviewee is interested. On the other hand, interview scheduling may be simpler in institutions, where the interviewee is an inmate or where the patient's time is at the disposal of the administration. In an institution an interview may be a welcome break in the boring monotonous routine or a sanctioned short vacation from a job. These secondary gains help to make an interview a desirable event.

In an institution or hospital ward the client's consultation with a social worker is difficult to keep confidential. If the inmate's or patient's group derogates those who see a social worker, the prospective interviewee may hesitate to make an appointment or may be uncomfortable when the social worker comes around. Clients are also aware that the interviewer has ties to other clients. If these people have any feelings of sibling rivalry in regard the interviewer, the interview will reflect such a competitive relationship.

In an institution interviewer and interviewee are likely to meet and interact outside the context of the interview. They have a relationship in which they occupy other roles vis-à-vis each other. It is difficult to keep these experiences from intruding in the interview. The interviewee may have seen and spoken to the interviewer on the grounds, on the ward, or in the prison yard. As a consequence even before the first interview contact the client may have developed some attitude toward the interviewer.

The social worker has probably been seen talking to and laughing with the executive director or the warden or the doctor, which firmly establishes the worker's relationship with those who are responsible for running the institution. Interviewees bring these perceptions into the interview, and if they have any feeling about the establishment and its representatives, the feeling will affect their initial interview behavior. Particularly in correctional institutions and residential treatment centers, clients are apt to strongly identify with the inmate subculture in opposition to the administration.

Johnston perceptively reviews some difficulties of interviewing in a prison setting:

> Many interviewers, though they have been in an institutional setting for a number of years, are very little aware of what the inmate goes through simply in coping with the mechanics of arriving for the interview and returning to his assignment. The searching by guards, the wisecracks of guards and inmates, the annoying red tape, a long wait in a stuffy anteroom, possibly changing clothes, being late for a meal or missing a recreation period because of the interview—these and other small things may make the prisoner less than anxious for the interview and may bring to it a bad frame of mind—antagonistic and irritable.
>
> The physical facilities for the interview itself are frequently poor, and undoubtedly affect the quality of the interview in many ways. For example, because of the internal routine of prisons, more often than not prisoners have a long wait in unpleasant surroundings prior to the interview. They may be sitting on benches in a stuffy hallway, subject to curious stares and deprecating remarks by passers-by. The talk among the men waiting for the psychiatrist or social worker frequently takes on a negativistic, cynical tone, probably a collective reaction against feelings of embarrassment and concern over contact with the "bug doctors," as all such professional workers are usually called. The writer has frequently overheard younger inmates affect an air of braggadocio upon leaving the interview, undoubtedly calculated to convince their cohorts that they are not a "bug" or a "rat" but, to the contrary, have put something over on the "doc." Such remarks can hardly be expected to put the waiting inmates in a receptive and constructive frame of mind for their interviews. . . .
>
> The stigma of staff contacts for the inmate likewise should not be underrated. Many prison officers and a great majority of prisoners look upon the frequent visitor to the "bug doctor," to the front offices, to the chaplain, or to the social workers with considerable suspicion.

(1956:44–45)

Hospital interviewing presents some atypical considerations. Scheduling an interview requires some knowledge of and concern for visiting hours, meal time, and physicians' rounds. The interviewee often is stripped of the usual marks of socioeconomic identification. The standard hospital gown further robs people of their identity and privacy. Patients may be hooked up to machines, drugged, and in some pain (Weiss and Elad 1993).

Interviewing a sick client presents some difficult status problems for the interviewer. The interviewee is lying down, the interviewer sitting or standing beside the bed. This accentuates status difference, as does the difference between the sick and the well. The interviewer is dressed in street clothes, the interviewee in pajamas, which make a person more childlike and dependent. The interviewee is immobilized, whereas the interviewer is mobile, which once again puts the interviewee at a disadvantage.

All these considerations that precede the actual interview leave residuals that may affect interaction once the interview starts.

The folk saying that well begun is half done has a good deal of truth in it. A good beginning starts the interaction in a positive direction. First impressions are strong and persistent; later perceptions tend to be added to earlier ones and consistent with them.

The Start of the Interview

At last the interview starts; interviewer and interviewee meet face to face, and the flow of communication between them is initiated. For the rest of what follows in the text the office interview is the context.

The interviewer has to decide whether to go out to the reception room and accompany the interviewee back to the office, whether to shake hands, and what to talk about while walking down the hall. Meeting in the reception room may not be necessary if the interviewee has been there before, but it may be a necessary courtesy in an agency with many offices and complex corridors.

Preinterview Amenities:
Meeting, Greeting, and Seating

The interview may begin during the journey from the waiting room to the interview room. One interviewer uses this time to make useful nonverbal observations. He notes how clients greet him and how they are dressed but mostly how they walk and carry themselves:

> Just watching Mr. W. walk to my office gives me an inkling to his mood. Sometimes, for instance, he walks in very determined and rapidly. I've

learned that this means he is anxious or angry, and that most of our time together may well be spent in verbal sparring.

With Miss T., who's depressed, I watch to see how slow her gait is and how drooped her posture is; together with her apparel she relays to me how badly she may be feeling that day.

(Hein 1973:159)

The interviewer will find it is helpful to greet the interviewee by name. Forms of address suggest status and level of intimacy.

Addressing the interviewer by name presents a problem. Honorifics and last names may be too formal; first names may be too informal. If the client is addressed by first name and the worker by last name or title (Dr.), the asymmetrical usage emphasizes the worker's more powerful position.

Use of first names by both interviewee and interviewer may suggest an interaction of familiarity and collegiality that belies a situation of inherent inequality. And reciprocal first-name use might confuse a professional relationship with a social relationship. It suggests an offer of friendship that the interviewer does not truly intend.

Because parents address children by their first name, whereas children generally address parents by their parental title, some interviewers feel using a client's first name is regressive and infantilizing. Age is a factor in the decision. If the interviewee is much older than the interviewer, deference to age dictates a more hesitant use of first names.

Timing is a factor. The interviewee may resent as presumptuous the use of first names before a relationship has been established. Later in the interview, when both parties are more comfortable with each other, this may be more acceptable. The interviewer can more frequently use the client's first name without violating the norms of interview etiquette. Interviewers generally need to obtain interviewees' explicit permission call them by their first name. Once again this clearly suggests the interviewer is first among equals.

Some interviewers who feel a strong need to define the interview as a cooperative interaction of equals feel uncomfortably formal in using surnames and courtesy titles (Ms. and Mr.). They feel the use of surnames is inhibiting, communicating distance, coldness, and rigidity. The anxiety this creates for them may be greater than the caveats we have noted in regard to the use of first names.

A study of name usage that included about ninety social workers found that about half preferred that both parties use last names and courtesy titles (Senger 1984). Almost none of the social workers used the interviewee's first name or asked to be addressed by surname and honorific. The researcher notes that "the social work profession, predominantly women [is] in the forefront of the women's movement [and] appear[s] particularly sensitive to egalitarianism in naming" (p. 41).

In resolving the problem workers should note that the use of names is only one way the interviewer can communicate what needs to be communicated. The interviewer can use honorifics and surnames and demonstrate warmth, informality, and closeness in other ways.

The handshake, a symbolic greeting ritual, often accompanies the introduction. Some interviewers deliberately refrain from initiating a handshake but respond readily if the interviewee initiates the gesture. The interviewer's hesitance is based on the recognition that some interviewees may not want to be touched. Other interviewers refrain from initiating a handshake because they want the interview clearly differentiated from a social encounter.

Having arrived at the interview room, the worker invites the interviewee into the office and goes through the familiar social amenities—taking a coat, offering a chair, and demonstrating concern that the interviewee is reasonably comfortable. The interviewer gives the interviewee a chance to get settled. The client needs a little time to get used to the room and the interviewer.

The interviewer acts in effect like a gracious host offering the elementary and expected courtesies. But the worker needs to temper the degree of hospitality because this is not a social visit. Also, the greeting should be appropriate to the client. An exuberantly cheerful greeting to the depressed client or a firm handshake with a 6-year-old are inappropriate. As Oldfield suggests, the interviewee may be made "uneasy by his perception that the interviewer is trying to set him at his ease" (1951:56). The admonition is to try not to try too hard. The ritualistic noises we make at each other at the beginning of a contact have been technically labeled "phatic communications." "How are you," "Nice day," and "How goes it?" all mean "I see you, I acknowledge you, I am friendly." Phatic communications serve primarily to establish contact.

Particularly at the beginning and the end of the contact interviewers find it helpful to make general conversation rather than engage in an interview. At the beginning we are making the transition from the way people relate to each other in an everyday social relationship to the formal interaction of the interview. It is temporarily a social occasion before it becomes an interview. At the end we are making the same transition in reverse.

During the initial conversation interviewer and interviewee have not yet officially assumed their roles, and they observe the rules that normally apply to conversation. Any event or situation that is widely shared may be the subject of conversation—the weather, parking problems, cooking, baseball, or the high cost of living. The subject of the icebreaker should be of some interest to the interviewee and a familiar topic. Saying something about the weekend all-star game to a male interviewee who is not interested in sports may intensify his feelings of inadequacy. That is why interviewers so often comment about the weather. It is something everyone knows about and is the least controversial of topics available to stimulate the feeling of togetherness.

This socializing is not wasted time. It eases clients' transition from the familiar mode of conversational interaction into a new and unfamiliar role that demands responses for which they have little experience. The conversation has the additional and important advantage of permitting the interviewee to size up the interviewer as a person. This opportunity makes for a more comfortable start to the formal interview, which demands by implication that clients entrust themselves to the interviewer. Small talk establishes the interviewer's interest in the interviewee as a person and reinforces a sense of human mutuality. Like the cocktail party chatter sometimes called "circling," both parties are really talking about getting ready to talk. Small talk is sometimes called a "reconnaissance dance" during which people size each other up.

Small talk serves another important purpose: it gives us an opportunity to explore possibilities of shared membership and social identities. We establish on sight some shared membership in a significant social group. We can see whether we share membership in the same gender, race, and age group. But small talk may further establish that we share membership in a religious group or that we are both movie enthusiasts, and so on. The more the participants find they have in common, the greater the reduction in social distances and the increase in interviewees' expectations that they will be understood and accepted. "Co-membership involves attributes of shared status that are particularistic rather than universalistic" (Erickson and Shultz 1982:35), such as age, sex, and race. And it is small talk that brings these common denominators to light.

If the transition to the interview is too abrupt, the interviewee may be off balance, as the following hypothetical interview beginning suggests:

INTERVIEWEE: Where shall I hang my coat?

INTERVIEWER: Where do you want to hang it?

INTERVIEWEE: Where shall I sit?

INTERVIEWER: What difference does it make to you?

However, too long a conversation robs time from the interview. It also tends to puzzle interviewees. They recognize that although the interview is a social situation, it is not a social visit. Prolonged conversation makes them wonder what the interviewer has in mind. They might regard undue prolongation as indifference to the urgency of their problem.

Even in the initial informal social conversation the interviewer should make an effort to indicate the direction of attention. The emphasis is on the interviewee's experience: "Did *you* have trouble getting the car started in this freezing weather?"; "Did *you* have any difficulty finding the office?"

The Opening Question

The opening phase of the interview is concerned with an initial general exploration of the problematic situation. It represents the interviewer's effort to gather preliminary data in order to understand the general nature of the problem. The interviewer should make some effort to determine what the client has done so far in dealing with the problem, the effect of those efforts, and what prompts the interviewee's contact with the agency at this time. The interviewer should seek to determine the extent, duration, and intensity of the problem.

The opening phase of the interview is likely to include primarily open-ended general questions. The interviewer is trying to find out what the interviewee believes the situation to be. The interviewer does not as yet have enough information to warrant asking specific questions or responding to details.

The opening interview gambit, which signals the end of the conversation and the beginning of the interview proper, should be a nonthreatening general question to which the interviewee is capable of responding easily and one that serves to develop the mutuality of interaction: "What do you think we can do for you?" Using words like *problem* and *service* in the opening question may have negative consequences. The interviewee may resent being asked, "What's your problem?" "How can we be of service?" may sound too formal.

A general and unstructured question grants the interviewee the freedom to choose how to communicate. An opening question that interviewees can field successfully encourages their confidence in their ability to perform creditably in their role.

Subtle differences in the opening question may determine the direction the interview takes. The interviewer might say, "What brings you here?" or "Why have you come here?" or "What would you like from us?" The first puts the emphasis on a description of the trouble, the second on the explanation for the trouble, the third on the treatment. The interviewer's inflections in asking the first question can signify three different concerns. "*What* brings you here?" focuses on the problem; "What brings *you* here?" focuses on the interviewee; "What brings you *here*?" focuses on the agency.

The interviewer might phrase the opening question in a way that forces specificity in response: "Could you tell me about the situation that prompts you to see a social worker?" This question specifies that the response should describe the situation, why the interviewee needs help, and why the client believes that a social worker can be of help.

Clarifying the Purpose

The initial phase of the interview should clarify the purpose that will engage the participants. The purpose needs to be of manageable proportions, and the interviewer should state it in such a way that its achievement is specific and identifiable. Frequently, the purpose of an interview is either far too ambitious or too ambiguously stated. The following statements of interview purpose from social work interview protocols are good examples of some of these difficulties:

> My purpose in this interview was to become acquainted, to get to know Mrs. P.
> During this interview I planned to help him with his anxieties.
> My visit with the client was to establish a relationship.

In contrast, the following statements of interview purpose are circumscribed and the objectives are definite. The statement identifies the purpose, so the probability of achieving such purposes is greater:

> The purpose was to help the client more adequately budget both her time and her money.
> To determine what service the client wanted from the agency.
> The purpose was to help Art with his feelings about leaving the foster home.
> My purpose was to establish Mr. Y.'s level of motivation for job placement and, if time permitted, to explore what type of work he felt he was suited for.
> The purpose was to obtain the needed information to make a decision on relicensing the foster home.

It is not only helpful but necessary to be explicit about the purpose of the interview.

In the following example, taken from the beginning of an interview, the statement of purpose is ambiguous and muddled. The social worker is interviewing an 11-year-old boy who was recently placed in a group home:

INTERVIEWER: What I wanted to talk to you about was to figure out how you are feeling about the home and where you see yourself going and if you want to stay here. If you don't want to stay here, what type of situation you do want so we can make a recommendation for placement. Have you been thinking about this?

Both participants should make every effort to formulate the purpose in operational terms. What specifically are they attempting to achieve by meeting, what will change—is the purpose to arrange for housing, find a job, select parents for adoptive children, prepare a mother to place her child in day care, resolve ambivalence about an operation? If the participants know clearly and unambiguously the purpose of the encounter, they can know when they have more or less achieved the purpose.

If the interview is being conducted at the initiative of the interviewer, the interviewer needs to make the purpose clear as early as possible: "I asked you to meet with me today because the teachers are having a difficult time with Robert"; "I wanted to talk with you because Dr. _____ indicated you had some questions about your Medicare entitlement."

In addition to stating the purpose the interviewer must obtain some agreement that interviewees want to engage in an interview directed toward this purpose. The interviewer actively searches for any basis for mutual engagement. In interviews with collaterals and in advocacy interviews the statement of purpose might also include the reason for choosing this particular interviewee. The statement should be simple and concise:

Female, 23, school social worker.

I visited Tommy's second grade teacher. I said I had made this appointment because I should like to find out more about how Tommy behaved in contact with other children. I said I thought that she had a good chance to observe this, since this was the second year she had had him in class, and I thought her observation could be helpful to us in getting to understand him better.

The interviewer attempts to elicit a definition of the interviewee's purpose that is compatible with the service the interviewer's agency can offer. If the problem cannot be defined so that it is relevant to the service, the interviewee needs to be referred elsewhere.

Studies of social work intake interviews show that the focus of first interviews is on the applicant's request as it relates to the purpose and goals of the agency (Day 1985; Morton and Lindsey 1986). Statements of feeling and allusions to other problems not relevant to the agency's service tend to evoke sparse response from the interviewer.

Inducting the Interviewee

Another task for the interviewer during this opening phase of the interview is to induct clients in their role of interviewee. Because people have less actual and vicarious exposure to the role of social work interviewee as compared with, say, medical patient interviewee or legal client interviewee, many people come to the social work interview with ambiguous or erroneous expectations. Relatively few people have ever participated in a social work interview, and few have seen or heard a social worker doing social work in a movie or on the radio or TV. In inducting the interviewee into what is for many an unfamiliar social role, the interviewer reinforces some responses and refrains from reinforcing others. When the client talks about feeling, the interviewer becomes active verbally and nonverbally—leans forward and says, "Yes," "Good," and "That's it." When the client is talking about some irrelevant matter, the interviewer is passive and unreceptive.

Interviewers can use explicit instructions to help the client be a "good" interviewee: "During our meeting together it would be most helpful if you talked about . . . "; "I will be asking you questions about . . . and hope that you will feel free to share with me what you think and what you feel about it"; "In such interviews people who have come here with concerns similar to yours have talked about. . . ." The interviewer inducts the interviewee into the role by demonstrating effective interview procedures and by signaling the order in which participants speak, how much, about what, and when. The following extracts illustrate socialization to the role of interviewee:

The interviewee is male, 27, lower middle income, and has come to an agency that offers family service–marital counseling.

WORKER: Just a little while ago you were telling me about this argument you had with your wife about the way she spends the money and the trouble you two have in budgeting. How does it make you feel, the way she spends the money?

MR. R.: You want me to tell you how I feel?

WORKER: Well, yeah. What happened is important, but how you feel about what happened is important too.

MR. R.: So I am supposed to say how I feel.

WORKER: Well, it would help to understand the situation.

The interviewee is female, upper lower income, seeking the assistance of a child guidance clinic.

MRS. E.: Well, I have been talking since I came in here, but you haven't said hardly anything at all.

WORKER [*Laughs.*]: What do you want me to say?

MRS. E.: At least more than you have been saying. Am I supposed to do all the talking? Doesn't anything come back from you?

WORKER: Like what?

MRS. E.: Well, like if we are doing anything wrong and advice about what to do.

WORKER: I am not sure that advice would be much of a help.

MRS. E.: You don't give advice?

WORKER: Not in the way you mean it, no.

In addition to the tasks of establishing a consensual purpose, gathering data for a preliminary understanding of the problematic situation, and inducting clients in their role of interviewee, a principal and significant task of the interviewer during the opening phase is establishing a positive relationship with the interviewee.

The procedures that are valuable in achieving a positive relationship require a separate chapter, which follows.

Summary: Chapter 4

The backgrounds of the participants to a large extent determine the interaction in the interview. Gender, race, socioeconomic, ethnic, religious, and cohort group affiliations influence the behavior of the client in the interview. In addition, the worker brings reference group affiliations to the interview; however, the principal reference group affiliation that should influence the worker's behavior in the interview is that of the profession.

Despite the importance of background variables, once the interview begins the most potent factor determining the behavior of one participant is the behavior of the other. Thus understanding the factors that lead to the interview is important. The client's decision to contact the agency is often the result of a series of complex and interrelated decisions. These decisions may affect the client's initial behavior in the interview. An irritating experience in scheduling an interview might cause a prospective client to develop a negative attitude that contaminates the beginning of the actual interview. In addition, interviewees bring expectations about how the interviewer will behave. Clients' stereotypes of human service professionals, for example, suggest that psychiatrists have more expertise, whereas social workers are warmer and more caring. The location of the agency, its physical appearance, and its state of repair may also influence the client's attitude. Frustration and resentment generated by a long waiting period and lack of consideration for the client's privacy in obtaining information in the reception area may cause negative feelings.

The interviewer prepares for the session before seeing the client. The physical setting should optimize the likelihood of undistorted communication. Preparation for the interview should include reviewing case material, reading the relevant professional literature, and clarifying a purpose for the interview and a professional role in the interview.

The social agency office is only one of several interview settings. Conducting an interview in the client's home furthers our diagnostic understanding of the client and the situation. However, the home visit transfers a measure of control to the client. The interviewee controls seating arrangements and interruptions and can temporarily move out of the interview psychologically and physically by concentrating on household tasks. Home visits may also complicate the worker's ability to draw the line between professional and social behavior.

In arranging for an interview in a hospital or in a prison the interviewer needs to have information about the institution's routines in order to schedule the interview at a time convenient for the client. Other factors that influence the interaction between worker and client in institutional settings include a lack of confidentiality and the identification of the worker as a representative of the institution. In the hospital the "sick role" assumed by the interviewee may present some difficult status problems for the interviewer.

As the interview begins, the interviewer should be conscious of social amenities—how to address the client, whether to shake hands or not, and helping the client get settled in the interview room. Making general conversation is a good transition from everyday social interaction to the formal interaction of the interview. At the end of the interview we go through the same process in reverse. The interview should open with a nonthreatening question that the interviewee is capable of answering and that develops the mutuality of the interaction. Tasks during the initial phase of the interview include clarifying a shared purpose, inducting the interviewee into the role of client, and developing a positive relationship.

SUGGESTED READINGS

Anthony Hall. *The Port of Entry: A Study of Client's Reception in the Social Services.* London: Allen and Unwin, 1974. (147 pp.)
An empirical study of the experiences a prospective client encounters en route to an interview with the social worker.

Anthony N. Maluccio. *Learning from Clients: Interpersonal Helping as Viewed by Clients and Social Workers.* New York: Free Press, 1979. (322 pp.)

Stuart Rees. *Social Work Face to Face.* London: Edward Arnold, 1978. (154 pp.)
The books by Rees and Maluccio are based on research interviews with workers and clients that illuminate the problems (and some solutions) in getting good communication going between the two groups. The emphasis is on what actually happens when workers and clients first get together.

FIVE

Beginning the Interview: First Phase Objective— Establishing a Relationship

Every interview involves two related components: the techniques that move the participants toward achieving the objectives of the interview, and the relationship, which defines the nature of the emotional, attitudinal atmosphere in which the techniques are implemented.

The effectiveness of the interviewing techniques used by the interviewer depends to a considerable extent on the nature of the relationship. Because establishing a positive relationship is a prerequisite for effective use of interviewing techniques, this chapter is devoted solely to discussing relationships; we discuss interviewing techniques in subsequent chapters. In this chapter we define a relationship, establish its significance, validate empirically the prime significance of the relationship in interviewing, and review interviewer behavior that is associated with establishing a positive relationship.

Defining the Relationship

Social workers have historically been concerned with relationships and have attempted to define the term. Biestek defines *relationship* as "the dynamic interaction of attitudes and emotions between the caseworker and the client" (1957:12). Perlman (1979) speaks of it as an emotional bond between people. The *Social Work Dictionary* ,defines it as "the dynamic interaction and affective, cognitive, and behavioral connection between the social worker and the client to create the working and helping atmosphere" (Barker 1991:199).

Relationships in the interview can be defined as the manner in which participants express the feelings and attitudes they have for each other that establish the context in which they do the work of the interview. Relationships do not just happen. They are created and recreated by the behaviors the participants engage in. Relationships are never static but always changing as a consequence of what people do and say in the interview.

A preponderance of research on the nature of the helping relationship was for a time based on Rogers's 1957 conceptualization of the core facilitative conditions—unconditional positive regard, warmth, and genuineness. Since 1986 the concept of the helping relationship has expanded, and the literature now more frequently refers to it as the therapeutic alliance, the working alliance, or the helping alliance (Gelso and Carter 1985; Gaston 1990; Horvath and Symonds 1991; Marziali and Alexander 1991; Horvath and Luborsky 1993; Horvath and Greenberg 1994). Horvath and Luborsky, in noting the overlap, write that "recent research shows the Rogerian facilitating conditions [are] closely associated with the working alliance" (1993:563).

Traditional social work conceptualizations of the relationship mirror the essential elements of the facilitative Rogerian relationship, although the terms used are somewhat different (Biestek 1957; Perlman 1979). Coady (1993) notes that social work's traditional concerns with relationship are precursors of the current interest in the helping alliance. For our purposes the overlap is sufficient to allow us to ignore the subtle distinctions between the terms.

Both traditional and recent conceptualizations emphasize the emotional bond, the mutual affective attachment that results from the positive interaction of the participants in the interview. This is the expressive component of the therapeutic alliance.

Significance of a Positive Relationship

The relationship is the communication bridge between people. Messages pass over the bridge with greater or lesser difficulty, depending on the nature of the emotional interaction. Clients lower their social and emotional screens or allow them to become more permeable in the context of a good relationship. This in turn heightens the client's readiness to return to the agency and willingness to participate in the interviews.

A positive relationship acts as an anesthetic to the sharing of painful material. It heightens the salience and credibility of the communication coming from the interviewer. It frees clients to reveal themselves without defensiveness or distortion because a good relationship promises acceptance, understanding, and freedom from punishing criticism, rejection, or reprisal. Such a relationship reduces the possibility that the interview will become a competitive struggle and increases the likelihood that it will become a collaborative endeavor.

A good relationship encourages and facilitates the active involvement and participation of the interviewee. It also fosters feelings of trust, security, and safety while decreasing anxiety, tension, and threat. A good relationship affects the perceptual set that the interviewee uses to filter communication. It results in imputing a benign coloration to the interviewer's interventions. The interviewee biases the communication in a positive direction: "She is saying it to help me, not hurt me."

The interpersonal relationship is the field through which an encoded message is communicated. A good relationship facilitates getting the message from sender to receiver and conditions the receiver to receive the message. In a poor relationship the field over which the message travels is filled with affective potholes, barbed wire, and briars.

In the interview the protective functions of the ego, which counsel concealment, conflict with the adaptive functions of the ego, which counsel revelation to obtain help. The conditions that make for a good relationship encourage those components of the ego that support revelation. Without the psychological safety provided by a positive relationship the interviewee would be reluctant to assume the risks and pain associated with openly revealing personal problems and engaging in efforts to change.

When such a relationship has been achieved, interviewer and interviewee can feel the rapport. Rapport suggests that the participants are in tune with each other, on the same wavelength, in sync with each other.

A good relationship amplifies the consequences of any interaction in the interview. It makes workers' influence greater, their suggestions more appealing, their techniques more effective. If the relationship is positive, the interviewee is likely to perceive the interviewer as trustworthy, attractive (likable, friendly, approachable), and competent. The social psychology literature has identified these characteristics as enhancing the influence potential of the interviewer (Corrigan et al. 1989; Heppner and Claiborn 1989; Heppner and Frazier 1993; Beutler, Machado, and Neufeldt 1994:246).

Empirical Confirmation of Relationship's Significance

Research has repeatedly identified a positive relationship as the factor most consistently associated with positive outcomes of human service helping. A nationwide study of the results of family service contacts notes that "one of the most striking findings of the present study is the marked association of outcomes with the counselor-client relationships" (Beck and Jones 1973:129). This association is highly significant statistically. Analyzing a variety of service factors thought to be related to outcome, the researchers found that "the overpowering influence of the counselor-client relationship was startling. It had more than doubled the predictive power of the second highest factor" (p. 146).

Other research studies of how clients view their experience with social agencies confirm a clear recognition of the crucial importance of the worker-client relationship as the basis for effective helping (Maluccio 1979; Sainsbury 1975:116, 125). Orlinsky, Grawe, and Parks (1994) reviewed the research on psychotherapy outcome from 1950 to 1992. They identify 2,354 separate studies. In their summary they identify the therapeutic bond as the variable showing the "strongest evidence linking process to outcome" (p. 360). They see this as one finding in regard to the relation of "various facets of process to outcome which are so well replicated that they can be accorded the status of established facts" (p. 352). In support Beutler, Machado, and Neufeldt, reviewing similar research, note that "the quality of the therapeutic relationship by its various terms was consistently found to be a central contributor to therapeutic progress" (1994:224).

A separate review of studies between 1985 and 1992 of therapist variables associated with outcome concludes that "collectively the quality of the therapeutic relationship by its various terms has consistently been found to be a central contributor to therapeutic progress. Its significance transverses theoretical schools theory, specific concepts and a diversity of measurement procedures" (Beutler, Machado, and Neufeldt 1994:244). Reviewing eight-five studies of psychotherapy sessions, Luborsky and Auerbach conclude that there is "consistent evidence of the predictive power of the therapeutic relationship on the outcome of psychotherapy" (1985:553).

In a subsequent review updating the relevant research Luborsky says, "The therapeutic alliance is now the most popular in-treatment factor in terms of the number of studies significantly predictive of the outcome of psychotherapy" (1994:45). Reviewing seventy-six relevant research studies, Sexton and Whiston conclude that "of all the techniques, client-counselor characteristics, and procedures that have been studied, it is only the counseling relationship that has consistently been contributed to the success of the therapeutic process" (1994:6, 7).

Detailed studies of doctor-patient interaction support the singular and primary importance of a good relationship in professional interaction. The repetitive finding of such studies is that patient satisfaction with the doctor correlates highly with the nature of the doctor-patient relationship (Harrigan and Rosenthal 1986; see also Hall and Dorman 1988; Buller and Buller 1987; and Nicholi 1988).

Although research supports the contention that psychotherapy is helpful, the results also suggest that differences in techniques and in theoretical assumptions about etiology and therapy contribute little to differences in outcomes (Stiles, Shapiro, and Elliot 1986). The element common to all the diverse psychotherapies that makes a significant contribution to outcome is the nature of the worker-client relationship (Horvath and Symonds 1991).

The various approaches to human service helping do differ in the emphasis and the priority they give to relationships. The humanistic psychodynamic procedures give the relationship a higher priority and emphasis than do behavioral, cognitive, rational, and emotive procedures. However, without exception all human service helping approaches regard the relationship as a significant nonspecific factor in determining treatment outcomes (Lambert and Bergin 1994:164).

Developing a Positive Relationship

Thus, having met the client and begun the interview, interviewers face the most important primary task: establishing a positive relationship.

Although the available research is ambiguous about the specifics of interviewers' attitudes and behaviors associated with development of a positive relationship (Gelso and Carter 1985; Beutler, Crago, and Arizmendi 1986; Sexton and Whiston 1994), theory and practice wisdom offer some consensus regarding desirable interview attitudes and behaviors.

All the human service professions have recognized the central importance of the worker-client, therapist-patient relationship to their work. Although describing the core conditions that characterize the relationship in different terms, the essence of what they describe is essentially similar. (In identifying the elements of the relationship we will use the terms and concepts generally used in the social work literature.) There also is a consensus about the characteristics that differentiate interviewers who are good and bad at building the relationship.

We have many adjectives that describe the interviewer who is *not* likely to develop a positive relationship—*critical, impatient, aloof, uninterested, controlling, dogmatic, detached, judgmental, insensitive, egotistical, opinionated, uncaring, businesslike, mechanical, punitive, authoritarian, condescending, rude, patronizing, unresponsive.*

In contrast, the interviewer who *is* likely to develop a positive relationship *is* characterized as *respectful, attentive, interested, caring, trustworthy, friendly, genuine, unpretentious, sympathetic, warm, concerned, empathetic, accepting, compassionate, understanding, supportive, reassuring, patient, comforting, solicitous.*

We are reminded of Aldous Huxley's remark that after a lifetime of studying what makes an effective relationship, he was chagrined to find that it all boils down to "being a little nicer."

Acceptance

What specifically should the worker do to develop and maintain a positive relationship? An accepting nonjudgmental attitude helps in developing and maintaining a positive relationship.[*] Workers manifest acceptance by behaving in a manner that shows their respect and concern for the client as a person, regardless of behavior, which workers may reject; workers are compassionate, gentle, and sympathetic. They give clients the freedom to be themselves, to express themselves freely, in all their unlovely as well as lovely aspects. The worker is not moralistic, cold, aloof, derogatory, or disapproving. The nonjudgmental attitude is one that suggests that the interviewer is not concerned with praise or blame but solely with understanding. The accepting worker seeks to explain the individual's behavior rather than to determine the worth of such behavior. The "object of acceptance is not the good or the bad but the real; the individual as he actually is, not as we wish him to be or think he should be" (Biestek 1957:70).

Blaming is counterproductive; it solves nothing and increases the interviewee's defensiveness and opposition. Striving to understand what explains, motivates, or supports the behavior that needs changing does not imply approval of the behavior. In fact it suggests disapproval because the behavior is what the worker targets for change. Thus the interviewer must surmount the difficulty of accepting people as they are while working to helping them change, which implies a rejection of them as they are.

Accepting clients as they are and leaving them there does not achieve the purpose of helping. Accepting clients as they are while helping them to achieve what they can and want to be is what the social work interviewer is being asked to do.

The trick is to distinguish between the person of the interviewee and the behavior of the interviewee. Acceptance relates primarily to the person. The distinction reflects the biblical injunction to reject the sin but not the sinner. A person's inherent worth is not subverted by that person's behavior.

Acceptance, when incorrectly interpreted, suggests that we are entirely

---

[*]We have phrased the conditions for a good relationship in terms that reflect social work usage. Other groups also vitally concerned with relationships have used somewhat different terms to designate essentially the same attitudes. Perhaps the best-known comparable phrase for acceptance is the Rogerian "unconditional positive regard."

neutral toward all behavior, neither approving or disapproving. But social work values make some behavior unacceptable. In supporting the profession society charges social work with responsibility for attempting to change socially unacceptable behavior, and people come to agencies in the hope that they can achieve changes in dysfunctional behavior and attitudes.

Although acceptance does not necessarily mean agreeing with or condoning the client's frame of reference, point of view, and concept of reality, it does involve granting their validity. It implies interpreting others in terms of themselves.

Stated negatively, acceptance is declining to judge; stated positively, it is an active attempt to understand interviewees as they truly are.

In the following example a protective service worker sets aside the question of blame and agonizes over an effort to understand:

> I am looking at her and listening to her tell me how she left the three kids—2, 3, 5—alone in the house to meet with her boyfriend for a drink at the local bar. She had planned to come back within an hour, but never got back until the next morning. During the time she was away, a fire broke out and the three kids were just barely rescued. And I am listening and thinking that clearly this was irresponsible child neglect, but why did she do it? What explains her behavior? What motivated her to neglect the kids? What? Why?

The following poem expresses a client's conception of an accepting worker:

> This woman
> talks to me
> in a warm language
> between her feelings
> and mine.
> This woman,
> seeing the gap
> in my face,
> walks through it
> knowingly; and I,
> I let her stand in my
> field,
> unharmed.
>
> *C. Anatopolsky* *

*Reprinted with permission from the American Association of Psychiatric Social Workers (AAPSW) *Newsletter* (Winter 1937).

The client feels accepted when the worker evokes the following kinds of responses:

She made me feel free to say whatever I was thinking.
I could be very critical of her or very appreciative of her without it chang-ing her good feeling toward me.
I could talk about most anything in my interview without feeling embar-rassed or ashamed.
I had the feeling that this is one person I can really trust.
I feel I don't have to be afraid to be very honest with him—or myself.

The feeling of acceptance is described by an interviewee who says that the interviewer "let me say what I felt," "didn't accuse, criticize, or condemn me," "didn't hold anything against me," "didn't put me down" (Maluccio 1979:124).

Male, 46, middle income, client of a family service agency.

INTERVIEWEE: It's just that I can't keep my hands off the stuff. I run into the slightest trouble and I reach for the bottle.

APPROPRIATE RESPONSES

1. There is trouble and you feel you need a drink.
2. You reach for the bottle.
3. How does reaching for the bottle help?

INAPPROPRIATE RESPONSES

1. Well, drinking doesn't solve the problem, does it?
2. That's not so smart, is it?
3. You ought to have more will power than that.

Male, 45, lower income, general assistance client.

INTERVIEWEE: All you social workers are alike, one goddamn question after the other. Why do I have to tell you so much just to get the help? You could see I need it if you only used your eyes more and your mouth less.

APPROPRIATE RESPONSES

1. You think I talk too much?
2. We make it hard for you to get help you feel you need.
3. You're sore because you feel much of this is none of my business.

INAPPROPRIATE RESPONSES

1. I don't like having to ask them any more than you feel like answering them.
2. You're making my job harder to do.
3. Well, I'm afraid you'll just have to let me get this information if you expect us to help you.

Being accepting and being nonjudgmental are different aspects of the same basic attitude—acceptance is an act of commission, being nonjudgmental an act of omission. The literature offers extensive discussion of the difficulties of implementing this attitude.

As Janis (1983) points out, noncontingent acceptance is difficult to enact because it runs against deeply ingrained social norms. The norm of fairness suggests that rewards should be given to those who have earned them. Acceptance suggests offering the social rewards of positive regard and respect even to those whose behavior may not merit them.

Perlman suggests that the attitude that the term acceptance identifies might be better named *nonblaming* or *noncensorous* (1979:56). Because interviewers are supposed to make "judgments" about what changes they hope to achieve with the client, their work cannot be "nonjudgmental." But the judgment, the assessment of the client in the situation that needs changing, is without blame. A truly nonjudgmental attitude would express a neutral indifference to the client's behavior—it really doesn't matter. To the interviewer who cares about clients it really does matter that clients may be acting in a way that is dysfunctional or destructive for themselves and others in their family.

The interviewer's acceptance of behaviors that differ to some marked degree from usual social norms may leave the interviewee with suspicions about either the sincerity or the competence of the interviewer.

The interviewee is generally keenly aware of community attitudes toward dysfunctional behavior. Rather than being helpful, the interviewer may be creating additional difficulty by condoning behavior that is problematic for the client. Thus we clearly need to make a distinction between accepting the individuals, their thoughts, and their feelings and responding with some concern to behaviors that create and maintain social problems.

If, with the help of the interviewer, the interviewee finally says openly, "I hate my child," and the worker reassuringly and acceptingly says, "It's all right to say that you hate your child," the interviewer is not necessarily approving the feeling or the behavior that may follow from the feeling. Acceptance here means that the relationship between interviewer and interviewee will not be adversely affected by the interviewee's sharing of this information. What the worker has not implied and should not communicate is a suggestion of condoning the idea of parents hating their children.

Admittedly and parenthetically (because an adequate discussion of acceptance would require a book in itself), this does not settle the matter. We can raise questions about behaviors, labeled dysfunctional by the community, that derive from a pathological society in need of reform or about behaviors such as homosexuality, which may have considerable community disapproval but may not be dysfunctional for the individual. In general social work has been ready to accept a wider range of behaviors than has the lay community (Pilsecker 1978). Broader acceptance does not imply an absence of limits, however. Reactions to rape, incest, and child and spouse battering are testimonials to this.

Because so much human service work involves moral and ethical questions, M. D. Rhodes notes that "we have to come to recognize that a nonjudgmental stance is only imperfectly possible and not always desirable" (1992:42)

Empathic Understanding

In using empathic understanding workers are responding to the latent as well as the manifest content of a client's communication. The worker understands sensitively and accurately the nature of the client's experience, the meaning of this the client, and the client's world cognitively and empathically from the client's point of view. The interviewer manifesting affective empathy reflects how the interviewee feels.

The interviewer manifesting empathy understands what the interviewee is thinking and feeling. This worker understands with, as well as about, the client and has the capacity to communicate that understanding to the client in words attuned to the client's feelings; the worker really hears what the client is saying, so the worker's responses have an "I am with you" quality, fitting in with the client's meaning and mood. Even if empathic workers do not always understand, they are always sincerely striving to understand, to reach out and receive the client's communication.

The interviewer feels *with* rather than for the client. Feeling *for* the client would be a sympathetic rather than an empathetic response. Somebody once said that if you have a capacity for empathy, you feel squat when you see a squat vase and feel tall when you look at a tall vase. Empathy is entering imaginatively into the inner life of someone else.

"Empathy allows one to sit in a movie theater and blubber over the death that never happened to a character that never lived," is how one *New York Times* reporter describes it (Angier 1995:C1). But it is not enough simply to be empathically understanding; workers also need to communicate that they accurately perceive and feel their client's situation. The client perceives that the worker is acting in response to empathic understanding when, in the client's words, "She was able to see and feel things in exactly the same way I do"; "He appreciates how the things I experience feel to me"; "She realizes what I mean even if I have difficulty saying it."

Empathic responses from the interviewer give interviewees the feeling that the interviewer understands them and their situation. The client feels emotionally closer to the worker, which strengthens the relationship.

Here are some examples of appropriate and inappropriate uses of empathy:

CLIENT: So I met with Dr. J. and he told me the child needs another operation. After all that, it's enough to make you downright disgusted.
WORKER: Did Dr. J. think this operation would make a difference?

This worker's response reflects little recognition that he is sensing the parent's disappointment and anguish.

CLIENT: So if I don't pass the test and don't get the job, how long do you think my marriage will last, given the way Mary feels about finances?
WORKER: You have a lot riding on the test, so I can feel some of your disappointment and anxiety if you don't pass.

Although the client has not overtly expressed disappointment and anxiety, the worker is empathically responsive to those feelings.

Female, 37, upper lower income, child guidance clinic.

INTERVIEWEE: I know I am supposed to love him, but how much can you put love in a kid without getting some back? You can't just go on feeling love without his showing you some love, too, in return.

APPROPRIATE RESPONSES

1. It's very disappointing for you.
2. It must be hard to do what you have to do under such circumstances.
3. That must hurt.

INAPPROPRIATE RESPONSES

1. Well, he is only a kid and he doesn't understand.
2. Still and all, you are his mother.
3. Many kids don't show their love for parents.

Empathy is the conscious awareness of another's feelings by the act of transposition. In sympathy we recognize the person's feelings but have our own feelings about what is taking place. In empathy the feeling we have about what is taking place is like the other person's feeling.

The term *empathy* has not as yet achieved a clear definition. Many writers use it to mean the interviewer's ability to understand the interviewee from the client's frame of reference or point of view. The interviewer's response is "on target" or "tuned into" the meaning and significance the experience has for the interviewee. The worker is on the same "wavelength" as the interviewee and "knows where he is coming from." Workers put themselves in the "other person's shoes."

This suggests that the interviewer demonstrates accurate interpersonal perception. Empathy in this sense is a cognitive process. Through empathy we share the state of mind of the interviewee. What is supposedly involved in this kind of empathy is a relatively conscious control that permits us to become absorbed in another person's thinking.

Others use the term empathy to point to a process that has stronger affective elements. Empathy here involves not only accurate perception of the other person's feelings and attitudes but, further, the mobilization of feelings in the interviewer that correspond to the emotions the interviewee is feeling. This suggests a more affective process of understanding, to not only to "see with the eyes of another" and "hear with the ears of another" but also to "feel with the heart of another."

Empathy can be both cognitive (I am thinking what you're thinking) and affective (I am feeling what you are feeling). The thoughts and feelings of the interviewer resonate with the thoughts and feelings of the interviewee. Cognitively, the interviewer takes the role of the interviewee; affectively, the emotions are contagious. When interviewers telegraph their empathic responses in one way or another to interviewees, the latter are assured that they are being understood, that they have an alliance.

In empathizing we categorize the client's experience and locate an analogous personal experience. Foster care placement is an experience of separation and loss for the parent. Categorizing this as a general experience of separation and loss, the interviewer, who has never experienced foster placement, evokes the feeling associated with going off to college. The client's pain and fright at learning about the need for an operation may prompt the interviewer to evoke analogous feelings of pain and fright at having to take an important exam.

The situations interviewers might recall in trying to be empathic may be quite different from the interviewee's situation. But the feelings the different situations evoke might be similar. Giving birth and passing a doctoral preliminary examination are different occasions, but both evoke great joy and relief. Empathy is vicariously experiencing another person's world while retaining the orientation of an objective observer.

The danger is that projection may be mistaken for empathy—"this is the way I would feel in this situation, so this must be the way he is feeling." Interviewers must discriminate between their own feelings and the feelings that originate in the interviewee. Empathy requires the ability to oscillate between subjective enmeshment with the interviewee and effective distancing, sensing the client's inner world of meanings as if it were the interviewer's own while recognizing the separation implied by "as if." An excess of empathy would imply overidentification and a loss of the objectivity necessary for effective interviewing. As Mattinson notes, the interviewer's "psychological skin needs to be sensitive enough to pick up some of the psychic difficulties of his client but it needs to be firm enough around his own being to be able to distinguish between what belongs to him and what is, in fact, some feeling he has introjected from the client" (1975:31).

Distancing does not imply detachment. We can be distant and affectively concerned. A suggestion that we be objective does not imply that we should be without feeling. Distancing and objectivity include being concerned about the interviewee's situation but infusing that concern with a cognitive component. Distancing involves emotion controlled by the need to understand intellectually so as to be optimally helpful. Heart is not absent, but its responses are tempered by giving priority to what the head is thinking.

We should note that empathy is a complex concept, and efforts to study the nature and effects of empathy have not been very successful (Greenberg, Elliott, and Lietaer 1994:521–22).

Genuineness and Authenticity

The Rogerians, existential therapists, and others concerned with the interview, particularly the therapeutic interview, have identified genuineness, or authenticity, as an essential condition for a good relationship.

In defining the concept human service professionals use words such as *genuineness, authenticity,* and *congruence* interchangeably. The concept reflects Shakespeare's admonition "to thine own self be true" without pretense or deception. Interviewers' responses are not canned, contrived, or artificial. An interviewer perceived as genuine is down to earth, not uppity, and is sincere, open, and spontaneous, without front or facade.

Genuineness tends to diminish social distance between interviewer and interviewee. The interviewer is less a professional with position, status, and power and more another human being with whom to share secrets.

Interviewees talk of genuineness in the interview when they say "He does not put on a front with me"; "She doesn't put on her social worker role"; "She seems willing to express whatever is actually on her mind with me, including any feelings about herself"; "He is not artificial or pompous but natural and spontaneous." Rather than being wooden and unresponsive to interviewees' expressions of sorrow or elation, the genuine interviewer is humanly responsive and spontaneous in reacting with appropriate feeling.

Authenticity requires that the interviewer be real and human. Authenticity implies spontaneity, the readiness to share with the interviewee our own reactions about what is going on in the interview. Genuineness means that workers are striving for congruence in their feelings and behavior. Paradoxically, the more deliberate the genuineness, the less genuine it is likely to be. A deliberate effort to be genuine and authentic is an oxymoron. As La Rochefoucauld said, "Nothing so much prevents our being authentic as our efforts to seem so."

Genuineness is manifested by judicious self-disclosure. Interviewers perceived as genuine have no need to share their feelings if such sharing is not important to the conduct of the interview. Where sharing feelings is helpful to achieving the objectives, genuine interviewers share openly without resistance, defensiveness, or self-protective apology. They do not deny their feelings. Interviewers perceived as genuine are able to openly acknowledge mistakes and ignorance when they do not know the answer to a question.

An interviewer manifesting high levels of authenticity openly provides information upon request and, when appropriate, initiates the sharing of information. Authentic interviewers answer spontaneously, candidly, and fully, sharing information that might be helpful to the client.

A medical social worker says,

> We had been planning the client's older mother's discharge from the hospital, and she kept returning to the question of finances. I said I had a real sense of what she faced because I had the same problem with the care of my mother. I said that applying for SSI [Supplemental Security Income] had been helpful. The interviewee had never heard of SSI, so I spent part of the interview cluing her in on this.

This worker used disclosure to emphasize empathic understanding, facilitating development of their relationship. Disclosure reduces the status difference between interviewer and interviewee and reveals the person behind the professional. This facilitates the development of a positive relationship.

An interviewer manifesting low levels of authenticity is guarded, defensive, and reticent about making any personal disclosures. This worker seems detached, depersonalized, and anonymous. In answering any question raised, the worker either fails to answer or answers briefly and ambiguously without communicating any information except the most superficial. And the answers appear to be evasive. The atmosphere generated is formal and professional; social and psychological distance are at a maximum. Self-disclosure facilitates the development and enhancement of a positive relationship. It is also a technical procedure to facilitate the achievement of interview objectives. Here we discuss disclosure as it relates to the development of the relationship; see chapter 7 for discussion of self-disclosure as a technical procedure.

Authenticity is related to, but separate from, the problem of interviewer self-disclosure. We can be authentic, that is, without pretense, while not sharing too much about ourselves. The supposition is, however, that if we are authentic, we will have a greater readiness to be open and sharing with the interviewee.

Although genuineness has received limited explicit consideration in the social work literature, Bradmiller found that honesty, straightforwardness, and sincerity by the interviewer—all elements of genuineness and authenticity—were seen by social workers as of almost equal importance to "respect," "warmth," "empathy and understanding" as "necessary elements of a helping relationship" (1978:34).

In his studies of worker-client interaction Lawrence Shulman found that "the worker's ability to 'share personal thoughts and feelings' ranked first as a powerful correlate to developing working relationships" (1991:137).

Interviewee Self-Determination

To the extent possible, interviewers should maximize interviewees' self-determination.

In adhering to and encouraging clients' self-determination the interviewer establishes an atmosphere of mutuality, encourages clients' participation in problem-solving efforts, and respects clients' initiative. Interviewers' behavior implements their belief that clients have the right, and the capacity, to direct their own life; they work *with* the client in problem solving; they communicate confidence in clients' ability to achieve their own solutions and actively help clients to achieve those solutions in their own way. Self-determination guarantees the interviewer's help without domination.

Interviewees who are hesitant to reveal their situation because they fear being controlled, that they might be coerced into doing something they would rather not do, are confronted by the interviewer's assurance of respect for their independence.

In developing the atmosphere of psychological safety required for establishing a positive relationship, interviewees need to feel that interviewers respect their autonomy and will not subject them to controlling tactics. Adherence by the interviewer to client self-determination communicates the message that clients are free to make decisions in their own way toward their own ends.

The interviewer has neither the authority or power to "grant" self-determination. At best interviewers can respect the interviewee's self-determined behavior and decisions and act as assiduously as possible not to threaten or encroach on it.

Aside from self-determination as an ethical right our concern here is with self-determination as a pragmatic vehicle for making it possible for the interviewee to share freely in the interview, to reduce as much as possible constricting inhibitions to self-disclosure.

The discussion here is in terms of negative freedom—the interviewee's freedom from being controlled or coerced. Positive freedom is concerned with enabling interviewees to do what they want to do. This implies a recognition of, and confidence in, the client's capacity for constructive self-determination. It shows a respect for the interviewee's autonomy.

Some argue that *self-direction* might be a more accurate term to apply to this concept. What is involved is a recognition and an implementation of interviewees' clear right to make their own decisions, that they should not be controlled overtly or subtly to do or feel what the interviewer prefers.

There is wisdom in the adage that "a man convinced against his will is of the same opinion still." Clients see this in terms of the worker's behavior in the interview: "She acted as though we were coworkers on a common problem"; "He encouraged me to work on my problems in my own way"; "She didn't seem to think it was necessary for me to accept her idea, opinions, advice, if I wanted her to like me."*

---

*Some of the phrasing is adapted from G. T. Barrett-Lennard, "Dimensions of Therapist Response as Causal Factors in Therapeutic Change," *Psychological Monographs* 76, no. 562 (1962): 1–36.

The case examples here are followed by a series of interviewer responses, some illustrating an attitude respecting self-determination and some illustrating an inappropriate violation of this approach:

Female, 27, lower income, public assistance client.

INTERVIEWEE: So I don't know. I think I should try to put the kids in a day center or maybe even in a foster home and get a job and make some money so we can get back on our feet again— but that might not be so good for the kids.

APPROPRIATE RESPONSES

1. You're puzzled about what to do.
2. It's hard to know what would be best.
3. "Not so good for the kids"?

INAPPROPRIATE RESPONSES

1. Well, if you got a job you would be off relief.
2. My own feeling is that it would be better to stay home.
3. It wouldn't be so bad for the kids.

Female, 55, middle income, client at a medical social work agency.

INTERVIEWEE: I know I have to have this operation, but I would rather not talk about it.

APPROPRIATE RESPONSES

1. It's hard to talk about.
2. Thinking about it makes you anxious.
3. Okay, perhaps there is something else you would rather talk about.

INAPPROPRIATE RESPONSES

1. But I was supposed to discuss this with you.
2. Not talking about it won't make the problem disappear.
3. Well, it has to be discussed sooner or later, so why not now?

Despite the desirability of promising clients freedom from control, this is a promise that is quite difficult to live up to. Perlman's statement that client self-determination is "nine-tenths illusion and one-tenth reality" has validity (1979:651). Studies have established empirically that, despite the brave words about self-determination, social workers in practice do honor the right provisionally and with limitations (Kassel and Kane 1980). The social work literature extensively discusses problems and limitations regarding adherence to and encouragement of client self-determination (Biestek 1951; Biestek and Gehrig 1978; Kassel and Kane 1980; Reamer 1987, 1995; Freedberg 1989).

In studying social workers' application of the principle of self-determination in actual practice, Rothman et al. (1996) found that the results reflected a continuum from least to most restrictive practice strategies. Practitioners might be completely nondirective, suggest direction, prescribe direction, or be clearly directive. Most practitioners used each of these strategies in response to different client situations. Risks to health and welfare, the presence of threatening consequences, questions about client capacity for autonomous decision making and legal and agency requirements were factors determining modifications in the application of nondirective self-determination.

Adherence to the principle that the client is entitled to self-determination requires a presumption that the interviewee is reasonably competent to make decisions. We do not grant infants the right to self-determination. We limit the autonomy of people who are clearly psychotic, and we do not accept a person's decision to commit suicide. We do not accept a self-determined decision of a 14-year-old girl to engage in incest. A girl of that age is not capable of informed consent because of a limited knowledge of what is involved.

Conflict may and often does exist between the client's preference and the worker's responsibility to the agency and to the community. The right to self-determination conflicts with the social worker's "paternalistic" responsibility to protect the interviewee from self-inflicted harm. The whole point of establishing a positive relationship—to increase the interviewer's influence in getting the interviewee to change self-defeating behavior—can sound like a subversion of self-determination (Abramson 1985). Abramson's study of the practice of protective service workers in dealing with this dilemma found that "when safety and freedom conflict, paternalistic beneficence prevails over [client] autonomy" (1989:101). The conflict is between honoring the promise of freedom for the client and meeting the professional responsibility for clients' needs.

Clients' self-direction does have limits, which are imposed by professional responsibility to clients' well-being. Self-determination does not obligate the worker to assist the client in obtaining crack if this is the client's choice.

Human services have a community mandate to try to influence the client-interviewee to change from socially dysfunctional to functional behavior, that is, to stop physically or emotionally abusive behavior, illegal activity, or substance abuse.

Human service workers have a professional responsibility to protect people from potentially self-damaging behavior or causing harm to others (suicide, unprotected promiscuous sex, dropping out of school in early adolescence, taking drugs while pregnant, and the like).

When a client seems to be leaning in the direction of a decision that is exploitative or irresponsible, the worker might suggest alternatives. However neutral workers in this situation might attempt to be, they are likely to favor an alternative in line with social work and/or community values. Because of the power difference in favor of the worker the client might perceive worker's stated alternative as a pressure to comply. This once again reflects the difficulties involved in nondirective interaction.

A medical social worker confers with a 32-year-old mother who is reluctant to schedule an operation she needs because she is concerned about caring for her three young children while she is hospitalized. The worker has offered homemaker service, but the mother is rejecting the idea. The worker comments,

> I could understand her objections, but I also realized that unless she accepted the service she might delay scheduling the needed medical care. Frankly, I wanted to throw the weight of my influence in favor of inducing her to accept homemaker service, but I was deterred by the dislike for manipulating and denying her maximum freedom in determining her own decision. Despite everything, my bias in favor of getting her the necessary medical attention without undue delay got past my professional safeguards. The questions I asked in discussing this with Mrs. R. were formulated in a way to suggest answers in favor of homemaker service. Instead of neutral questions starting [with] "What do you think . . . ?" I tended to ask questions starting with "Don't you think that . . . ?" My verbal skirts weren't long enough to keep my bias from showing.

Because the right decision is not, and cannot be, the worker's to make, the best that the interviewer can do is be mindful of the interviewee's right to self-determination and strive as diligently as possible for its maximum implementation.

Recognizing the variety of considerations—biological, practical, and philosophical—that limit the client's freedom, adherence to client self-determination or self-direction remains an important attitudinal component in developing a positive relationship. A worker convinced of the desirability of maximizing client self-direction approaches the client by trying to push against the limits that restrict the client's choices. This worker seeks to determine the preferences of the client, even if these preferences cannot always be accepted; to get the client's reaction to any inevitable restrictions on the client's choice; increase the number of feasible choices for the client's choice-making; make a decided effort to be aware of personal preferences and any tendency to impose these on the client; respect the client's preferences even though, for a variety of reasons, it may be necessary to modify them; and exercise the absolute minimum of interference necessary to balance conflicting responsibilities to the client and the community. This attitude is in contrast to workers who are convinced that only they know what is right for the client and have little interest in, and/or respect for, the client's choice or preference.

The result may be the same. Clients may be required or induced or influenced to do some things different from their preference. But the process by which this is achieved can either make the client feel esteemed, respected, and individualized or dehumanized, stereotyped, and denigrated. An attitude that communicates sincere consideration for the client's entitlement to self-determination results in an interaction of positive feeling between interviewer and interviewee, even if the entitlement may sometimes have to be modified, curtailed, or even denied.

In actual practice social workers adhere to a narrowly qualified definition of self-determination, violating it only at its edges (Williams 1982). Self-determination is a means to an end—the initiation and development of a positive relationship. Acting to assure interviewees of their autonomy facilitates this. Even if it were not a right in and of itself, practice needs would require honoring the entitlement to self-determination.

Confidentiality

A strong assurance for interviewees that, in revealing themselves to the interviewer, they are not making such information available to a wider public reduces the level of ego threat and facilitates communication. Threats to self-esteem resulting from disclosure of unflattering material is limited if the interviewer alone will know this potentially damaging material. Personal information is a private possession. In sharing it with the worker the client is not giving permission that it be broadcast and used indiscriminately.

The Social Work Code of Ethics states that social workers will "respect the privacy of clients and hold in confidence all information obtained in the course of professional service." But the right to privacy is not only an ethical professional obligation; it is a legal right.

Adherence to confidentiality is in effect a corollary to acceptance of the interviewee. It demonstrates that the interviewer respects the interviewee's rights and entitlements as an individual and that the worker can be trusted.

The pragmatic basis for adherence to confidentiality is that if social work interviewers are to perform their functions effectively, they need to know a great deal about the personal intimate life of the interviewee. The assurance of confidentiality facilitates the disclosure of such information. The absence of such assurance would discourage some people who might need and be able to use the agency's services. Knowledge of a person, particularly intimate knowledge, gives others power over that person—for potential damage, to hurt and embarrass, as well as for potential assistance.

Reviewing the research regarding the effects of confidentiality on clinical interaction, Miller and Thelen note that "the overall findings of laboratory research suggest negative behavioral and attitudinal reactions to those who do not maintain the confidentiality of communications" (1986:15). Safeguarding the interviewee's privacy through adherence to confidentiality increases the sense of trust the interviewee feels.

Studies show that promises of confidentiality are associated with an enhanced perception of the interviewer as trustworthy. Doubts about confidentiality make for initial hesitance about seeking help and are a disincentive to interviewee disclosure (Miller and Thelen 1987:77–78). In fact, one justification for granting legal protection to confidentiality is that it is essential to maintaining the working relationship between client and professional (Watkins 1989a:134).

On June 13, 1996, the U.S. Supreme Court found that "confidentiality of psychotherapy serves important public as well as private interests" and upheld the protection of social workers' confidentiality in federal courts. The decision was based on an effort by a licensed clinical social worker in Wisconsin "to protect records of a therapy session from being disclosed" (Greenhouse 1996:1A)

The right to privacy is a professional ethical obligation, a legal right, and a pragmatic requirement for developing a positive working alliance. Like self-determination, it is a useful principle of practice.

A study of inpatient and outpatient psychotherapy clients found that they both value and expect that their disclosure to the interviewer will be held in confidence. However, they accept case-handling practices regarding such information (secretarial typing, case supervision) as within the bounds of confidentiality (McGuire, Toal, and Blau 1985).

The ethical basis for adherence to confidentiality is that personal information is a possession of clients, analogous to their hat and coat. In disclosing, clients lend information about themselves to the worker in exchange for being helped. But such information still belongs to the client and cannot be "lent" by the interviewer to others without permission.

Confidentiality guarantees that private affairs do not become public property. It might be advisable for the interviewer, when establishing the ground rules for participant interaction early in the interview, to say something about the confidential nature of the encounter.

The worker has an obligation to guard confidential information discreetly; the worker may share it with others, after obtaining the client's permission, only when doing so is necessary to help the client more effectively. Obtaining clients' permission is not a simple procedure but involves great emphasis on *informed consent*—which means the client clearly understands what information is to be shared, with whom, and for what purpose. The worker informs the client that such information, although disclosed to the interviewer in privacy, may be shared with supervisors, typists, and colleagues who might at some point be involved with the case. The greater use of the team approach in offering services increases the need for inter- and intra-agency sharing of information.

As is true for the right to self-determination, the right to privacy is limited and qualified, not absolute. Promises of full confidentiality are not consistent with the requirements of child abuse and neglect reporting laws. Some have suggested that the interviewer share with the interviewee the limits of confidentiality in those situations where the law may obligate the interviewer to share some information. But clinicians in general believe that such a warning would have an inhibiting effect on self-disclosure.

Promises of confidentiality are also limited by court decisions, which have dictated a "duty to warn." The case of *Tarasoff v. Board of Regents of the University of California* (1974) established a legal requirement that therapists break confidentiality if they learn from clients that they might do harm to another person. The *Tarasoff* decision (529 P.2d 553 [1974]) found that the "protective privilege ends where public peril begins" (Kopels and Kagle 1993:103).

Two cases illustrate some dilemmas associated with confidentiality:

> I had been seeing Mr. P. over a period of three months at a mental hygiene outpatient clinic. He was a voluntary patient suffering from severe depression. During this interview he told me in strictest confidence that he had touched the breasts and buttocks of his thirteen-year-old daughter. He was

no longer living with his daughter since the divorce from his wife two years ago. He was, however, living with an eleven-year-old daughter of the woman he had married last year. If I reported him for sexual abuse, as I think I am required to do, he would terminate the contact and a chance to "cure" his behavior. If I failed to report him, I perhaps jeopardized the safety of the eleven year-old with whom he is currently living. What to do? An enigma wrapped in a dilemma. I yearned for some discretionary flexibility on this one.

Harry came in looking anxious and upset. In response to my inquiry, he very hesitantly said that he had learned last week that he was HIV positive. When after some discussion of this I asked whether he planned to tell his wife, he said explosively, "Are you crazy?" I was burdened with the conflict of keeping confidentiality or protecting Harry's wife.

The proliferation of health maintenance organizations, which provide counseling as one of their services, has complicated the problems of confidentiality. Insurance companies paying treatment benefits may request patients' files in order to determine the legitimacy of claims (Lewin 1996). As Kayle and Kopels note, "In recent years (social workers) have seen their ability to protect client confidentiality further diminished by increasing demands for accountability, widening access to information in records, mandated child abuse reporting, and expanded court involvement in professional decisionmaking" (1994:217).

The problem is exemplified in the finding that the third most-frequent malpractice claim against social workers (after sexual impropriety and incorrect treatment) is breach of confidentiality (Watkins 1989a:134, table 1; see also Zadik 1993).

Finally, despite assurances of confidentiality, agency records may be opened by court order. Social workers do not generally have the protection of privileged communication. Privileged communication is a special legal concept in support of agency confidentiality. It provides legal protection to professionals' refusal to share information obtained in the confidential worker-client interview and/or agency records. The statutes of many states grant such privileges to clergy, lawyers, and doctors. Some states have extended this privilege to social workers, but only with considerable extenuating provisions. This trend grows stronger with the spread of social work licensing and certification. In general the protection accorded social workers is less broad than that for other professions (Herlihy and Sheeley 1987; see also Watkins 1989a).

The limits of any realistic promise of confidentiality lie, then, in saying that you will not willfully or carelessly share a client's information with anyone who in your best judgment does not need to know it or can possibly hurt the client.

Although we do not have available any research providing information about how social workers explicitly handle the question of confidentiality with the interviewee, a study of the responses of psychologists to this question is instructive. Although they have a variety of ways to inform clients about confidentiality and its limits, psychologists responding to a nationwide survey "indicated a high regard for the confidentiality of the psychotherapy relationship" (Baird and Rupert 1987:351). In only one situation, the possibility of harm to others, did most respondents say they would be likely to violate confidentiality.

A study of the responses of social workers to vignettes that pose dilemmas in adhering to confidentiality suggests that they are more ready than psychologists or psychiatrists to breach confidentiality. The study found that social workers regard their position as more vulnerable and more ambiguous when dealing with socially threatening behavior (Lindenthal 1988).

Respect for Clients' Individuality

Demonstrating respect for the interviewee's individuality helps to establish and maintain a positive relationship. This involves behavior that supports the client's self-esteem. The atmosphere between interviewer and interviewee is one that suggests that as people they have equal value. The worker responds to the client as a unique individual rather than as one of a class of persons. The orientation toward the interviewee is not "as a human being but as *this* human being with his personal differences" (Biestek 1957:25). It involves the personalization of any generalization and suspension of its application until the evidence is clear that it applies to this particular individual.

Some contend that individualizing the interviewee's problem is a personalistic bias. In warning against routine individualization the critics argue that the interviewee's problem is often a group problem. Individualizing the problem depoliticizes the problem and suggests that the difficulty is the result of some individual personal shortcoming.

The interviewee perceives respect for individuality when an interviewer behaves in a way that elicits the following comments: "She was friendly and had great regard for my feeling"; "He was interested in my individuality"; "He didn't talk down to me"; "She never made me feel I was just another client"; "He not only was interested in trying to help me with my problem, he was interested in me as a particular person."

Appropriate and inappropriate worker responses follow this case:

Female, 19, lower middle income, client of a child care agency.

INTERVIEWEE: Well, Catholics are against abortion, and here I am pregnant and all.

APPROPRIATE RESPONSES

1. How do you yourself feel about abortion?
2. What are your ideas about what you want to do?
3. And you, what do you think?

INAPPROPRIATE RESPONSES

1. Well, I guess, as a Catholic, abortion is not a possibility for you.
2. Okay, so abortion is out then.
3. What is your thinking about adoption?

Individualizing the client is an act of respect. Interviewees say, "She treated me not as a number or as representing some group but as a separate human being unlike any other, distinguished from others"; "He seemed to see me not as another client but as *this* client."

Stereotyping is the reverse of individualizing the client. On the basis of a limited amount of information we assign a client to a group and then attribute to that person the attitudes, feelings, and behavior generally attributed to members of the group. Having classified and labeled, we tend to perceive the interviewee not as a special individual but in terms of the pattern drawn from the stereotype. Stereotyping reduces our ability to differentiate this interviewee from others and to make precise discriminations.

Stereotypes of positive characteristics are as antithetical to individuality as are negative characteristics. A worker in a mental health clinic says,

> I am alert to negative stereotyping but an interview with Mrs. Yung brought me up short. A Korean family owner of a restaurant, she was having constant conflict with an adolescent son. Assuming that all Asian parents were high on education, I somehow assumed that part of the trouble related to the kid's trouble in school and probed this area for information. We miscommunicated in her hesitancy and evasiveness about this. It turned out that what she was trying to tell me, in opposition to my stereotype, was that part of the problem was that her son was too involved in schoolwork and she needed him to work more hours in the restaurant.

The persistence of the tendency of interviewers to stereotype presents a problem because to some extent it is functional. Workers could not possibly meet every interviewee without some generalizations to organize the complex data they have to process. Although we are opposed to stereotyping, we recognize the utility of generalizations, scientifically derived, that professionals apply in using all sorts of diagnostic labels. Stereotypes are lay generalizations derived from empirical lay experience. As such they have an element of validity. Members of a particular age, sex, race, or ethnic group do have some elements in common. At the same time each member of the group is different from every other member. The scientifically derived generalization emphasizes group characteristics and is useful in that it tells us something about the interviewee that is likely to be true. Individualization emphasizes the unique aspects of the interviewee.

Because it is functionally useful and necessary in organizing the world around us, stereotyping is likely to continue to be a problem despite all our exhortations. The best we can hope for is that interviewers will be explicitly aware of the stereotypes and generalizations they hold and that they will hold them lightly and flexibly, applying them only when sufficient data clearly warrant their use. Such an interviewer gives the client the freedom to communicate data that contradict the generalizations.

The "halo or horns" syndrome also leads to denying some aspect of the client's individuality. The "halo effect" suggests that the interviewee who is considerate in one situation will be considerate in all situations; conversely, in the "horns effect" the client who is selfish in one situation is likely to be selfish in others. This denies people their tendency to be wonderfully inconsistent and to act differently in different situations. Like a generalization, the halo or horns effects make our job easier because we presume to know more about the individual client than we in fact do.

Consistent application of the principle of individualization implies a contradiction to everything we have written about the principles of interviewing. Every principle of interviewing that we have suggested is a generalization. Although the principles are likely to work for most interviewees most of the time, the principle of individualization cautions the worker to be sensitive to the exceptions, to look for and monitor feedback carefully, and adjust the application of the principles to the individual instance.

Interest, Warmth, Trust, Respect

Genuine *interest* is a great help in establishing and maintaining a positive relationship. A worker expresses interest by showing concern about a client's needs, showing a readiness to help, and communicating the feeling that the worker really cares what happens to the client over and beyond the formal responsibility to the job.

Interest and concern imply a heightened special attention, an enhanced intensity of the interviewer's presence. They manifest an attitude that demonstrates that what the interviewee has to say is worth the interviewer's efforts.

Clients testify to a worker's high level of interest: "He was ready to do things to help me even if it meant some bother for him"; "She didn't rush to finish the interview"; "He seemed to *want* to hear what I had to say."

We demonstrate interest by asking interviewees for their story, their feelings, their reactions, and their responses and by making replies that demonstrate how well we have been listening, how much we have remembered of interviewees' statements, and how carefully we have heard them. These examples include both appropriate and inappropriate worker responses:

Male, 22, lower income, probation agency client.

INTERVIEWEE: I'm not sure if I can explain how I got into this jam.

APPROPRIATE RESPONSES

1. Take your time.
2. Tell it your own way and perhaps I can help if you get stuck.
3. Uh-huh. [*Expectant silence.*]

INAPPROPRIATE RESPONSES

1. Well, we have very limited time. . . .
2. Well, then, perhaps we can go on to something else.
3. Well, it may not be so important.

The appropriate response demonstrates an interest in hearing what the client has to say; it encourages communication. The inappropriate response shows lack of interest and impatience to end the interview.

Female, 26, lower income, public assistance client.

INTERVIEWEE: All those things you asked me to bring—some of them I have, some of them I can't find. I don't know how I can get them, where to go. I have the rent receipts and gasoline bills and for the electricity, but like the marriage certificate, and the birth certificates of the two boys—these I don't know about.

APPROPRIATE RESPONSES

1. I'll be glad to show you how to get what you need.
2. Let's go over this and see what can be done.
3. Try again to find them. We'll help you get duplicates if you can't.

INAPPROPRIATE RESPONSES

1. Well, I am afraid that until you bring these things, we cannot make out a check for you.
2. Well, you'll just have to find them.
3. I thought it was clear that we needed this for your eligibility.

The line between interest and curiosity is thin. Curiosity implies seeking access to information to which the interviewer is not entitled because it does not further the purpose of the interview. The focus of legitimate interest is selective and discriminating. Principled adherence to confidentiality would suggest that we need to help the interviewee to be silent about anything that is none of our business.

Interviewers can communicate *warmth* by using eye contact, leaning forward, smiling, using verbal responses that are frequent, short, and encouraging, and by making positive statements about the interviewee. Their speech is calm, modulated, and soothing and has a friendly overtone. Posture is relaxed.

Interviewers display *respect* by adhering to the appropriate social amenities—but not by resorting to effusive overdemonstrative friendliness. Affirming the client's worth and uniqueness through acceptance is a sign of respect.

Respect implies that we regard the interviewee as having intrinsic value, not as a means to some end. Respect involves manifesting a courteous regard for interviewees and a consideration of them as worthy of esteem. In respecting interviewees we take them seriously and listen attentively. We demonstrate respect by being punctual for the interview, attending to interviewees' comfort, and addressing them by name.

The interviewees who felt that the interviewer communicated warmth and respect for them said, "She was friendly and polite, and she seemed to have a regard for my feelings"; "She treated me like the adult I am"; "He didn't try to act smug and superior as though he were trying to outsmart me."

Trust is more likely to develop when interviewees perceive that the interviewer is favorably disposed toward them, has good intentions, wants to be helpful, demonstrates competence and expertise in being helpful, and can be relied upon. Trust suggests a feeling that interviewers are dependable and predictable; the client can have confidence in what they say: "She could be trusted to do what she said she would do."

Trust, warmth, and respect are hard to separate from each other and from the other components that comprise the orientation that makes for a positive relationship. The overlap is considerable.

The facilitative factors we have discussed thus far—self-determination, acceptance, individuality, genuineness, empathic understanding, confidentiality, attention, warmth, trust, respect—are associated with the development and maintenance of a positive working alliance relationship. This association has been recognized as substantially valid. "Virtually all schools of therapy accept the notion that these or related therapist relationship variables are important for significant progress in psychotherapy and in fact fundamental to the formation of a working alliance" (Lambert and Bergen 1994:164; see also Orlinsky, Grawe, and Parks 1994:335, table 8.46).

Relationships as an Interactional Event

Although we have been focusing on interviewers and how they need to behave in developing a positive relationship, we emphasize once again that relationships are reciprocal, interactive, and contingent. The interviewee is very much a codeterminant of how the relationship will develop.

The interviewee is an equally important factor. The worker may offer the necessary conditions for an optimum relationship, but it may fail to develop because the client lacks the capacity or the desire to interact.

The worker's actions may not be the sole determinant of the client's response. The interaction may be the result of transference as well as objective elements in the interaction. *Transference* means that the client reacts to the worker as though the worker were another person. The client may perceive the interviewer in terms of a relationship with another person at another time and place.

Interviewers have control only over the attitudes they communicate. They have no control over how their communication is perceived. Interviewer-offered conditions may not be the same as interviewee-received conditions. A discrepancy can exist between objectively rated therapeutic conditions and the client's rating of them (Gurman 1977). Generally, we can count on some congruity between the two. But the ultimate test of the effect of facilitative conditions is not what the interviewer does but what the interviewee perceives the worker as doing.

As Sexton and Whiston note in a review of the research, "Client factors have been found to be a contributing factor in the development of the alliance and also appear to mediate the relationship between the alliance and outcome" (1994:42). This is seconded by Bergin and Garfield who, in a summary of reviews of psychotherapy research, conclude that "client characteristics do make a difference with respect to outcomes—if the client does not absorb, utilize and follow through on the facilitative efforts of the therapist, then nothing happens" (1994:825).

Inner Attitudes and Expressed Behaviors

We need to discuss one more important consideration regarding the good relationship. The portrait we have painted here of the ideal interviewer may strike you as an intimidating paragon of virtue.

Consistently manifesting this saintly attitude may be difficult, given the realities of the social worker's job. We interview child abusers and neglectful parents, spouse beaters and rapists, psychopaths, habitual criminals, and chronic substance abusers. We dislike some clients because they are overly demanding, manipulative, excessively passive, intimidatingly assertive, hostile, resistant, or cloyingly dependent.

Perlman says plainly what we find difficult to acknowledge: "It is honestly not possible to like everyone" (1979:103).

Studies confirm that therapists experience feelings of anger, annoyance, frustration, boredom, and resentment in response to some clients and some client behaviors (Fremont and Anderson 1986, 1988; Pope and Tabachnick 1993).

It is contrary to the human condition to expect that interviewers will be able to like and feel concern for all the different kinds of people who come to their social agency. Similarly, interviewers will like and care for some clients more than others and be turned off by some clients (a limited number, it is hoped).

Be assured that interviewers' behavior rather than their attitude or feeling tends to be of more critical importance. The interviewee reacts to the overt behavior the interviewer manifests rather than to the worker's underlying attitudes or feeling. It is of course most desirable for the overt behavior and underlying attitude to be congruent. This would eliminate the possibility that the overt behavioral message is contradicted by the covert attitudinal message. It would also reduce psychic stress on the worker who feels one way but is constrained by the professional role to act in another way. But if the two messages are contradictory, the message of behavior seems to have clear priority, according to studies in which researchers interviewed both worker and client about their experiences after their interview together (Hyman 1954). In some instances the workers confessed that, although they acted in an accepting manner, they did not feel accepting, that although they acted as though they liked the interviewees, they did not really like them. The interviewee's perception of the same interview rarely reflected any recognition that the worker's underlying attitude was negative. The clients perceived and reacted to the worker's positive verbal and nonverbal behavior toward them.

A similar conclusion results from another careful study of interviewee-interviewer interaction in a health interview survey, based on independent reports of the same interview from interviewer and interviewee. "The study started with the assumption that the attitude and feeling variables were the most important and significant factors determining interview interaction. The results of the study contradicted the hypothesis and indicated that the actual behavior of both interviewer and interviewee were the variables of greatest importance in determining the course of the interview" (Cannell, Fowler, and Marquis 1968:5).

The findings of studies of the relation between a therapist's genuineness and a positive psychotherapy outcome have relevance here. A review of such studies by Orlinsky and Howard found that the relationship between genuineness and positive outcome is strongest when "measured from the patient's perspective" (1986:340). The implication is that the interviewee's perception of the interviewer's behavior is more significant than what the interviewer feels.

Genuineness can apply to interviewers' interaction with themselves or to the interaction between the interviewer and the interviewee. Interviewers can be congruent within themselves. They are aware of what they feel. they are not deceiving themselves about their feelings, and they accept what they feel. At the same time they may be incongruent in their interaction with the interviewee because they may be feeling one way but communicate a different feeling to the interviewee. We can differentiate between being honest with ourselves and being honest with others. Interviewers can feel genuinely congruent as a person within themselves toward interviewees, recognizing and accepting that we dislike them but act, as professionally required, in contravention of the personal feelings. What is involved is not a denial of our true feelings but rather judicious restraint in the open expression of such feelings.

The social work literature recognizes that on many occasions our feelings are inappropriate to effective interview interaction requires. We are admonished to develop a self-awareness so that we recognize when we have such inappropriate feelings and attitudes. The objective of developing self-awareness is to control the expression of inappropriate feelings and attitudes. In effect the control that self-awareness permits us to exercise is similar to the kind of dissimulation we suggest here. We control the expression of inappropriate feelings and attitudes so that we can overtly express the appropriate feelings and attitudes.

Saying that a person has acted like a professional social worker is an acknowledgment that professional behavior is consciously managed behavior. No matter what our internal feelings and attitudes are like, our professional role prescribes the appropriate external behavior to display. What is involved is behavioral conformity to the role requirements even if we do not achieve affective and/or attitudinal conformity.

Discussing the emotional work required of service personnel, Wharton notes that the "central emotional task for these workers is to publicly display an emotion they may not necessarily privately feel" (1993:208). Studies show that professionals who are successful in managing their feelings are effective on the job. For instance, researchers evaluate as better nurses those who appear not to be upset or frightened by what are truly unpleasant and anxiety-provoking experiences that cause them to feel disgust and fear (DePaulo, Stone, and Lassiter 1985:348; see also Hochshild 1983).

And in fact, while generally not explicitly noted, human service professionals, including social workers, often behave in interviews in contradiction of their feelings and attitudes (Whitley 1979). Discussing human service interviewers, Epstein notes that "interviewer behavior tends to be a compromise between what they really feel and what is expected of them in their occupational role and their situational identity" (1985:24). A study of the use of self-disclosure by social workers found that they avoid disclosing to the client their negative reactions to the client (Anderson and Mandell 1989:266).

Detailed interviews with child welfare social workers show that "they carefully restrict their assumptions, diagnoses and attitudes when in the presence of the clients—suspicions and impressions are never fully shared. They keep a tight rein on assessments and assumption which, if shared with the client, might lead to unmanageable reactions" (Pithouse 1987:94–95).

Woods and Hollis found that

> when workers fail to achieve understanding and acceptance and instead feel hostility, aversion, or some other anti-therapeutic emotion, they usually try to avoid translating it into speech and action. . . . Whether the feeling is one

of anger, boredom, sexual attraction or intense like or dislike, the seasoned psychosocial worker makes every effort to guide the expression of personal feelings according to their value to therapeutic work. (1990:206)

What we are suggesting here may evoke misgivings and objections on the part of the reader. We are suggesting that we act in one way, although we feel another way. The ethical justification for this approach lies in its purpose: helping the client. The dissimulation is not self-serving. It is not designed to provide personal gain. Rather, professionals engage in it to help the client. Deception for the purpose of helping may "constitute a higher form of moral behavior than does the simple injunction to tell the truth," no matter what the consequences (Saarni and Lewis 1993:14). Such dissimulation is analogous to the doctor's use of the placebo, which helps many patients even though it is a lie. We are faking toward benevolent ends. Sophisticated management of self-presentation is justified as being in the best interests of the client.

Aside from the concern with ethical considerations, a principal objection to what we are suggesting is pragmatic. Some contend that feeling one way and acting another does not work because the interviewee will discern and react negatively to the duplicity. Despite the myth in social work that the client is so perceptively sensitive, research repeatedly shows that discrepancies in attitudes and behavior are difficult for most people to detect.

A long-term student and prolific researcher of nonverbal aspects of deception, Paul Ekman, says, "Our research and the research of most others have found that few people do better than chance in judging whether somebody is lying or truthful. We also found that most people think they are making accurate judgments although they are not" (1986:162). In general people are not good judges of other people, despite our consistent conceit to the contrary (Cook 1982; DePaulo et al. 1987; DePaulo, Stone, and Lassiter 1985; Ekman 1992).

The reassuring implication of these findings for the student of interviewing is that success in establishing good relationships is possible without being angelic. Although admittedly desirable, it is not necessary to feel invariably respectful and accepting. It is enough to *act* respectful and accepting. All we can ask of interviewers is that they be capable of a disciplined subjectivity, not that they resolve all their prejudices,dislikes, and antipathies. They are asked to control negative feelings in the interview so that they are not obvious. If the research has validity, this control is likely to be sufficient for establishing and maintaining a good relationship that facilitates communication.

What is involved is the behavioral management of feelings we wish we did not feel but that we do feel. We manage our behavior in this way in response to our commitment to be optimally helpful. We cannot teach you how to experience the facilitative feelings. What we can teach, and what you can learn, is how to behaviorally manifest a therapeutic stance.

There is a further implication. It is true that if we truly feel the correct attitude, we are likely to say the correct word. However, oddly enough, the reverse also can be true. If we keep saying the correct word, we are likely to begin to feel the correct attitude. Cognitive dissonance is a strain that is resolved by bringing behavior and attitude into congruence, this time by bringing the attitude closer to the word (Halmos 1966:55–56).[*]

Transition from Opening Phase to the Body of the Interview

A study by Luborsky et al. (1985) that confirms the crucial significance of relationship to effective psychotherapy further found that the relationship, when combined with skillful interviewing technique, increases the likelihood of a positive outcome.

A good relationship makes change possible. It is like heating steel to shape a horseshoe. While the steel is hot, the blacksmith uses technical skill to shape the metal into a horseshoe.

Sometime between 2700 and 2200 B.C. Vizier Ptah-Hotep wrote to his son in recognition of these considerations:

> If thou art one to whom petition is made, be calm as thou listenest to what the petitioner has to say. Do not rebuff him before he has swept out his body or before he has said that for which he came. The petitioner likes attention to his words better than the fulfilling of that for which he came. . . . It is not necessary, that everything about which he has petitioned should come to pass, but a good hearing is soothing to the heart.

Four thousand years later this statement remains true. But social workers need to be more concerned with "the fulfilling of that for which he came" than was a grand vizier. Interviewees want more than expressive satisfaction

---

[*]Dissonance theory posits a tendency toward psychological consistency. Inconsistency between behavior and feelings creates a psychological tension that is resolved by efforts to reduce the inconsistency. James Lange's theory of emotion also supports this; it suggests that although we act in response to our feelings, we also feel in response to our actions. See R. B. Zojonc, Sheila T. Murphy, and Marita Inglehart, "Feeling and Facial Efference: Implications of the Vascular Theory of Emotion," *Psychological Review* 93, no. 3 (1989): 395–416, for a recent confirmation of the James Lange theory.

from their contact with the interviewer. They want help with their problem. A relationship is not enough; a good relationship is a necessary but not sufficient condition to provide what the interviewee needs and wants from the agency—some actual help in dealing with a socially problematic situation. To achieve this technical skill is necessary.

Summary: Chapter 5

The relationship can be defined as the expression of the participants' feelings and attitudes for each other that establishes the interactional context in which they do the work of the interview. A good relationship increases the likelihood of self-disclosure and amplifies the influence of the interviewer. Research has identified a positive relationship as the most consistent and ubiquitous factor associated with positive outcomes in human service helping.

The elements of a positive relationship include acceptance, empathy, genuineness and authenticity, self-determination, confidentiality, individuality, interest, warmth, trust, and respect. The relationship, however, is an interactional event. If the client does not absorb, facilitate, or follow through on the efforts of the worker, positive outcomes will not result.

Consistently manifesting the qualities necessary for the development of a positive relationship can be difficult if clients are demanding, manipulative, dependent, hostile, and otherwise unpleasant. However, if the interviewer's attitudes and behavior are contradictory, the message of behavior has clear priority. If a worker feels rejecting but acts accepting, the client is likely to respond to the worker's positive verbal and nonverbal behavior rather than the negative underlying attitude. Success in establishing a good relationship is possible without being godlike. It is not necessary to always feel respectful and accepting. It is only necessary to act respectful and accepting.

A good relationship is a necessary but not sufficient condition to ensure successful outcomes. Workers must also apply technical skill to solve the client's problem.

SUGGESTED READINGS

Felix P. Biestek. *The Casework Relationship.* Chicago: Loyola University Press, 1957. (149 pp.)
   First published in 1957, this book is still one of the clearest statements of the components of the effective interviewer-interviewee relationship.
Lawrence M. Brammer. *The Helping Relationship: Process and Skills*, 3d ed. Englewood Cliffs, N.J.: Prentice-Hall, 1985. (174 pp.)
   Written for the counseling psychologist by a counseling psychologist. In describing

the helping process it clarifies the nature of the helping relationship and the skills used within the relationship to help people.

Counseling Psychologist. Special Issue: The Relationship in Counseling and Psychotherapy 13, no. 2 (1985). (294 pp.)

A scholarly delineation, presented in a series of articles, of some essential aspects of the helping relationship.

F. E. McDermott, ed. *Self-Determination in Social Work: A Collection of Essays on Self-Determination.* London: Routledge and Kegan Paul, 1975. (245 pp.)

A sophisticated and critical analysis by a group of social work philosophers and theoreticians of a key component of the helping relationship.

H. H. Perlman. *Relationship: The Heart of Helping People.* Chicago: University of Chicago Press, 1979. (236 pp.)

Written with warmth and wit by an eminent social worker, the book clearly details the importance of relationship for social work.

SIX

Problem Exploration Phase

Interviewers have achieved the principal objectives of the opening phase when they have established the purpose for the interview, gathered some preliminary data about the problem, inducted the client in the role of interviewee, and determined that a positive relationship has begun.

We have noted that a positive relationship is essential for an effective interview—but it alone does not guarantee success. *Technically skillful interviewing* in the context of the positive relationship is what ensures that the objectives of the interview are likely to be achieved. Within the context of the relationship the interviewer has to apply effective techniques to propel the interview in the direction of success. Techniques in the absence of a positive relationship are sterile; relationships in the absence of technical skill are impotent. As Mahoney and Patterson note in citing the ubiquitous research findings on the importance of the relationship, "Therapeutic techniques can effectively be employed only within the matrix of a well functioning therapeutic relationship" (1993:680). But technical competence in interviewing is necessary in order to fulfill the hope and expectation for help that the relationship provides.

The Meaning and Sequence of Techniques

Techniques are conscious and deliberate interventions that the interviewer selects because some research or some theory has shown that a particular intervention will have effects that further the objectives of the interview.

A technique is a procedure by which a task is accomplished. Certain techniques are in the toolkit of almost every human service interviewer of any theoretical persuasion—reflection and paraphrase, questioning, summarizing, transition, clarification, silence, humor, confrontation, interpretation, providing information, offering advice and suggestions, and modifying the environment. *Skill* is the ability to use techniques effectively. Skills involve not only knowing what to do but how to do it.

Although we have, for the purpose of clarity in presentation, sharply separated relationship development and maintenance from interviewing techniques, they in fact overlap. For instance, the techniques we use to help clients share their problem with us work more effectively in the context of a good relationship. But we enhance a good relationship if we use the techniques in a basically supportive and respectful manner.

In selecting the sequence in which to present and discuss interviewing techniques, we have been guided by the problem-solving process. The interviewer selects the change-oriented interventions after reaching an understanding (assessment) of the problem that derives from the facts (data gathering, social study). Thus the process starts with the facts—obtaining the information that will enable us to know the interviewee's story, the situation for which the client is seeking the interviewer's help.

Consequently, we first must explain the set of skills primarily designed to help interviewers help interviewees share the details of their situation, in other words, provide the information the interviewer needs in order to be helpful.

A variety of techniques is designed to encourage the client to maintain the flow of communication: attending behaviors and minimal encouragements, reflecting and paraphrasing, summarizing or recapitulating, making transitions, and questioning. Because *questioning* is a general procedure used to both broaden the range and intensify the depth and implementation of the problem-solving process, this book devotes an entire chapter, chapter 9, to questions and questioning. We discuss a second set of skills—interpretation, confrontation, information sharing, advice, and disclosure, which we call "problem-solving interventions"—in chapter 7.

Early in the interview the worker uses exploratory skills. The interviewer and interviewee are trying at this point to explicate, as clearly as possible, the nature of the problem and its context. Once they have identified the problem, the worker is likely to use skills designed to influence the client to change; this is more likely to occur in the latter part of the interview when interviewer and interviewee are trying to do something about the problem.

But before we can review these skills, we need to briefly discuss two ideas. First, the skills we use to obtain information about the interviewee's problem and the skills we associate with helping the client deal with the problem often overlap. Information-soliciting skills often have a problem-solving component. Problem-solving skills often help to elicit additional information. Still, there is a logic to grouping the skills as we have. A particular skill may be best used as a primary technique to achieve a particular purpose, even as it performs a secondary function. The primary objective of paraphrase and reflection is to help interviewees tell their story. At the same time, because paraphrases and reflections are selective in their emphasis, they may help the interviewee see solutions to problems more clearly.

Second, there is an intermediate step between the data-gathering and problem-resolving interventions: *data assessment.* In order to be truly helpful the interviewer not only needs to *know* about the interviewee's situation but *understand* the problem. Data gathering provides the informational units of a jigsaw puzzle. Assessment puts the pieces together to form a picture that explains the situation. Assessment organizes and interprets the information obtained during the first step, data gathering.

In making an assessment we impose order on discrete data, interweaving and making connections between units of information. This step is not, however, an element of interaction in the interview. Assessment takes place in the mind of the interviewer rather than as a result of interacting with the interviewee.

Before we move on to the skills that help interviewees detail the facts and feelings surrounding their problem, it bears repeating that, although the helping process involves some clearly identifiable steps—data gathering, assessment, and helping interventions—such steps do not occur in a uniform and ordered sequence. An interview is not like an assembly line, which has an invariable and necessary sequence of fixed steps. The helping steps in the interview interlock, appear out of turn, and reverse themselves.

Attending Behaviors and Minimal Encouragements (Expressions of Attention and Interest)

Attending behaviors are those observable actions of interviewers that show that they are interested and paying attention. An important component of attending behaviors is nonverbal, manifested in eye contact and body posture.

The interviewer is comfortably relaxed but not slouched. The body faces the interviewee squarely and has a slightly forward lean. Interviewers do not cross their arms and legs—their position should suggest openness, a receptivity to what the interviewee is saying. The interviewer speaks in a clear voice, using various inflections to evidence animation and involvement, and uses expressive hand gestures.

The distance between interviewer and interviewee is such that the interviewer is not intrusively close and not unapproachably distant.

Good attending behavior communicates the interviewer's involvement in and commitment to the task of the interview. It suggests an intensity of presence, attentive listening.

The interviewer initiates and maintains comfortable eye contact with the interviewee. A determined effort at constant eye contact, amounting to a stare, is not desirable. The interviewer should show a willingness to maintain eye contact but vary it in response to the flow of communication, which dictates an occasional break in eye contact at appropriate points. Constant eye contact is intrusive; frequent shifts in eye contact suggest discomfort with or rejection of the interviewee.

The acronym SOLER—straight, open, leaning, eye contact, relaxed—is an easy way to remember the posture of involvement, the relaxed alertness characteristic of good attending behavior (Egan 1986). One study videotaped physicians rated as high and low on rapport to determine differences in their nonverbal behavior. High-rapport doctors were observed to manifest SOLER behavior to a greater degree than the low-rapport doctors (Harrigan, Oxman, and Rosenthal 1985).

The verbal component of attending behavior is manifested in what has been termed *verbal following*. Interviewers demonstrate attentiveness to the client by commenting in ways that follow from what the client is saying. The client's comment cues the worker's response. Client stimulus and worker response share the same content.

Interviewers exhibit poor verbal following when they frequently interrupt the interviewee and initiate frequent changes of topic that are unrelated or only peripherally related to what the client has been saying—the worker's responses do not have as their antecedents the client's immediately preceding statements. Thus the interview lacks continuity. Failures in following are analogous to the situation in which one person extends a hand for a handshake and the other does not accept it. The following example demonstrates poor verbal following, giving the impression that the interviewer has not been paying attention:

At the start of an adoption application interview, the interviewer asks how long the couple has been considering adoption.

MRS. C: Oh, I think it's always been on our minds. We've been trying for a child for, oh, almost four years. I think from the time we realized nothing was happening [*nervous laugh*], then we always had adoption at the back of our minds.

INTERVIEWER: Do you know anyone with adopted children, any friends
          or relatives?

Following involves intensity as well as content. The affect of the interviewer's statement must reflect the level of affective intensity of the interviewee's preceding statement. If the interviewee says, "I was very upset,
practically immobilized when I heard about the accident," and the interviewer says, "You were somewhat anxious, then?"—we see a discrepancy
in following.

Different people have different representational systems for expressing
their world. Some people think kinesthetically, others aurally, others visually.
Following is more effective if the sender matches the representational world
of the receiver. An interviewee who says, "That rings a bell," is matching the
interviewer who introduced a comment by saying, "I hear you saying . . ." or
"How does this sound to you?" The best response to an interviewee who talks
about "things being heavy" and "difficulty of getting a good grasp on things"
is to talk about "feeling your way." The client who comments, "Everything
looks bleak," is matched by the interviewer's response: "I see what you mean."

Good attending behavior also involves a slight pause—two to five seconds—between the interviewee's statements and the interviewer's response.
The pause communicates that the interviewer is not rushing and is giving
some consideration to the client's statement before replying.

Minimal encouragements are short utterances—"gurgles"—with little
content that encourage interviewees and reinforce their desire to continue—"uh-huh," "hmm," "go on," "and then . . . ," "so," "I see," "sure," "that's
so," "and . . ." Gurgles include nonverbal nodding.

These essentially meaningless sounds assure the interviewee that the
interviewer is psychologically present, is involved, and is in effect showing
interest in what the client is saying.

Once the client has started talking and is actively involved in communicating, the interviewer uses minimal encouragements. These are like the
pats you give to a swing in motion to keep it moving. They lubricate the
interaction.

Although the word *minimal* refers to the activity of the interviewer, the
effect on the interviewee is more than minimal. Such utterances have a
potent effect in reinforcing the interviewee's behavior. Because they are
meaningless interventions without content, they are unintrusive. They do
not impede the interviewee's flow, and they do not cause the interviewee to
shift the nature of the material being shared.

The uh-huhs and hmms are neutral ambiguous encouragements. Unlike encouragements such as "Good"; "That's interesting"; and "Fine," the uh-huhs and hmms do not tell the client that this is the kind of content the interviewer is looking for. They tell the interviewee little about the interviewer's reactions other than that the worker is interested and acknowledges what the interviewee is saying. The responses of "I see" and "I understand" also are ambiguously encouraging. "Good" and "That's interesting," on the other hand, suggest more explicitly that interviewees should continue to focus on the kinds of content they have been discussing. The different minimal encouragements convey subtly different messages. Saying uh-huh assures the interviewee you are paying attention. "I see" claims that you understand the client's meaning. "Yes"; "Okay"; and "Of course" suggest approval of what the client is saying. "Go on" obligates the interviewee to continue. Interviewers may need to give more conscious attention to exactly what message they want to communicate rather than, as so often is the case, responding automatically as though the minimal encouragement used makes little difference.

These responses also are delaying tactics. They keep the interviewee talking and give the interviewer an opportunity to build a picture of the situation. The responses permit interviewers to refrain from committing themselves before they know enough to decide what is best to do, yet these responses suggest that the interviewer is with the interviewee and is not ignoring what is being said. On reaching an impasse an interviewer says, "I didn't know what to say so I used a safe 'uh-huh.'"

Shepard and Lee summarize some additional functions served by hmm-hmm:

> [Hmm-hmming] allows the patient to hear the sound of the therapist's voice; allows the therapist to hear the sound of his own voice; provides the therapist with a feeling of usefulness; provides the therapist with an outlet for stored-up energy; makes the therapist sound non-committal and therefore extremely professional. . . . When the patient hears 'hhmmnn' he knows for certain that he is in therapy and getting something for his money.
>
> (1970:65)

These interventions are one step beyond an expectant silence. They are somewhat selective, whereas silence is indiscriminate. They emphasize a response to some content, highlighting and encouraging elaboration of the material to which the interviewer has responded, "Uh-huh."

The danger is that minimal encouragement can become ritualistic or automatic when an interviewer responds to every statement with uh-huhs and hmms whether these are appropriate or not.

A similar problem relates to head nodding, which can act as a minimal encourager. Appropriate head nodding does show interest and acts as a nonverbal reinforcer to keep the interviewee talking. Automatic continuous head nodding has been negatively characterized, however, as therapeutic Parkinson's syndrome.

Minimal encouragements have a cognitive effect, conditioning effect, and motivational effect. The interviewer's encouraging response tells interviewees that they are acting as good interviewees should act, that they are talking about things that are relevant. An encouraging response reinforces the behavior. The interviewer's encouragement further motivates the interviewee to continue because the approval implied in the response is rewarding.

Brief encouragement also communicates that the interviewer is not interested in taking a turn to speak at this point in the interview and is giving the interviewee the uncontested opportunity to continue.

Paraphrasing

A step beyond repetition of a word as a minimal encourager is the technique of paraphrase. In *paraphrasing* the interviewer restates the essence of the interviewee's statement, although not exactly, as an echo. Paraphrasing is a selective restatement of the main ideas that resembles but is not the same as the statement by the client. *Para* means 'alongside,' and a paraphrase parallels what the client said:

INTERVIEWEE: Ever since I've been taking the drugs they gave me to take when I left the hospital, I just can't seem to keep awake. It's getting so I really neglect my kids.

INTERVIEWER: Because of the effects of the drugs on you, the kids get less care.

INTERVIEWEE: Ever since Bob lost his job, he's around the house more and we get into arguments more frequently than before.

INTERVIEWER: Bob's being unemployed and home increases the amount of conflict between you.

A good paraphrase is a condensation and crystallization of the client's communication:

INTERVIEWEE: You make out applications one after the other, and you go out for interviews one after the other, and they take one look at you, and because you're African American you don't get any consideration for the job.

INTERVIEWER: You make every effort to find work, but you feel discrimination prevents you from getting a job.

The best paraphrases tend to be concise because they reflect not everything the interviewee has said but the essence of what the interviewee
has said:

INTERVIEWEE: Sometimes I really want to stay with him because he is so
nice and caring, and other times I really want to split
because he behaves in a punishing inconsiderate way.

INTERVIEWER: He is inconsistent, and you are ambivalent about what you
want to do.

INTERVIEWEE: Jack is no angel and he doesn't like schoolwork, but his
teacher can't seem to control the class and seems to have a
poor grasp of how to teach.

INTERVIEWER: Jack makes some contribution to the situation, but you see
the teacher as being somewhat responsible for his difficulty
in school.

Paraphrase is a restatement in the interviewer's words of what the interviewee has said. It is a concise and accurate condensation that uses the
interviewee's frame of reference. A good paraphrase has a high degree of
interchangeability with the interviewee's statement.

A paraphrase is different from parroting, however. The following
exchange in an interview of a 22-year-old woman does little, if anything, to
help move the interview along:

INTERVIEWEE: I should never have become a mother.

INTERVIEWER: You should not have become a parent.

INTERVIEWEE: That's right. I shouldn't have become a parent.

The following paraphrase is more helpful:

INTERVIEWEE: I should never have become a mother.

INTERVIEWER: You don't like being a mother.

INTERVIEWEE: Well, I like being a mother, I just don't think I have enough
patience.

INTERVIEWER: You like it, but you have some questions about your ability.

INTERVIEWEE: Yeah, I wish I could be less impatient with Sheri.

A well-chosen paraphrase highlights the significant aspects of the client's statement. It thus ensures visibility of the important aspects of the client's communication. If done well, a paraphrase is an unambiguous distillation of the essence of the client's communication.

Because paraphrasing requires accurate restatement of the interviewee's communication in the interviewer's words, it requires that the interviewer listen carefully and digest what is being said. Thus paraphrasing is not a mechanical process but a complex cerebral one.

Paraphrasing reflects what the message means to the listener, how the interviewer has received the message. A variety of different lead-ins avoids sounding mechanical when paraphrasing:

> If I get you right . . .
> It seems to me . . .
> In other words . . .
> As I understand it . . .
> I hear you saying that . . .
> I gather that . . .

A paraphrase helps interviewers check their understanding of what the client is saying. The client might accept, confirm, correct, or modify the paraphrase.

Paraphrasing also helps interviewees to see more clearly what they have said because it holds a mirror up to their communication. Even an incorrect paraphrase may be a productive response because it stimulates the interviewee to elaborate further.

Paraphrase responses are formulated as statements, not as questions. The reflecting statement is affectively neutral, reflecting neither approval nor disapproval. As much as possible the interviewer should use interviewees' words in order to reflect their thinking or feeling.

One danger in the use of paraphrase is that it may lead to finishing the interviewees' thoughts for them. Instead of reflecting accurately and without distortion we unintentionally add some gratuitous interpretive comment.

To summarize, paraphrasing is a special form of reflecting. In paraphrasing you are reflecting what the interviewee said, but you are not using the words of the interviewee. A paraphrase is a restatement of the interviewee's communication in the words of the interviewer. As such it shows that the interviewer has not only listened to the interviewee but has understood what the client said well enough to formulate this understanding in new words. A paraphrase is a kind of translation of the client's message in the interviewer's words.

Reflection

In its simplest manifestation *reflection* is a selective repetition of what the interviewee has actually said. It pushes the interview ahead because it demonstrates that the interviewer is interested in what the client has to say, has actually been listening, and by echoing what the client has said encourages the interviewee to continue.

Reflection of Content

Reflection is selective in that it does not mirror all that the client has said. The interviewer assesses the aspects of the interviewee's communication that are most likely to further achievement of the interview's purpose and uses that content in the reflection:

INTERVIEWEE: I dropped the course and my parents were upset.

INTERVIEWER [*Reflecting.*]: Parents were upset.

The interviewer comments, "I reflected 'parents were upset' rather than 'dropped the course,' because I thought focusing on Jim's relationship with his parents would be more helpful.

Unlike a paraphrase, simple reflection repeats verbatim a key word or a phrase from the interviewee's last response. The word or phrase selected for repetition gives it greater visibility, encouraging the interviewee's selection of material to pursue:

INTERVIEWEE: My mother keeps after me about my drinking.

INTERVIEWER: Drinking?

The interviewer might have repeated "mother" or "keeps after you" rather than "drinking." The choices propel the interview in different directions.

The repetitive comment shows that the interviewer is willing to hear more about a particular topic. Through the reward of the interviewer's attention it reinforces the client's choice of that content for discussion.

Frequent mechanical repetition is undesirable in reflection:

INTERVIEWEE: I know I shouldn't drink.

INTERVIEWER: Shouldn't drink.

INTERVIEWEE: Sure, it's killing me at home and on the job.

INTERVIEWER: At home?

INTERVIEWEE: Yeah, 'cause my wife and I fight about it all the time.

INTERVIEWER: Fight all the time.

INTERVIEWEE: Is there an echo in here?

Simple reflection of content is somewhat difficult to distinguish from paraphrase. The examples that follow illustrate the difference between a verbatim reflection and a paraphrase.

INTERVIEWEE: I just can't seem to get going. I find it difficult to get organized to give the kids breakfast and get them off to school and start the housework. I just fuss around a lot.

VERBATIM REFLECTION

Fuss around a lot.

PARAPHRASE

You know what you need to get done, but it is difficult for you to get to do it.

GROUP HOME PARENT: I think that if Betty continues to run with that crowd, sooner or later she'll get pregnant and have to drop out of school.

SIMPLE REFLECTION

You think Betty might get pregnant and drop out of school.

PARAPHRASE

You think Betty's peer group presents a risk for Betty, a risk that involves the possibility of pregnancy and an end to her education.

Reflection of Feeling

Reflection of feeling is somewhat more distinguishable from paraphrase. We can reflect feeling; we cannot paraphrase feeling.

Reflection of feeling is an intervention designed to intensify the depth of the interview. *Depth* refers to how the interviewee feels about what is happening. Reflection of feeling is similar to paraphrase because both procedures feed back to the client the interviewer's perception. They differ in that they focus on different aspects of the communication.

Paraphrasing is a response to the interviewee's verbalized thinking. Reflecting is more frequently a response to the interviewee's verbal and nonverbal expressions of feeling. We paraphrase thinking and reflect feeling.

Paraphrase relates to the content of the communication, information about clients and their situation, a description of an incident or event. Reflection of feeling elicits from the interviewee feelings about the incident, event, or information being shared. Consequently, interventions that reflect feeling are more appropriately related to depth in interviewing.

Attending behavior says, "I am with you." Minimal encouragers say, "I am with you, please go on." Paraphrasing says, "I am with you, please go on. I understand what you're saying." Reflection of feeling says, "I am with you, please go on. I understand what you are saying and recognize how you are feeling."

These examples illustrate the distinction between paraphrase and reflection of feeling:

An aged client applying for Supplemental Security Income.

INTERVIEWEE: The inflation is killing us. We had to come here because we just can't get along on the lousy small company pension.

WORKER [*Paraphrasing.*]: You need to apply for supplementary income because it's difficult to make ends meet.

WORKER [*Reflecting feeling.*]: You seem to feel uncomfortable and unhappy about having to apply for help.

A preteen talking to a social worker at a runaway shelter.

INTERVIEWEE: I had had it at home—up to here. I wanted out, but it's hard to know where to go, what to do, and be sure you're going to eat.

WORKER [*Paraphrasing.*]: You wanted to get away from your family, but it's not so easy once you do.

WORKER [*Reflecting feeling.*]: Sounds like you feel confused and scared.

Accurate reflection of feeling is more difficult than paraphrase. In paraphrasing you are acting on words the interviewee has actually said. In reflection of feeling the communication to which the interviewer responds is more ambiguous. Clients do not, for the most part, identify or label their feelings. The translation of the emotion being displayed by the client requires some inference on the part of the interviewer. Acting in a certain way, speaking in a certain tone of voice, and gesturing in a certain manner are signs the interviewer reads to learn what the interviewee is feeling—sad or glad, friendly or hostile, hurt or delighted. Having made some decision about how the interviewee is feeling, the interviewer reflects that emotion in responding to the interviewee.

Reflecting that follows from what the interviewer feels rather than what the interviewee said can make for problems. An interviewer in reflecting said, "I hear you saying you feel sad that your husband would leave." The interviewee responded with some asperity, "I don't know how you heard that because I don't feel that."

Sometimes the interviewer does not need to infer feelings because they are explicit in what the client has said. A father, in discussing a rough spanking of his 10-year-old son, said, "Sure, I was angry as hell at the little bastard for coming home five hours after school was out and stinking like a beer barrel." The interviewer, reflecting, says, "You sure were angry and upset."

In reflecting feeling the suggested paradigm is this format: "You feel . . . because . . ."—"You feel guilty because you drink too much"; "You feel inadequate because you find it difficult to cope with your developmentally disabled daughter."

The interviewer needs to have available a rich vocabulary of nuances of feelings. Emotions are like colors: there are many of them and many different shades. A rich vocabulary of emotional terms enables the interviewer to name, in reflecting, the best approximation of the feeling the interviewee is expressing.

Accurate reflection of feeling is difficult because feeling states are often a combination of feelings. A symphony has a dominant theme and somewhat muted other themes. So it is with feelings. Death of a aged parent may evoke sorrow, guilt, relief, regret, and annoyance, all at the same time.

We can reflect feeling by observing nonverbal behavior alone. The interviewee slumps in the chair and hunches his shoulders; his eyes are downcast and his facial expression is dejected. The interviewer, reflecting feeling, says, "You look like you're feeling sad and lost, discouraged, and distressed."

Subtle choice of wording in phrasing a reflection may have significance in shaping the interaction. In helping a teenager who attempted suicide to clarify her feelings the interviewer said, "You say you felt alone and abandoned when you took your mother's sleeping pills." In retrospect the interviewer notes the words "took your mother's sleeping pills." "Why didn't I say more directly 'when you attempted suicide'? I feel that I have been denying and avoiding facing what this girl has done, and my denial tended to reinforce her own denial."

Feelings have a continuum of intensity. The words used in reflecting feeling need to be congruent with the intensity of feeling expressed. If clients say they feel "overwhelmed" or "devastated" and the interviewer uses "down" or "blue" in reflecting, there is a discrepancy between the feeling expressed and the feeling reflected. Interviewees who say they feel "frantic" or "terrified" are not likely to appreciate the interviewer who reflects by using "uneasy" or "apprehensive."

Despite the differences in focus intended, paraphrase and reflection of feelings may overlap. It is hard to exclude from a paraphrase some reflection of feeling and equally difficult to exclude from a reflection of feelings some objective contextual elements of the client's communication.

Both tend to increase the bond between interviewer and interviewee. Both intensify the feeling of sharing, of mutual understanding. The interviewer's being in tune with the interviewee in reflecting accurately is a confirmation of the worker's empathy. The reflective comment affirms that the interviewer does understand the interviewee's thinking and feeling.

Hearing the interviewer's accurate and sensitive reflection of the thinking and feeling gives interviewees an opportunity to listen to themselves through the echoes of the interviewer's comments.

A social worker in a family planning clinic interviewing a 16-year-old high school senior who suspects she is pregnant.

INTERVIEWER: What do you think you might do if you are pregnant?

INTERVIEWEE: Oh, I don't know—I guess I am not sure.

INTERVIEWER: You're not sure?

INTERVIEWEE: No, I've thought—um, about an abortion—but it's just—I don't know.

INTERVIEWER: Uh-huh, so although you have thought about an abortion, it seems like you are not totally comfortable with that option.

INTERVIEWEE: Right. [*Silence.*] I guess that in a lot of ways an abortion would probably be the best, but it's just that—even though I think women should be able to get them—abortions—I just wish that I didn't have to think about it.

A senior citizen in a nursing home discussing her reaction to group activities.

INTERVIEWEE: Well, it gives us something to do, I guess. Like the awareness group, I don't know if I like that group or not. I don't like hearing other people's problems. I feel uncomfortable in the group sometimes.

INTERVIEWER: You feel uncomfortable when other people are talking about their problems?

INTERVIEWEE: I don't like hearing all that stuff.

Good reflection of feelings is associated with some concern for concreteness and immediacy. The interviewer's reflection has greater credibility if it is clearly tied to some definite situation that has evoked the feeling the client has discussed, as in the cases of the student and nursing home resident.

Reflection of feeling, like the previously discussed responses, has the effect of assuring the client the worker is striving to understand, but it has the additional effect of reinforcing discussion of feelings. The interviewer's response gives emphasis to the feeling communicated by interviewees and suggests they should continue with it.

Reflection of feeling has the additional effect of clarification. In reflecting feeling the interviewer attempts to give a name to unclear sensations. Interviewees may become more aware of what they feel as the interviewer explicitly labels feelings in reflecting them.

Accurate reflection of feeling also has the advantage of sanctioning negative feelings. The interviewee may express the feelings directly. The interviewer, in reflecting, identifies and shows acceptance of them more directly.

A woman discussing her problems in getting a sibling to share responsibility for the care of aged parents.

INTERVIEWEE [*With some exasperation.*]: He doesn't want to know about it, he doesn't want to help me with them, he leaves it all up to me, he is completely and totally uncooperative.

INTERVIEWER: It sounds to me like you are mad at him and resent him now for what he is doing.

Reflection and paraphrase interventions push the interview ahead because they encourage participation and disclosure on the part of the interviewee. Interviewers also use these techniques to focus the interview productively and encourage emotional exploration by the client of the situation.

Summarizing

Summarizing is a selective condensation of what has transpired in the interview over a period of some time.

Partial or detailed summaries and recapitulations help to extend the range of communication. The interviewer briefly reviews what has been discussed and gives the interview its direction. A summary tends to pull together a section of the interview, makes explicit what the participants have covered, and flags what they have not covered. It clears the agenda of items that they have adequately discussed so that they can devote attention to items that have not:

> It seems to me that we have adequately covered what we need to talk about regarding your school situation. Let me summarize what I think you have been saying, and if you agree with the summary, perhaps we can then move on to something else.

> So far, we have considered dealing with the income situation by applying for SSI and the problem of job training in our discussion of referring you to vocational rehabilitation. But we need to discuss something about housing if you are certain about wanting to move out of your parents' apartment.

Summarizing requires a sifting out of the less relevant, less significant material. It also shows the interviewee that the interviewer has been listening attentively and knows what has been going on.

Throughout the interview brief periodic summaries of sections of the interview are helpful in making transitions. Such brief summaries give unity and coherence to a section of an interview and signal the interviewer's intent to move on to something else. Brief summaries during the interview highlight and give greater visibility to important points. Summaries provide an organizational structure for the variety of content that might have been covered and suggest patterns and themes.

A good summary requires of the interviewer considerable informational and theoretical knowledge of the problem under discussion. An interviewer who has this knowledge can select, for inclusion in the summary, the most important elements of the situation. Knowledge also enables the interviewer to link seemingly different but actually related aspects of the client's presentation.

In summarizing a series of interactional units you are not only recapitulating what has been discussed but also reviewing and giving emphasis to the content selected for summarizing.

If the summary is to include, as it should, a salient theme, worker and client need to have discussed some aspect of the interview for a reasonable length of time:

> Let me summarize what we have been doing over the last half hour. We have talked about some of the problems in your marriage which concern you most—loss of affectionate responses from your husband, your feeling about your in-laws, the conflicts about money and sex.

Generally, people present their story in a disjointed manner, and they include both relevant and inconsequential material. A summary pulls together the most significant aspects of the presentation and gives these elements explicit visibility.

Summaries are important when interviewees tend to ramble through many digressions in recounting their situation. A good summary may give the account the coherence required for a productive interview.

An interviewer summarizes the first twenty minutes of a discursive interview with a divorced woman with three children who is receiving AFDC:

> Okay, this gives me a little of an idea of your situation. After your divorce, you were forced to go on AFDC because your former husband did not make the support payments he should have been making. All this time you've been faced with the terrific and lonely responsibility of being a single parent.

Because summarizing requires a sifting out of the less relevant, less significant material, summaries must be selective. The interviewer's selection of material might be biased. The interviewee may regard other content as significant. Thus feedback from the interviewee is important.

A behavior modification–oriented social worker summarizes what she has identified as the problematic behavior of a 4-year-old girl whom the mother wants to work toward changing:

> Well, we've identified five or so areas of behavior that you see as problems. So far, we've got: Alice stools in her pants; Alice follows Mom around and clings, cries, whines; Alice frequently refuses to comply with requests and commands made of her; Alice has shown dangerous behavior with the baby; Alice reverts back to baby talk on occasion. Can you think of any other behaviors that you would like to see changed?

The interviewer, in moving into a summary or recapitulation, might say, "Let me make sure I understand you. As I hear you, your situation is like this"; or "To sum up what we have been talking about . . ."; or "During the past ten minutes we have been discussing . . . and it seems to me that you are saying . . . " Having summarized, the interviewer asks, "How does that sound to you?"

Mutual participation in summarizing is desirable. It engages the interviewee in thinking about the interview, and it ensures that both participants are identifying what they have discussed. In confirming and/or correcting summaries the interviewer might ask the interviewee to modify it:

> You describe—I'll tell you how it sounds to me and you can correct me if I've misunderstood—you describe to me a little boy who was deserted by his mother and who was adopted. Things didn't go very well, especially between you and your adoptive mother. You felt pretty much rejected and alone. You felt thrown out to whoever would take you—that maybe you were the forgotten child. I get the picture of a really unhappy little boy.

The interviewer can invite interviewees to summarize, intensifying their participation: "I would be very much interested if you would be willing to try to summarize our discussion during the last fifteen minutes."

Chapter 10 discusses summarizing as a technique in termination; see box 6.1 for guidelines for summarizing.

Box 6.1 Guidelines for Summarizing

1. Summarize when the content is sufficient to suggest a general theme in the presentation.
2. Summarize when you have sufficiently explored an area of content and transition to new content is appropriate.
3. Summarize when content has been diffuse and disjointed and when pulling the scattered related content together would be useful.
4. Ask interviewees to participate, either by suggesting that they summarize or by inviting them to respond to your summary.
5. In summarizing select the data that appear to be most significant for achieving the purpose of interview and organize that information for coherence.

Transitions

At times during the interview the interviewer may decide that a change in the material being discussed is appropriate. The interviewer then faces the problem of engineering a transition without disturbing the relationship. Transitions help extend the range of the interview.

Interviewers decide for a number of reasons that a change is advisable. They might have exhausted the content under discussion—the spontaneity and interest with which the interviewee discusses it have clearly diminished. The content might have proved to be a dead end. The interviewee might have introduced some clearly irrelevant material that cannot possibly further the purpose of the interview. Some material might have been introduced prematurely. The interviewee might appear to be distinctly uncomfortable, and rather than risk endangering the relationship the interviewer makes transitional comments to move away from the sensitive material. Sometimes transitions are the result of a deliberate effort to avoid creating anxiety.

A woman is applying to become a foster parent.

MRS. P.: I would imagine it is a difficult thing if foster parents get too attached to their foster children, and no matter how hard you prepare for their leaving, I would think it's still pretty hard.

INTERVIEWER: Yes it is. Could you tell me how you heard about our program of foster care?

Commenting on her question, the worker says,

This was an extremely poor question as I failed to acknowledge the interviewee's anxiety and in fact completely ignored it, making a transition to something entirely different. At the time I was thinking that I didn't want to make Mrs. P. more anxious about the need to give up the foster child. I didn't want to emphasize this by encouraging discussion. I think I went too far in my concern about her.

Interviewers may initiate a transition if they sense that the interviewee is sharing material of a more emotional nature than is desirable at this point in the contact. Recognizing that neither the worker nor the interviewee will be able to handle this much affect now, the interviewer might say, "You seem to be getting quite upset about this. Perhaps we can table it at this point and talk a little more about the job situation you were telling me about before."

Interviewers frequently initiate transitions to serve their own purpose rather than the purpose of the interview. Here social workers explain transitions they initiated during an interview:

P. has been discussing the problems with her son and solutions that were suggested and/or tried. She is asserting herself as knowing what is best for her child. This is a common response given by natural parents. This is touchy ground with natural parents, and I was treading very lightly. I felt uncomfortable agreeing or disagreeing with her at this point, so I changed the subject.

I was physically and mentally worn out from trying to keep up with the client. I introduced a somewhat neutral topic in order to give myself a breather.

I was feeling frustrated since the client hadn't been giving me any answer I could work with or had expected. I introduced another subject in the hope that I would have somewhat greater success.

We were getting close to an area we had discussed before and about which I knew the agency, because of lack of resources, could do very little. I therefore made a transitional statement, taking us further away from the area I wanted to avoid.

All these social workers violated the cardinal operative principle that whatever the interviewer does should serve the purposes of the interview and the needs of the client.

The problem of transition derives from the time limits for interviews. Out of respect for both participants, time has to be used productively. Interrupting the interviewee's flow of communication of inconsequential material and suggesting a transition to more meaningful material is not a derogation of the client or an exercise of arbitrary authority. It spares both the client and the worker a fruitless expense of time and energy and increases the confidence of the client in the worker's competence.

Types of Transitions

Transitions refer not only to a change in topic but also to a change in affect level within a content area.

Woman, 26, upper middle income, family service, marital counseling.

WORKER: Well, let me kind of see where we are now. You have been telling me about your husband, the kind of man you think he is, his education, his work, the kinds of interests you have in common, the kinds of things you do together or the kinds of things you hope he would do along with you. But I am not sure what the feeling is between you, what about him makes you glad, what about him depresses you, what about him that makes you happy, what makes you sore as hell. Maybe now we can talk about the feelings between you and your husband.

The interviewer may also shift the time reference, discussing the same relationship in the past as well as the present, making a transition from one time period to another.

Psychiatric social worker talking to 20-year-old male about plans for release from mental hospital and return to his home community.

GEORGE: The thing I really hate is, when you're in a place like this, you get out and people call you stupid and nuts and everything. Tease you about being here and all that.

WORKER: I imagine that makes you pretty angry. [*Client nods. Pause.*] That hurts. [*Pause.*] That really does. [*Pause.*] But how about before you came here, George? They couldn't say that about you then. [*Client shakes head no.*] What was the trouble then in your relationship with the guys back home?

Making Transitions

Steering messages, road signs that prepare the interviewee for a change in direction, often precede transitions: "I would like to change the subject now"; "There is something of importance that we haven't as yet had a chance to discuss."

People generally introduce a transition by prefacing it with "All right"; "Okay"; or "Well," followed by a slight pause. Shifts in posture or distance from the client generally accompany transitions.

Sullivan (1954) classifies interview transitions as smooth, accented, or abrupt; Merton, Fiske, and Kendall (1956) label them as cued, reversional, or mutational. In the *smooth* or *cued transition* the interviewer adapts a remark the client has just made in order to effect a transition. There is no, or little, apparent break in continuity, but the focus of the interview shifts.

One form of cued transition is a short question or comment that leads the interview back from irrelevant to relevant material by linking the two. In effect such comment makes the irrelevant become pertinent. Technically, the smoothest transitions are related associations rather than real transitions.

The association may concern topics that are related psychologically. The classic transition from talking about our father to talking about our employer or supervisor is based on the emotional association of our father with other authority figures on whom we are dependent.

Reversional transitions use content touched on but not discussed at some earlier point in the interview:

> WORKER: You remember, a little while ago, near the beginning of the interview, we were talking about the foster home you were in before you came here. And you said it wasn't an easy place. Remember that? What difficulties did you have there?

It is best wherever possible to use the comments and even the exact wording of interviewees. This suggests that they have shared some responsibility for the decision and that to some extent they have consented to the transition.

A *mutational* or *abrupt transition* is a clear break with what is under discussion. It has no obvious associational ties with the material that preceded it, as in a cued transition, or with anything previously raised in the interview, however briefly.

Transitional Interruptions

Having made the decision to effect a transition, the interviewer has to watch for a logical point at which to smoothly terminate the topic under discussion and introduce a new topic. This raises the question of perhaps the most abrupt "transition" of all—interruption of the interviewee by the interviewer.

In the face of a determined nonstop interviewee, interruption to effect a transition may be difficult. The interviewer may need to be unequivocal in regaining the initiative. This may require a sentence like, "Permit me, I know I am interrupting, but I wonder if I can say something about this?" or "May I interrupt for a moment, please?"

On some occasions the interviewer actually needs to interrupt the interviewee. If the interviewee has embarked on a prolonged digression that the interviewer is convinced is not likely to contribute to achieving the purposes of the interview, an interruption is called for. The interviewer needs to do this gently but firmly and insistently. At the same time the interviewer owes the client an explicit explanation for the interruption.

Permitting talkative interviewees to ramble on when what they are saying clearly is repetitious or inconsequential is a disservice. The rambling intrudes on the time that might be available to other clients and is a threat to the relationship. We all are likely to become increasingly impatient and annoyed at the interviewee who talks and talks about things that are of little consequence to the objectives of the interview.

In trying to regain control of the interview from a garrulous interviewee the interviewer needs to use a transition with a lead-in:

> I appreciate your sharing these experiences with me, but I wonder if we can continue our discussion of . . .
> It is very nice hearing all about your grandchildren, but because we have limited time, we should focus more directly on . . .
> I recognize that this is important to you but we have gone over this before, as you know, and I think I can be more helpful to you if we move on.

But be cautious. Interrupting when you cannot justify the interruption in terms of the needs of the interview derogates the interviewee's autonomy, and a struggle for status and control of the direction of the interview may ensue. Interviewees may feel they have been squelched and that what they have had to say is of secondary importance. Thus the interviewer must keep interruptions to a minimum and make certain that they are justifiable.

Frequently, however, inexperienced interviewers tend to interrupt when such an intervention is not clearly warranted. The interviewer intervenes and takes control of the interview before it is clear that the interviewee has finished. This tendency is another carryover from some habits of conversation, when we interrupt each other frequently—with impunity and without apology. There is some ironic justice in the oft-made comment that nothing is quite as annoying as to have somebody go right on talking when you are interrupting.

Transition Caveats

A transition is like a scene change in a play. One topic ends, another is introduced. In a book on the psychiatric interview Harry Stack Sullivan comments,

> When I talk about how to make transitions I simply mean how to move about in the interview. It is imperative if you want to know where you are with another person that you proceed along a path that he can at least dimly follow so that he doesn't get lost completely as to what you are driving at. . . . It is ideal, if you can, to go step by step with sufficient waving of signal flags and so on so that there is always something approaching a consensus as to what is being discussed.
>
> (1954:46)

Transitions that are abrupt—for which there is no preparation and that might appear to the interviewee to be illogical—are apt to be upsetting. Interviewees know what they were doing and why; suddenly, the interviewer moves them to something else, and they aren't clear how they got there or why.

If the relationship of the new content to the purposes of the interview seems clear, noting this may be talking down to the interviewee. Frequently, however, the significance of the topic the interviewer is introducing is not clear to the interviewee, no matter how obvious the connection is to the social worker. "Transitions to new topics require [interviewees] to stop and think, to relocate themselves; this may be necessary, but it tends to be unsettling" (Weiss 1994:80).

Preparation for transition, then, should include some explicit statement of the relationship between new content and the purpose of the interview.

Couple, upper middle income, man aged 33, woman aged 28, adoption application interview.

WORKER: We have been talking about the different kinds of children for whom you both seem to have a preference. Perhaps we might discuss now your feelings about unmarried mothers and illegitimate children. You might wonder what relevance this has to your wanting to adopt a baby. You may know, however, that most of the infants we have available for adoption are illegitimate, so that your feelings and attitudes about illegitimacy are relevant to our meetings together. What comes to mind when you hear the words "unmarried mothers"?

When a transition leads to a new frame of reference, the act of making the transition has to explicit. This is because frames of reference of previous content tend to persist. For instance, the interviewer might say, "We have been talking about how you feel about having the abortion. Try now to shift in your mind to thinking about the father. How do you think he feels about it?"

The interviewer should be aware that the need for focus that is served by using transitions may be antithetical to the need for rapport. Transitions by the interviewer tend to restrict the spontaneity of the interviewee and emphasize that the contact is interviewer controlled. In some instances the interviewer may have to sacrifice focus for rapport and permit the interviewee a greater freedom, even though this is clearly unproductive in achieving the specific interview purposes.

It is best not to make a transition to other content unless you can spend some time on the new material. Whenever the context of the interview shifts, both participants have to readjust their perception of the situation.

Becoming accustomed to the change takes a little time and some psychic energy. Unless time is available to work on the new content, the investment pays no return.

Transitions that are too rapid and too frequent may signal that the interviewer has no clear idea of how to conduct the interview and does not know what is most relevant to discuss. Rapid and frequent transitions suggest a buckshot approach, that the interviewer is trying many things in the hope that one topic will prove productive.

Before actually initiating a transition, the interviewer should mentally review the area under discussion to check for failure to cover any significant aspects. The interviewer then checks with the interviewee to see whether the client wants to discuss anything else that is relevant to the content area.

The mother of a 14-month-old, Sue, and a 4-year-old, Andrew, who is developmentally disabled, is discussing with the worker the problems she is having rearing the children as a single parent. The discussion has first focused on Sue and includes some talk about feeding and toilet training.

> INTERVIEWEE: I really don't have many problems with Sue, not like I have with Andrew.

> INTERVIEWER: Right. I'd like to talk about that in a minute. Anything else about Sue?

Commenting afterward the worker says,

> I wanted to get some closure on the subject of Sue before we moved on to Andrew yet still assure the client that she would be provided the opportunity to discuss him.

Effective transitions result from mutual agreement. Hackney, Ivey, and Oetting (1970) perceptively divide the purpose of transition into "islands" and "hiatuses." An island is a section of the interview in which both participants are mutually engaged in attending to some content. Having momentarily said all they need or want to say about this, they reach a hiatus, a respite. The hiatus is "a period of negotiation between the counselor and the client, a negotiation in which new response classes or topics are sought" (p. 343). In short, it is a period of transition. The client may tentatively offer something as new content; the worker may tentatively suggest new content by asking a question or making a comment. Each waits to see if the other responds with acceptance or rejection.

Male, 20, parole interview.

WORKER: That's about it on the job situation then.

ANDY: Yep, that's about it. [*Pause.*] It's sure been hot lately.

WORKER: Yeah. [*Pause.*]

ANDY: Good weather for swimming. Carol [Andy's girlfriend] and I were at the lake last night, and there sure was a big crowd out.

WORKER: I would imagine so.

ANDY: Saw a couple of guys from [the correctional school] there.

WORKER: What did they have to say?

Here the interview has achieved closure on the topic of the client's job. The client offers the weather, his relationship with his girlfriend, and leisure time activities as potential next topics. The worker is indifferent to these possibilities. She picks up, however, on the client's contact with young men he knew in the institution. This became the topic on which the interview focused during the next fifteen minutes.

In making a transition, even with the apparent agreement of the interviewee, the interviewer must be sensitive to any changes in interaction immediately after the transition. If the interviewee subtly reverts to the previous content area, if the flow from the interviewee seems to reflect a resistance that was not there earlier, if the interviewee seems to display some resentment, the interviewer may need to reconsider the transition. It is more efficient for the interviewer to be flexible and follow the interviewee's lead back to the previous content area than to stubbornly dragoon a client into discussing something else.

Interviewee-Initiated Transitions

Transitions are not the exclusive prerogative of the interviewer. Interviewees often take the initiative in making a transition. They might be bored by the topic under discussion; they might have something else to discuss that worries them more; they might want to avoid the topic under discussion; they might feel a need to exercise some control over the interview.

With interviewee-initiated transitions interviewers have to decide whether to go along with the change and modify their ideas about content and sequence of the interview accordingly. Interviewers also have the problem of understanding what prompted the transition. Sometimes this is obvious. At other times the emotional logic of the interviewee's thinking may not be apparent. An interviewee-initiated transition often seems warranted. However, when interviewers go along with it, they need to make a point of mentally filing for future reference the material they wanted to discuss.

When the interviewee introduces apparently irrelevant material, the worker should stay with it long enough to explore whether a transition is necessary. Sometimes apparently irrelevant material has a pertinence that only gradually becomes clear. Interviewees' interest in the material, manifested by their introducing it, acts as a constraint on rapid transition away from it. Interviewees sometimes perceive rejection of the new content area as a personal rejection.

If what prompted the interviewee-initiated transition is unclear and the interviewer is uncertain about what to do, asking an explicit question about the transition may be helpful.

Male, 19, lower middle income, parole preparation interview.

WORKER: Help me out here. I think I lost you somewhere a little further back. We were talking about the guys you used to know at [the reformatory] who got out and made it. Now we're talking about the changes your father plans to make around the farm. I don't get it.

GEORGE: Yeah, how did we get to this?

WORKER: As I say, I don't know, but maybe you could think back on this.

GEORGE: Well, I don't know either. [*Pause.*] What was I saying about this? [*Long pause.*] Yeah, oh hell, I don't know.

WORKER: Okay, maybe you don't.

GEORGE: It may be that those guys who made it, some of them got a lot of help from their family, money for things they wanted to do or needed, so if my old man puts all that dough in the farm, maybe he can't help me out so much, or maybe I feel I can't ask him because he won't have it, see.

Here's what the interviewer said about the exchange:

George had me puzzled on this. I really didn't know how we got from his reformatory peer group to his father's farm. I turned over a couple of things in my head as he talked, but nothing seemed to click. I didn't want to cut him off because he seemed to want to talk about it, but I couldn't see that this stuff about the farm was going to get us anywhere. That's when I decided to risk having it out with him. For a while I thought he didn't know either. The pauses seemed long, and he seemed to get more annoyed. He fidgeted a lot in his seat. That's why I decided to let up the pressure by saying, "Well, maybe you don't" [know why you shifted the focus]. But maybe my letting up on him by saying that helped ease his tension so that he was able to tell me.

If the digression is apparently unproductive, the interviewer may want to acknowledge it but not accept it as a focus for discussion. The interviewer might say, "That is very interesting and may be helpful. Perhaps if you like, we can come back to it later. However, it may be more helpful to you if we could talk about the way you get along on your job."

Sometimes the interviewee-initiated transition is designed to frustrate the purposes of the interview. It is an attempt to evade painful work that must be done. When an interviewee-initiated transition seems clearly designed to be an escape, going along with a temporary digression to neutral material may be advisable. This provides interviewees with a breather during which they can pull themselves together for another try. But if the difficult content is important, the interviewer should try again. If the interviewer fails to try to make this transition again, clients may be pleased but disappointed at the interviewer's collusion in their evasion of painful material. Clients may be annoyed at but gratified by the unyielding but compassionate interviewer who holds them to the purpose.

Clients may initiate a transition to meet their own needs and the interviewer may decide, for good reason, to accept the transition even though it might blur the focus of the interview. An interviewer notes the value of apparently unproductive digressions initiated by interviewee transitions:

> I learned that I had to be flexible in response to a person's concentration ability. At first, when a person started in on a story about life in the Navy during the war, or an account of the dog's prowess as a watchman, I panicked a little: I felt that the interview was going to splinter off into small talk and long stories. Then I began to realize that this was an integral part of the process. The interview was a strain for some of the people and they needed a chance to retreat from it for a short time. They seemed to need a shift in focus and I usually drifted with them until they seemed ready to return to the questions.
>
> (Converse and Schuman 1974:46)

Sometimes a rambling digression is merely the equivalent of a mental coffee break. Good interviewing is hard work for both participants. The interviewee may just need time to talk about something pleasant, even if it is not relevant. Interviewers who, recognizing this, mentally sigh and settle back to listen are ultimately likely to get where they want to go faster than if they try to stop the process. See box 6.2 for guidelines for transitions.

Box 6.2 Guidelines for Transitions

1. Planning a transition involves a decision about why this transition would further the interview's objective.
2. Having decided that a transition is necessary, be sensitive to a point in the interaction that would be appropriate for introducing a transition.
3. Prepare the interviewee for your intention to make a transition.
4. If the reasons for the transition are not obvious, explain the rationale.
5. Transitions tend to be unsettling. Make the transition in a manner that is the least disruptive for the flow of the interview.
6. Do not impose a transition if the interviewee signals that a lack of readiness to make the change.

Reaching for Feelings

The techniques we have been discussing—attending behavior, paraphrasing, reflecting, summarizing, making transition—tend in common to extend the range of the interview's content. They help the interviewer to learn more about interviewees and their problem. However, we also need to learn how interviewees feel, how they are reacting to the problem they are detailing. In order to understand the situation, which of necessity precedes helping interviewees do something about it, we need to help interviewees to provide not only a range of information about their problem but also information about how they feel about their situation. *Range* is concerned with what is happening; *depth* is concerned with how the interviewee feels about what is happening.

Identifying and Calling Attention to Feelings

Various techniques have been developed to help the interviewee move from a descriptive informational level to a more emotional and intimate level. Encouraging the discussion of feelings by asking about or commenting on feelings is the simplest and most frequently used technique for achieving depth. "How do you feel about it?" is a good example. Such questions tend to focus the interviewee's attention on emotions. They offer stimulus and invitation to discuss content at greater depth.

A mother had been describing at some length the experiences her 16-year-old son had had with drugs. He had been recently arrested for selling heroin, and the mother was detailing her efforts to obtain legal assistance. The social worker assigned to juvenile court said to her, "A lawyer is very important, and I am glad you were able to get such help. But what were your feelings when they told you that William was arrested?"

Social work interviewers are quick to call attention to feelings.

Woman, 29, lower lower income, foster care agency.

MRS. Y.: So when the doctor said I needed the operation and I knew I had to go to the hospital, I thought what am I going to do with the kids? Who will take them, take care of them? I mean, there's nobody. Half the people, like relatives, I know, far away, they can't come.

WORKER: You feel all alone.

In response, the interviewee shifted from the problem of child care to discussing her feelings of fright at facing an operation without the support of anyone close to her. The interviewer's comments on the emotional aspects of the situation encourage the interviewee to discuss them. The worker identifies the feelings, gives them recognition, and attempts to keep the interviewee's attention centered on emotional responses.

A 30-year-old mother on public assistance, discussing her relationships with her children.

MRS. D.: And John more or less is inclined to favor Mary, and my mother-in-law favors the twins. Everybody favors the twins, and Mary. But then these two are left out. I guess I'm more or less inclined to favor Mary, too.

WORKER: What makes you feel this way?

MRS. D.: Well, we all love them the same. We buy them things, we buy them all nice things, but yet when that one's hurt or something, I just sort of ache more. I don't know why, is that selfish, or something? I don't know. I even feel guilty about that and maybe I'm doing wrong.

WORKER: You feel guilty?

MRS. D.: Yes, but as long as I try there's nothing wrong. Okay?

WORKER: I think so, but how do you mean wrong?

MRS. D.: Am I doing wrong because I favor Mary above the others? I don't try to favor her. Well, I think I have my own answer, really. But I hate to look at it sometimes.

WORKER: What's your own answer to what makes you feel this way about
    Mary?

The interviewer may take the initiative in calling attention to or making
explicit feelings the interviewee seems to be manifesting but which the
client has not identified. The interviewer in this situation might say, "You
seem to be upset"; "You kind of winced when you said that"; or "What were
you feeling then?" Reaching for feelings is what the interviewer does when
suggesting the reaction that is likely to be evoked in most people by a particular situation: "That would be very depressing"; "That would make most
people feel anxious." It is a process of identifying latent feelings and making them manifest.

    In helping the interviewee to articulate feelings that appear to be present
but unexpressed, a sensitive noncoercive nudge may be necessary:

> That must have hurt.
> It would seem that something like that might make you very angry.
> I imagine that was very upsetting.
> That kind of reaction would normally be very disappointing.

What is involved is a gentle pressure to express emotion guided by sensitivity to intrusion.

    Once the interviewee begins to discuss material with some intensity of
affect, rewarding encouragement may help the client to continue. "I know
it is hard for you to talk about this, and it's a sign of your strength that you
can discuss it"; "It must be painful for you to discuss this, and I admire your
courage in making the effort." Part of what may be involved here is a
process of modeling. When interviewers demonstrate that they are ready
and willing to discuss feelings, they acts as a model for interviewees to emu-
late by being open about their feelings.

Sanctioning Feelings

One of the barriers to self-revelation is that such sharing makes a person
vulnerable to rejection by others. Content about which the client is sensitive is often content that is likely to seem, at least to the interviewee, to be
self-incriminating, embarrassing, or associated with shame, guilt, or blame.

    One approach to such content is to sanction in advance any feelings that
might provoke shame or guilt. This technique makes acceptable the seemingly unacceptable and frees interviewees to share that which they would
have withheld. A legitimate explanation or excuse may preface the comment that is offered as stimulus to the exploration of feelings. Thus the

interviewer might say to a daughter struggling with the problem of helping her elderly parents find a place to live, "I can understand that there might be a conflict between what you feel you owe your children and what you feel you owe your parents. How do you feel in looking for a nursing home for your parents?" Such prefacing has a face-saving effect; it softens the potential threat involved in self-disclosure of feelings.

Another sanctioning procedure is to universalize the emotional responses that are known to be common. Thus a worker might say to a teenage mother, "Most women are anxious about many things related to pregnancy. How do you feel about it?" Or to an unhappy wife, "All married people hate each other on occasion. How do you feel about your husband?"

Kinsey, Pomeroy, and Martin (1948) used such a procedure to encourage discussion of material about which the interviewee might otherwise have been reticent. Instead of asking whether the interviewee masturbated, followed by a question about frequency, their interviewers asked only, "How frequently do you masturbate?" The question incorporated the presumption that the practice is universal.

What is involved in sanctioning socially unacceptable responses is projecting such feelings onto others and depersonalizing what are regarded as socially unacceptable feelings: "Some people feel that parents cannot always love their children. How do you feel about your child?"; "Even happily married men think of extramarital adventures. Have you ever felt this way?"

Interviewers may explicitly sanction feelings and at the same time present themselves as a model by stating their own response to the situation: "If anybody treated me like that, I know I would really get sore"; "I don't think I could face a situation like that without feeling depressed and upset."

Explicit expressions of empathy help the interviewee to verbalize feelings: "I can imagine how frustrating it must feel to be ready, willing, and able to find employment, only to find no jobs are available."

By explicitly articulating the different kinds of feelings that might be associated with some problem, the interviewer signals that all are equally acceptable. "Some families do institutionalize their Down's syndrome children. Some maintain them at home. What is your own feeling about this at this time?"

The interviewee has no difficulty in sharing positive, socially sanctioned feelings. Encouraging the articulation of such feelings might then make it easier for interviewees to verbalize feelings that they perceive as unacceptable. Having discussed what they like about their marriage, interviewees might be ready to discuss what they dislike. Children might be ready to express their dislike for their parents after describing some of their affectionate feelings. The interviewer then gradually move from focusing on the acceptable feelings to asking about less acceptable feelings.

Using Euphemisms and Indirection

Euphemisms are helpful in moving into more sensitive areas. Euphemisms are a way of communicating offensive words or ideas in a socially accept-able form. *Euphemism* is derived from the Greek word that means 'good-speak.' Social workers who once spoke of the *retarded child* now speak of the *developmentally disabled child*. Workers in adoption replaced the *hard-to-place child* with *children with special needs*, which was then replaced by the *waiting child*. A mother who is reluctant to discuss her feelings about *hit-ting* a child may be ready to discuss her feelings about *disciplining* a child. Adolescents who retreat from talking about their feelings associated with *stealing* may talk more readily about their response to *taking things*. Felicitous euphemisms soften reality with an acceptable gloss.

Euphemism, metaphors, and similes soften the threatening nature of the questions, trigger less resistance, and reduce the probability that the interviewee will avoid discussion of certain feelings. For example, in talk-ing with an older client about moving to a group home, the worker refers to it as a "nursing home." The client reacts negatively and shifts the inter-view to more neutral material. A little later in the interview the worker reintroduces this content but now refers to a "home for senior citizens." The client picks up on this and readily engages in a discussion of plan-ning for the move.

Interviewers may approach personal emotional reactions gradually and indirectly. One way of doing this is by initially depersonalizing the discus-sion. Instead of asking a new mother how she reacted to the experience of accepting a homemaker's assistance after her return from the hospital, the worker asks about her husband's response to the homemaker and about their children's feelings. Only after such discussion, which desensitizes the woman to the emotional aspects of homemaker service, does the worker ask the woman about her feelings.

Sensitivity to and labeling of latent content is one approach to depth in the interview. The latent content behind the manifest comment suggests the accompanying deeper, more intimate feelings associated with the con-tent. The very sick patient who says to the medical social worker, "This has been a very hard winter. I wonder what next winter will be like," may be ask-ing for assurance that he will live to see another winter. The 6-year-old who asks the foster care worker, "Did my brother cry when you took him to the [foster] home?" may be asking for acceptance of his own need to cry.

Discouraging Expression of Feelings

Although interviewers may stimulate the interviewee to introduce more intense emotional content, they may also block further exploration of feeling. As is true to some extent for all of us, the beginning interviewer is more comfortable with concretely factual material than with affective content. The initial tendency, then, is to retreat from emotional material into the reportorial "who, what, when, where" kinds of response, discouraging further discussion of feelings.

> **A 13-year-old boy describing a family fight involving his parents and older brother to worker of family service agency.**
>
> PHIL: Jim wanted to go out; some one of his friends called him up and he wanted to go out. But Mom didn't want him to go out, and he pushed her away and he slapped her, and then they just started fighting and hollering, and it was all sort of scary.
>
> WORKER: What day did this happen?
>
> PHIL: I think it was Wednesday, no Thursday. I can't picture it in my mind.
>
> WORKER: What time was it?

In the next example the worker's feelings are affecting an interview. The mother of an emotionally disturbed 3-year-old boy is discussing the child with an intake worker at a day care center for disturbed children. She has just suggested, with considerable affect, that the child was unplanned, unwanted, and is rejected. She feels guilty about her attitude because she recognizes that it may explain the boy's behavior. She is leaning forward tensely in the chair, twisting her hands together, looking at the floor. The worker responds by introducing a series of questions about the onset of walking, talking, and toilet training, saying, "Let me ask you some questions we need for our records." The worker says in retrospect, "I felt that the mother and myself needed the emotional relief of a fairly objective line of questioning. But what made me feel that? As I think about it, she seemed ready to explore it further. Maybe I wanted out."

According to Weiss, "the interviewer does best to convey a middle distance in response to the respondent's feelings, in touch with them, responsive to them, but not overwhelmed by them" (1994: 128).

Asking about the emotional reactions of everyone but the interviewee can be another evasion. It permits discussion of the issue but does not risk that the interviewee will display any strong feelings to which the interviewer will have to respond.

Correctional social worker talking to a 19-year-old male charged with drug abuse.

WORKER: So when you dropped out of school, how did your parents feel about this?

GREG: Well, they didn't like it, of course. They were upset and hollered a lot and we argued.

WORKER: What was your girlfriend's reaction?

The worker fails to ask about Greg's feelings about his decision.

The interviewer can also avoid discussion of emotionally laden material by shifting the focus to a person outside the interview:

MARY: I was over at my boyfriend's house, watching TV, and my father came busting in and said I had to go home with him. He was shouting and everything and made a big scene. I was so embarrassed.

WORKER: Why did he do it?

Summary: Chapter 6

Techniques are conscious deliberate interventions selected by the interviewer because they have effects that further the objectives of the interview. Using the relationship as the necessary context, the interviewer has to apply effective techniques to propel the interview in the direction of success. The interviewer uses a variety of techniques to encourage the client to maintain the flow of communication.

Attending behaviors are those observable actions of the interviewer—eye contact and body posture—that signal that the worker is interested and paying attention. The verbal component of attending behavior is manifested in what has been termed verbal following. Minimal encouragements are short utterances with little content that encourage interviewees and reinforce their desire to continue talking.

Paraphrasing is a selective restatement of the interviewee's communication that reflects the essence of what the interviewee has said. Paraphrasing helps interviewees see more clearly what they have said, because it holds a mirror up to their communication. It also helps interviewers to check out their understanding of the interviewee's communication.

Reflection of content is a selective repetition of the content of what the interviewee has said. Unlike paraphrase, simple reflection of content repeats verbatim a key word or a phrase from the interviewee's last response.

Reflection of content encourages interviewees to elaborate on the content area to which their attention is being called. Reflection of feeling is an intervention designed to intensify depth in the interview by focusing on the interviewee's feelings about the problem. Reflection of feeling is similar to paraphrase, because both procedures feed back to the client the interviewer's perception. They differ in that they focus on different aspects of communication. Paraphrase relates to the content of communication, reflection to the affect.

Summarizing is a selective condensation of what has transpired in the interview over a period of some time. Summarizing helps to extend the range of the interview. It is advisable to summarize when content has been sufficiently explored and transition to new content is appropriate or when the content presented has been disjointed and there is a need to pull together scattered related content.

Transitions extend the range of the interview by making a change in the material under discussion. Transitions should be used to further the objective of the interview. Preparing the interviewee for the transition is important, as are being sensitive to the most appropriate place to introduce a transition, explaining the rationale for the transition, making a transition as smooth as possible, and not imposing a transition on a reluctant interviewee.

Identifying and calling attention to feelings move the interview from a descriptive informational level to a more emotional and intimate level. This technique also extends the depth of the interview. Using this technique, the worker identifies feelings, gives them recognition, and attempts to focus interviewees' attention on their emotional responses. Advance sanctioning of feelings that may provoke shame or guilt is one method of encouraging the client to share sensitive information. Using euphemisms, figures of speech, and indirection in the interview also help the client to discuss threatening feelings and content. The inexperienced interviewer who is more comfortable with concrete material may attempt to discourage the client's expression of emotion by asking factual questions or shifting the focus to someone outside the interview.

SUGGESTED READINGS

Gerard Egan. *The Skilled Helper: A Problem Management Approach to Helping*, 5th ed. Monterey, Calif.: Brooks/Cole, 1994. (357 pp.)
   Written by a professor of counseling and counselor oriented, this book has an introductory section on theories of helping, after which most of the book is devoted to specific helping skills such as empathy, confrontation, self-disclosure, and the like.

Readers will be on familiar ground. The book is accompanied by a separate hand-book, *Exercises in Helping Skills: A Training Manual.*

Dean H. Hepworth and Jo Ann Larson. *Direct Social Work Practice: Theory and Skills*, 3d ed. Homewood, Ill.: Dorsey, 1990. (734 pp.)

This book does not focus directly on the interview, but it discusses and aptly illustrates many direct practice skills that are, in effect, interview-related skills. The illustrations are primarily from social work—the authors are faculty members at a graduate school of social work.

SEVEN

Developmental Phase:
Problem-Solving Interventions

The manifestation and effective communication of facilitative attitudes toward the client help the interviewer establish the positive relationship so necessary to social work. Attending behavior, minimal encouragements, paraphrasing, summarizing, and effective transitions extend the range of the interview. Identifying and calling attention to feelings and reflections of feelings help the client deepen the emotional level of communication. No matter how skillfully social workers have demonstrated their acceptance, empathic understanding, and warmth, no matter how competently they have helped interviewees to broaden and deepen their sharing of problems, the purpose of the contact is yet to be achieved. Interviewers also need to demonstrate problem-solving skills.

Clarification, interpretation, confrontation, self-disclosure, information sharing, advice and suggestion, silence, support and reassurance, humor, and environmental modification are among the skills the interviewer needs in order to achieve the problem-solving objectives of the interview. This chapter and the chapter that follows discuss such interview interventions. Questioning skills are of sufficient importance to warrant a separate chapter.

Clarification

Clarification and interpretation go a step beyond reflection and selective restatement. *Clarification* mirrors what the interviewee has said but translates it into more familiar language so that it is more understandable; it amplifies without falsifying. Clarification involves helping clients to restructure their perceptual field. All the elements of the clarification are already within the interviewee's level of awareness. Clarification distinguishes subjective reality from objective reality and presents various alternatives for consideration, including the consequences of different choices. The dominant note is cognitive understanding.

The objective of clarification is to bring into sharp focus otherwise vague communication. A side benefit of many interventions discussed earlier, such as reflecting and paraphrasing, is that they clarify what clients are thinking, feeling, and saying to themselves and to the interviewer. When the interviewer says, "Do you mean that . . . ?"; "In other words . . . "; "Let me see if I have this right . . . ," the interviewer is clarifying what the client has said.

Clarifying efforts increase specificity. When the client says, "I think my husband really dislikes me," and the interviewer asks, "What does he do or say that suggests this to you?," the interviewer is asking the client to clarify by being specific. When the client says, "I feel depressed," and the interviewer asks, "What depresses you most—your job, your marriage, your children, your social life?," the interviewer is attempting to get the client to be specific.

Interviewers seek clarification when they want to check out their understanding of what the client is saying and/or when they feel the client's thinking and feeling are not clear. In this case the request for clarification is designed to help both participants.

The interviewer's requests for clarification appeal for the interviewee's help in dispelling the interviewer's confusion and/or ignorance and have the positive effect of increasing mutuality—the interview becomes more of a joint endeavor. Seeking clarification also motivates the interviewee to participate more actively. Declining to respond to a person seeking to do a good job is difficult.

A word of caution: as always, the art of interviewing calls for *judicious* use of such intervention as "I don't understand"; "I am not sure I know what you mean"; and "I am not clear about . . ." Using these phrasings too frequently may suggest that the interviewer is not particularly bright or not listening carefully.

Many interviewees have not clearly defined their problems. Clarification helps them reduce their ambiguity, which helps them to get a clearer picture of their situation.

The following illustrates an interviewer's attempt to obtain clarification:

MALE SENIOR CITIZEN: I don't know. There are so many things bothering me, I hardly know where to begin. The house has gotten too big for us. The stairs are hard to climb, given my arthritis. My wife needs to go in shortly for an operation for gall bladder. The Social Security and pension together don't amount to much,

INTERVIEWER: Mr. Applegate, you have listed a number of different problems, all of which are real cause for concern. Of those you mentioned, which one do you think troubles you most?

INTERVIEWEE: Well, I think my wife's need for an operation gives me the most trouble.

INTERVIEWER: What about that bothers you more than the other problems you mentioned?

INTERVIEWEE: Well, I am dependent on her for companionship, for support. We've been together a long time and you never know about an operation.

INTERVIEWER: That makes a lot of sense, and I can see the reason this problem would trouble you most. If we focus on that problem, in what way do you think I or the agency can be of help to you?

Interpretation

Interpretation goes a step beyond paraphrasing, reflecting, or clarifying. In paraphrasing, reflecting, and clarifying the interviewer works with the interviewee's frame of reference; in interpreting, the interviewer offers a new frame of reference for the client's consideration. The interviewer relabels the client's comment so that it has a different meaning. A clarification, paraphrase, or reflection stays close to the message presented by the client. Interpretation takes off from the message and includes an inference derived from it, one added by the interviewer. It is what the interviewer heard plus what the interviewer inferred.

Information offered by the interviewee plus theory are the ingredients of inference. Using theoretical constructs about human behavior, the interviewer puts different pieces of information together so that they make psychological sense.

In arriving at an interpretation the interviewer is more directive than in clarifying or reflecting. In effect, interviewers have developed and are attempting to lead the client to an explanation (developed by the interviewer) that they think has some validity.

Clarification and paraphrase are more descriptive. Interpretation adds explanation. In reflection the worker does not seek to suggest an explanation for the behavior being highlighted and does not go beyond what the interviewee has presented. However, going beyond is the essential feature of interpretation.

In the following excerpt a social worker in a residential institution for emotionally disturbed children is faced with a resistive interviewee, a 12-year-old boy. The worker reflects the client's statements a number of times and then makes an interpretation in the form of a question:

INTERVIEWEE: I don't like talking to grown-ups. I like talking to kids.

INTERVIEWER [*Reflecting.*]: You don't like talking to grown-ups. How come?

INTERVIEWEE: I don't like to talk seriously. . . . I just like to talk "goofing around."

INTERVIEWER [*Reflecting.*]: Um-hum . . . you don't like to talk seriously.

INTERVIEWEE: Nope.

INTERVIEWER [*Interpreting.*]: Kids don't ask you a lot of personal questions?

INTERVIEWEE: Yeah, that's part of it.

In making an interpretation the worker offers a connection of which the client may not be aware.

GIRL, 12: I am not the easiest kid on the block to live with—I know that. My schoolwork and running around. They give me a hard time with that and it makes for a lot of conflict. But did they have to get divorced?

INTERVIEWER: You are honest in recognizing that you contributed to the difficulties in the family. But are you blaming yourself for your parents' getting divorced?"

A high school student is having difficulty in a chemistry lab class supervised by a male teacher. She resists following the teacher's instructions in doing the required lab work. She discusses her anxious feelings about her relationship with her authoritarian father:

INTERVIEWEE: My father makes me feel uneasy. Even when he's not criticizing me, I feel he's criticizing me.

INTERVIEWER: As you talk about this I keep wondering if there is any connection between your feelings about your father and your antagonistic behavior toward Mr. P. [the lab teacher].

If the interviewer here had reflected or paraphrased, she would merely have described in somewhat different words the way the client was relating to her father. Instead the interviewer interpreted psychologically related items of information, suggesting an explanation for the problem in the lab and making a link that the client had not made.

Interpretation can be hazardous because the explanation depends only partly on what the client has actually said at different points; it also depends on the theoretical constructs basic to the inferences.

Applying different theoretical constructs to the same client's statements could result in varying interpretations. For instance, the last interviewer had preconceived ideas about parents and teachers as authoritarian figures and about displacement and transference. The interviewer saw her client's behavior toward the teacher as resulting from feelings in the parent-child context that the client had transferred to the teacher-pupil context. An interviewer oriented to behaviorism might see the problem as resulting from learning certain patterns of behavior in the family and repeating them in the school setting. An interviewer with a feminist orientation might interpret the conflict as another illustration of the socialization of women to a subservient role in relation to men. An interviewer oriented to transactional analysis might interpret the child self as being in conflict with the adult self.

Interpretation is a reconceptualization in terms of the interviewer's theory of the details of the situation as offered by the interviewee.

Because different explanations have somewhat equal plausibility, depending on the interviewer's theoretical orientation, the ultimate determinant of the utility of an explanation in helping the client is the client's reaction to and use of the interpretation.

Although the same content can be interpreted in different ways, all the interpretations provide the interviewee with a new way of looking at the problem.

Here is another example of how the process works:

The worker has been discussing with a foster mother the possibility of converting the status of the foster child, Norman, 11, to that of a subsidized adoption. The foster mother has had an ambivalent relationship with the child during the five years he's been in her home. She is resisting the idea of adopting Norman despite the guarantee of a maintenance subsidy. She says, "I don't want to do it, but then I wonder if maybe Norman will reject us if we don't."

The worker, piecing together his knowledge that the woman sometimes feels she is rejecting Norman and his knowledge of concepts of projection, interprets what she is saying and responds, "Could it be that some of your reluctance about this is related to the fact that you sometimes feel that you reject Norman?"

Interpretation also requires sufficient information from the interviewee about the specific situation. Unless an interpretation is firmly grounded in information provided by the client, it is likely to be more of a guess and may be invalid.

In the following instance the worker offers an interpretation without sufficient preparation. A correctional social worker is talking to a 32-year-old inmate:

MR. R.: But I just go on resenting authority.

WORKER: Why do you resent authority?

MR. R.: I don't know. I can't answer that.

WORKER: Was your old man pretty tough on you when you were a kid?

MR. R.: No, he was pretty easy on me. That may be why I don't like authority. My father never gave authority to me so why should I take it off of these people?

If in error, the client might perceive the interpretation as a lack of understanding on the part of the interviewer. A client may reject an interpretation because it is too close to the truth—it creates considerable anxiety for the interviewee. Thus clients sometimes reject an interpretation either because it is inaccurate or because it is uncomfortably accurate.

In offering an interpretation the interviewer presents a view of the situation that is challenging because it disagrees with the view of the interviewee. Consequently, interviewers are advised to attempt interpretation in the context of a positive relationship, inherent in which is that the interviewee has respect for and confidence in the interviewer.

Clients are more likely to accept an interpretation that results from a collaboration. If this is the case, the interviewee is likely to respond by saying, "Am I to understand that you mean . . . ?"; "Are you telling me that . . .?"; "Did I hear you to say that . . .?"; "Did you mean . . . ?"

Every interpretive statement has an element of inference. The interviewer is establishing some connection in thoughts, feelings, and attitudes that the client has not perceived as being related. It is often, in effect, a translation of "manifest behavior into its psychodynamic significance."

Every inference is more or less conjectural. The best interpretation is the one that has the fewest components of conjecture and that is most clearly substantiated by evidence from the client's communications. It is what the client has almost said.

Interpretation makes explicit that which interviewees have communicated at such a low level of awareness that they are not aware they said it. It is often a latent affective message translated into words. Frieda Fromm-Reichmann, a psychoanalyst, defines interpretation as the translation of the "manifestations of that which is barred from awareness into the language of consciousness." The dominant note is emotional understanding.

In interpreting, the interviewer acts as a mental obstetrician, helping the client give birth to an understanding that is on the edge of recognition. If accepted, interpretation provides clients with a broadened perception of their behavior and perhaps a different angle on how to deal with it.

Interpretations that focus on content close to the margins of the interviewee's consciousness help to encourage self-exploration and expand self-awareness.

Interpretations are problem-solving interventions. They help the interviewee better understand the problem and in doing so aid in dealing with it more effectively. A changed perspective on the problem opens up previously unrecognized possibilities for solution.

The goal of interpretation is for the interviewee to accept the interviewer's definition of the situation as accurate. The worker cannot force acceptance of an interpretation. The client needs to reach it. When this happens, interpretation may lead to insight.

Because interpretation comes partly from what the client has said and partly from the sense the interviewer gives to the message, it is best to present it tentatively. Interviewers often offer interpretation as a suggestive question: "Would it be fair to say that . . . ?"; "Might you consider the possibility that . . . ?" Or the interviewer might introduce an interpretation by using qualifiers such as "I wonder if . . ."; "Maybe . . ."; and "Perhaps . . ." The interviewer presents the interpretation as a hypothesis for consideration rather than as a conclusion for acceptance.

Clients are more likely to accept an interpretation if it is within their grasp—"sensed but yet not clearly understood"—and results from an understanding developed by the interviewer and interviewee working together.

Interviewers sometimes introduce an interpretation by asking questions designed to stimulate the client to make connections between seemingly unrelated behaviors and feelings: "How do you figure that. . . ?"; "How do you understand this . . . ?"; "What are your own ideas about this . . . ?"

If the client rejects the interpretation—"No, that's not the way it is" or "I don't buy that"—the interpretation was a either off the mark or presented before the client was psychologically ready to consider it. The client may not reject it overtly but may ignore it, respond defensively or with resistance, or become confused. In these instances the interviewer probably ought to back off and not press the interpretation. Negative reactions suggest that the client is not yet ready or that the interpretation is invalid. Interpretations that are only slightly different from the interviewee's view of the situation are more likely to be effective (Claiborne, Ward, and Strong 1981).

In the following interchange the worker tentatively offers an interpretation and explains it, and the client ultimately accepts it. The social worker is talking with a young mother who is anxious about a continuing conflict with her 6-year-old daughter:

INTERVIEWER: Okay. Just to help me understand, when she complains like that and she's feeling miserable, and you get angry at her, is there a feeling that somehow you have to, want to, make things ideal for her so that she's happy?

INTERVIEWEE: Yeah.

INTERVIEWER: And that when she then complains like that, it makes you face the fact that things are less than ideal?

INTERVIEWEE: Yeah.

INTERVIEWER: And you get angry because they're not ideal, that there are difficulties and limitations in your situation?

INTERVIEWEE: That's really accurate. Cause I—you know, I fantasize that—in my fantasies everything is, you know, peaceful, loving, happy, and—and—it is. It's like a slap in the face when these disappointments come up. And then I think—I brush 'em off, like, you know, it's not going to be this way all the time. And I keep struggling to make things better. Even though it's just a minor thing like, you know, getting upset over, you know, having broken a promise or something. It just seems too much to look at.

In the next example the interviewer recognizes the danger of making interpretations for the interviewee. The client is a teenage, single, pregnant adolescent:

RUTH: Like, at a party I can talk to people, but inside I am afraid.

WORKER: Of what? [*Pause.*] Maybe you're afraid that people won't like you?

RUTH [*Blowing her nose.*]: Yes, I guess so.

The worker comments,

I think I could have waited out a longer pause before giving an interpretation. Perhaps she might have stated this reason herself—or maybe another reason— if I had let her.

Because interpretations are hazardous interventions interviewers should consider their interpretations carefully. And because interpretations vary in the degree of validity with which they are perceived, it may be best to introduce such statements provisionally:

It seems to me that . . .
It appears that . . .
It sounds like . . .

A social worker in a mental health clinic is reporting to her supervisor about one of her clients. Concerned about an interpretation she is considering, she says,

He had detailed a tragic litany of bad luck—an auto accident due to drunk driving, loss of a loan to a ne'er-do-well friend whom he met at a bar, a small fire in his apartment started by a lit cigarette, and several other equally disastrous happenings. It all seemed to suggest a pattern of self-punishment and self-destructiveness. I am considering offering this as an interpretation for his consideration.

Interpretive statements or questions are usually constructed as two statements linked by the word *because* or a similar conjunction. The statement following the conjunction embodies the inference that the interviewer recognizes but that is unrecognized or only partially recognized by the interviewee:

Maybe you spank Roger the way you do because this is the way your parents disciplined you.
Perhaps you feel guilty and anxious about your brother's accident because sometimes you hoped he would be out of your way.
As I get it, while you knew about contraceptives, you failed to take precautions because maybe you wanted to get pregnant.

Sometimes two pieces of current data are connected. Or the connection might be between something happening now and something that happened in the past, perhaps during childhood. In either case the worker hypothesizes two apparently unconnected events as having some relationship.

Summaries may have interpretive significance. In organizing the information the interviewer "positions" some units of information with reference to some other items. Furthermore, in selecting certain pieces of information for inclusion in the interpretation the interviewer highlights and emphasizes these items. Thus the interviewer is presenting a particular perception of the problem for the interviewee's consideration. This may be somewhat different from the way the interviewee perceived the problem and may result in shifts in perception.

Interviewers can offer interpretations at various levels of psychological depth and distance from the content presented by the client. Because the interpretation has to be acceptable if it is to have any effect, the initial interpretations should be close to the level of the data presented.

> INTERVIEWEE, *a 15-year-old*: My parents fight all the time and they talk of divorce. If they do, which they might, what's going to happen with me? I just feel terrible.

> INTERPRETATION, *level 1*: You're worried about who will provide the love and care that you still need?

> INTERPRETATION, *level 2*: You're worried about being abandoned like the time we talked about when you were in foster care?

> INTERPRETATION, *level 3*: You're feeling upset about the things you did that might have increased the fighting between your parents, like your dropping out of school?

In offering an interpretation interviewers confirm to the interviewee that they are trying to understand, that they are actively employing their expertise by offering for consideration some explanation of the interviewee's behavior based on workers' knowledge. Because interpretation is an active effort to be of help it has a positive effect on the relationship. Studies of interviewers delivering interpretation confirm that the clients saw the interviewers as empathetic and caring (Claiborne et al. 1981). See box 7.1 for guidelines for interpretation.

Box 7.1 Guidelines for Interpretation

---

1. Consider interpretation interventions only after you have established a positive relationship.
2. Consider an interpretation only after you have sufficient information to suggest that the interpretation may have validity.
3. Offer interpretation tentatively as a hypothesis for the client to consider, not as a statement that the client must accept.
4. Monitor interviewees' response to determine their level of receptivity of interpretation.
5. Accept rejection without defensiveness or apology.

Confrontation

Confrontation deals with incongruities—what clients say at one point and another statement they made later on; incongruities lie between what they say and how they say it, between clients' fantasy of how they see themselves and the reality of the effect of their behavior on others, between what clients say they want and behavior that suggests otherwise.

Confrontation tends to disrupt habits of thinking that permit discrepancies to exist. It forces rethinking. Confrontation inevitably evokes some feelings of disequilibrium or, as some have termed it, "beneficial uncertainty" for the interviewee. But disequilibrium is a necessary antecedent to change. This points to the value a confrontationist intervention may have in instigating change. It sets out the contradictory elements in the client's presentation. It presents discrepancies for acknowledgment, explicit examination, and resolution. The definition of the word *confront* implies 'bringing together to the front' so that what is communicated is clear and visible.

Confrontation has the effect of pulling the interviewee up short. The confrontation does not change behavior. It does, however, initiate reconsideration of behavior and suggests need for change. By acting contrary to the usual social expectation that they will ignore inconsistencies, interviewers set up a new situation that requires resolution.

Confrontation calls attention to observed discrepancies, inconsistencies, contradictions, distortions, evasions, and "stinking-thinking" rationalizations. It makes denial more difficult.

Confrontation stimulates self-examination. It presents interviewees with a contradiction that they are invited to resolve. It is a challenge to interviewees to face themselves more realistically—an unpleasant and difficult exercise. Like interpretations, confrontations increase self-awareness in order to enable interviewees to deal more realistically with their problems. An awareness of inconsistency is a prerequisite to considering change. As with interpretation, a confrontation is not productive unless the interviewee accepts it and attempts to resolve the inconsistencies. An Interviewer often makes an explicit invitation to the client to deal with the problem, concluding the confrontation statement with "What do you think about what I just said?" or "What do you feel about this?"

Confrontation, as contrasted with interpretation, is more focused on description than explanation. Confrontation invites clients to provide an explanation. Interpretation provides for the interviewee's consideration the interviewer's explanation of the meaning of the interviewee's behavior. Confrontation goes a step beyond interpretation. It is a more forceful, more active presentation of a hypothesis for the interviewee's validation or rejection.

Confrontation may be a necessary intervention with involuntary interviewees who deny any problems and resist the worker's attempts to help. Interviewers use confrontation to deliberately develop some uneasiness in the client.

Confrontation calls unmistakable attention to what the client is avoiding or not saying. It lets clients know what the interviewer thinks about the situation and what they need to talk about openly. To a client referred for counseling because she neglected her children and who spent the first twenty minutes of the interview consistently talking about the rise in the cost of living, the interviewer might say directly, "I think we both are aware that we are together to discuss your care of the children. We need to begin to discuss that now."

The interviewer may confront clients by pointing out clear differences between what clients say and what they do: "Talking the talk and not walking the walk."

A client who has been unable to hold a job for more than a few months because of his heavy drinking persists in describing himself as a social drinker. In confronting the client the worker says,

> I notice that you keep calling yourself a "social drinker," as you did just now. You have been drinking about a quart a day for some time now. How much do you think you would need to drink in order to consider yourself an alcoholic rather than a social drinker?

Other discrepancies occur in the way we perceive that other people are acting toward us and the way we describe their behavior.

Discussing a school problem with an adolescent, the interviewer says,

> You said a number of different times, and with some vehemence, that the main instructor dislikes you, is not concerned about you, couldn't care less whether you passed or not. How does that square with what I just understood you to say, that she was willing to stay after class to go over the assignment with you and that she asked you about your interest in being tutored? I don't get it.

Some discrepancies occur between what we say we value and the way we act, between what we are and what we profess we wish to be.

In discussing a marital conflict the interviewer says,

> You say you feel men should give women greater opportunities to fulfill their potential, yet from what you tell me you didn't change your pattern of household activities once your wife started working. Did I hear you wrong?

Discussing social problems with an obese adolescent, the interviewer says,

> You have talked quite a bit about how you don't like the way you look, how you think it makes for social difficulties for you, but you don't seem interested in a diet or exercise program or something like that. How come? The two things don't go together.

The worker uses confrontation to point out differences between verbal and nonverbal behavior.

A lesbian is talking about her relationship with other women in the bank where she works:

INTERVIEWEE: Since I accept my sexual preference and feel comfortable about it, I am pretty relaxed when I have to work with other people.

INTERVIEWER: I wonder if you noticed that when you said what you just said, you lowered your eyes, turned your head away from me, and clenched your right hand into a fist. What you said doesn't seem to go with all that.

Another way to confront is to suggest disbelief. "Did I understand you to say that you *never* felt any anger toward your children?"

A good confrontation involves more than explicitly pointing out that the client's presentation seems to have some discrepancies. It includes some details that provide the basis for the worker's statement that a discrepancy exists.

A mother of a 6-year-old boy, Carlo, who is so fearful of other children that he has been unable to remain in school, sees herself as an accepting, loving, permissive mother. The boy recently received a bike from his grandmother for Christmas. The mother has just finished detailing how, fearful that Carlo may have an accident, she locked the bike up until he is older. This is one of several overprotective actions on the part of the mother. In response the social worker says,

> You know, I don't get it. On the one hand, you say that you would like Carlo to grow up and you would like to help him to be less dependent, and on the other hand you do things—like this thing with the bike and your not letting him sleep overnight at a friend's house that we discussed last week—that

tend to keep him dependent. The two things seem contradictory to me. How do you explain to yourself the inconsistency between what you say you want and what you tell me you do?

The social work interviewer is obligated to raise for discussion the questions that the interviewee would rather not think about. Forcing the interviewee to consider these questions has an element of confrontation.

A college senior, Gail, with a long-standing relationship with a boyfriend by whom she is pregnant, is discussing the possibility of abortion with a social worker in a family service agency. The worker asks whether the boyfriend has been involved in the decision. Gail says she has not told him she is pregnant and does not plan to tell him. The worker asks,

Have you thought at all about how you would feel later on? That is, like . . . do you think that by not telling him, it would affect your relationship later in the future? I guess what I am asking you is if, say, you stayed together and got married, would it bother you in later years to have a secret from him? And how would it affect your relationship if, say, you told him or he found out about it after it was done?

In commenting on this intervention the worker notes,

The way I came at the question was hesitant and somewhat garbled, but the idea behind the question was good. I felt it important to confront Gail with this type of question since I didn't think she would confront herself with it.

The decision to confront a client is based on something the interviewer has observed the interviewee to actually say or do. Confrontations should have smaller elements of inference than interpretations have.

Confrontationist statements, like interpretations, should be somewhat tentative. However sure you are of the correctness of your perception of discrepancies, you might be wrong. You want to provide a climate that permits the interviewee to disagree with your observation.

The principle of contiguity suggests that confrontation should use the client's most immediate statements and behavior: "Thinking about what you just said . . ."; "Seeing what you are doing now with your hands and feet and your facial expression, and comparing that with what you are saying, it seems to me that . . ."

A male adolescent in a training school for delinquents had had a preliminary discussion with the residential social worker about his suppression of feelings about his parents. The worker is attempting to follow this up in the next interview, but the client is resisting, saying he really doesn't feel strongly about his parents. The worker is attempting a confrontation:

INTERVIEWER: What about your angry feelings?

INTERVIEWEE: Aaagh . . . I stopped that . . . Oh God, let's talk about something else.

INTERVIEWER: Like the weather, bowling, snowmobiling . . . fun stuff, huh? It sounds to me like you don't feel safe talking about your angry feelings, so you want to change the subject.

INTERVIEWEE: I don't get angry anymore. [*His face is turning red; he is very angry right now. His voice is raised almost to a shout.*]

INTERVIEWER: Oh yeah? Aren't you angry at me right now?

Like interpretation, intervention by confrontation is best done in the context of a firmly established relationship when the interviewer has enough information to feel confident that the confrontation statement has some validity and when the client has signaled some early perception of the mixed messages at which the confrontation is directed.

A young battered wife is ambivalent about leaving her husband and has discussed her feelings several times with the worker but has taken no action. In confronting the woman the worker says,

You've got to make up your mind, Dolores. Every time we talk about it, you say the same thing, but you never do anything about it. I realize that you might not be able to make that decision for good right now, but you have to do something to keep yourself from getting so upset all the time.

In commenting on her action the worker says,

I'm pushing her pretty hard. I can only do this because my love and approval are very important to her. When her psychiatrist starts pushing her, she walks out on him. I was pretty sure of my position, or I wouldn't have been quite so strong.

A sensitivity to the interviewee's emotional state is a determinant of when to use confrontation. When the interviewee is feeling momentarily low self-esteem, it is not a good time to introduce the discomfort inherent in any confrontation.

Confrontation is not forced. It is not designed to break down defenses, to shove unpalatable content down the interviewee's throat, or to force a client to face facts squarely. Confrontation is designed to stimulate the interviewee to take a careful look at the situation and to help the client feel free enough and safe enough to take that look.

The focus of confrontation is behavior, not the person of the interviewee. There is a difference between assertiveness that makes for a helpful confrontation and aggressiveness that arouses anxiety, defensiveness, and hostility. The most important consideration is the spirit in which the interviewer intervenes, not out of a desire to intimidate but out of a desire to do whatever can be done to help the client. It is a neutral description of a significant aspect of the client's behavior presented forcefully and unambiguously, making it difficult for the client to avoid dealing with it.

Confrontation risks alienation. An approach sympathetically attuned to the effect the confrontation is likely to have on the interviewee reduces the risk. If the confrontation is an attack merely to provide ego satisfaction for the interviewer, or to force the interviewee to make a change to meet the needs of the interviewer, it is likely to evoke hostility. If engaged in out of empathic understanding of the needs of clients, understanding of what may induce clients change to meet their needs, clients may resist but less actively.

Confrontation is a loaded word and rightfully so because it can be, and often is, used as a sanctioned opportunity for acting punitively. This interviewer justifies telling people off and putting people down by rationalizing that doing so is in the service of a helpful confrontation.

Once again the basic attitude is as important or even more important than the content of the confrontation. Interviewers who making a challenging statement out of narcissistic desire to display how smart they are ("See how I can psyche you out?") are likely to be resented. Interviewers who confront with an intent to satisfy their aggressive feelings toward the client ("How are you going to weasel out of this?")are likely to communicate a desire to hurt. However, when interviewers confront out of desire to understand the client better, out of a sense of puzzlement, a hope that the confrontation will enable the client to more effectively deal with the problem, the intervention comes across differently, and the client is likely to react differently. The best confrontation mirrors the Bible's admonition to "speak the truth in love."

Confrontation creates less of a threat to the worker-client relationship if the confronting statement focuses on strengths rather than limitations. Mr. P., a supervisor in a machine tool plant, is assertive on the job when supervising his employees or when facing plant administrators about workers' grievances, but he expresses considerable resentment because he generally feels he has to do what his wife wants to do on his time off. The interviewer says,

Look. How is this? You act one way on the job—assertive, verbal, kind of courageous, and another way off the job—unassertive, meekly going along. It's like you're two different people.

Because confrontation risks impairing rapport confrontationist interventions should not follow each other closely. The interviewer should devote some effort to repairing rapport after a confrontation. And because not all discrepancies are of equal significance or relevance to the objectives of the interview, the interviewer must be selective in targeting discrepancies for confrontation.

Because confrontation nakedly exposes what interviewees are often most eager to hide from themselves and others, successful confrontation depends not only on interviewers' skill or a good relationship with the client but also on the interviewee's readiness to explore whatever the confrontation involves.

The interviewer's presumption in making a confrontation is that the interviewee is able but unwilling to deal with the content. If the client is unable to deal with it, confrontation would be futile and injurious.

Confrontation must openly violate the etiquette of social conversation wherein we make a deliberate effort not to face people with inconsistencies we observe. Because we have been trained to regard such probing as impolite and because it is contrary to our patterns of learned social behavior, confrontation may be difficult for the interviewer. And the tendency to evoke a hostile reaction in the interviewee reinforces interviewers' reluctance to use such an intervention.

Because confrontation does involve a measure of unmasking self-deceptions, we need to recognize that it is painful for the interviewee and feel some concern. The interviewer should be candid but not coercive or punitive. The principle is to "confront without affronting."

On balance, and when in doubt, it is better to hesitate to use confrontation than to be eager to use it.

When the interviewee might benefit from a valid confrontation, the interviewer may be hesitant for several misguided reasons. The interviewer might see the client as vulnerable to damage. Eager for the interviewee's approval, the worker might not want to risk rejection. Sometimes interviewers fear their own impulses and may be anxious about their ability to control hostile impulses in using confrontation. When these factors determine whether to use confrontation, interviewers' concern is primarily with their own needs rather than the interviewee's.

The risk in failing to confront when appropriate is that the interviewee will continue to act in a dysfunctional way and by our dereliction assume that we support such behavior. See box 7.2 for guidelines for interpretation.

Box 7.2 Guidelines for Confrontation

---

1. Confront only to meet the objectives of the interview.
2. Confront only when you have sufficient and valid reasons to support a supposition that contradictions that need to be resolved exist.
3. Be selective in the frequency and timing of confrontation and the choice of discrepancies.
4. In confronting identify explicitly the behaviors on which the confrontation is based.
5. Base your spirit of confrontation on a desire to be helpful.
6. Confront softly, without affronting, "speaking the truth in love."
7. A positive relationship is a necessary context for confrontation.

Self-Disclosure

Self-disclosure by the client is expected during an interview. It is a necessary cost for obtaining the help the client seeks. Self-disclosure by the interviewer is not as commonplace.

Interviewer self-disclosure is related to an interviewer's authenticity and genuineness, as described in chapter 5. Feelings of openness, spontaneity, and congruence predispose us to self-disclose. Although it is related to interviewer authenticity and genuineness, self-disclosure is a separate intervention.

Authenticity and genuineness are *intra*personally focused. They suggest that interviewers are aware of their negative as well as positive feelings toward the interviewee, that they accept responsibility for these feelings and accept ownership of them without being defensive. Interviewers may or may not disclose these feelings to an interviewee. If, however, a direct question or the purpose of the interview requires disclose of such feelings by an interviewer, the interviewer shares the feelings honestly without defensiveness or apology. Self-disclosure is thus *inter*personally focused. The interviewer's sharing, intentionally and voluntarily, of personal information is a social act.

Of course interviewers may unintentionally and not always entirely voluntarily disclose a good deal about themselves. Gender, approximate age, race, and socioeconomic group are disclosed on observation. A ring discloses marital status. Diplomas and membership certificates from professional organizations hanging on the wall disclose information about education and experience. But parenthood status, life failures, frustrations, disappointments, and satisfactions can be disclosed only voluntarily and intentionally. Thus *self-disclosure* generally refers to these aspects of communication.

Interviewees may seek information about the interviewer that is not available through casual observation. In orienting themselves to the person of the interviewer clients may ask direct questions about the worker's personal life.

Interviewers self-disclose when they share information about their personal life and beliefs. But another group of self-disclosing statements relates to what happens during the interview—when interviewers share information about their feelings and their perceptions of interviewees and their behavior.

Clients ask questions about the interviewer's personal life and experiences ("Are you married?"; "Do you have children?"; "Have you ever been divorced?"; "Have you ever flunked a course?"; "Any experience with drugs?"; and the like). But they also ask questions about the interviewer's reaction to them ("Do you like me?"; "Am I boring you?"; "Do you see me as an attractive person?") and the interviewer's assessment of them ("Do you think I am intelligent?"; "Am I making as much progress as most of your clients?"; "Do you think I can lick this problem?")

Interviewers often feel uncomfortable with personal disclosure because it may mean sharing information that puts them at a disadvantage. Learning that the interviewer is unmarried, childless, or a student may erode some of the worker's potential for influence, some social workers believe.

Interviewers may also be uneasy about self-disclosure of their reactions to the interviewee because it may threaten the relationship.

A worker in a family service agency says of a client,

> She tells everything unselectively with every single irrelevant detail packed in along with whatever is relevant. She goes on and on and on and I get bored out of my skull searching the details for significant items. I have often been tempted to point out to her what she does but have always been hesitant (scared) to tell her she's boring. My supervisor, however, suggested that maybe she's not aware that she bores people and maybe coming from me, with whom she does have a good relationship, she might appreciate knowing this. Maybe. Can I take the chance?

On the other hand, interviewer self-disclosure may create some anxiety for the interviewee because it blurs the boundaries of the relationship Sharing intimacies is characteristic of a friendly, not a professional relationship (Wells 1994).

Objectives of Self-Disclosure

Interviewers engage in self-disclosure to achieve a variety of objectives.

1. Authenticity coupled with a readiness to self-disclose facilitates the client's willingness to communicate and reduces barriers to intimate communication. Interviewers cannot fully expect openness from an interviewee unless workers set an example of openness, spontaneity, and responsiveness.

Considerable research supports the contention that disclosure by interviewers of some personal information, their difficulties and deficiencies, encourages a greater flow of such disclosures from the interviewee (Chelune et al. 1979). Lawrence Shulman found that clients feel that when a worker shares personal thoughts and feelings, clients feel they know the interviewer better as a person. Shulman found that such self-disclosure correlates highly with perception of social workers as helpful, and he found it to be important in developing the worker-client relationship (1977:78). Research from psychology tends to suggest that moderate, judicious, and appropriate self-disclosure by the interviewer facilitates an effective working relationship and encourages greater self-disclosure by the interviewee (Simon 1988).

This interaction is generally known as the *reciprocity effect*—the interviewee reciprocates the self-disclosure offered by the interviewer. Researchers have offered a variety of explanations for this phenomenon.

A social norm of reciprocity carries into the interview room. Self-disclosure by the interviewer obligates the interviewee to share as well. Personal information is the price of the exchange to keep the situation equitable. Another explanation derives from the effect of modeling. Because the social work interview is an ambiguous situation, interviewees are not always clear about what is expected of them. The worker's self-disclosure presents a model of appropriate behavior.

2. Interviewer self-disclosure can encourage clients to self-disclose when other less intrusive measures have failed. After a client said she had to have an operation for an ovarian cyst, a medical social worker began by saying, "From what you said, I get the feeling that the operation scares you." When the client was silent, the worker universalized by saying, "I would imagine that most women would be frightened in thinking about having the operation." After a pause and the client's continued silence, the worker said, "I think I know a little bit about how you might feel. I remember when I had a hysterectomy last year, I was really nervous and upset for a week before the operation." The worker reported later, "After a short pause Ms. P. asked some questions about my operation, and after I briefly answered what she

wanted to know, she began slowly and in a depressed voice to talk about her own feelings."

Interviewer self-disclosure encourages interviewees to self-disclose because it establishes a bond of shared experiences.

3. Interviewers can use self-disclosure to deliberately provoke a catharsis for the client.

A worker in a protective agency had helped an abusive mother obtain a job as a typist and day care for her child so that the woman would have some relief from child care. A short time later Mrs. F. was laid off because her typing speed was too slow. The worker said,

> As we discussed what happened, she seemed unable to express any feelings about being let go. She discussed it in an indifferent matter-of-fact way, although I had the feeling she was hurt and upset. So I said, "Gee, if I were in your place, I think I would feel lousy, upset, angry, sad. I know I would feel that way because I once had your experience and I know how it affected me." I then told her about the time I had been fired from a job in a dress factory because I couldn't sew a straight seam and how lousy this made me feel. Sharing this seemed to help Mrs. F. open up. Even before I finished telling about my experience, she started to slump, hunched over the desk, and started to cry.

4. Interviewers may self-disclose to support the client and offer reassurance—the worker can understand the situation because of having been there.

An adolescent has just shared with a social worker that she told her mother off "in no uncertain terms" when her mother objected to her going out with a certain boy.

CLIENT: I don't think she was mad, but she was upset. I don't think she's going to leave me alone. Sometimes I hate her.

WORKER: I've felt the same way about my mother sometimes. The worst times were when I was trying to break away from her and form some opinions of my own.

The worker, commenting on her decision to share this with the client, says,

> I think Ann feels very guilty and hates her mother for making her feel guilty but probably also might feel guilty because she shouldn't hate her mother.
>
> I think she needed to be reassured that she isn't the only one who has ever had feelings of hatred for a parent. I also wanted to let her know that I know what it is like and can understand her feelings.

5. Interviewers may use self-disclosure to relieve feelings that are getting in the way of an effective interview.

A female social worker in a mental health center is engaged in an initial interview with a middle-aged male engineer who is considering divorce and is anxious about its implications. Throughout the interview the interviewee has made a number of classic sexist remarks. The social worker notes that she was becoming increasingly upset. She felt that she was expending energy in controlling herself to the detriment of the interview. Afterward she says,

> I felt that I was not acting as effectively as I might have in the interview because of the feelings the client generated by his remarks. When he said that he thought a woman's place was in the home taking care of the kids, I took advantage of this to raise the question with him of how he thought I might be responding to his remarks. I said I wondered what he thought about my working since I was obviously "not home caring for the kids." In response to his ambiguous answer I pursued it further by wondering if, given his feelings about this, he thought I could be helpful to him. While I did not disclose directly how I felt about his male chauvinist remarks, raising it indirectly for discussion permitted me to resolve some of my feelings so as to be able to conduct the interview more effectively.

6. In self-disclosing the worker becomes a model of a person who is open and comfortable with feelings and is not defensive. The worker demonstrates problem-solving techniques and approaches as by sharing successful resolutions of problems similar to that faced by the client (Simon 1988:408).

In summary, self-disclosure facilitates development of the relationship; encourages, stimulates, and helps the interviewees tell their story; and provides access to problem-solving techniques.

Dangers and Disadvantages

Self-disclosure entails dangers and disadvantages. The interviewer needs to pay attention to timing, appropriateness, and relevance. The worker should be aware that with some clients self-disclosure may impede rather than facilitate relationship development. So in what situation, with what interviewees, might interviewers appropriately disclose what kinds of information about themselves and with what precautions? The interviewer who indiscriminately engages in self-disclosure to encourage self-disclosure may not always be doing the client a service. One scholar notes, "Not everybody is benefited by the opportunity to let it all hang out. Some indeed may need help in tucking it all in."

One danger is that, unless controlled, worker self-disclosure may shift the primary focus onto the interviewer and the interviewer's problem.

A female social worker in a child welfare agency was discussing day care with a divorced mother of two young children. She comments,

> I lost control of the interview for an extended period because I talked too much about myself and had to struggle hard to get back on course (which I am not sure I really did).
>
> Mrs. B. asked me where I lived and if I had a family. I said on the west side and have one child but, I went on to say, I was divorced too. Mrs. B. then wanted to know if I was divorced for some time. I told her three years. And before I knew how it came about, I was discussing the problems that led to my divorce and the problems I had in being a single parent now.

Clients deserve honest answers to their questions, but the interviewer's responsibility then is to return the focus of the interview to the interviewee.

In ensuring that self-disclosure will be interviewee related, the self-disclosure should follow from an interviewee's statement and should end with a return to the interviewee's situation.

After a five-minute tirade about her adolescent son's misbehavior an interviewee says, "I am so frustrated I could spit. Nothing seems to be getting to him." After a pause the interviewer says, "I think I share some of your feelings. We have a thirteen-year-old daughter and a fifteen-year-old son, and life is more of a problem now than when they were younger. But I wonder if you could focus on one recent specific incident of difficulty. Could you tell me what happened?"

Too much interviewer self-disclosure blurs the boundaries of who is interviewer and who is interviewee.

Another problem is determining when the client is seeking self-disclosure by the interviewer and when the client is asking a different question.

Urdang describes a client, a young woman whose mother has been mentally ill for years, who asks the worker, "'What is your opinion of me?' She looked up at me. I said I was beginning to like her a lot. I said we've just known each other a short while but she's really done some good work" (1979:7). Note that in asking, "What's your opinion of me?," the client may be asking, "Do you think I am crazy like my mother?" Returning the focus of the interview to the client and exploring the meaning of her question may have been the more productive option. In this instance the latent significance of the client's question got lost in the eagerness of the interviewer to self-disclose.

Another disadvantage in an interviewer's sharing personal information is that this increases the interviewer's vulnerability. Becoming humanly fallible leaves an interviewer open to derogation. Also, a client may perceive excessive and/or inappropriate self-disclosure as evidence that the interviewer is not well adjusted. If this happens, the interviewer loses credibility.

However, the literature notes that interviewees can more easily excuse weakness than they can deal with a worker who, by failing to share, projects an image of perfection and invincibility.

If an interviewer refuses to self-disclose and rigidly differentiates the status of interviewee and interviewer, the interviewer enhances the power distinctions. Self-disclosure that comes exclusively from the interviewee generates the kind of negative feelings about participant inequality exposed by this client:

> With half a laugh of hearty zest
> I strip me of my coat and vest.
> Then heeding not the frigid air
> I fling away my underwear.
> So having nothing else to doff,
> I rip my epidermis off.
> More secrets to acquaint you with
> I pare my bones to strips of pith.
> And when the exposure is done
> I hang, a cobweb skeleton.
> While you sit there aloof, remote,
> And will not shed your overcoat.
>
> *(Menninger and Holzman 1973:60–61)*

Another pitfall lies in the worker's honest disclosure of feelings of shock and disapproval in response to what the client is saying. Here, interviewers must be judicious.

A young female worker in a protective service agency interviewed a middle-aged man reported for committing incest with his 7-year-old stepdaughter. The worker reports,

> This really was a hard one for me. As he talked about what had happened I kept saying to myself, "How could you? How could you?" In my own mind his behavior was unacceptable and despicable. I had to exercise conscious deliberate control over what I said and how I thought I sounded. I knew that if he could read how I felt, he would clam up and withdraw from the interview.

Weiner, in a careful evaluation of his prolonged clinical experience with self-disclosure, concludes that "one cannot naively be one's self with patients in spite of the Rogerian notion that genuineness is the sine qua non of successful psychotherapy" (1978:2). Self-disclosure is not a license for a full expression of feelings. The interviewer is obligated to be in control of feelings which, if expressed, may be contrary to the therapeutic needs of the interviewee.

Interviewers may use selective self-disclosure, partial self-disclosure, or refuse to disclose, based on their assessment of which alternative is better for accomplishing the objectives of the interview.

A study based on questionnaires sent to therapists at counseling centers found that they do become angry, annoyed, exasperated, and vexed by interviewees. Interviewees who blame others for their problems, who are uncooperative or resist the counselor's efforts to help, or who are openly critical of the counselor are high on the list of those who evoke counselors' anger. Most therapists express some hesitation in sharing these negative feelings with the interviewee. Some believe the interviewee would be hurt; others feel uncomfortable expressing anger, this despite their frequent exhortation to clients to be freer in expressing negative feelings. Those who share their anger try to communicate the difference between anger and hostility and between anger at behavior and anger at the person. The study adds the caution that disclosure should be made to interviewees with reasonably intact self-esteem and in the context of a positive relationship (Fremont and Anderson 1986).

Yet another danger is unintentional manipulation. When interviewers, in relating a personal situation analogous to the one faced by the client, reveal how they resolved their problem, the client may interpret the information as a strong hint to go and do likewise.

On the other hand, if the client does not see the worker's disclosure as bragging or as coercive, it may be encouraging, a sign that positive change is possible.

Another risk in self-disclosure is that interviewers will misuse it as a tactic for ingratiating themselves with the interviewee by offering their personal secret as a present. Clients may perceive as manipulative indiscriminate self-disclosure that is not obviously related to the requirements of the situation.

That willingness to self-disclose is an indication of maturity and superior mental health is a conceit. Interviewers' self-disclosure may be a subtle way of reassuring themselves that they are indeed mature, mentally healthy, openly human. Thus narcissistic gratification may be parading as self-disclosure in an exhibitionistic display. See box 7.3 for guidelines for self-disclosure.

Box 7.3 Guidelines for Self-Disclosure by an Interviewer

Because self-disclosure by the interviewer involves danger as well as advantages, here are some guidelines that may prove useful:

- Too much self-disclosure too soon by the interviewer is as bad as too little too late. Although interviewees may be uncomfortable and anxious with interviewers who remain sphinxlike, they are equally discomforted by an interviewer who is a Niagara of self-disclosure. Interviewees see the latter as indiscreet, self-involved, indiscriminate, and unstable and are concerned about their competence to be of help.
- Timing is important. Intimacy in the relationship needs to be developed gradually, and the client's need for some psychological distance early in the relationship needs to be respected.
- Context, dosage, and timing are the principal factors that determine whether and when self-disclosure might be helpful. The most important question is whose needs are being served. If the only answer is the client's needs, interviewer self-disclosure is justifiable. This also implies that an interviewer's failure to disclose when the needs of the interview require it is as much a failure as overdisclosure.
- Use of self-disclosure should be sparing so that it does not overwhelm the interviewee. Interviewers should offer it discriminately, delicately, with some sensitivity to the client's readiness for such information, with a conscious idea as to what is likely to be helpful. An interviewer needs to handle self-disclosure so that the interviewer does not, in the digression, become the focus of the interaction.
- Monitoring the effects of interviewer self-disclosure is important because each interview is a highly individualized encounter and because no one interviewee is like any other interviewee. Feedback from the interviewee helps the interviewer to tailor self-disclosures so that they are timely, appropriate, and helpful.
- Although interviewer self-disclosure facilitates disclosure by the interviewee, it is only one way to get a client to open up. Given the dangers inherent in self-disclosure, it may not be the most effective way.

An atmosphere of psychological safety, acceptance, and respect and the interviewer's manifestation of empathic understanding facilitate interviewee self-disclosure. Well-timed, well-formulated questions and open invitations to talk also have this effect. Using these interventions may be better than the trickier tactic of self-disclosure. Interviewees generally recognize that their sharing of personal information is not contingent on the interviewer's reciprocal sharing. Thus affective neutrality may be the safest initial orientation of the interviewer, discarded briefly for self-disclosure when the needs of the interview clearly would be better served by the change.

Because self-disclosure implies increased intimacy, this factor affects the frequency with which some social workers self-disclose. In a study of self-disclosure by social workers Bradmiller (1978) found that unmarried female social workers are least likely to share personal information with clients. Although married female social workers may feel that their marriage "offer(s) a form of protection against misrepresentation of their personal or intimate disclosures," unmarried female social workers might be concerned that clients will perceive self-disclosure as an invitation to greater familiarity outside the interview situation (p. 33).

Another study of the use of self-disclosure by social workers echoes Bradmiller's finding that social workers are guarded in their use of such intervention. Borenzweig (1981) found this particularly true of social workers who regard themselves as psychoanalytically oriented. Social workers are reluctant to share with their clients information about their political, sexual, or religious orientation. They more freely share information about their marital status, parenting, and significant experiences of loss such as divorce and death. Respondents expressed a feeling of resentment that clients manipulate and/or coerce the workers into self-disclosure. They feel that emphasizing the elements of a common humanity in disclosing secrets about themselves diminishes some of the clinician's charismatic power to help the client.

A 1989 questionnaire study by Anderson and Mandall of the use of self-disclosure by clinical social workers found that they most often use it to increase the interviewee's awareness of options, to increase interviewee self-disclosure through modeling, to decrease the interviewee's anxiety, and to increase the interviewee's perception of the interviewer's authenticity and empathy (p. 265). The workers most frequently disclose information about their personal history and current relationships and least often discuss their sexuality and finances.

A questionnaire study of the self-disclosing practices of psychotherapists found that reasons for self-disclosure most often relate to providing a "model for appropriate client behaviors and to increase similarity between counselor and client" (Edwards and Murdock 1994:387).

Studying counselors' perception of their use of self-disclosure, Robitschek and McCarthy (1991) found counselors most frequently disclose information about their training and counseling style, about their marital status, and about family experiences as children and adolescents. They are least likely to disclose about their finances and political affiliation, sexual relations, and experiences with drugs and alcohol (Robitschek and McCarthy 1991:219, table 1) Most self-references are of a positive nature, acting to reassure interviewees and show them that their situations are normal. When counselors use negative references, they often do so to challenge a client.

Social workers oriented to psychodynamics are mindful of the caveat that disclosure interferes with the proper development of transference. Because social workers, in disclosing, are no longer a blank screen, clients are likely to find them more difficult to perceive as a representative of some past significant other.

Some interviewers have ideological commitments to self-disclosure. Some humanist-oriented interviewers are uncomfortable with a relationship in which sharing of personal information goes only one way. To redress the inequity of such a situation, to restore a greater sense of mutuality, and to reduce social and psychological distance between interviewer and interviewee, they feel impelled to share information about themselves (Simon 1990).

Sharing Information

Although almost every interview involves some flow of information from the interviewee to the interviewer, some interviews involve a reverse flow of information. Social work interviewers provide information that clients need, such as the eligibility requirements of some social service programs, procedures for applying for benefits, the nature of foster care service, the legalities of adoption, and alternative family planning techniques.

Videotapes of interviews to determine eligibility for public assistance show that a high percentage of such interviews involve getting, giving, and clarifying information (Morton and Lindsey 1986). Providing information is an intervention that contributes to problem solving.

The significance of sharing information relevant to the problem may be too easily dismissed. Sometimes people have difficulty in dealing effectively with their problems simply because they lack information. Providing information may show the client the problem in a new perspective or may provide alternatives. Correcting misinformation may prevent mistakes. Sharing specialized information is an important and relevant intervention procedure in social work interviewing. Information is power.

Accurate information can help to reduce a client's anxiety and alleviate depression by countering unfounded concerns ("HIV is not transmitted through kissing"). The interviewer can provide information that the client lacks and that may be helpful ("You are entitled to file for earned income credit with the Internal Revenue Service"). Social workers also can provide clients with information about the kinds of behavior to expect from children at different ages.

The social worker experienced in a particular field of practice should have a good deal of specialized professional knowledge that may help the client find more options and avoid dangers that are not easy to recognize:

INTERVIEWEE: He's out there mentally ill and doing God knows what. I want him in an institution for his own good.

INTERVIEWER: I can appreciate your worry about him, but I have to tell you that Bob is an adult and as such cannot be institutionalized because you think it's best for him. [Worker then goes on to provide information about procedures and criteria for institutionalization.]

In communicating information the interviewer has to know the facts—the specific eligibility requirement of a program, the actual procedures in making application, and the like. The worker must judiciously select the nature and amount of detail to communicate to the client so that the worker shares only the most pertinent information. The danger lies in information overload, and too much information too quickly may leave the interviewee more confused than before.

An interviewer discussing with a pregnant unwed teenager the effects of drugs, alcohol, and tobacco on the fetus felt that she had given the interviewee too much information:

I'm not sure Ms. B. was able to absorb it all. I dumped quite a load of information on her all at once. While I tried to keep it simple and use nontechnical language, I felt it was just too much. But once I got started I think I got some pleasure from showing how much I knew. Next time I am going to talk less and supplement what I say with the pamphlet the agency puts out.

The best approach is to tailor the information you provide to the specific needs of clients and their situation. Communicate information so that it is consistent with the interviewee's educational and vocabulary level.

Timing is important because receptivity to information depends on the interviewee's readiness to hear it. Communicate information when it is most meaningful and when the interviewee is highly motivated to listen. Provide information in digestible dosages as the client needs it. You may have to repeat the information. What is crystal clear to interviewers because of their familiarity with it may be confusing to the interviewee. Soliciting feedback while providing information may help the interviewer determine what is getting across and what is being missed. If available, brochures, pamphlets, and the like are helpful supplements.

Take special care in sharing information that may be hurtful or derogatory. Interviewers sometimes are purposely vague and indirect. Having to tell parents that their child has been found to be developmentally disabled, for example, can create anxiety for the interviewer and hostility in interviewees. This is termed a *bad news interview*. Here the interviewer has to be sensitive not only to whether interviewees understand the communication but also to how they react to the communication. Because the interviewer is delivering bad news, the client is likely to have a highly affective reaction that makes comprehension difficult. In reacting to the information the interviewee may reject the message, disputing its validity with the interviewer. The interviewer may wish to introduce the full implications of bad news gradually, building toward acceptance.

The following is an interview between a clinician and Mr. and Mrs. R. in which the interviewer presents diagnostic findings about their son's mental disability:

INTERVIEWER: I think—you know I'm sure you're anxious about today and I know this has been a really hard year for you. And I think you've really done an extraordinary job in dealing with something that's very hard for any human being or any parent.

MRS. R.: True.

INTERVIEWER: It's HARD when there's something not all right with a child, very hard. And I admire both of you really and, and as hard as it is seeing that there IS something that IS the matter with Donald, he's NOT like other kids, he IS slow, he is retarded.

MRS. R.: HE IS NOT RETARDED!

MR. R.: Ellen.

MRS. R.: HE IS NOT RETARDED!

MR. R.: Ellen. Uh, please.

MRS. R.: NO!

MR. R.: Maybe—look—it's their way of—I don't know.

MRS. R.: HE'S NOT RETARDED [*sobbing*].

INTERVIEWER: He can learn and he is learning.

(Maynard 1991:162–63)

Although informing the parents about the disability appears here to be direct and blunt, the interviewer introduces it by recognizing how difficult such a situation is for parents. Further, they end by beginning to point to some of the positives of the situation. The interviewer might then go on to develop in greater detail the possibilities for adequate development within the limits of their son's disability. Because clients are more likely in such instances to deny and distort the information, interviewers have to be extraordinarily clear in what they say. See box 7.4 for guidelines for offering information.

Box 7.4 Guidelines for Offering Information

1. Make sure that you *know* what you're talking about.
2. Be clear that the information is relevant to the interviewee's problem.
3. Offer information in digestible dosages so as not to overwhelm the client.
4. Present the information at a level aligned with the educational and vocabulary skill of the interviewee.
5. If possible, back up the information you present with relevant written material.
6. Present information in a manner that maximizes the client's understanding and acceptance.
7. Use appropriate pauses and expressions to emphasis the significant items in the information you offer.
8. Consider the interviewee's culture in selecting information for sharing.
9. Present information with some sensitivity to the interviewee's emotional readiness to accept it.
10. Provide relevant information with some sensitivity to the client's level of motivation to receive it.

Additional problem-solving interventions are discussed in the next chapter.

EIGHT

Developmental Phase: More Problem-Solving Interventions

Support and Reassurance

The primary objective of another kind of intervention is support of the interviewee. Interviewers evidence their support by overt expressions, both verbal and nonverbal, of their understanding, reassurance, concern, sympathy, and encouragement. Showing support includes expressions of praise and appreciation of the client's abilities, qualities, and coping efforts. This technique demonstrates the interviewer's active approval of the client's qualities and achievements.

The psychological safety of a good relationship is in itself supportive. The interviewer's attitude toward the interviewee, discussed earlier, is supportive. The interpersonal atmosphere created by using this approach makes the client feel comfortable, safe, and relieved. The involvement of the worker in helping with the problem is also supportive. The interviewee is no longer struggling with the problem alone.

However there are more explicit acts of support that help a client solve a problem.

Specific supportive interventions go beyond a general supportive context. They are designed to affirm that the worker sees the client as capable, on the right track, and in possession of some of the strengths necessary to deal effectively with the problems (Nelsen 1980). This is what interviewers are saying, in effect, when they praises the client, show approval of certain things the client has done or said, and express confidence in the client's plans.

Supportive intervents communicate confidence in clients' ability to cope with their problems. The hoped-for outcome is that clients then are in a better position to mobilize their resources.

The intent of support is to relieve psychological pain, to affirm and reinforce the client's ego strengths, and to replenish depleted self-esteem.

Emotionally supportive statements increase interviewees' motivation to work on the problem, increase their confidence that they may be able to resolve the problem, and encourage clients in feeling that they can resolve the problem. Support and reassurance tend to reduce anxiety, shame, and guilt, which are among the negative feelings that divert psychic energy from dealing more directly with the matters of concern. Such intervention helps clients to move the interview ahead.

Interviewers demonstrate support by communicating an appreciation of interviewees' efforts to solve their problem despite the real difficulties they are encountering. Support includes short interactions, such as "I think I can understand that"; "That must have been very difficult"; "I think anybody would get upset as you did about a situation like this"; or "You seem to have handled that very well."

Following a client's statement that she thinks her son's daydreaming in school is related to his overhearing fights between she and her husband, the worker says, "I see you have given this a great deal of thought. You might be right."

A worker uses praise to support an older client who has joined a senior citizens club after considerable hesitance: "I know that it takes a lot of courage to do this, and I am glad that you were able to join."

An inhibited preteen who had expressed little of his feelings became agitated when he learned he might be removed from a foster home he liked and returned to his parents' home. He expressed considerable feeling about the move and talked openly about his negative feelings toward his parents. Throughout, the interviewer nonverbally encouraged him to continue by nodding and using facial gestures. At the end the interviewer complimented the client on his awareness of his feelings and his ability and willingness to articulate them.

Statements that universalize ("Many people are encountering your problem"; "Most women faced with your situation react the way you do") are supportive because they reassure interviewees that they are not deviant or atypical. We reassure by saying that it is human and natural for people to feel hostile and rejecting in some situations.

Because such interventions come easily and interviewers have often used them in social situations, these interventions carry a danger of indiscriminate overuse. If misused, they may lead clients to feel the interviewer disrespectfully minimized the problem or that the interviewer failed to understand the real difficulties in their situation.

Rather than helping a client feel less anxious, supportive interventions might increase clients' anxiety because clients might perceive that the worker perceives them as more capable than they actually are. Clients sometimes react by feeling an increased burden of having to live up to the worker's unwarranted expectations.

Reassurance and expressions of support are often appropriate, but they can also inhibit a more helpful expression of feeling.

A single parent concerned about finances says with disappointment that she failed to get a teaching assistantship for which she had applied. In response the interviewer says supportively, "But it is a tribute to your motivation that despite that you're still planning to go back to school." In commenting on her response the interviewer says,

> Not getting the position was obviously a great disappointment to Ann. I should have shown her empathy here and then encouraged her to express her feelings of failure. Instead, I played Pollyanna, attempting to get her to see that she was doing positive things to improve her situation, and the setbacks were temporary—but really, the effect was to minimize her feeling. I failed to consider how very depressed Ann felt about her inability to support herself and her family, even if it was only a temporary circumstance.

The principal caution to observe in the use of support intervention is that it must be based in reality. Offer praise, approval, and expressions of confidence that the client is capable or that the situation will get better only if the assessment squares with the facts.

Clients regard as dishonest and disrespectful expressions designed to cheer them up if that support is based on little but hope. "Don't worry—I am sure things will get better and that you're going to be all right" has a hollow ring and leads the client to worry about the worker's understanding of the situation. To be effective, support requires that the client have some confidence in the worker's judgment.

Supportive statements are most likely to be effective if the interviewer can specifically identify the interviewee's feeling or the behavior for which the interviewer is expressing approval or encouragement. Finally, interviewer statements designed to be reassuring are most likely to be effective if a trusted interviewer gives them when they are needed and the interviewee is receptive. Congruence between verbal and nonverbal communication, although important in all situations, is of critical importance in offering support.

Advice

Advice can be defined as a "noncoercive recommendation for some decision or course of action based on professional knowledge." *Suggestions* are a mild form of advice. Advice is an intervention that contributes to meeting the problem-solving responsibilities of the interviewer.

Reviewing tapes of interviews and categorizing interviewers' responses shows that 5 to 8 percent of social work interview interventions can be classified as advice (Mullen 1969; Reid and Shyne 1969; Ewalt and Kutz 1976; Kassel and Kane 1980).

Giving information is neutral. It provides resources for decision making. Advice is biased and directs a decision. However, interviewers advise and suggest by selectively presenting information that favors a particular course of action. In doing this interviewers often are not explicit that they are advising.

The word *advice* covers a number of different, albeit somewhat similar, activities. It covers explicit directions as to what the client "should" or "ought" to do. It includes "suggestions" of alternatives for the client's consideration, and it includes questions worded to point to the direction the interviewer hopes the client will go.

Thus you might say,

It seems to me, having heard how senile your parents are, that you should find a nursing home for them.

It seems to me the physical condition of your parents as you described it is like many other families I have known who found a nursing home to be a desirable solution to their parents' problem.

Given the physical condition of your parents, have you ever thought of a nursing home as a possibility?

The recommendation is essentially the same in each instance. The gradation is, however, from an imperative statement that dictates to the client, through a tentative suggestion that raises the recommendation for consideration, to an even more tentative question that manipulates the client's mind-set to focus on the recommendation. The interventions are progressively less directive.

Advice can vary in the degree of directiveness and also in the degree of explicitness; some advice is more subtle than other advice. The technique of modeling is, in effect, a subtle nonverbal form of suggesting that the client adopt certain behavior.

Advice giving comes in a variety of attenuated soft forms:

As a question: "How do you think it might work out if you tried . . . ?"
As self-disclosure: "I once faced a similar kind of problem and what worked for me was . . ."

Interviewers often give advice without being explicitly aware that they are doing it:

INTERVIEWEE: So I had to work late and Doris had to stay with the babysitter till seven o'clock, and she was very upset, and I felt very sorry and guilty.

INTERVIEWER: You really shouldn't feel guilty because coming home late wasn't your fault.

The interviewer is advising the mother to change her feeling about the incident.

Simple statements like "Perhaps you need to get out more by yourself" or "You should try picking up on your knitting again because it seemed to give you so much satisfaction" embody advice.

In each instance the intervention seeks to influence the interviewee to take a particular course of action. This is the essence of advice. It is designed to encourage or discourage some behavior, attitude, or feeling on the part of the interviewee through the open expression of the interviewer's opinion. It is, in its varied forms, a procedure of direct influence.

The advisability of offering advice has been controversial in social work for some time. Some feel that offering advice to the interviewee is a manifestation of the interviewer's arrogance. How could the worker possibly know enough about the interviewee's total situation to be able to give advice? Others base their objections to giving advice on the inherent shift of responsibility for solving the problem from the interviewee to the interviewer and point out that giving advice encourages greater dependency on the part of the interviewee. Furthermore, giving advice may be ineffectual—the interviewee is not likely to take it. Many see giving advice as a violation of social work ethics because it denies clients the right to make their own decisions.

Offering advice is also controversial because it clearly reflects differences between the professional interviewer and lay interviewee. Advice given by a social worker, like a doctor's prescriptions and instructions to a patient, suggests greater knowledge and expertise on the part of the professional. Giving advice emphasizes the inherently nonegalitarian nature of the interview. Giving advice is a manifestation of the power and status difference between interviewer and interviewee. The interviewee does not offer advice to the interviewer.

Some who derogate advice like to say, "If it's free, it's advice; if you have to pay for it, it's counseling." Advice in general has a bad reputation. One witticism has it that the best thing that we can do with advice is to pass it on, unused.

Here is an example of a worker who is reluctance to offer advice. A child welfare worker in contact with a mother who was pressing for specific advice regarding institutionalization of her mentally handicapped child shared the following parable with the client:

> A young man approached a sage and said, "I am holding a bird behind my back. Tell me, is it alive or dead?" If the sage said the bird was alive, he planned to crush it. If the sage said the bird was dead, he was going to present a live bird. After pondering the question for a short time, the sage said, "The answer is in your hands."

Empirical studies of clients' expectations regarding advice and their response to it show that such interventions are useful problem-solving procedures. Although some interviewees do not expect advice, do not welcome it, and resent it, most interviewees come to the social agency with some expectation that they will get advice. They are receptive to advice and generally make effective use of it in working on their problems (Reid and Shapiro 1969; Mayer and Timms 1970; Ewalt and Kutz 1976; Maluccio 1979).

Feedback from clients shows that they are more frequently dissatisfied when they receive too little advice but almost never complain of getting too much. Maluccio, in summarizing client feedback, notes,

> Clients from diverse socio-economic groups indicated that they expected the worker to play a more active role by expressing opinions, giving advice and offering suggestions. While they accept the ultimate responsibility in resolving their problems, they clearly looked to the social worker as the expert to suggest options and guidelines. Over half of the clients expressed dissatisfaction with what they perceived as the worker's failure to offer advice and guidance. (1979:74)

Research summarizing the client's definition of the "good therapist" concludes that good therapists are "keenly attentive, interested, benign and concerned listeners—a friend who is warm and natural, *is not averse to giving direct advice,* who speaks one's language, makes sense, and rarely arouses intense anger" (emphasis added; Strupp, Fox, and Lessler 1969:117).

Seventy-nine percent of the clients of an outpatient mental health clinic, asked to list the curative factors associated with their therapy, listed advice as a factor (Murphy, Cramer, and Lillie 1984). Advice and "talking to somebody who understands" correlated most highly with outcome (Murphy, Cramer, and Lillie 1984:190).

A detailed analysis of the research on factors associated with successful social work practice in outpatient mental health clinics notes that advice is one intervention associated with "better client outcomes" (Videka-Sherman 1988:328).

What has sometimes been said of teaching might be paraphrased for giving advice, namely, that although people don't like to be taught, they may be ready to learn. Even if the client does not follow the advice, the explicit suggestion may stimulate the client to find alternatives to solve the problem. Advice has the effect of actively engaging the client in problem solving if only by providing something specific to react to. Furthermore, we underestimate the capacity of the interviewee and overestimate the influence of the social worker if we think our advice is an imposition. If people have a great capacity to reject the doctor's prescriptions, checking them against their experience and that of friends and neighbors, they have equal or greater capacity to critically evaluate the advice of social workers (Rees and Wallace 1982:39–42).

Withholding advice the client expects has its disadvantages. The client may evaluate the worker as someone who is without understanding and incompetent. Because social workers present themselves as a professional, the client is likely to perceive workers as having some special expertise that qualifies them to offer advice.

In a meta-analysis of thirty-eight research studies of social work practice in mental health Videka-Sherman concluded that the research supports the idea that "practitioners should consider their advice and direction to be important resources for the client" (1988:330).

We are expected to have some knowledge, some expertise, about social problems and the variety of alternatives for resolving them. We are supposed to have had some experience with the probable consequences of the various solutions available. All this gives the social worker legitimate grounds for offering advice. However, the interviewer needs to be sensitively aware of the limits of the profession's knowledge base, which sets parameters for legitimate advice. The knowledge base of the profession does not provide pat answers when Mr. Lipton wants to know whether he should marry Ms. Cole or when Mr. and Mrs. Evans are trying to decide whether she should take a job offer that entails moving to another state.

It would seem, then, that rather than reject advice out of hand as an intervention procedure that has no legitimate place in the social work interview, we need to give advice and its variations more positive consideration. Box 8.1 provides some guidelines to observe in offering advice.

Box 8.1 Guidelines in Offering Advice

---

1. The request for advice must clearly come from the client and not be a manifestation of the needs of the worker. Giving advice, whether it is accepted or not, is intrinsically pleasurable: it parades the worker's smartness and wisdom; it is a gift to the client with the expectation that the client will like the worker more for having offered it; it enables the worker to "do something" for the client if the client isn't sure how the worker can be of help. All these speak to workers' needs for offering advice without reference to whether clients want it.

2. As much as possible the worker should ground in the knowledge base of the profession the advice offered in response to a client's need. The advice should derive from some knowledge that what the worker is suggesting has a high probability of having the desired effect, and the worker shares the nature of the effect with the client. If we advise the parent to take some particular course of action in dealing with a hyperactive child, we should know something of the research and/or practice wisdom that shows that certain ameliorative effects are quite likely to result.

3. The worker must consider the client's situation, culture, the social norms of the client's group, and the degree of support or opposition the suggestion is likely to elicit from the client's significant others. However objectively sensible a recommendation might be, the particular context in which the client has to implement the suggestion may make it difficult.

4. In most instances the worker should offer advice tentatively, giving the client freedom to reject it and encouraging honest feedback. The worker should offer the advice in such a way that the client does not feel obligated to accept it. Interviewers have to feel comfortable about having their advice rejected. The most desirable approach is to use the least coercive, least restrictive degree of influence necessary to achieve the objective.

5. Wherever feasible, workers should give advice in conjunction with other interventions, such as support: "If you do decide to attempt to learn an occupational skill through the WIN program, as I am suggesting, I think you are capable of succeeding in the program." Furthermore, we need to indicate our willingness to help the client implement the decision or course of action we are advising.

6. A worker should offer advice only after helping clients to explore their own suggestions. Doing this answers the objection that giving advice preempts clients' opportunity to solve their problems on their own, which is clearly desirable. Rather than a first resort to the client's problem, advice should be a last resort. The first response to a direct request for advice should be an offer of help in reviewing any responses the client may have pondered for dealing with the problem. Accepting the client's request for advice at face value is not always advisable. Initially exploring with clients the reasons that prompt the request for advice may be helpful.

7. A worker should not give advice too early in the interview. A good relationship maximizes receptivity to and acceptance of advice (Stone 1979:39; Ewalt and Kutz 1976:16). When participants have some opportunity to know each other, the interviewer has the opportunity to learn enough about the situation to offer sensible advice.
8. Interviewers should restrict their advice to content about which they have some special knowledge and expertise. Interviewers should give some reasoning or rationale to the client to explain the basis for the advice.

Silence

Both interviewer and interviewee use silence as an intervention that could move the interview ahead. Although more likely to be useful as a data-gathering intervention, silence has problem-solving potential.

We should note at the outset that silence presents a problem because of its cultural connotations. The American cultural emphasis on self-expression—speaking our mind, having our say—makes silence seem an unacceptable form of behavior. In general social interaction we feel compelled to talk even if we have nothing to say. Those who are silent are suspect and regarded as unfair for their failure to contribute to the conversation. The usual social meaning of silence is rejection. We use the "silent treatment" to punish by denying ourselves to others. We also use silence to communicate that we think so little of the other person that we will not exert ourselves even to converse.

The norms of interpersonal etiquette define silence as impolite. Silence that suggests we are boring others unnerves us. We regard silence as a manifestation of social failure. To suggest that you should never break a silence unless you have something worth saying would be regarded as un-American.

When people come together with the intent of talking to each other, silence generates social anxiety and is embarrassing. But the social worker feels a professional anxiety at the thought that continued silence signals a failing interview. It is no surprise, then, that inexperienced interviewers tend to feel uncomfortable with silences and tend to terminate them prematurely. It takes confidence for the interviewer to let a productive silence continue. It also requires that interviewers accept that a silence is not necessarily an attack on them.

Because we can think faster than we can talk, silence seems to expand time. Five seconds of silence seem considerably longer than five seconds of talk. Even silence of limited duration builds up anxiety in interview participants.

Sometimes pauses and silences are different. Pauses are regarded as a "natural rest in the melody of speech," a kind of verbal punctuation similar to a change of paragraphs. Silence, unlike a pause, is a temporary deliberate withholding of speech. Silence is a paradox in that ostensibly nothing seems to be happening. But something is happening all the time, even when the participants appear to be totally passive. Silence is a period filled with lack of speech, in which both interviewer and interviewee participate. Silence is different from being unresponsive.

Silence is a significant meaningful communication. One of the most significant sounds that requires listening is the sound of silence and the associated messages of omission. What interviewees avoid saying is as important as what they do say. Not talking is a special way of talking.

Just as speech can conceal as well as reveal, silence can reveal as well as conceal.

The words used to describe silences graphically illustrate the variety of silences. We speak of *tranquil* silence, a *pregnant* silence, an *ominous* silence, a *tense* silence, an *embarrassing* silence, a *reverent* silence, an *attentive* silence. A person can be silent out of reticence or indifference. The catalogue of silences includes the silence of rebuke and the silence of defiance. Although the act is the same in each case—refraining from talking—the meaning that each communicates is far from the same. A silence is dynamic, subject to change. What was a pregnant silence can gradually become an embarrassing silence; what was a tranquil silence can become a tense silence.

The problem for the interviewer is to decide which kind of silence the interviewee is manifesting. Interviewers need to predicate their response on some understanding of the meaning of the interviewee's behavior in maintaining the silence. The meaning of silence varies from interviewee to interviewee and may be different for the same interviewee at different points in the interview.

Interviewees' Use of Silence

Differences in social status between interviewer and interviewee in some interviews may result in silences that are culturally determined. Silence in the presence of a higher status person of some authority may be a consequence of learned patterns of respect. The admonition "Don't speak until you're spoken to" and the silence in the courtroom and church are similar expressions of respect. This might suggest that lower-income clients need more active encouragement to break their silence.

Silence can result from uncertainty about who has the responsibility for continuing the interview. Silence is a nonverbal way of jockeying for status.

The interviewee can use silence to control the situation. More effectively than words, silence can often hurt, discomfort, or create anxiety. It can be an effective form of passive aggression.

Interviewees may be silent because nothing further readily occurs to them to say about the topic. The interviewee stops to think things over, to review the content mentally, to determine whether anything else needs to be said.

Silence may be the result of normal difficulties encountered in enacting the complicated and demanding role of interviewee. Interviewees may reach a point at which it is not clear in which of a number of different directions they might want to go. This silence is an expression of indecision; it gives the client time to resolve any uncertainty.

Silence may have an organizational aim. The story is complicated, responding to the question the interviewer raised is difficult, and the interviewee is silent while trying to organize a coherent answer.

Sometimes silence permits synthesis. Having talked about material that has considerable emotional meaning, interviewees want a chance to pull themselves together. They sit in silence while sorting out their feelings, absorbing them, and asserting control over them.

Silence can be the pensive consideration of some interpretation of the dynamics of the client's behavior that the interviewee has encountered in the discussion. The interviewee needs a period of silence in which to think over its validity.

Silence provides time for assimilation. The interviewer has suggested to the client that her frequent illness may be a test of her husband's willingness to care for her. She says, "You know, I never thought of it in just that way. I'd hate to think that you just might be right. Give me a chance to think about that for a moment."

Interviewers' Use of Silence

Interviewers make deliberate use of silence to further the objectives of the interview. At the most basic level an interviewer's silence optimizes the interviewee's opportunity to talk. An interviewer's silence increases the flow of information from the interviewee. Silence from the interviewer acts as a stimulus that encourages the interviewee to continue talking. Interviewees who know and accept their role are conscious that they have the major responsibility for talking. If the interviewer refrains from talking, the interviewee feels pressure to fill the silence. In the case of some overtalkative clients we want to encourage more silence. Gentle inattention or a gentle request for the floor may induce silence.

During a period of silence the interviewer has an opportunity to observe the interviewee and any nonverbal messages without distraction.

Judicious use of silence slows the pace of the interview and gives it a more relaxed mood, a more informal atmosphere. Because silence does slow the pace, using silence may be counterproductive in an agency where time for interviews is limited. A relaxed pace eats up time.

Silence is an ambiguous intervention technique. It gives the interviewee no direction, no specification of what the interviewer wants other than that the client will continue talking. If the interviewee needs some direction, silence enhances the uncertainty. For the interviewee who is capable and desirous of taking the initiative, however, the interviewer's silence offers the freest selection of content.

Silence is like a blank screen. We can fill it in any way. It is a neutral non-verbal probe that neither designates an area for discussion nor structures what might come next.

Sometimes silence reflects interviewers' uncertainty and frustration. In retrospective review of their periods of silence interviewers said,

> I would like to say that this long period of silence was maintained because of its therapeutic, thought-provoking potential, but actually I felt frustrated because my questions weren't getting the material I thought we needed to discuss and I couldn't think of how I could get the client to discuss this.

> This silence meant that we had reached the end of a thought and both did not know what to say next. I had lost my way temporarily and did not know how to proceed. This made me feel nervous and out of control.

Ending the Silence

Because people can get lost in silence, and because too much silence is as bad as too little, the interviewer sometimes has to accept responsibility for ending the silence. Tension as a consequence of too prolonged a silence might make it difficult for the interviewee to continue. If the silence results from some uncertainty or because the interviewee has said everything that needs to be said, letting the silence continue has little point. If silence is the result of hostility, prolonging it might engender guilt; if silence is the result of resistance, prolonging it might solidify the resistance. In these instances, instead of a pregnant pause that leads to productive communication, the silence is unproductive.

The problem for the interviewer is not only to help the interviewee resume the flow of communication but also to help the client understand, if this is appropriate to the goals, what prompted the act of silence. Rather than nagging the interviewee to start talking, the interviewer can engage the client in a joint search to understand the silence.

Wolberg (1954) offers a series of graded responses to silence in psychotherapy that is equally applicable to the social work interview. When the interviewer encounters a pause appreciable enough to regard it as silence (more than five seconds), Wolberg (1954:164) suggests the following:

1. Say "mm-hmm" or "I see" and then wait for a moment.
2. Repeat and emphasize the last word or the last few words of the client.
3. Repeat and emphasize the entire last sentence or recast it as a question.
4. If repetition or recasting is unsuccessful, summarize or rephrase the client's last thoughts.
5. Say "and" or "but" with a questioning emphasis, as if something else is to follow.
6. If the client remains silent, the therapist may say, "You find it difficult to talk" or "It's hard to talk." This focuses the client's attention on the blockage.
7. In the event of no reply the interviewer may ask, "I wonder why you are silent?"
8. Thereafter the interviewer may remark, "Perhaps you do not know what to say?"
9. If the client still is silent, the interviewer might say, "Maybe you're trying to figure out what to say?"
10. This may be followed by, "Perhaps you are upset?"
11. If still no response is forthcoming, the interviewer may make a direct attack on the resistance: "Perhaps you are afraid to say what is on your mind?"
12. The interviewer's next comment might be, "Perhaps you are afraid of my reaction, if you say what is on your mind?"
13. Finally, if silence continues, the interviewer may remark, "I wonder if you are thinking about me?"
14. In the extremely rare instances in which the interviewee continues to remain mute, the worker should respect the client's silence and wait it out. Under no circumstances should the interviewer evidence anger with the client by scolding or rejecting.

The interviewer is responsible for effectively managing silence, using silences so that they contribute to achieving the purposes of the interview. Instead of seeing silence as a threat interviewers should see and use it as an opportunity. The interviewer should preserve the silence when it is appropriate and interrupt the silence sensitively when it is productive to do so.

Interviewers may use nonverbal gestures to help stimulate the interviewee to break an unproductive silence. Leaning forward, making eye contact, or smiling illustrates an expectancy and receptivity to whatever the
client might want to say.

Lawrence Shulman's studies of worker-client interaction found the
exploration of silence is a skill that is characteristic of more effective interviewers (1991:119–23).

Humor

Some researchers are giving serious consideration to the therapeutic effects of
humor and laughter. Norman Cousins, former editor of the *Saturday Review*,
gave the trend respectability with his 1979 book *Anatomy of an Illness*. The
book describes his recovery from a crippling spinal disease—a recovery that
Cousins attributes in no small measure to self-prescribed daily doses of
humor from watching the movies of Laurel and Hardy, the Marx Brothers,
and the like. Advocates of these effects, sometimes described as "ho-holistic
medicine," have succeeded in formalizing the procedure. Jane Brody, reporting in the *New York Times* in 1988, describes how the "nuns at St. Joseph's
Hospital in Houston are required to tell each patient a funny story, each day."
At Oregon Health Sciences University members of a local group wear buttons that read, "Warning: Humor May Be Hazardous to Your Illness."

Positive physiological changes are associated with a response to humor
(Martin and Dobbin 1988; Fry 1994). Laughter produces beneficial physiological effects on the respiratory, muscular, and cardiovascular systems. It
results in the release of mood-changing hormones that produce a sense of
well-being.

Some large corporations have sponsored seminars on humor in the
workplace to reduce employees' tension and stress (Collins 1988). Blau
details the use of humor by social workers to relieve job stress (1955:91–95).
Previously perceived as frivolous, humor and its therapeutic effects have
become a matter of serious consideration.

Fry and Salameh list a 306-item bibliography of relevant citations in
their *Handbook of Humor and Psychotherapy* (1987). Shaughnessy and
Wadsworth (1992) list of sixty-seven references relating to humor in counseling and psychotherapy.

The judicious use of humor can help to achieve the purposes of the interview. Humor has received little attention in social work; only a few scattered
references appear in the literature (Orfanidis 1972; Dewayne 1978; S. L.
Rhodes 1978:128; Nelsen 1975; Farrelly and Brandsma 1974; Siporin 1984;
Pollio 1995).

Humor serves a variety of significant purposes in human interaction. It permits indirect expression of irreverent and impertinent ideas. The metacommunication is "It's all a joke; don't take it seriously." The role of court jester and April Fool's Day are societal manifestations of this function of humor.

In permitting the open expression of the impermissible humor liberates the repressed. Humor provides an end-run around the superego. La Rochefoucauld said that humor "permits us to act rudely with impunity." It is sanctioned taboo breaking, a momentary liberation from everyday inhibitions. That helps explain why so many jokes are based on sex and aggression.

Humor permits the worker or client to act as though the norms of the interview interaction are temporarily suspended, and either or both can act with impunity, putting aside the usual constraints of logic, language, and conduct. Because humor gives an element of indirection to communication interviewers and interviewees can disallow something by implying, while saying it, that they do not really mean what they are saying; this makes humor a useful tactic for transitions. Either party can tentatively introduce sensitive or potentially embarrassing material through humor. If it proves too threatening, its humorous statement permits the speaker to back off, to withdraw without penalty. Thus the interviewee might use humor to challenge the authority of the interviewer. Because such an approach is anxiety provoking the use of humor permits interviewees to do so while denying that they are doing it. Humor permits us to circumvent inhibitions through ambiguity, metaphors, and symbols.

Humor promotes acceptance of the inevitable irrationality and illogic of some of life's circumstances. Humor enables us to objectify and cope with some of the absurdities of the human condition, the injustice and capriciousness of life. Humor enables us to deal with feelings that we find too painful to confront directly. Humor relieves anxiety and makes us better able to handle frightening situations by making them appear less frightening. Gallows humor is an example of this function. We joke at death when we talk about the man who, about to be executed, refused a last cigarette, saying he was trying to give up smoking. In laughing at the intractable difficulties of everyday life we transcend them. Humor thus has a cathartic effect. Proverbs 14:3 says, "In laughter the pain of the heart is eased."

One story about Freud's use of humor in dealing with tension and anxiety is probably apocryphal. The Nazis, having occupied Vienna, sent the Gestapo to interrogate Freud. Not finding him home, they searched the house. When Freud arrived, he found his wife understandably upset, as he was. "Did they take anything?," he asked his wife. "Yes," she said, "some six hundred dollars." "Why, that's more than even I get for a single visit," Freud said. And both laughed. Joking about our problems tends to make them appear less formidable.

Humor, artfully used, provides a gentle way of dissolving tension in the interview:

> A young worker with the Red Cross, assigned to a rural area hit by a tornado, felt uncomfortable about asking clients detailed questions about their background when "the whole world around them lay in ruins." The client said he was a Creole. I questioned, "Creole?" "What," he said, "you never heard of it?" I said, "No, I have led a sheltered life." This broke both of us up, and the laughing made us feel easier with each other.

A psychiatrist who has advocated the use of humor in therapy (Mindess 1976) reports an instance in which he used humor to reduce the anxiety of a new client. At the beginning of the first interview the client said with some anxiety that she had heard that therapists not only failed to help people but that some who had gone into therapy "had been destroyed." Mindess responded, "Well, you're in luck. I've already destroyed my quota for the week." The client laughed with relief at the understanding response of the therapist and at the absurdity of her statement (p. 336).

Humor can counteract anxiety. A social worker in a family service agency writes,

> Deb wanted to change her behavior but was anxious about what the changes would imply for her relationship with her husband. Reflecting this anxiety, she said at the end of one interview, "It's just my bad luck that you have been very helpful." In response I said, "Sorry, I'll make every effort to be less helpful next time we meet." We both laughed, and I thought she seemed less anxious.

A study by Falk and Hill (1992) on the use of humor in counseling found that humor is most often successfully used to release and reduce tension in the interview. Humor is also used as a device to socialize the interviewee to the tasks and procedures of a social work interview. A family agency caseworker says,

> Despite my best efforts, I could never get Mrs. A. to be specific about any of her dissatisfactions with the marriage. Her responses to my questions were always very vague, very general, very ambiguous. In desperation, I said her answers to my questions reminded me of a joke. Somebody asks their friend, "How is your spouse?" The person answers, "Compared to what?" She laughed and said she thinks she got it—I wanted to know the details. Eureka.

In explaining to a client that social workers cannot always accommodate what the client wants done the correctional social worker told of another client who had said she felt guilty and anxious whenever she hit her child. "And so you want us to help you to stop abusing your children?" the social worker said. "No," said the mother. "I want you to help me feel less anxious and less guilty when I beat them."

Clients sometimes use humor to help the interviewer obtain a clearer assessment of the situation. A high school counselor says,

> Harry, seventeen, was trying to describe his relationship with his mother. He felt that nothing he could do would really please her. He said if she gave him two ties for his birthday and he wore one, he knew she would say, "What's the matter, you don't like the other tie?" It's an old joke, but it really helped me get a picture of how Harry saw his mother.

Humor makes it easier to use problem-solving techniques effectively. An interviewer can use humor as a compassionate kind of confrontation. Formulating a confrontation in a humorous manner makes it less hurtful and easier to receptively consider.

A social worker in a community mental health center used a humorous confrontation to help a client accept some responsibility for her employment problems. Fired repeatedly, the client consistently blamed her supervisors and her colleagues for her difficulties.

> I said, "You know, Sarah, somehow, your situation reminds me of the man who never won the lottery. Complaining to God about his predicament, he said, 'I can't understand it, I pray to you regularly. I keep all of your commandments, I do everything you say I should do, but I never win the lottery.' After hearing this complaint week after week, God, either in exasperation or compassion, spoke. 'Morris,' he said, 'I hear your complaint, but do me a favor: buy a lottery ticket.'"
>
> Although we both shared a hearty laugh at this, I don't know if it made a difference. But, at least, I got my point across by confronting Sarah in a way that was more comfortable for me.

Because humor makes a point in a comical, sharply focused manner, it can help the client make sense of a situation from a novel perspective. Humor is potentially insightful. It is not a trivial distraction but can be a potent procedure for facilitating interview objectives. Levine cites such an instance:

> A forty-year-old female patient constantly complained about her unfaithful and inconsiderate husband. The marriage was a failure since she disliked her

husband, found sex with him disgusting, and generally considered his behaviour contemptible. The therapist felt moved to comment that she still chose to live with him and did not consider divorce. The patient responded that she was afraid that she would not be able to replace him and, as bad as he was, she felt that loneliness would be worse. The therapist remarked that he could understand her fears of loneliness but felt that there was another aspect of her preference for remaining married, which was suggested by the story of the man who worked in the circus cleaning up after the animals and giving enemas to constipated elephants. An old friend of his, observing the menial type of work that he was doing, offered to help him get another job. To which he replied, "What, and give up show biz?" The patient at first was indignant about this analogy but then began to laugh about it. She was able to come to grips with some of her covert motives in her complaints about her husband. She came to recognize that despite these constant complaints her marriage had some redeeming features and did satisfy some of her needs, not the least of which was the opportunity to complain and to blame others for her unsatisfied needs. (1977:133)

The joke is in the nature of an astute interpretation offered to the client for thoughtful consideration. Use of humor by the interviewer in an interpretative or confronting intervention gives the message a more benign, less threatening quality.

A psychiatric social worker in a mental health clinic says,

I was once delighted by a reaction I got to one of my very infrequent attempts to use humor in an interview. Ruth was a young college student who turned every victory into defeat. If she got an A in a course, she was depressed because it was not an A plus; when she got the best part in a play, she was depressed because, while it was the best part, it wasn't the best play. Every effort to help focus on the positive aspects was rejected. In desperation, I told Ruth that she reminded me of a story I had heard about a kid who lost a quarter in the street. A passerby, seeing him crying and finding out the reason, gave him a quarter to replace the lost quarter. At first the kid brightened up but then burst into tears again. When the man, in surprise, asked him what was the matter now, the kid said, through his tears, "If I hadn't lost the first quarter, I would have fifty cents now." Neither one of us laughed, but Ruth looked thoughtful and there was a long silence. In the next interview Ruth was somewhat more ready to consider positives.

Incongruity often provokes laughter. Playfully violating habitual patterns of thought, a joke has an element of insightfulness because it puts two ideas together that generally do not go together.

There is an analogy between humor and insight. In both instances we see, as William James noted, "the familiar as strange and the strange as if it were familiar." The mind makes a sudden transposition of two ideas previously unrecognized as perhaps being related. Both humor and insight may occur in a sudden shifting of mental gears. Humor, like poetry, makes us see the familiar differently. In using humor to further insight we are going from "ha ha" to "ah ha." Humor, like insight, presents an element of incongruity that induces a cognitive disequilibrium that the person has to resolve. Humor, like insight, often involves the condensation of two seemingly incongruous elements into a meaningful hybrid. It enables us to see the logic in the illogical, the possible in the impossible. Discovery of a relationship when we least expect it creates laughter and, like insight, involves a recognition of a connection not previously perceived. It stimulates cognitive reframing.

The resolution of incongruities, the basic source of humor in a good joke, is similar to the cognitive process involved in clarification and insight. Both involve a reorganization and restructuring of the perceptual field, permitting a corrective cognitive experience. Humor may involve the reconciliation of seemingly incompatible ideas in an unexpected manner:

> The rich Texan bought his nephew two golf clubs, but one had only nine holes.
> A medium asked me if I wanted my palm read, and when I said yes, she painted it red.

The comments simultaneously occupy more than one frame of reference. They communicate simultaneous multiple layers of meaning.

Because humor tends to make incongruous ideas congruous, it tends to break up routine patterns of thinking and aids in problem solving. Consequently, the interviewer might use humor to stimulate clarification.

A variety of humor is a central ingredient in some psychotherapeutic programs in which therapists exaggerate clients' problems and applaud their dysfunctional behavior (Farrelly and Brandsma 1974). The purpose is to make clients see their behavior as paradoxical and absurd. Ridicule, sarcasm, and irony are among the principal interventions in such therapy. In exaggerated overemphasis of the worst aspects of the client's situation the interviewer forces the interviewee to make explicit and define some of the positive aspects (Farrelly and Matthews 1981).

The interviewer might say,

> With all the trouble your parents are giving you, I am surprised you haven't run away from home.

I am not sure I understand why you fail only these two courses. Wouldn't it be easier to fail all of them and drop out of school altogether

Humor is used to exaggerate a condition so that its dysfunction is graphically apparent. To a client who was apologetic and self-effacing the interviewer at one point said, "Sometimes you remind me of a man who got on the up elevator and said to a man who got on along with him, 'I am going up. I hope it's not out of your way.'" There is an important caveat associated with this approach. As Farrelly and Lynch note, "For provocative therapy to be successful, the client must experience the therapist as warmly caring and essentially supportive" (1987:90).

Interviewers may also use humor to provide information to clients. An informational message encapsulated in a humorous aphorism or anecdote is likely to have a greater influence and be remembered longer than if merely didactically stated.

A worker in a child guidance program says,

> I have had misgivings about the use of humor in my work, but I did have real success when I once chanced it. My client was complaining about the fact that her son distorted everything she told him. I was trying to get across the point that what we say is often not what children hear. So I told my client about a mother who was trying to teach her kid the danger of disobedience. She said that against instructions, a neighbor's child went out sledding one day without his coat, caught pneumonia, and died. Hearing the story, the kid, after a pause, asked, "Where's the sled?"

Laughing together tends to increase the sense of solidarity in the interview. It heightens the sense of being involved in a small social system that is special and unique, the sense of "we" as contrasted with "them." Humor here has the effect of being supportive.

Megdell tested the effect of counselor-initiated humor on the client's perception of the counseling interaction. He found that "client's attraction ratings to counselor significantly tended to increase both in frequency and magnitude when the counselor initiated humor which the client perceived and rated as humorous. . . . These results indicate that shared humor may be a viable intervention facilitating a more positive counselor-client relationship" (1984:522).

The use of humor tends to reduce social-psychological distance and formality. Joint appreciation of the joke solidifies a sense of common membership in the human race. A psychiatrist tells a client about a postcard he had received from another psychiatrist on vacation: "Having a wonderful time. I wonder why?" The psychiatrist seems more humanly accessible as a consequence. Humor, like self-disclosure, increases the sense of intimacy between interviewer and interviewee. Self-deprecating humor from interviewers makes them appear less formidable and more accessible.

As Victor Borge says, "Laughter is the shortest distance between two people." Humor is an equalizer. It deflates pomposity. Workers' capacity to laugh at themselves without embarrassment or shame communicates genuineness in the relationship. It introduces a desirable element of informality and spontaneity into an essentially formal encounter.

A social worker in a family service agency says,

> I recognize that the best use of humor in clinical situations comes spontaneously out of the interaction. However, I once used a canned incident very effectively as a self-disclosing ploy. My client had suffered a series of personal setbacks that reinforced his feelings of being a loser and a failure. I was recapitulating some of his successes and trying to mitigate the effects of his setbacks by noting that failures are ubiquitous and inevitable and need to be seen in perspective. What about you, he said, did you ever fail? "Sure," I said. "When?" he challenged. I then told him of a client who had a recurrent fantasy that there was a threatening somebody underneath his bed. He had to get up several times a night to reassure himself that nobody was there. Despite my best efforts over weeks of contact, I was unable to help him resolve this. On the eighth visit he came in beaming triumphantly and said, "You couldn't help, but my wife solved the problem." How? "She cut off the legs of the bed." The client and I laughed together in our joint alliance in failure.

Humor tends to intensify group identification, making people feel closer to each other. Much humor is concerned with disparagement of out-group members by in-group members, making in-groupers feel better about themselves. Ethnic humor has an element of this. Disparagement of self and particularly of others is a frequent cause of laughter. In both cases the disparagement is an expression of hostility and aggression made socially acceptable in some quarters through its expression in humor. On the other hand, self-denigrating humor may be used as a weapon of appeasement or ingratiation.

Caveats Regarding Use of Humor

Because humor comes in all shapes, sizes, and colors, and has different effects on different people we need to use it with considerable caution (Kubie 1971). What seems funny to one person may be mockery to another.

The insensitive use of humor can communicate contempt. It can be antitherapeutic and potentially destructive. Consequently, we must be especially careful with some groups of clients, such as those who are paranoid or obsessive. In addition, jokes that disparage any group are obviously offensive and should be avoided.

The need for caution is particularly acute in the social work interview. Because clients are seeing us because they have a problem, the situation is inherently not funny. No matter how bad a problem is, it generally is worse for the person who has it, so that the client is least inclined to see any humor in the situation. The joking interviewer may appear to be insensitive and unfeeling.

Humor should never be used at the expense of the client. Laughing *with* a client is very different from laughing *at* the client. Goodman suggests "going for the jocular rather than the jugular" (1983:11).

Interviewers who maintain their "superior" position through the use of supposedly humorous sarcasm are using humor inappropriately. But every intervention can be abusive in the hands of a punitive interviewer, and humor is no exception.

Because humor can inadvertently have the effect of belittling or trivializing the interviewee and/or the problem and has the potential for being hurtful and disrespectful, we tend to avoid its use. But if treated with caution, used appropriately with the intention of helping, humor has value in achieving the objectives of the interview.

Because the effects of humor are difficult to predict the interviewer is on safer ground in responding to humor introduced by the client than in initiating a humorous intervention. A female social worker helping a woman on AFDC with difficulties in budgeting says,

> One of the things Mrs. W. said early in the interview helped increase our sense of rapport with each other. She said she keeps struggling with the budget, and it seems to her that it's like trying to help elephants have intercourse. She just can't seem to get on top of things. The picture this spontaneously seemed to invoke in both our minds had us laughing together uproariously.

Dosage, timing, sensitivity, and good taste with regard to humor, as with all other aspects of the interview, are important considerations. Dosage has been likened to yeast in bread—an appropriate amount leavens the bread; too much yeast spoils it. The best use of humor comes in a sensitive response to the immediate situation and reflects the needs of the situation. The interviewer needs to be aware of the possibilities of humor in the situation and blessed with a sufficiently spontaneous sense of humor.

Humor in the interview is most effectual if it is a spontaneous response to the needs of the moment. However, a joke, an anecdote, or a wisecrack that the worker brings to the interview can have a similarly positive effect if artfully used to appropriately meet the needs of the moment. Planned spontaneity has value. The interviewer might have a repertoire of humorous remarks or anecdotes to use when appropriate.

Clients might regard interviewers who use humor as frivolous or insensitive. Worse, they might regard the interviewer as unprofessional—the deadliest of sins. Yet laughter contributes to the objectives of the interview by highlighting contradictions and challenging sacred ideas and feelings so that they become approachable and discussable. Humor makes the unbearable bearable.

Humor is a social lubricant, a safety valve, a liberator, a shock absorber.

In summarizing the benefits of using humor in therapeutic interviews Rosenheim and Golan found that the "major merits elucidated were enabling emotional catharsis, alleviating anxiety and tension, overcoming excessive earnestness, creating an atmosphere of closeness and equality, developing a sense of realistic proportions, exposing the absurdity of stereotypes, increasing flexibility and confronting hidden emotional processes" (1986:111).

The very nature of humor makes it difficult to discuss abstractly. Context and timing are most important. All we can do here is to raise your consciousness about the contributions humor might make to a good interview and to encourage its sensitive use as an acceptable and appropriate interview procedure (see box 8.2).

Box 8.2 Using Humor in the Interview

VALUES OF HUMOR

1. Humor helps to establish and maintain positive relationships.
2. Interviewers can use humor to stimulate clients' insight.
3. Humor reduces the negative aspects of confrontation.
4. Humor increases egalitarian feelings among interview participants.
5. Humor helps us recognize that we all face common problems.
6. Humor reduces feelings of frustration, anxiety, stress, and defensiveness.
7. Humor permits the acceptable release of hostility.
8. Humor helps interviewees to accept that which is difficult.
9. Humor helps reduce the discomforting aspects of the formal interview.
10. Humor helps clients to learn the information offered in the interview.
11. Humor reduces inhibitions about disclosing sensitive material.

Problems in the Use of Humor

1. Humor may tend to trivialize content that should be approached seriously.
2. Clients may use humor to avoid difficult content.
3. Humor may tend to equalize the relationship, eroding the authority and leadership of the interviewer.
4. The interviewer's humor may appear to the interviewee to be disparaging or ridiculing.

Figures of Speech

Using appropriate figures of speech has some value similar to that of humor. The figure of speech presents the situation in a way that prompts a shift in perspective, furthering understanding. A simile compares two different things on the basis of some underlying aspect(s) that unites them. Similes include "he is as unmovable as a mountain"; the solution to the problem fits like a glove"; and "the organization is like a good mother." Metaphors "capture complex themes in concise and memorable ways . . . highlighting briefly and graphically the essence" of some significant interview content (Cirello and Crider 1995:511). Metaphor enables us to express one thing in terms of the other: the unity of the two presents a third perception of the situation. Metaphors also enable us to express abstract concepts through some concrete representation so that they can be more readily perceived. Metaphors include "He put me in the basement of his mind"; "It's a real family earthquake when Bob acts up"; "His mother was an albatross"; and "She has a grasshopper mind." Figures of speech give us another way in which to present information or frame an intervention.

Environmental Modification

Environmental modification—changing the circumstances of the client by providing such concrete resources and services as public assistance, access to health care, and subsidized housing—is a unique aspect of the social work helping process. Social workers can provide, mobilize, and facilitate access to such services as foster homes, residential treatment centers, day care, nursing homes, adoption services, homemaker and respite services, and the like. Social work interviewers have, or should have as part of their responsibility, knowledge of entitlement programs such as Aid to Families with Dependent Children; Supplementary Security Income; food stamps; Old Age, Survivors and Disability Insurance; Medicaid; earned income credit; job training programs; and housing facilities.

The intervention phase of the interview includes providing information about such programs, referring clients to and preparing them to use such resources and expediting their access to such resources and programs.

Environmental modification often involves other agencies that provide specialized resources or specific entitlements. The interviewer might steer or refer the interviewee to such agencies. Referring, rather than simple steering, is more effective. Unlike steering, referring involves a formal contact by the interviewer with someone at the associated agency, an introduction of the client to a contact person at that agency, some preparation for what the interviewee might encounter at the agency, and simple directions for finding the agency.

Empirical Studies of Interventions Used

Now that we have reviewed the variety of interventions that social workers might use in the interview, what does the research show about what workers actually do?

In their review of psychotherapy research Orlinsky, Grawe, and Parks identify confrontation, interpretation, reflection, clarification, and self-disclosure as among the techniques that therapists use frequently (1994:302–307, 358–59).

Reviewing the social work training programs concerned with interpersonal skills, Dickson and Bramford note, "There is no single commonly recognized anthology of interpersonal skills for social work. Those that have been included in programs of training have seldom been identified by empirical means" (1995:96). Specific skills identified in reviewing such programs include verbal attending, questioning, reflecting feeling, listening, and nonverbal communication.

Hollis (1967) developed a systematic categorization of the activities of the social work interviewer. She applied the system in her research on what social workers do in the interview, and other social work researchers have used modifications of her system in their examination of social work interviews (Mullen 1969; Reid and Shyne 1969; Cohen and Krause 1971; Sherman et al. 1973; Reid 1978; Fortune 1979; Rosen and Mutschler 1982). Other social work researchers have used alternative systems of categorization in studying what workers do when interviewing (L. Shulman 1977).

Although the definitions of interventions are not standard, some general overall agreement exists regarding the frequency with which social workers use various interventions.

The findings of such research tend to be diverse. In general, however, the workers are found to be involved, with varying degrees of frequency, in four different kinds of activity. They say and do things to *explore* the client's situation, to learn about the nature of the problem. They say or do things to *structure* the interview situation in clarifying the role of interviewer and interviewee. They say and do things in providing emotional *support* to the client, reassuring, encouraging, sympathizing, showing concern, understanding, and acceptance, and they say and do things designed to *effect some change* in the client's perception of the situation, some change in the client's attitudes, feeling, and behavior. In doing this they offer advice and suggestions, provide information, raise questions, make comments that encourage selective reflection, and engage in clarification, interpretation, and confrontation. Thus social work classifies interventions as exploratory, supportive, structuring, directive, or reflective.

The interventions frequently used by social workers include exploring the client's situation (obtaining information from the client about the problem and giving information to the client about resources and services) and supportive expressions of reassurance, understanding, encouragement, or sympathy with regard to the clients' situation and their efforts to cope with their problems (Sherman et al. 1973:259; Grinnell and Kyte 1975:315; Jones, Neuman, and Shyne 1976:68). Although providing information to the social worker may have therapeutic, cathartic, and reassuring implications for the client, the worker's primary purpose in using an intervention is to gain information rather than effect change in the client's behavior or attitude.

Directive interventions, during which the worker attempts through advice, recommendations or suggestions to promote or discourage particular client behaviors and courses of action, are frequently used in social work interviews (Sherman et al. 1973:59, 138; Jones, Neuman, and Shyne 1976:68).

Social workers less often use reflective interventions during which the "worker raises questions or gives explanation to increase the client's understanding of his own behavior attitudes, of his situation, the consequences of his behavior and the reactions of others to him." These include confrontation and interpretation.

Fortune (1981) reviewed and organized the findings of nine different research projects that by 1981 had attempted to use interventionist typologies to explicitly identify what social work interviewers do when they interact with the client in the interview. The summary of findings suggests a somewhat different picture of the worker's activity than that outlined earlier.

Combining the research results of the various projects, Fortune found that the worker's principal communications by far are concerned with exploring with clients their situation and their behavior and attitudes regarding it (40 percent overall) and with communication designed to help clients understand the causes and consequences of their behavior (38 percent overall). Social workers give little emphasis to exploring data about early life development. Social workers give somewhat more emphasis (6.4 percent overall) to direct influence—suggestions, advice, and recommendations designed to influence clients' decisions and behaviors in a specific direction.

The difference in frequency found by different studies for particular interviewer interventions may be related to when in the relationship the interview took place. The balance of intervention in the first or second interview is likely to be considerably different from the balance of intervention in the fifteenth or sixteenth interview.

You might envision a sliding scale that reflects a change in the nature of interventions used during a sequence of interviews. At the beginning of the contact the interviewer places more emphasis on interventions that are supportive and accepting, that express concern and a willingness to help. Intervention at this point follows rather than leads the client and uses the client's frame of reference. These interventions include reflection, paraphrasing, and minimal encouragements.

As a relationship develops, the emphasis on the sliding scale gradually shifts more to leading rather than following actions by the interviewer. These include more active interventions designed to effect change, such as more frequent challenges to the client's frame of reference. The emphasis shifts from activity concerned with establishing a relationship and learning about the client's situation to a problem-solving orientation while still being supportive, accepting, respectful, and empathic. The interviewer places more emphasis on interventions designed to help interviewees progress from where they are to where they want to be in reference to their problem. Interviewers more actively use advice, suggestion, interpretation, and confrontation.

The same shift might take place in an attenuated form within a single interview. At the acceptance end of the sliding scale is the early part of the interview, which emphasizes communication of the core facilitative conditions and those interventions designed to help interviewees share their problems. As the interviewer confirms for clients that this is a psychologically safe, understanding, and respectful context, and as the interviewer develops a clearer picture of the problem, the interview shifts toward the directive end of the scale. The shift is toward the interviewer's more active involvement in problem-solving and helping interventions directed at influencing changes in feelings and behaviors. At this point the interviewer may sound less accepting and more judgmental. If early in the contact clients are free to be themselves, now interviewers need to be challenging so that change will occur. If early in the interview interviewers need to communicate a willingness to help, in the later part of the interview they must demonstrate a competence in actually being helpful.

Summary: Chapters 7 and 8

Social workers must master and use a number of skills to help clients achieve the problem-solving objectives of the interview.

The objective of clarification is to bring otherwise vague communication into focus. Clarifying increases specificity. Clarification increases the interviewer's and client's understanding of the problem.

Interpretation goes beyond paraphrasing, clarifying, and reflecting. Paraphrasing, clarifying, and reflecting maintain the frame of reference of the interviewee; interpretation offers a new frame of reference to the client for consideration. Clarification, paraphrasing, and reflection are close to the message presented by the client. Interpretation takes off from the message and includes an inference derived from it, one added by the interviewer. Interviewers should offer interpretations only after they and their client have established a positive relationship and workers have gathered sufficient information to support the validity of the interpretation.

Confrontation addresses incongruities in the client's thinking, behavior, and/or feelings. Confrontation tends to disrupt habits of thinking that permit discrepancies to exist. Confrontation presents interviewees with a contradiction and invites them to resolve it. Like interpretations, confrontations should occur only in the context of a relationship after sufficient information has been gathered to establish the validity of using confrontation. An interviewer should use confrontation sparingly to achieve the objectives of the interview and in a spirit of understanding.

Self-disclosure is a social act in which the interviewer intentionally and voluntarily shares personal information. Interviewers may use self-disclosure to help a client communicate, provoke a catharsis for the client, demonstrate that the worker is capable of understanding the situation because of having "been there," relieve tension through sharing feelings that are obstructing the interview, and demonstrate problem solving and open communication. However, unless the worker pays attention to timing, appropriateness, and relevance, self-disclosure may impede rather than facilitate problem solving.

Sharing information has the effect of enhancing a client's problem-solving ability and reducing anxiety based on misinformation. Information that is shared should be factual, relevant, offered in digestible doses, pitched to the education and vocabulary level of the client, consistent with the client's culture, and reinforced with written material.

Interviewers may demonstrate support through overt expressions, both verbal and nonverbal, of understanding, reassurance, concern, sympathy, and encouragement. Such interventions signal active approval of the client's qualities and achievement. Support reduces anxiety, shame, and guilt, which divert energy from dealing directly with the problem under consideration.

Advice can be defined as a noncoercive recommendation for some decision or course of action based on professional knowledge. Advice can vary in the degree of directiveness and also in the degree of explicitness. The worker should ground advice in the knowledge base of the profession, consider clients' context, offer advice tentatively and in conjunction with other interventions such as support, and wait until clients have explored their own suggestions. Workers should offer advice only in the context of a good relationship and at the request of the client.

Interviewers may use silence as a data-gathering and problem-solving intervention. Silence in the interview may have several meanings. It may result from differences in status, uncertainty about how to enact the role of interviewee, the need to sort out feelings, think over a problem, or frustrate or control the interviewer; Silence may also represent a defense against anxiety. Interviewers use silence to encourage the interviewee to keep talking. In ending a silence interviewers should engage interviewees in a joint search to understand the silence.

Interviewers use humor to address painful feelings, dissolve tension, socialize the interviewee to the tasks of the interview, and provide educational information. They may also use humor to formulate a confrontation, interpretation, or clarification. The use of humor also tends to reduce social-psychological distance and formality between interviewee and interviewee. However, in using humor in the interview the worker should consider dosage, timing, sensitivity, and good taste. Figures of speech share some qualities with humor. By comparing two different things on the basis of some underlying aspect that unites them, a simile prompts a shift in perspective and therefore furthers understanding.

Environmental modification—changing the client's circumstances by providing concrete resources—is a unique aspect of the social work helping process. By providing information about programs and services social workers facilitate access to a range of resources.

Empirical studies of the variety of interventions that social workers actu-

ally use suggest that their repertoire changes during a sequence of interviews. At the beginning social workers use more interventions that are supportive and accepting, such as reflection, paraphrasing, and minimal
encouragement. As a relationship develops, they use more active problem-
solving interventions designed to effect change, such as advice, suggestion,
interpretation, and confrontation. Within the frame of a single interview
the same shift might occur in an attenuated form.

SUGGESTED READINGS

Self-Disclosure

Myron F. Weiner. *Therapist Disclosure: The Use of Self in Psychotherapy.* Boston:
   Butterworth, 1978. (175 pp.)
   An engaging presentation of the implications of self-disclosure for the interviewer.
   The author, a psychiatrist, shares his doubts and problems.
George Stricker and Martin Fisher, eds. *Self-Disclosure in the Therapeutic Relationship.*
   New York: Plenum, 1990. (295 pp.)

Humor

Thomas L. Kuhlman. *Humor and Psychotherapy.* Homewood, Ill.: Dow Jones, Irwin,
   1984. (129 pp.)
   The values and dangers of the use of humor in psychotherapy.
William F. Fry and Walred A. Salameh, eds. *Handbook of Humor and Psychotherapy:
   Advances in the Clinical Use of Humor.* Sarasota, Fla.: Professional Resource
   Exchange, 1987. (355 pp.)
William F. Fry and Walred A. Salameh, eds. *Advances in Humor and Psychotherapy.*
   Sarasota, Fla.: Professional Resource Exchange, 1993. (295 pp.)
   Fry and Salameh, the editors of both volumes, have collected articles that demon-
   strate the relevance of humor to psychotherapy.
Herbert Stream, ed. *The Use of Humor in Psychotherapy.* Northvale, N.J.: Jason Aronson,
   1994. (232 pp.)
   A collection of articles with a somewhat psychoanalytic orientation.

NINE

Developmental Phase:
Questions and Questioning Techniques

Asking questions is a multipurpose intervention. Interviewers use questions to extend the range and depth of the interview, to help in problem solving, and to make transitions. Questions stimulate and energize the interviewee to share both factual and affective information. Questions instigate exploration of different areas and different levels of emotionality.

Interviewers use questions to encourage interviewees to tell their story. Once interviewees start their presentation, interviewers use questions to encourage clients to elaborate on what they are saying. Good questioning helps interviewees to organize their presentation and ensures that they include all the relevant material.

Interviewers also use questions to stimulate problem-solving thinking and feeling. Questions help interviewees think about their situation in an explicit and systematic way. Questions designed to clarify the situation for the interviewer also clarify the situation for the interviewee.

Questions encourage the interviewee to consider alternatives. Questions solicit and obtain feedback from the interviewee. They help to structure the interview and help interviewees to be systematic in their presentation.

Questions have a latent training function. They model for the interviewee the interviewer's approach to problems. For instance, a series of questions that directs clients' attention to how they reacted to a particular situation, what they thought about dealing with it, and how they finally decided what action to take implies that their behavior was not haphazard or accidental, that people's behavior is purposive. Interviewers base the sequence of the questions on their presumption, implicitly communicated by their questions, that reasons exist to explain people's behavior.

Questions serve to socialize an interviewees to the requirements of their role. A question asked about some content communicates the significance of the material. If the interviewer elects to ask about it, it must have some importance. Questions that focus on feelings signal the interviewee that this is a matter of relevance to social work interviews. A question that follows up on what the interviewee is saying by requesting further information shows that the client is on the right track. Questions from the interviewer are an implicit guide to the interviewee, offering instruction regarding the appropriate content of social work interviews.

Questions may be directed at exploration, understanding, or problem solving (see box 9.1). In the sequential process of the interview, questions focused on exploration precede those focused on understanding, which in turn precede those concerned with problem solving. Thus when an interviewer asks early in the interview, "Can you tell me more about it?," the worker is focusing on exploration. Somewhat later, as the interviewer is seeking to understand the information, the worker may ask, "What sense do you make of the way you are reacting to the problem?" Following this, problem-solving questions are appropriate: "What do you think can be done about this?" or "How do you think we can be of help?"

Box 9.1 The Purpose of Questioning

Questions are flexible instruments that serve a variety of purposes in the interview. We ask questions to

1. Obtain information.
2. Check the validity of information.
3. Assess the interviewee's knowledge about and familiarity with the situation.
4. Focus attention on some aspect of the interviewee's situation and to structure the direction of the interview.
5. Encourage and stimulate an interviewee's more active participation in the interview.
6. Encourage the interviewee's consideration of some alternatives.
7. Encourage client's feedback.
8. Act as an icebreaker—to get the interview rolling.
9. Communicate and solicit agreement on a value or point of view: "Doesn't it seem clear that unless the two of you start communicating with each other, you're not going to be able to resolve your marital disagreements?"

10. Influence: "Can we both agree about that?"; "Will you two think about that till our next meeting?"; "Does that make sense to you?"
11. Help organize and systematize the client's presentation. Questions help clients to recall relevant material.
12. Confirm or disconfirm an assessment hypothesis.

General Classifications:
Open and Closed Questions

We can classify questions in a number of ways. One is according to the amount of freedom or restriction the question offers the interviewee. By focusing on specific aspects of the situation the closed question restricts the scope of the answer. Open questions provide the interviewer with greater freedom and less restriction.

Note that questions are not either open or closed. A continuum of degrees of freedom exists between wide open questions such as "What brings you here" to closed questions such as "Do you have any children?" Questions also are open ended, moderately closed, or tightly closed.

"What brings you to the agency?"; "What would you like to talk about?"; "Where would you like to begin?"; and "What seems to be bothering you?" are all relatively open-ended questions. "What seems to be bothering you about the children?"; "What seems to be bothering you about what the doctor told you?"; and "What seems to be bothering you about school?" are all more restricting questions that define the frame of reference for the content of the response.

"What would you like to talk about?"and "Where would you like to begin?" are the most neutral nondirective openings. "Could you tell me something about your problem?" directs the client's attention and focuses on the word *problem*. "Could you tell me how you think we can be of help?" directs clients' attention to what they want from the agency. The latter two questions are more restrictive than the first two.

The following series of questions moves from an open to a progressively more closed format. The setting is a child guidance or family service interview:

Before this happened, what was your life like?
What was your life like as a child?
When you were a child, how did you get along with your family?
When you were a child, how did you get along with your parents?
When you were a child, how did you get along with your mother?

When you were a child and you did something wrong, what did your mother do in disciplining you?

When you were a child and you got into fights with your brothers and sisters, how did your mother handle it?

When you were a child and you got into fights with your brothers and sisters, how did you feel about the way your mother handled the situation?

Each question successively narrows the area of interviewees' experience to which the interviewer is directing their attention. The first question is open to any period before the event that brought the client to the agency. The second question restricts the scope temporarily to childhood but permits the interviewee to select for discussion any sector of the childhood experience—relationship with parents, siblings, peers; school experience; leisure time activities; attitude toward the community; economic situation; and so on. The final questions direct attention to one particular relationship during one time period—the mother-child relationship during childhood in a specific context, such as disciplining in response to sibling conflict. The final questions solicit a scope of answers narrower than that permitted by the first questions. The next to last question calls for an objective description of the client's mother's handling of the situation. The last question calls for a subjective emotional response to the same situation.

The phrasing of open-ended questions calls attention to the cognitive aspects of the interviewee's experience ("What do you think about . . . ?"), to the affective aspects ("What do you feel about . . . ?"), or to the experiential aspects ("Could you describe for me what happened . . . ?").

Open-ended questions have advantages and disadvantages. Although appropriate in some situations, they are clearly inappropriate in others.

Advantages of Open-Ended Questions

Open questions have the advantage of giving the interviewee a measure of control over the interview. The interviewer invites the client to talk about some broad area of concern and suggests interest in anything the interviewee may select to say about this.

Such questions permit the interviewee greater discretion and thus permit the interviewee to introduce significant material that interviewers may not have thought to ask about. Interviewers may as a consequence learn more of pertinence about the interviewee's situation than if they had asked a series of more closed questions. Interviewers who fail to ask such questions may miss much of interest and concern to the client because the client did not raise pertinent matters and had no autonomous opportunity to introduce them.

The open question allows interviewees to select their answer. An open question gives interviewees an opportunity to reveal their subjective frame of reference and select those elements in the situation that they regard as of greatest concern. Open-ended nondirective questions also communicate clearly that the interviewee has considerable responsibility for and freedom in participating in the interview and determining interview content and direction.

Open-ended questions permit interviewees to select for early discussion the matters of greatest concern to them. If these matters are not raised early in the interview, interviewees' strong unexpressed concerns interfere with their ability to focus on questions raised by the interviewer.

Open-ended questions are more likely than closed questions to provide information about interviewees' feelings and intensity of feelings and are more likely to provide information about interviewees' explanation of their attitudes and behavior.

Open-ended questions have a positive effect on clients' feelings about an interview. Interviewees are gratified when they have a greater measure of freedom to tell their story in their own way. They respond warmly to the implication that they are capable of adequately exploring their situation. Such questions further communicate a respect for the individuality and uniqueness of the interviewee. A standardized series of questions tends to suggest uniformity in the problems people face. Open-ended questions imply that this interviewee and problem are somewhat unique.

Open-ended questions permit a greater degree of catharsis than close-ended questions, providing a greater element of support and relief.

Open-ended questions generate an atmosphere of greater mutuality in the interview interaction. By contrast, a series of closed questions evokes a feeling that the interviewee's role is that of passive supplier of answers.

Because interviewees often respond to closed questions with limited information such questions impose a heavy burden on the interviewer. Interviewers who ask closed questions have to be constantly formulating the next question. Open-ended questions shift the burden of activity to the interviewee.

Disadvantages of Open-Ended Questions

Open-ended questions have a high component of ambiguity. Interviewers are deliberately vague about the answer they are trying to elicit. Ambiguity encourages interviewees to be verbally productive. At the same time the interviewee who has a limited tolerance for ambiguity may find open-ended questions puzzling.

Box 9.2 The Open-Ended Question

ADVANTAGES

1. Takes advantage of the fact that interviewee is the participant who has the most detailed knowledge about the situation.
2. Maximizes clients' freedom regarding choice of content to disclose.
3. Maximizes clients' participation.

4. Provides the interviewee's cognitive and affective view of the problem.

5. Increases the likelihood that the interview will proceed from the client's frame of reference.

6. Demonstrates the interviewer's respect for autonomy and competence of the interviewee.
7. Allows the interviewer to observe what interviewees select to share, what content they give priority, and how they organize the content in communicating it.
8. Requires the interviewee to provide elaboration in responding.

DISADVANTAGES

1. Provides inefficient access to data, particularly when the interviewee is rambling, disorganized, and garrulous.

2. Risks failure to obtain specific detailed content.

3. Presents difficulty for interviewees who need structure and assistance in telling their story.

4. Presents a more difficult format for inexperienced interviewers, who have to share control with interviewee.

5. Are difficult for the interviewee because they require a memory search, retrieval, and organization of response. Closed questions merely require recognition and response.

Open-ended questions are threatening to the interviewee who has little experience and/or competence in the role of interviewee. For such interviewees open-ended questions provide little structure, little guidance for what they supposed to talk about and how they are supposed to talk about it. They may be embarrassed because they do not know how to organize their presentation and find they have little to say.

If the interviewee responds to an open-ended nondirective question with a detailed account of some relevant aspect of the situation, the interviewer has no problem. However, a client might respond to a beginning questions such as "Could you tell me about the situation that brings you to the agency?" by saying, "Well, I really don't know where to begin." The interviewer then faces the problem of helping the interviewee to tell the story. Such situations require a more specific general question, such as "What has been troubling you recently?" or "What made you decide to come here?"

One client responded to the open-ended question "Would you like to tell me something about your situation" by asking for clarification: "What would you like to know?" Moderately broad closed questions may help such a client to focus, to recall relevant material, and to structure the presentation.

Open questions may be less desirable in time-limited interviews, with talkative interviewees, or with the resistant nervous interviewee. See box 9.2 for a list of the advantages and disadvantages of open-ended questions.

Closed Questions

Interviewers use open questions to open up some new, hitherto undiscussed, aspect of the situation. They use closed questions when they have obtained a good deal of information but some details are missing.

Closed questions are appropriate when the interviewee is uncertain about how to proceed, the situation appears confusing, and the interviewer needs specific information. Closed questions can help the reticent interviewee get started and develop some momentum.

Closed questions are appropriate for providing greater clarity and focus to the interview. The interviewer uses the closed question at some point to exercise greater control of content. The closed question helps narrow the scope of the interview and limits the introduction of extraneous and irrelevant content.

Interviewers may use a series of closed questions to slow down the interaction and reduce the degree of emotionality of an interviewee who is displaying an intensity of feeling that might create problems for achieving the purposes of the interview. Closed questions help "cool" interviewees who are too open too early, sharing content they may later resent having shared.

On the other hand, interviewers sometimes use closed questions to introduce a sensitive topic that the client may be hesitant to mention in response to open-ended questions.

Closed questions provide cues that stimulate the memory to retrieve information. Open questions require clients to retrieve information but do not offer much guidance.

Box 9.3 The Closed Question

ADVANTAGES	DISADVANTAGES
1. Helps clients to complete and clarify vague, diffuse, contradictory, superficial, or inappropriate responses.	1. Leads to short answers because clients can answer satisfactorily with a brief response, often yes or no.
2. Elicits precise explicit details of the interviewee's situation.	2. Provides interviewees with little opportunity to volunteer potentially significant information.
3. Helps initiate participation of reticent, unexpressive, non-verbal, or laconic interviewees.	3. Encourages passive restricted participation on part of interviewee.
4. Helps motivate reluctant or resisting interviewees to participate.	
5. Helps to elicit content that the client may have forgotten and/or is hesitant to share.	
6. Provides more efficient access to content when time is limited.	
7. Provides inexperienced interviewers with an easier format.	
8. Helps interviewers regain control of the interview from a rambling and talkative interviewee.	

An interviewer with limited time may deliberately opt for closed questions. Open questions may be time consuming in that much of the client's response may have limited relevance.

As is true of most interview techniques, the different kinds of questions are not good or bad. They are merely appropriate or inappropriate at different stages or with different kinds of interviewees.

Open questions are generally more appropriate in the early part of an interview. At this point the interviewee knows everything about the situation and the interviewer knows nothing, so the interviewer should extend maximum freedom to the client.

After using broad open questions to help interviewees say what they want and need to communicate, the interviewer can use more restricted closed questions to fill in details. Even later in the interview it is best to start with an open-ended question when a new subject area is introduced.

The interview as a totality may resemble a funnel, beginning with more frequent open-ended questions, ending with more detailed closed questions. But within the interview may be a series of smaller funnels, as the interviewer introduces each new area with open-ended questions and follows up with increasingly more narrow questions.

The appropriateness of open or closed questions varies with the interviewee. Open questions may be appropriate with sophisticated interviewees who have a clear grasp of their role and the capacity to implement it. They need little direction from the interviewer. Open questions impose heavy demands on the interviewee to organize responses, demands that experienced interviewees can meet. See box 9.3 for the advantages and disadvantages of using closed questions.

Other Dimensions

We can further classify questions in terms of *responsibility*. Direct questions ask about interviewees' response to a situation, a response for which they take responsibility. Indirect questions solicit a response for which responsibility is ambiguous. The following questions are first asked directly, then indirectly:

How do you feel about your job?
What's the feeling in your unit about the job?
What's your feeling about applying for assistance?
How do you think most people feel about applying for assistance?

The *level of abstraction* is another way to differentiate questions. A question such as "What hobbies do you have?" is somewhat less abstract than

"What do you do in your leisure time?" "How do you discipline the children?" is more abstract than "Think back to the last time one of your children did something that made you mad. What did you do then?"

We also classify questions in terms of *antecedents*. Those questions that derive from interviewees' communications are said to have interviewee antecedents. Questions that derive from what the interviewer has said have interviewer antecedents. Once interaction has begun, the interviewer's questions or comments should derive from and respond to what interviewees have said, their interests and preoccupations, whenever possible and appropriate. Furthermore, questions are most understandable when they adopt the interviewee's words or phrases.

Another way to classify questions is in terms of their *differentiated focus*. For example, questions may focus on different time periods. The interviewer may ask about past events, current events, or future events. Questions can have the thinking, feeling, and behavior of the interviewee as their point of reference, or they can focus on the thinking and behavior of significant persons related to the interviewee. "How does your husband feel about having a homemaker in the house?" (time: now; person focus: other; activity: feeling). "Once the children are placed in foster care, in what ways do you think your husband's feeling toward you might change?" (time: future; person focus: other; activity: thinking). "What was your feeling when you learned your wife had been hurt in the accident?" (time: past; person focus: interviewee; activity: feeling). "What do you think is the cause of your reluctance to go to school?" (time: present; person focus: interviewee; activity: thinking).

Probing Questions

Probing ensures that the interviewer does not accept significant but general statements from a client. Probing is not a cross-examination technique. It is rather a judicious process of explication that permits interviewee and interviewer to see the situation in greater detail that clarifies what has happened. If an applicant for adoption says that she loves children and gets pleasure from her contacts with them, the interviewer tries to fill this statement out by probing. What kind of contact has she had with children? Under what circumstances? What exactly did she do with them? What was pleasurable in the contact for her? What was difficult? What kinds of children did she like best? Which children did she find hardest to like? How did the children react to her?

A school asks the protective agency to visit a woman whose children come to school hungry and inadequately dressed, and the mother says,

"That's a damn dirty lie; my kids are as well taken care of as anybody's." The worker replies, "Perhaps you're right" but goes on to probe the behavioral aspects of the woman's statement: "What did the kids eat yesterday?"; "Who takes responsibility for preparing the food and seeing that the children are fed?"; "What do you consider a decent meal?"; "What kinds of cold weather clothes do the children have; what kinds of rainy weather clothes?"; "What difficulties do you have in getting proper clothes for the kids?"

Probing questions that seek more specific information may be necessary because the initial answer is insufficient, irrelevant, unclear, or inconsistent with some information offered previously. The general picture of the client's situation has emerged but consequential details may be missing. Unless the interviewer obtains clear, complete, and relevant information regarding content of significance for achieving the interview objectives, the interviewer may incorrectly presume to know what the interviewee had in mind.

Keeping the content on a general level does not permit an understanding of individual clients in their individual situation. General statements like "It's a hard job" or "Marriage is very complicated" need specific follow-up questions: "What specifically is hard for you about the job?"; "What complications have you encountered in your marriage this past week?" These are probing questions.

Probing questions are successive approximations of the detail interviewers need to know if they are to be helpful. Probing questions direct interviewees in shaping a response. Open-ended questions followed by probes permit interviewees to tell their story in their own way and then help them amplify.

Although questions are the most common kind of probe, silence, minimal encouragements, paraphrasing, and reflecting can also act as probes. These varied interventions also result in more specific information.

The words *probe* and *probing* tend to evoke a negative reaction among social workers. The words suggest the antithesis of the kind of emotional response to the client that they regard as desirable. Probing implies an active interviewer and a passive interviewee who is required to answer questions. In reality probing is usually a gentle follow-up on what has been said. Probing most often is a legitimate request for further detail. Probing is different from a prying question, which would be characterized as more unwarranted, more intrusive. Although probing questions often are circumscribed and direct, they do not have to be asked in a demanding manner.

Interviewers use probing questions when the relevance of content is not clear and when they need to clarify ambiguous content or obtain more detail or greater specificity.

Answers that are evasive, superficial, vague, irrelevant, and diffuse require probing. Interviewers probe to obtain clear, complete, and relevant detail; these questions are designed to reduce the interviewer's uncertainty. Probes reflect the interviewer's recognition that gaps in information exist.

Interviewers use different kinds of probing questions in response to different problems in the interview.

Completion probes point to neglected or inadequately covered content and call on the interviewee to elaborate and fill in omissions. Complete probes include such questions as "And then?"; "What else can you think of about this?"; "Does anything else come to mind?"; "What happened then?"; "You said you left the hospital after the operation without the doctor's approval. What prompted you to do this?"

Completion probes are sometimes called "nudging probes" and include "Uh-huh?" and "Yes?," said with a rising inflection. "What did you do next?"; "What were you feeling at the time?"; "Can you tell me more about that?"; and "Anything else?" are examples of completion probes.

The use of completion probes suggests that the interviewer senses that the interviewee may say more if given additional encouragement.

Woman, 44, lower middle income, receiving AFDC because of husband's disability; agency is a vocational counseling service.

WORKER: How does your family feel about your going back to work?

MRS. H.: Well, the kids are all for it.

WORKER: All for it? [Clarity probe through reflecting.]

MRS. H.: Well, they think it would be good for me. I would get out and be less concerned about the house and have some interests. They know it will mean more cooperation on their part in the house-keeping. They say they are ready to do this.

WORKER: And your husband? [Completion probe—question was around family reactions, and interviewee had answered only in terms of the children.]

Interviewers use *clarity probes* to elicit a clearer explanation. These questions reduce ambiguities and conflicts in details; they help to further explain the situation. They include such questions as "Could you give me an example of that?"; "What do you mean by that?"; and "Could you tell me what you think leads you to feel this way?"

A psychiatric social worker is discussing a developmentally disabled 4-year-old girl with her mother.

WORKER: What problems did you have with her during this past year?

MRS. M.: No problems, but only that I feel she was too good a child, that there had to be something wrong.

WORKER: Well, when you say too good a child, could you give me some examples?

Some clarity probes permit the interviewer to specify the material to which the client should respond: "When you think about the shoplifting incident, what feeling seems dominant, shame or guilt?"; "Do you feel anxious about Roger [a mentally defective child] only when he is out in the street or when he is in the house as well?"

Vague or inconsistent responses to an open-ended question lead to probes that seek clarification: "What did you have in mind when you said your relationship with your mother left a lot to be desired?"; "When you said, 'We didn't have sex very often,' how often was it?"

Clarity probes help to get a clearer picture of the situation. People speak of being "somewhat depressed," "a little anxious," "a moderate drinker." Probes help to specify what they mean by modifiers.

Reaction probes focus on the interviewee's thinking and feeling and serve to increase emotional depth. These questions include "How did you react to it?"; "What do you think about it?"; "What are your feelings when this happens?"; and "How did you feel while this was going on?"

Answers to open-ended questions may *suggest* a feeling that is not explicit. Probing questions are designed to help the client make these feelings more explicit: "You said you thought you had good reasons for objecting to your mother's coming to live with you. How did you feel about refusing?"

The following excerpt from an interview shows the value of follow-up reaction probes:

INTERVIEWEE: I get upset about the decision to break away from the church and to miss mass and confession.

INTERVIEWER: What's upsetting about it?

INTERVIEWEE: I don't know.

(INTERVIEWER: Maybe she really doesn't know, but maybe it's something she's afraid I'll laugh at or be shocked at—so I'll probe further.)

INTERVIEWER: What comes to mind when you think about it?

INTERVIEWEE: Well, ah, I guess I really know. It's, well, I guess I'm, well, I'm afraid of going to hell.

INTERVIEWER: That can be upsetting.

(INTERVIEWER: I had to be careful to treat this very seriously, because it is a real fear of hers.)

Probing questions are less confusing when they are specific. An interviewee says, "I had problems with my daughter for a while. Not because of her behavior. It was because of my relationship with my marriage." The worker, using a completion probe, asks, "Can you tell me more about that?" The "about that" could refer to the daughter's behavior, the marital conflict, or the nature of the problems that the mother had with her daughter. A less confusing elaboration probe might have been "Your marriage was causing problems for you with your daughter. Can you tell me what kinds of problems it was causing?"

When using probes, the interviewer should first repeat the specific aspect of the interviewee's presentation about which the interviewer wants clarification or elaboration. In doing so it is preferable to use some of the interviewee's phrasing:

You were just mentioning the fact that your husband has annoying habits. Could you describe some of them to me?
When you were talking about your loss of achievement satisfaction on the job, I am not sure I understood what you meant. Could you help me understand that?

The timing of probing questions is important. It would not be advisable to stop the interviewee who has developed some momentum in order to ask for clarification or elaboration. Allowed to continue, the interviewee might answer some of the questions the interviewer had intended to ask. Waiting until the interviewee winds down poses a problem, however. A worker may need elaboration of some details that appeared early in the client's presentation. By the end of the presentation the client may have moved the focus to other areas. Attempting to probe the material introduced earlier requires a lead-in. "When you first started to tell me about this, you said that you felt . . . Could you tell me what led to your feeling that way?"

To ensure that they have covered all important points after completing a series of probes, the interviewer may ask the client an open-ended question, such as "Anything else—anything we missed?"

Formulation and Phrasing: Some Common Errors

Recurrent errors in question formulation include the leading or suggestive question, the yes or no question, the double question, the garbled question, and the why question.

The Leading or Suggestive Question

A frequent error is to phrase a question in a way that leads the interviewee to provide an answer that the interviewer desires. Interviewers formulate a leading question when they have a preconception of what the answer should be or a strong expectation of what the client may say. Leading questions make it difficult for interviewees to respond freely. They have to oppose the interviewer if they respond in a way that contradicts the answer that the question implies. Leading questions are not really questions at all but answers disguised as questions. The interviewer is not asking for an answer but soliciting a confirmation.

Leading questions actually provide the answer the interviewer is looking for—"But of course you love the child, don't you?" Suggestive questions are not as directive but nevertheless signal the response expected: "Don't you think foster care is best for Ann?"

Here are some more leading questions:

Applying for the job makes you anxious, doesn't it?
If your mother accepts nursing home care, you will feel better, don't you think?
Starting a new relationship is hard, isn't it?
You would be in a better position to keep your job if you stopped drinking, isn't that right?
If you found that your wife abused the child, you would petition for custody, wouldn't you?

Asking questions that provide their own answers is sometimes aptly described as "I'll tell you a question."

A social worker is talking with a 12-year-old boy who has run away from and been returned to an institution for emotionally disturbed children.

WORKER: You might as well face it, John: you're going to have to learn to deal with your anger in other ways. I can understand that you're very upset, but you saw how running away didn't accomplish anything. Don't you agree?

A school social worker is talking to a 7-year-old about her relationship to classmates.

WORKER: You play just with these two girls in the class. But you want more friends, don't you?

Here is the worker's retrospective comment:

As soon as I said, "But you want more friends, don't you?" I wished I hadn't. I felt I was putting words in Helen's mouth. It is true that she wants more friends, but I shouldn't be telling her; she should be telling me.

Interviewers also suggest responses by using negative or positive phrasing.

A worker in the social service unit of a public assistance agency is conferring with a young woman receiving AFDC.

WORKER: I don't suppose you have thought about working while the children are so young, have you?

The context of the question, rather than the question itself, also can suggest the interviewee's answer.

WORKER: Do you think Roger and Ruth [the client's preschool children] receive enough attention and care from your neighbor while you are working when she has three children of her own to take care of?

PAROLE OFFICER [*Speaking to parolee.*]: How about some old friends with a prison record that you aren't supposed to associate with. Do you see any of them?

A worker can bias a question by omitting an alternative.

A worker in a service for single pregnant adolescents is interviewing one of the teens.

WORKER: As you think about abortion or placing the child for adoption, which way seems best to you?

The question omits the alternative of the young woman's keeping the child.

Omissions are subtle but nevertheless significant. An interviewer asking questions about a woman's reaction to the possibility of getting custody of the children after a divorce follows up asking how she is likely to react if her ex-husband obtains custody. Failure to ask about joint custody biases the interview.

A leading question may influence the response because of the associations it evokes: "As a considerate son, do you think your mother would be happy in an old age home?"

Questions that start by suggesting implications exert even greater pressure for a particular response: "If you really feel that a good parent does not neglect her child, do you think you would have stayed at the tavern so late?"

Sometimes selective emphasis suggests the answer: "Do you *really* feel that your plans to keep the baby and find a job and housing are realistic?" *Really* is powerfully emotive in evoking a biased response to any question: "If you really loved your wife, do you think you would do that?"; "If you really wanted to finish school, would you keep cutting classes?"

Questions may prejudice a response by communicating the interviewer's annoyance: "What made you think that spanking Billy was going to do any good?"

Interviewers can influence the interviewee's response in more subtle ways. "How hard did you hit the child?" is more suggestive than "How did you hit the child?" "Do you hit him frequently?" suggests a different answer than "Do you hit him occasionally?" or "How often do you hit him?"

Even such subtleties as the use of a definite article can influence the response. In questioning a child who may have been sexually abused, asking, "Were you in *the* bed when it happened?" is likely to get more agreement than asking "Were you in *a* bed when it happened?"

However the bias is incorporated in the question, biased questions imply that certain answers are more acceptable than others, gently pressuring the interviewee to respond in a certain way.

Here are some questions taken from social work interviews and the more desirable neutral formulation of the same question:

BIASED FORMULATION	NEUTRAL FORMULATION
If you leave Mark at the day care center now, won't he act up again?	How do you think Mark will react to the day care center now?
Won't Sue be the most difficult one to care for?	What difficulties do you think you might have with Sue?
Well, I see you're making good progress. Don't you think so?	What progress do you think you are making?
I suppose Mrs. A. [the foster mother] treats all the kids the same?	How does Mrs. A. treat the different kids?

| You feel pretty comfortable with younger children? | What's your reaction to younger children? |

The dangers of leading questions can be exaggerated. Highly competent interviewers can and do use leading questions. When used properly, leading questions do not lead clients to distort their response. Clients with clear points of view and some self-assurance are unlikely to be intimidated by an interviewer's preference in a leading question (Dohrenwend 1965, 1970). However, Dohrenwend's research involved a general group of respondents. Social work interviewees are a particular group of respondents—particular in the sense that most of them want something from the agency. The power dif-ferential in the relationship is clearly in the interviewer's favor, and the interviewee is vulnerable. Consequently, the client's readiness to disagree is likely to be somewhat less in this situation than it might be in other interview situations.

Leading questions are least appropriate with interviewees who are eager to please or con the interviewer, who are afraid to disagree, or who have little motivation to participate responsibly in the interview. In these instances the interviewee will be willing to parrot back whatever the interviewer suggests. For such interviewees this is the least painful way to fulfill what is required of them.

Some questions that suggest an answer also suggest criticism: "Don't you think that . . . ?"; "Shouldn't you have . . . ?"; and "Wouldn't it have been better to . . . ?" are phrasings that suggest an answer and critically evaluate the interviewee's behavior. Such formulations impose the "tyranny of the should," and clients are likely to resent them.

Leading questions can be useful in communicating the social worker's position. They consequently tend to ally the worker with one aspect of the client's ambivalence. The worker may deliberately select a leading question. Social workers who want to emphasize that they favor an alternative procedure may ask, "Instead of refusing to talk to Sally, don't you think it might be better to consider other methods of discipline?" rather than the more neutral "What methods of discipline would you consider, other than refusing to talk to Sally?"

Leading questions may be useful and legitimate in some situations. When interviewers have good reason to believe that some event has taken place, such as sexual abuse, and a child is reluctant to discuss this, a leading question may encourage disclosure. The question gives the child permission to say what the child is resisting saying: "From your drawings and doll play,

I think I am getting a better picture of what happened. Didn't he touch you between your legs?"

Sometimes a question that suggests a response is a result of the interviewer's desire to be helpful. Rather than impose on the interviewee the burden of formulating an answer, the interviewer makes it less difficult by offering the question and answer simultaneously: "What explains her behavior? Do you think it might be because she was afraid to tell her parents?"

The Yes or No Question

The closed question that social workers use most frequently is one that can be answered with a yes or no. This is a desirable and legitimate approach when the interviewer needs specific information:

Are you a citizen?
Did you apply for unemployment insurance?
Were you retired at that time?
Will you be seeing your doctor tomorrow?

Although the yes-no format may be useful in some situations, the interviewer often has the option of converting the closed question to an open one that requires elaboration:

YES-NO FORMULATION	FORMULATION REQUIRING ELABORATION
Do you feel that when you go home your visits with your family are successful?	Tell me about your visits with your family.
Did you have to miss work a great deal?	What about absenteeism on the job?
Do you think there are some advantages in having this operation?	What do you see as the advantages in having this operation?
Do you ever do anything with your children?	What kinds of things do you and your children do together?

In general clients usually can answer closed questions in a few words. Questions that start with *is, did, have,* or *does* are more likely to get a simple yes or no answer and a limited response: "Have arrangements been made for the child's vaccination care?"; "Is he generally this way when his mother visits the foster home?"; "Have you ever made an application for adoption before?"

Similar questions that start with *what* or *how* are likely to require more detailed communication of the interviewee's experience: "What arrangements have you made for maternity-home care?"; "How does he generally behave when his mother visits?"; "What contacts have you had with adoption agencies before?"

Similarly, the formulation is not "Does he like his sister?" but "How does he get along with his sister?"; not "Did retirement lessen your contact with people?" but "What contacts with people have you had since you retired?"

Because yes-no questions are dichotomous, they do not provide information about gradients. A client who answers yes when asked, "Was there pain after the operation?," provides no information about the extent of the pain—whether it was slight, mild, extreme, or unbearable.

The Double Question

The beginning interviewer frequently asks more than one question at the same time. While asking the first question, the interviewer decides that another question would be better. Before the client can begin to answer, the interviewer asks a second question. The situation is confusing. Frequently, the second question changes the frame of reference, shifts the content, or asks something quite different. The interviewee then has the problem of deciding which of several questions to answer. Given a choice, the client often answers the least threatening question, ignoring the others. The least difficult question to answer is often the least productive because it encounters the least emotional resistance.

For the interviewer multiple questions pose another hazard: having asked a series of questions, the worker may forget that the client did not answer the original question. The worker may remember only that the question was asked and check it off the interview agenda.

Often it is not clear which question the client has answered:

WORKER: Are you managing better with your crutches, and how about your glasses, do they fit?

MR. W.: Oh my, yes.

Here are some examples of double questions asked during social work interviews:

Have you found the changes in customs from your country hard to deal with? How have you gone about adjusting to them?
What happened when you had a nervous breakdown? By the way, what do you mean by a nervous breakdown?

When do you think you and your dad started fighting? How long has it been? Has it been since your mom died or before that? Have you always not got along with your dad?

The worker, commenting on the last set of questions, says, "The client chose to answer the last question with a one-word answer, yes—about what I deserved."

Sometimes a single sentence includes more than one question because it offers more than one frame of reference for response.

Since coming home from the hospital, what difficulties have you had in finding a job, or finding housing, or even getting back in with your friends? Were you angry at what you were doing then or at the way you were treated then?
How do you and the children feel about moving out of the state? ["You" and "the children" are distinctly different reference points for an answer.]

Multiple questions are often formulated as an open question followed by a closed one: "How do you discipline John when he misbehaves? Do you use time-out?" The interviewee answers yes to the second question, and the first one is lost.

Good interviewees can save poor interviewers from their imperfections. In the following exchange the interviewee answers a double question sequentially:

INTERVIEWER: Okay, and then do you and your boy friend live here, and do you work, or do you have any job that takes you out of the house much of the time?

INTERVIEWEE: Yeah.

INTERVIEWER: You do? Okay—

INTERVIEWEE: And he's living here too.

The Garbled Question

Sometimes it is impossible for the interviewee to know what the interviewer is asking.

When interviewers are unclear about what they want to ask, they garble their message. The interviewee would be justified in asking, "What did you say?," or perhaps less kindly, "Would you please get the marbles out of your mouth." The following are verbatim examples from tape-recorded social work interviews:

INTERVIEWER: Yeah. So [*pause*] okay [*pause*] you said in the beginning of the interview that the frustrations that you are having [*pause*] are you finding that, well, is it cyclical? Have you noticed that? Is there any, you know what I mean?

A social worker in a divorce court setting, interviewing a 40-year-old male about the possibility of reconciliation.

INTERVIEWER: What do you think, what do you suppose she wants to do, like, why do you suppose she's acting the way she does?

The divorce court worker says of this question,

> My question was uncertain to the point of being incoherent. I felt something should be brought out and clarified, but I wasn't sure what and so I stumbled around. I am not sure what point I wanted to make—possibly something about his wife's deeper motive for [sharing his infidelities with the children], to justify herself or punish him, or erode the children's loyalty to him. What? I guess I had several ideas in mind but wasn't clear about how I wanted to develop this.

It takes an assertive interviewee to request clarification, as in the next interchange. The client has said that he has learned to control his embarrassment when someone praises him. Earlier the client had discussed problems in controlling anger. The worker attempts to establish a connection:

WORKER: How do you see to maybe perhaps learning from that experience of expression, transferring that to anger or anything that you can think of that would work in a similar way?

INTERVIEWEE: Would you repeat that? I didn't follow.

The "Why" Question

One kind of question that interviewers tend to overuse is the "why" question. This is a difficult question for the interviewee. It asks for a degree of insight, which, if possessed by the interviewee in the first place, might have obviated the need to come to the agency. A why question demands that interviewees account for their behavior in rational terms, but people often really do not know why. Figuring out the why is often one objective of the therapeutic contact.

Most people find it difficult to explain why they behave in the way they behave, particularly when the behavior is self-destructive and self-defeating. The why question increases their frustration, inadequacy, defensiveness, and sense of having disappointed the interviewer.

If sophisticated enough, the interviewee may attempt to provide reasons in retrospect to satisfy the questioner. The why question thus encourages a tendency to rationalize behavior, which may falsify the reality—the disordered impulses that prompted the client's behavior. That behavior may have come in response to unconscious or preconscious needs, to socially unacceptable impulses that the interviewee is trying to repress or suppress, and so is unable to share.

As rational people, most interviewees feel a need to defend their rationality by devising a rational answer—and one why question leads to another.

A school social worker, talking to Lil, an 8-year-old.

WORKER: What happens when you try to play with the other girls?

LIL: They say, "Go away."

WORKER: They tell you to go away. Why do you think they say that?

LIL: 'Cause they don't want more people to play with.

WORKER: Why do you think they don't want *you* to play with them?

LIL: 'Cause they have too many friends, and I was just learning how to jump rope, and I can't jump good. I always hafta take an end. I never get to jump.

WORKER: Why do the other girls always make you take an end?

Psychiatric social worker in an institution for emotionally disturbed children, discussing with a 16-year-old his attitudes toward the staff.

WORKER: You just said you're not going to, uh, like anybody around here again.

WILLARD: I'm not [*hostile tone of voice*].

WORKER: Why do you feel that way?

WILLARD: I just feel that way.

WORKER: Have people disappointed you?

WILLARD: Nobody's disappointed me.

WORKER: Then why do you think you feel that way?

WILLARD: I just do [*matter-of-factly*].

The worker comments,

> I continue to try to get Willard to verbalize his reasons for not liking anyone.
> I make a serious assumption here, and probably an erroneous one. I assume
> that Willard understands, or at least is aware of, the dynamics of his behav-
> ior. I push him to reason on a cognitive level as to the origins of his feelings.

Workers find that asking why is often counterproductive.

A social worker in a drug abuse center is discussing peer relationships
with a young adult male. She asks why he always has to follow what the
group wants him to do when it often gets him into trouble.

> I got the usual response: "I don't know." Then it dawned on me in the mid-
> dle of the interview that Jack became defensive whenever I asked the ques-
> tion "Why?" The word *why* seemed to imply that Jack had to justify his
> behavior, to hold himself accountable for his feelings. I realized then that
> asking why all the time was like pointing a finger at Jack and only resulted in
> his becoming more defensive and upset in the interview.

It is difficult to formulate a question in "why" terms without overtones
of blame. Reasons formulated in response to such a question may appear to
the interviewee as answers submitted for evaluation. Do the reasons appear
solid and acceptable to the listener? Why has a critical component as well
as an information-seeking component. As a consequence, it may prompt
the interviewee to respond defensively and focus counterproductively on
justifying rather than explaining the behavior.

Some alternatives to a why question may elicit the same information.
Instead of asking why, it may be better to ask what. What is easier for most
people to answer than why, which calls for self-analysis. What calls for
explanatory description. Not "Why do you have difficulty in telling your
husband about the things he does that annoy you?" but "What do you think
would happen if you told your husband about things he does that annoy
you?" Not "Why are you afraid of the medical examination?" but "What
scares you about the medical examination?" Not "Why didn't you use contraceptives?" but "What prevented you from taking precautions?" Such
interventions direct attention to some explanation without the direct challenge of why.

If an interviewer needs to ask a why question, it may be helpful to first
acknowledge the problem the question may pose for the client: "I know it
is difficult to put you finger on why you did it, but if you were to hazard a
guess, what would you say?"

Additional Guidelines for Formulating Questions

At this point we have some additional caveats and suggestions about formulating questions.

Questioning is a much abused art. Interviewers appear to find it difficult to ask a clear, unequivocal, understandable question and then be quiet long enough to give the interviewee an unhampered opportunity to answer.

Questions need to be understandable, unambiguous, and short enough that the interviewee can remember what is being asked. Any question of more than two sentences is apt to be too long. One sentence may permissibly set the context for the question, or explain the reasons for it, or motivate the interviewee to answer it. The second sentence should be the question itself. After that the interviewer should stop and wait, expectantly listening for the response and comfortable in the period of silence between the question and the response.

The best questions are those that are never asked because the client provides the answers in response to a facilitating atmosphere that stimulates the interviewee to share freely. The best answers to questions never asked are those that arise almost spontaneously from what the interviewee is saying. Facts and feelings are not so much actively sought as they are permitted to emerge. Such an approach reflects the worker's concentration on getting clients to talk rather than getting them to answer questions.

When you need to ask a question, you first must decide what it is you want to know and why you need to know it. Only then can you formulate the question. If you select and formulate a question that you think you may want to ask, what would you do with the answer once you got it? What purpose does the answer to that question serve? You should select questions in response to some need to know the answer rather than take a fishing trip that might turn up something of significance.

Formulating a question and selecting a question are two different processes. How do you actually put into words what it is that you want to know, so that it is likely to elicit the information you seek? The public opinion survey literature is littered with examples of how subtle changes in the formulation of a question elicit widely different responses (Bradburn and Sudman 1979).

The following anecdote illustrates the importance of selecting and formulating the right question:

A nursery school teacher is offering a breakfast of oatmeal to 4-year-old Michael, and asks, "Do you like sugar?" Michael says yes, so she adds some. "Do you like milk?" "Yes," says Michael, so she adds this. "Do you like butter?" "Yes," so this is added. However, Michael refuses to eat the oatmeal. The frustrated teacher says, "I asked if you like sugar. You said yes. I asked if you like milk. You said yes. I asked if you like butter. You said yes. So why don't you want to eat the oatmeal? And Michael says, "Because you didn't ask me if I like oatmeal!"

Asking the right question in the right way is important.

Questions should be crisp, lean, clearly phrased, and focused. Interviewers should phrase questions with regard for the interviewee's frame of reference and vocabulary level and the sociopsychological accessibility of content. Thus asking a woman with a third-grade education to discuss the "attitudinal orientation of her husband which creates difficulties in the role allocation of responsibilities in their marital relationship" is likely to be met with a blank stare—and should be, even by a person with a doctoral degree.

Questions should be formulated with concern for the interviewee's ability to provide an answer. Do not ask a question if the interviewee is unlikely to have the information at hand. Asking a man in a marital counseling interview whether his wife's parents were generally accepting of her during her childhood is asking for information that the interviewee may not know.

Rather than being hesitant, timid, or apologetic about questions, interviewers should be convinced of their entitlement to the information and communicate a sense of confident expectation that the interviewee will respond. "Would you mind if I asked whether you are married?" and "May I ask if you have any children?" suggest apologetic hesitance.

Every question has a command aspect associated with it. A question is more than an invitation to respond. It involves an expectation of response. Disclaimers, hedges, and qualifiers sometimes are appropriate in softening the demand inherent in a question. Hedge questions and qualifiers start with words and phrases, known as disclaimers, like "Maybe"; "I guess"; "It could be that . . ."; "I'm not really certain but . . ."; and "It may sound odd to ask about this but . . ."

Asking a question carries a variety of risks. The interviewer has to weigh the need for the information against the nature and degree of discomfort, anxiety, and the like that the question may evoke. The interviewer has to balance the value of the question against its effect on the relationship.

Interviewers can mitigate such risks by using appropriate *lead-ins*. Lead-ins reduce the threat to the client's ego , make it less likely the client will react defensively, and provide reassurance of the interviewer's understanding and acceptance. Prefaces, or lead-ins, to questions can make the question more palatable. The trick is to use face-saving prefaces and prefaces that universalize problems. A protective service worker says, "It must be difficult for you, without a husband to share the care of the children and to have to always be patient with them," and then asks, "What was happening just before you struck the child?"

Another worker may say, "Many people find it difficult to care for an aged dependent parent," and then ask, "How does it go for you?"

Exculpating lead-ins reduce the client's anxiety about answering:

Many parents have difficulty disciplining their children—what problems have you had with discipline?

Resisting peer pressure about drinking is a problem for most of the young people I talk to. How have you dealt with such peer pressure?

Every marriage that I am aware of faces the husband with the hard problem of making compromises. Have you encountered this in your marriage?

Interviewers also use lead-ins to telegraph that any answer is acceptable: "Some parents find it very difficult to accept a son's homosexuality; some parents are somewhat more accepting. How did you feel when Sid told you?"

Interviewers use lead-ins to motivate a client's participation. A school social worker says, "As Ed's mother, you have had the most continuing contact with him and know him better than anyone else. Could you tell me what he is like to live with?"

Interviewers use lead-ins to raise a client's self-esteem in preparation for dealing with a question that is apt to be deflating. A social worker in a corrections facility says in a first interview with an adult parolee, "From what you've told me, you have encountered many problems that you've dealt with successfully on your own. Which situations were hardest for you?"

The *attitude* with which a question is asked is perhaps as important as the question itself. The context and spirit of the question should reflect the emotional tone of the interviewee at the moment. If the interviewee is depressed, the question should show supportive understanding; if the client is anxious, reassurance; if the interviewee is hostile, recognition and acceptance of the hostility. In each instance interviewers use the lead-in to demonstrate that they are paying attention not only to the content of what the interviewee is saying but also to the feelings that accompany the interviewee's statements.

Male, 78, lower middle income, in need of assistance through Old Age, Survivors and Disability Insurance.

MR. Q.: At our age we have to depend on each other. As long as I'm around, she has somebody to depend on. But I don't know . . .

WORKER: It worries you. [*Pause.*] How do you think your wife would manage if she survived you?

Male, 19, upper lower income, probation interview.

MR. D.: And my mother is another one. She gives me a stiff pain in the ass.

WORKER: She really makes you sore. What does she do that gets you so mad?

When the subject matter is unfamiliar to the interviewee, it may be best to introduce the question by offering essential information.

The mother's group has about six to eight people, all in their early thirties, meeting for two hours every Wednesday evening to discuss the problem of how to live on a public welfare budget. What is your reaction to the idea of joining such a group?

Phrasing should avoid common words with vague meanings—*most, much, many, frequently*. The answers are easy to misinterpret because the interviewer is unlikely to know the interviewee's standards with regard to such words. "Do you frequently use corporal punishment in disciplining your children?"—"frequently" may mean once a day to the respondent who punishes once a week who then answers, "No, not frequently." Obtaining information by using such questions requires precision: "In the last month how often have you used corporal punishment in disciplining your children?"

Interviewers need to use some sensitivity to hot-button words—words that carry a lot of emotional freight—in formulating questions. Acceptable formulation can elicit the same information without the flak that such words provoke. "As you grow older, what kinds of things do you do more poorly?" is likely to evoke more defensiveness than "As you grow older, what kinds of things do you do less well?" "How do you feel about your wife's asserting her desire to work?" is not as neutral as "How do you feel about your wife's desire to work?"

Only subtle changes in wording can change inoffensive requests for information to antagonizing questions. To a client with a long-standing problem who comes for help during a crisis, asking "Why did you wait so long to get some help?" is antagonizing; "What made you hesitant about coming to the agency before now?" is more neutral. "Were you a school dropout?" is offensive; "What was your last grade in school?" is less so.

A skilled interviewer varies the format of questions so that no one pattern characterizes the interaction. If possible and appropriate, interviewers should ask some direct questions interspersed with indirect questions and leavened with comments. Even a series of open questions should have a few closed questions tucked in. Interviewers should make some effort to use novel formulations for questions, such as projective questions or those that offer choices.

Projective questions present a hypothetical situation that requires a decision. Such a question directed to a child might be, "If you were going on a vacation and could take either your mother or your father with you, whom would you take?" The interviewer might pose hypothetical but realistic situations and invite the client to react: "Suppose she did . . . ?"; "Suppose you had . . . ?"; "What do you think would happen if you said . . . ?"

A worker in a correctional agency is talking to a 17-year-old male.

BILL: They urged me to try it [shooting heroin] and so I thought, what the hell.

WORKER: Suppose you had refused. What do you think would have happened?

Interviewers can sometimes formulate questions in hypothetical terms that engage clients vicariously in experiences they are likely to encounter. The worker asks a male adolescent about to be discharged from a mental hospital, "Suppose you were to go back and live with your parents again—how would you imagine it would be now?"

The *indirect projective question* has the advantage of permitting the interviewee to answer without personalizing the response. It then permits the interviewer to introduce sensitive material without increasing the client's anxiety unduly. This type of question has the disadvantage of assuming that the answers represent the way the interviewee actually thinks or feels. This may not be the case.

WORKER: Think about a girl your age watching a favorite TV program. Her mother says, "Turn the set off, it's time for supper." What do you think the girl does—turns the set off and comes to supper, or sits there and continues to watch the program?

Alternative questions provide choices from which the interviewee is invited to select a response.

INTERVIEWER: How do you feel about your job?

INTERVIEWEE: It's okay!

INTERVIEWER: It's okay?

INTERVIEWEE: Yeah, that's about it.

INTERVIEWER: Well, as you know, for some people the thing they like best about their jobs is the work that they have to do; for others the best thing may be the people they work with; for others it's the pay; for others it's the location or the hours or the status and prestige of the job title. What aspects of your job do you like most?

Here, using the plural rather than singular form of the noun in the question gives the interviewee more freedom and nets a bigger answer.

Alternative questions need to offer choices that are approximately equal. To ask, "Would you rather make application for general assistance or continue without any money?" leads to one answer in most instances.

Interviewers sometimes use the alternative question in conjunction with hypothetical situations. In trying to clarify the preferences of an applicant for foster parenting the social worker says,

We have many different kinds of children who need a home. For instance, Bill is a shy, quiet, withdrawn seven-year-old who tends to play by himself and doesn't talk much. Timmy is very active, outgoing, talkative, seven years old, always on the go. Which kind of child is more in line with the kind of child you feel more comfortable with, Bill or Timmy?

Questions can be imaginative in terms of contrasts: not "How do you feel about Bob?" (a mentally retarded child) but "In what way is your feeling for Bob different from your feeling about the other children in the family?"

We can ask questions by making statements rather than using the interrogative mode. Instead of asking, "What prompted you to separate from your husband?," the interviewer may say, "I would be interested in the reasons that prompted you to leave your husband."

Interviewers often can reformulate questions to make them less challenging. Instead of asking, "What difficulties have you encountered in being both a mother and a fully employed teacher?," the interviewer may say, "Being both a mother and a fully employed teacher probably presents some problems. Tell me about those you have encountered." The remark is an indirect question without the inflection characteristic of the direct question. The reformulation of the question as a general remark reduces the risk that the session will seem like an interrogation. This technique increases the feeling of the interaction as a corroboration.

The art of asking questions, like the art of using any intervention, depends on the interviewer's sensitivity to what is appropriate at the moment. Artful questioning involves judicious variation in the formulation of questions to fit the occasion.

Relentless consistency in the use of any one particular style of question is likely to be counterproductive, however comfortable the interviewer feels with it. Because the demands at different points in the interview are so varied, the consistent use of one type of questioning is likely to be appropriate at one time but much less appropriate at another.

Interviewers' Preparation for Asking Questions

Many interview interventions we have discussed thus far can only be formulated during the course of the interview in response to something the interviewee has said. In contrast, interviewers can and should prepare questions in advance. If interviewers know the general problem that is the subject of the interview and perhaps some socioeconomic information about the interviewee, they can prepare the kinds of questions they might ask to obtain the information they need in order to help the client.

Here the need for expertise in some area of social work practice is evident. For instance, medical social workers with a caseload of older hospitalized patients need to know the psychosocial and economic problems of the aged and the psychosocial economic problems associated with planning the discharge of such patients in order to know what they need to learn from such interviewees to be of help. Knowledge of programs and their eligibility requirements for in-home and nursing home service and the psychosocial problems of the elderly—such as isolation, lack of economic resources, and issues related to loss—helps the interviewer to prepare for a discharge planning interview with an aged patient. The interviewer can anticipate the kinds of questions that are most productive, good ways to formulate such questions, and a sequence for asking them that makes sense to older patients.

Adequate preparation also requires an awareness of questions we might fail to consider because of our theoretical or ideological commitments. Interviewers fail to ask questions for many reasons. When they don't ask pertinent questions, they may not obtain information they need to be of help.

Sometimes doubt about their capacity to help makes interviewers reluctant to ask questions about a client's personal life. But because obtaining intimate information is necessary in order to help a client, the interviewer is entitled to inquire about such matters.

In other cases the agency may want its workers to obtain certain information, but the workers have no conviction that such data are necessary. Asking the client to discuss material the interviewer thinks is irrelevant is difficult. For example, adoption workers in a denominational agency who are themselves agnostics may find it difficult to explore seriously the religious practices of adoptive applicants. They lack conviction that such information is significant.

The introspective comments of a 26-year-old female social worker assigned to a terminal cancer ward of a large city hospital provide another example:

> As I review the tape of the interview, I am struck by how frequently I introduced a question or a comment with an essentially apologetic preface. At one point I said, "You probably don't see much sense in this question." Another time I said, "You might not want to answer this question," and again I said, "Would you mind if I asked you . . . ?" I even went so far as to say at another point, "I am supposed to ask you . . ."
>
> I think it's because I am new to the agency and I have a feeling that there is nothing we can do. The fact that these people are dying is the overwhelming consideration, and I am not sure talking to them and getting them to talk to us serves any useful purpose.

Some interviewers are highly sensitive to the pain occasioned by asking about failures and personal tragedies. Foran and Bailey note,

> Inexperienced doctors or nurses sometimes give an injection so slowly and gently that instead of avoiding pain they cause it. Student social workers, too, are sometimes too gentle to probe into (or even allow the client to probe into) sensitive areas and they offer reassurance or change the topic. The more honest of them will admit that, in truth, it was pain to themselves that they were anxious to avoid.
>
> (1968:45)

A middle-aged father, responding to the interviewer's questions, hesitantly and with considerable anxiety describes incest with his 14-year-old daughter. The worker says,

> It was almost as painful for me to ask the questions as it was for him to answer them. I have been socialized not to intrude into the private affairs of other people and here I was having to do just that. There are moments that

I felt really humbled because I am not sure I would reveal as much to a person who asked me similar questions.

When under pressure to make decisions about many cases, the interviewer may fail to ask questions or to hear answers that are likely to make the job harder.

An AFDC worker says,

I had a feeling of apprehension about asking how things had gone with Mrs. G. during the past week. I knew I had to ask, yet I was afraid of the answer. Aware that the situation had been precarious, I was afraid to find out that everything had fallen through. If she were having all sorts of problems, which I dimly suspected, I did not really want to know. Once I found out I would have to start working all over again putting Humpty Dumpty back together again. Just for once I wanted things to be nice and uncomplicated. As long as I did not ask and give Mrs. G. a chance to tell me, that's the way they were as far as I knew.

If they feel discomfort about a certain problem, interviewers may be reluctant to pursue it even when the interviewee initiates the discussion.

A 24-year-old disabled client, talking about his family's reaction to his disability while he was growing up.

MR. D.: They did not want the responsibility of a disabled person in the house. There were always arguments over who was going to put my shoes and socks on, which I couldn't do myself. Things like that, you know. It really hurt.

WORKER: How many brothers and sisters do you have?

The worker comments,

I was aware that I did not follow his lead about his strong feeling reaction to his experience. I demonstrated fright for what was for me a painful subject. I heard echoes of my own family's arguments about who was going to take turns in pushing the wheelchair of a paralyzed grandmother.

As Harry Stack Sullivan says, when interviewers communicate a reluctance to ask about some particular feeling or problem, "the records of their interviews are conspicuous for the fact that the people they see do not seem to have lived in the particular area contaminated by that distaste" (1954:69).

Questions formulated to test some hypothesis about the interviewee's situation run the risk of what has been termed a *confirmatory strategy*. Rather than being neutral about the validity of the hypothesis, the interviewer may have an answer in mind. The interviewer then formulates questions in a way that tends to solicit confirmation of the hypothesis. Similarly, interviewers may neglect to ask some questions that would disconfirm their hypothesis (Dallas and Baron 1985).

Thus, to cite an all-too-familiar example, if we are committed to the hypothesis that spouse abuse is initiated by the male, we ask questions about the male's behavior in confirmation. We fail then to ask questions about the female's behavior, which may weaken if not disconfirm the hypothesis. Ideological hesitance about "blaming the victim," added to theoretical preconceptions, puts certain questions off limits.

A final word of caution. Although questions can serve many purposes, social workers may be wise to use them sparingly. Interaction based on a persistent question-and-answer format tends to establish a type of relationship that contradicts the cooperative and collaborative atmosphere that is most often helpful. The interviewer speaks in questions. The interviewee speaks in answers (Dillon 1990).

A series of questions often leads to an undesirable perception of the respective responsibilities of interviewer and interviewee. It suggests an unrealistic situation in which, if the interviewee answers all the questions, the interviewer will provide a clear solution to the problem.

Summary: Chapter 9

Questioning serves multiple purposes in the interview, and asking questions is probably the intervention that social workers use most frequently. We can classify questions according to the amount of freedom or restriction they offer the interviewee. Closed questions restrict the scope of the answer; open questions provide the interviewee with greater freedom to respond.

Open-ended questions are advantageous because they give the client greater control over the interview, more discretion in introducing significant material, elicit more information about feelings and intensity of feelings, and instill positive feelings about the interview. However, open-ended questions give the interviewee little structure or guidance regarding what to talk about or how to talk about it.

Interviewers use closed questions to obtain greater clarity and focus, to obtain more definite or detailed information, and to reduce the degree of emotionality in the interview. The interview as a totality may resemble a funnel, beginning with open-ended questions and ending with more detailed closed questions. Additional dimensions for classifying questions include responsibility, level of abstraction, antecedents, and focus.

Probing questions are designed to get clients to explicate and clarify significant but general content. Interviewers use probing questions when the relevance of the content is not clear, when ambiguous content requires clarification, and when they need more detail and/or greater specificity. Types of probing questions include those that seek completion, clarity, and reaction.

Among the recurrent errors in question formulation are the leading question, the yes or no question, the double question, the garbled question, questions with ambiguous references, and the why question.

Additional considerations in formulating questions include the need for questions to be crisp, lean, clearly phrased, and focused. Lead-ins are useful in softening the demand inherent in a question, in motivating a client's participation, and in raising a client's self-esteem in preparation for a question that may be deflating. Interviewers need to formulate questions with sensitivity to hot-button words or words that have high affective connotations. A skilled interviewer varies the format of questions so that no one pattern characterizes the interaction. When interviewers ask questions to test a hypothesis, they should be aware of the risk of formulating them in a way that tends to solicit confirmation of the hypothesis. Interviewers can and should prepare questions in advance of the interview.

TEN

Termination, Recording, and Evaluation

The final phase of the interview is termination.

In discussing termination we are not discussing final contact between client and agency but rather ending any interview in a series of interviews.

Preparation for termination begins at the start of the interview. The interviewer should inform the client explicitly at the beginning that a specific period of time has been allotted for the interview, that the client is free to use some or all of this time but that going beyond the time limit is discouraged. Unless an unusual situation develops, the client should understand that the interview will terminate at the end of the allotted time.

Another aspect of preparing for termination is linked to the mutually agreed-upon purpose of the interview. The interview is an ad hoc social system created to achieve a purpose. When the purpose is accomplished, the system should dissolve. The purpose should bear some general relation to the time available, so that accomplishing it within the time limit is possible. If this is not possible, the interviewer should break the general purpose down so that they can achieve some subunits in one interview and schedule an additional interview or interviews. In a sense the interview does not end at the close of the first meeting; it has merely been interrupted.

Research findings regarding long-term and short-term worker-client contacts may be applicable to the interview situation. Such research suggests that if the agency establishes a limited time for contact with the client, both worker and client tend to work more efficiently to accomplish the tasks of the contact. If the period for a single interview is clearly limited, a similar concentration of effort may occur.

Termination Techniques

Throughout the interview the social worker has to be aware of time spent and time yet available. Because interviewers are responsible for seeing that the purposes are accomplished, they need to pace the interview so that there is some reasonable expectation of success. Interviewers might decide to make more rapid transitions; they might decide to focus less time on some areas; they might make less effort to evoke affect if time is growing short. If the interview proceeds faster than anticipated, interviewers may decide to conserve the interviewee's time as well as their own by ending early. In moving toward termination occasionally checking with the interviewee may be useful: "It seems to me that we have done what we set out to do and that we are coming to a close. How do you see it?"

We should note that the interviewee is as free as the interviewer to terminate the exchange. If clients feel they have accomplished their purposes or if they feel that the likelihood of accomplishing their purposes is small, they may not want to spend more time.

The best situation, of course, is that the decision to terminate is mutually acceptable, that both participants recognize that they have achieved the purpose of the interview and they have little reason to continue.

The pacing of affect as well as content is a factor in preparing for termination. In moving toward the end the intensity of emotion should ease. Toward the end of the interview interviewers should not introduce content that is apt to carry a great deal of feeling. The interviewee should be emotionally at ease when the interview ends, in contrast to this situation:

> A worker is discussing marital planning with a young adult. The woman is a carrier of a genetically transmitted anomaly and has discussed what she might do if she becomes pregnant. Toward the end of the interview the worker says, "Another option is just not having children, being married and having a husband but not having kids, remaining childless."

Commenting on this intervention at the end of the interview the worker says,

> I wanted to be complete, and by stating this final option I was completing the spectrum of options for Ruth. Yet it was very unfair of me to so casually drop this bomb on Ruth when I knew we wouldn't have time to deal with her reactions to the idea of never having children. Her facial reaction showed that this thought made her very sad. I wonder if I might have subconsciously waited with this option until the end of the interview so that I wouldn't have to deal with Ruth's hurt.

The interview should terminate before the participants become physically or emotionally fatigued. An hour to an hour and a half is a long time for most participants. The mind can absorb only as much as the seat can endure. Highly charged interviews may fatigue participants even sooner. If fatigue sets in, the risk of interviewer error is greater.

If it becomes clear that the interviewee is unaware of the limited time available, some gentle reminders may be necessary. Interviewers might signal movement toward closure by explicitly noting that they perceive the interview is coming to an end: "Well, I guess that's about as much as I think we can cover today." This legitimizes and sanctions termination. The tentative "I guess" and "I think" permit the interviewee the possibility of sharing another, perhaps different, perception about whether the interview is coming to an end. The interviewer might say, "Now that we are coming to the end of the interview, perhaps you . . ." Or, "I wish we could get into this more fully now, but given the time we have left it seems that . . . "

The word *well*, as in "Well, it seems to me . . . ," is a verbal marker that people recognize as signaling closure.

We can signal movement toward closure by explicitly noting external circumstances for terminating: "I am sorry, but there is another interview scheduled to begin in five minutes." Or "I think we have to finish up now. I am due at a committee meeting shortly" (Knapp 1973).

Nonverbal gestures that suggest the interview is drawing to a close reinforce verbal reminders. Breaking eye contact, interviewers collect the papers or forms used during the interview; they looks at their watch rather than glancing at it. Grasping the arms of the chair, placing your palms on your knees, moving to the edge of the chair, and assuming a readiness-to-rise stance are all nonverbal messages that flag your intent to end the interview shortly. These are courteous preparatory signals to the interviewee that things are coming to an end without having to verbally articulate this.

We can use verbal and nonverbal closure markers simultaneously. "Well [*glancing at your watch*], we are at about the time for ending [*straightening up in your chair*] and we can, as we said [*rising from chair*] continue to discuss this [*moving from behind your desk*] the next time we meet."

These verbal and nonverbal movements release people from contact with each other in a courteous manner, permitting each to go away without feeling dismissed. Such termination rituals preserve a sense of cordiality and emphasize the solidarity in the relationship. We are leaving each other now, but we will make contact again.

If the interviewer terminates the interview abruptly and without considerate warning, the client may perceive the interviewer as discourteous and rejecting. Separation is easily confused with rejection; the interviewer should make clear that termination of the interview is not the equivalent of wanting to get rid of the interviewee—although sometimes the worker may want to do just that.

Sometimes, despite the interviewer's best efforts, the interviewee fails to respond to the signals and appears likely to continue beyond the point where the interview should have ended. The interviewer needs to be concerned about and understanding of the interviewee's reluctance to leave. Sometimes this reluctance is a hostile gesture toward the interviewer. Sometimes it reflects the time the interviewee needs to feel comfortable about bringing up the most important problem. Clients may delay mentioning a difficult problem until the end of the interview to avoid having to explore it fully. Sometimes the reluctance to end the interview expresses a desire to prolong a satisfying experience; sometimes it is an expression of sibling rivalry and reluctance to share the interviewer with the next sibling/interviewee. The problem may result from different perceptions of how the interview has progressed—the interviewer believes they have accomplished the purpose, whereas the interviewee believes that much still needs to be done.

The following account illustrates an interviewee's reluctance to terminate and the worker's difficulty in handling it:

> She began to talk about the boys, and as I began to break in at a pause or start a concluding sentence that would indicate a termination of the interview, she became extremely tense, talking faster and in a dissociated manner. I asked what she thought of my getting hold of her again, and she replied that she would be able to hear the phone ring. I then stood up to indicate termination and she began to list relatives and their careers. I perhaps should have stated that I must return to other work, but I was rather cowed by her sudden extreme talkativeness, and so I just walked her to the stairs and she continued to talk all the way downstairs and as she walked out onto the street. I had avoided interrupting her or being firm—those are not my usual ways of dealing with people—and I also was afraid to, but I did no favor to her to allow her to become so anxious at that point.

Whatever the interviewee's reasons for acting to prolong the interview, the interviewer needs to follow some specific procedures in terminating. Here, as always, the worker would do well to explicitly recognize the behavior manifested:

> I can see that you would like to continue longer.
> It seems like you are reluctant to end the interview.
> It appears to me that you wish we had more time.

While holding without equivocation to the need to terminate, the interviewer should express a desire to maintain communication; it is not that the interviewer does not want to hear more, it is that the interviewer does not want to hear it at this particular time. Consequently, the interviewer should make an offer to continue during another specified time period. The offer confirms the interviewer's continuing interest. If the client already understands that this is one in a series of interviews, the promise of continued discussion is implicit. The interviewer may say, "I am very sorry but we have to wind this up. I would like to continue now but it's not possible. I would be glad to schedule another appointment so that we could continue talking about this together."

Sometimes the imminence of the end of the interview overcomes the client's resistance to making a significant disclosure. In preparing to exit interviewees mobilize themselves to share something that they have been reluctant to disclose all along. The interviewer explicitly recognizes the concern raised and explicitly suggests that it be the first item on the agenda of the next interview.

If the interviewer plans to continue contact in another interview, the worker should provide explicit recognition and support for the continuing relationship by saying, "Till next time"; "See you next week"; or "See you soon" rather than "Good-bye."

When scheduling a subsequent interview, the interviewer should make specific arrangements for the next steps, such as time, date, and place of the next interview or the time, date, place, person to see, and how to get there, if the interview terminates in referral to another agency.

If worker and client have no plan to continue, terminating the interview and signaling a break in contact might seem like an impersonal dismissal unless the interviewer softens it by making supportive comments: "Well, I hope things work out for you" or "Good luck in your efforts to deal with this."

If the interview is with a collateral, or is an advocacy interview, it is advisable to thank the interviewee, recapitulate the significance of the contact, and reassure the client about how you plan to make use of what they have discussed.

Interviewers needs to apply all these suggestions flexibly, with sensitivity to the individual situation and a generous helping of common sense. The interviewer should consider the interviewee's needs in moving toward termination. Interviewers must also consider their own needs because those needs may indirectly affect the interviewee adversely. Interviewers' balanced concern for their schedule is the highest courtesy to the interviewee. If interviewers are too compliant, yielding, or compassionate, and the interview runs beyond the scheduled time, workers begin to worry about the interviewee who is waiting, the things they need to do,and begin to listen to their mounting anxieties and forget to listen to the client. In this case the extra time is not productive.

The least desirable alternative involves the interview that has ended as far as the interviewer is concerned, but the worker does not have the courage or the skill to say so. By withdrawing their attention and being pre-occupied and disengaged these interviewers leave the client forgotten but not gone.

Sometimes interviewees take the initiative in signaling what is for them the end of the interview. An interviewee might say, "Well, that kind of wraps it up for me. I think I know how to take it from here." Or, signaling nonverbally, clients might take off their glasses, or stand, gathering up their belongings or searching for their car keys. Clients might prepare the interviewer for termination by expressing appreciation: "Well, this has really been helpful" or "Thanks very much for giving me your time."

Summary and Postinterview Conversation

As part of the termination phase the interviewer briefly recapitulates what they have covered in the interview, decisions they have reached, questions that remain to be resolved, and what, if any, steps for action one or both are to take. A summary tends to consolidate the work of the interview and give participants a feeling of satisfaction as they look back over what they have achieved. But if they have not accomplished much, a summary may lead to a sense of despair.

Summarizing is always a selective process. Consequently, a summary tends to highlight those aspects of the interview that the summarizer, generally the interviewer, regards as most significant. For this reason the interviewer should explicitly solicit the interviewee's response. The interviewer should invite clients to revise the summary if it does not agree with their perception of what was significant during the interview. Or the interviewer may ask interviewees to recapitulate what *they* thought the session accomplished. Such recapitulations might include a statement of what they need to do in subsequent interviews. The summary should enable both participants to get a perspective on the interview, highlighting the relationship of the many different, perhaps seemingly unrelated, aspects that they have discussed. The summary is an opportunity to give a sense of coherence to what has taken place.

Here is an example of how a social worker in a university counseling center used a summary to move toward termination of an interview:

INTERVIEWER: Okay, that's fine, okay. Anything else you can think of that might be helpful?

INTERVIEWEE: Nothing more right now. [Period of silence.]

INTERVIEWER: Okay. I think I'm starting to get a general picture from this early information, which is where we have to start. And right now I'm seeing two or three areas that, that I see as potential areas of importance as far as, uh, exploring with you. Definitely your relationship with your boyfriend—I think it's something we have to talk about more in depth. Uh, I think perhaps, too, another area I would like to explore a little bit, uh, your perceived expectations, which you might feel are based in reality, or how much aren't based in reality. Uh, I think that's just going to take us a little bit of time to look at. Um, that's what I see as the important areas. How do you feel about that?

INTERVIEWEE: Um, I agree.

INTERVIEWER: Another thing that I see is that you seem to have an excellent support system—friends, family, et cetera. That should be most helpful to you. [*Pause.*]

INTERVIEWER: So I'm getting a few ideas. What I'd like to do now is assimilate what you've told me and ask you to think about these things also, and also set up a time for next week. Then we can start to look into some of these situations in more depth. How does that sound to you?

INTERVIEWEE: Yeah, that really sounds great.

INTERVIEWER: Okay, then let's set up that appointment for next week.

Just as a short social conversation may precede the interview as a transition, a similar short conversation may follow termination of the interview. This exchange acts as a transition out of the interview and helps to restore emotional equilibrium if the interview has been emotionally charged. Such postinterview conversation permits interviewees time to regain composure and restore their ego, which may have been somewhat battered during the interview.

Termination small talk eases the transition from formal professional interaction to the more informal social interaction: "Nice talking to you"; "Hope the weather clears up"; "There isn't likely to be too much traffic on your way home."

Toward the end of an interview a correctional social worker discusses the best fishing spots with a male client. Listening to the interview on tape later, he notes,

> The content is pretty much small talk. However, Bob seemed to need this neutral conversation after expressing the previous emotional material. It also gave me an opportunity to learn something about his interests and show him I was interested in him as a person with hobbies, et cetera, and not merely interested in him as a probationer.

As at the beginning of the interview, if such a conversation goes on too long, it tends to confuse a formal interview with a social encounter. Because the rules for communication are different in the two situations, the interviewee may be puzzled about which rules are appropriate. Even though the conversation may be pleasant, gratification is not what brings people together for the interview and should not be the determinant of when it ends.

The best termination occurs in a friendly, collaborative, and definite manner, showing the interviewer's professional confidence. Adherence to the procedures we have suggested ensures a greater likelihood that the interview will terminate rather than just peter out.

The interviewer should conduct the leave-taking in a manner that brings a sense of closure to the encounter, effects a release for participants from each other with a feeling of support rather than rejection, and provides a sense that they have achieved something. The interviewer may deliberately stimulate postinterview rumination by assigning some "homework" by suggest that the interviewee think over something they discussed in preparation for continuing to explore the problem.

Endings, the last unit of the interview interaction, may condition the interviewee's clearest perception of the interview in retrospect.

Just as an interview starts before it begins, it terminates before it ends. Both participants carry something of it away with them, mulling over what they said and continuing the interview in their minds afterward.

The "song is over, but the melody lingers on" is another way to describe the difference between interview termination and ending. See box 10.1 for guidelines for termination.

Box 10.1 Guidelines for Termination

1. Prepare for termination from the start of the interview.
2. Set objectives and pacing to maximize the possibility of achieving the objectives within allotted time.

3. Clearly inform the interviewee of time limits.
4. Prepare the interviewee for termination through verbal and nonverbal communication when interview objectives appear to have been achieved.
5. Summarize what the session has accomplished and solicit the interviewee's feedback on summary.
6. Remember that the interviewee has the option to decide on and implement termination.
7. Conduct the termination in a manner that preserves a positive relationship.
8. When appropriate, build bridges to a future contact.

Review and Evaluation

Interviewers need to schedule some client-free time between interviews to enable them to clear their mind in preparation for the next interview. We noted the importance of this in discussing the beginning of the interview. A respite also serves the needs of the interview just concluded. The worker may need time for review and evaluation to absorb some of the less obvious aspects. Evaluation is a responsibility of the interviewer. An interview has not ended until interviewers mentally recapitulate the encounter and attempt to assess their performance critically. Interviewers may want to ask themselves a number of questions in making such an evaluation:

1. In retrospect what were the purposes of this interview—for the interviewee and for the agency?
2. To what extent did we achieve the purposes?
3. Which interventions helped to achieve the purposes? Which interventions were hindrances?
4. What was my feeling about the interviewee?
5. At what point was my feeling most positive? Most negative?
6. How might my feelings have been manifested in what I said or did?
7. If I now empathize with the interviewee, how did the client seem to see me? What seemed to be the client's reaction to the interview?
8. When did the interview seem to falter? When was it going smoothly?
9. At what point did the interviewee show signs of resistance, irritation? What had I said or done just before that?
10. At what point did the session cease to be an interview and become a conversation, a discussion, or an argument?
11. If I had the opportunity to do the interview over again, what changes would I make? What justifies such changes?
12. What in general did this interview teach me about myself as an interviewer?

Note Taking

After terminating the interview the social worker in most social agencies has some obligation to record the interview. The worker translates the language of the interview into the language of the file, the computer program, or the agency's forms. Before we get to recording, however, a word about note taking during the interview.

The more an interviewer takes notes taken during the interview, the less the worker has to do afterward. The immediate caveat is that note taking can be distracting. When interviewers look down to write, they break eye contact, a sign that their field of awareness has shifted. When taking notes, interviewers' focus is generally on what the client *has* said rather than what the client *is* saying. If interviewers are looking at a notepad, they may lose some potentially significant nonverbal information. The dictum is to interview the interviewee, not the notepad.

Another pitfall in note taking is that it may direct the interviewee's attention to certain content. If after talking for some time the interviewee says something that mobilizes the interviewer to make a note, the interviewee will naturally wonder about the significance of this item and begin to focus on it. This focusing may be good if the interviewer is deliberately reinforcing concern about this particular item. However, the client's focusing may be an inadvertent and unintentional by-product of note taking.

As interviewees see an interviewer taking notes, they are unsure whether they should continue to speak. They hesitate not only because the interviewer is apparently not listening but also because they do not want to interfere with what the interviewer is doing.

Sensitive interviewees have been known to slow down or stop talking while the interviewer takes notes in order to give the interviewer a chance to catch up. It may be necessary to assure interviewees that taking notes does not affect the conduct of the interview and that they should continue to talk.

In some measure note taking is self-defeating. When the most important things are happening is when the interviewer can devote the least amount of attention to note taking. When what is happening is less significant, the interviewer has more time for notes. Hence the most complete notes may highlight the less important interchanges.

There are exceptions. Some interviewers can take notes unobtrusively, without looking away from the client and without seeming to shift their attention. They have learned to set down key phrases that serve as reminders of blocks of interview content. And they have learned to write without looking at the notepad. They take notes easily and without much show. On the other hand, some interviewers may use note taking as defense against contact with the client, in effect hiding behind the notebook.

A pencil poised over a notebook is a nonverbal message that says, "Tell me more." As such it emphasizes the difference in status between interviewer and interviewee. The interviewee usually has no pencil, no pad, and takes no notes.

Interviewers need to apply these considerations differently with regard to different content. If the interviewee is offering specific necessary information such as dates, names, addresses, and telephone numbers, the interviewer must note them. If the interviewer fails to do so, the interviewee, aware that the interviewer is unlikely to remember this information, concludes that the worker is uninterested and indifferent. The client might well wonder why the interviewer asked about these matters in the first place. Taking notes at this point validates the importance of what the client has said and shows that the worker is taking it seriously. Notes about actions the interviewer has promised to take are essential. If the worker has promised to obtain an interpretation of some regulation, make a hospital appointment, or check the availability of a homemaker, the worker should make a note.

When interviewers plan to take notes during the interview, they should share this with the interviewee and obtain permission to do so. Generally, interviewers do this in a manner that suggests that the interviewee will have no objections and includes some explanation of the purpose: "You don't mind if I take some notes while we're talking? I'll need to do this if I am going to be most helpful to you." Especially with a suspicious interviewee, the request for permission may include a statement of a willingness to share the notes if the interviewee wants to look at them. The interviewer may even encourage the interviewee to take notes. Always take notes in full view of the client rather than surreptitiously.

Interviewers should assess the effect of note taking periodically during the interview. If at any point the interviewee appears to be upset or made hesitant by note taking, the interviewer should mention the reaction for explicit discussion. If, despite the interviewee's stated assent, note taking appears to be a disruptive tactic, the interviewer may be well advised to abandon it.

The principle is that the purpose of the interview has clear priority over note taking, and in any conflict between the two the interview interaction has priority. When taking notes is disruptive, the interviewer should do it selectively, inconspicuously, flexibly, and openly. If taking notes during the interview is difficult, the interviewer should make some notes immediately afterward. Waiting until the end of the working day to make notes risks a considerable loss of essential detail. After a series of interviews it is easy to confuse what occurred in one with interaction in another.

Taking notes during home interviews presents greater problems. Interviewers may have to make notes in the car after the interview or during a coffee break at a nearby restaurant.

Recording

After conducting and completing the interview the interviewer is responsible for recording it in some manner. Recording is an organized presentation of the interviewer's notes for the agency's files.

Recording is an act of accountability to the agency and its clients. In recording the content interviewers "evaluate the progress and outcomes of their activities with and on behalf of the clients" (Kagle 1995:2027).

Recording is a legitimate part of the interview process. Recording what occurred continues the interview in the mind of the interviewer afterward. Recording is a retrospective reliving of the encounter. Recording the interview requires the interviewer to select which aspects of the interview were most significant. The interviewer has to systematically organize a somewhat chaotic experience.

Recording helps the worker become a more effective interviewer. Recording imposes the need to structure the information obtained. It also helps to more clearly individualize interviewees and their situation for subsequent recall. It helps interviewers recognize what they did well, what they covered adequately, and what they missed. Recording in whatever form permits and contributes to analytical reflection about the interview experience. It encourages cognitive and affective integration of the experience.

The importance of recording lies as much in the process as in the product.

> The record reflects practice and through the process of making the record the [interviewer] has cause to reflect upon practice. Writing takes place at some distance from the practice it documents, thereby allowing for a new perspective on the [interview]. Recording at its best can help the [interviewer] to reconstruct what has taken place, to re-evaluate plans for the future and to give form and precision to ideas which have been inchoate. (Kagle 1984:100).

Here Kagle is suggesting that recording the interview achieves the practice objective of planning for the next interview. Reviewing the record of the last interview before the next one helps the interviewer to achieve immediacy.

One purpose of recording the interview is to justify a decision the worker has made and to cover the worker in case an action is challenged (Pithouse 1987:33). What a statesman once said about memoranda may be said of some interview records, namely, that they are written not so much to inform the reader as to protect the writer.

What the worker reports in the record is often a subjective account of fallible recollections of complex interactions by a participant actively and emotionally involved in the interaction. Records are often exercises in retrospective redefinition of the original experience. The reconstructive memory bias tends to be greater if time elapses between the interview and the recording. Computerized agency operations, the need to document activity for third-party payers, such as Medicare and Medicaid, and the courts' definition of evidence in actions that frequently involve social workers (e.g., termination of parental rights, divorce proceedings, adoption, etc.) have affected the way workers record the information they obtain in the interview.

Computerized record keeping requires standard approaches to recording. The emphasis on uniformity means the inevitable loss of the interviewee's individuality in the recording (Kagle 1987:465).

The expense associated with record keeping, the imposition on the worker's time, and the chronic dislike workers have for recording has resulted in changes in agency practice. The changes move in the direction of less concern with recording as a process and more concern for recording as a managerial product. The changes are toward abbreviation and standardization. Agencies have been modifying recording procedures to streamline content and to focus more sharply on the specifics of service, much of which involves what actually is accomplished in the interview. Outlines, checklists, and brief forms are replacing detailed narratives. Agencies ask for opening summaries, social history outlines, progress summaries, and closing summaries (Kagle 1993).

Summary: Chapter 10

The final phase of the interview is termination or the ending of one interview in a series of interviews. The interviewer should tell the client at the beginning of the interaction that a definite period of time has been allotted for the interview. The interviewer is responsible for pacing the content and affect so that they can reasonably expect to achieve the objectives of the interview in the time allotted. The interviewer should prepare the interviewee for closure by using a variety of verbal and nonverbal cues. In some cases the interviewee may fail to respond to the signals that the interview is coming to a close. In this instance the interviewer should hold without equivocation to the need to terminate but express a desire to maintain communication.

As part of the termination process the interviewer briefly recapitulates what they have covered in the interview, what decisions they have reached, what questions remain, and what, if any, steps for action they plan to take. Just as the interview itself may be preceded by a short social conversation as a transition, termination may be followed by a similar short conversation. Once the interview is concluded, the interviewer should spend some time reviewing and evaluating what occurred.

Note taking during the interview may be distracting and self-defeating. However, note taking is appropriate if the interviewee is offering specific information such as dates, names, addresses, and telephone numbers or when interviewers note actions they have promised to take between sessions. Interviewers planning to take notes during the interview should share this with the interviewee and seek permission. If note taking disrupts the interview, it is advisable to discontinue the activity.

SUGGESTED READINGS

Suanna J. Wilson. *Recording: Guideline for Social Workers.* New York: Free Press, 1980. (238 pp.)
  A detailed account of social work recording with an interesting variety of examples.
Jill Kagle. *Social Work Records*, 2d ed. Belmont, Calif.: Wadsworth, 1991. (225 pp.)
  A comprehensive overview of the why's, wherefore's, and how's of social work records.

PART THREE

Some Special Problems in Interviewing

ELEVEN

Nonverbal Communication

Throughout this book we have pointed out that verbal content is only one channel that interview participants use to communicate their messages. In this chapter we discuss those other channels. "I *hear* you talking" is supplemented by observing the nonverbal message "I *see* what you mean."

Those concerned with the interview have always been interested in nonverbal communication. Freud commented, "He who has eyes to see and ears to hear may convince himself that no mortal can keep a secret. If his lips are silent, he chatters with his fingertips; betrayal oozes out of him at every pore" (1959:49). However, lack of technology that would "capture" nonverbal communication for analysis hampered its systematic analysis.

Today the tape recorder, movie camera, and videotape have made possible the preservation of the interview almost intact and allow different observers to replay each moment for scrutiny. Technology also permits the electronic analysis of the characteristics of vocal communication—its exact pitch, volume, "roughness," quavering, and the like. As a result recent decades have witnessed the rapid development of interest and research in nonverbal communication of all kinds.

Nonverbal communication can be an expressive channel for those who have a rich gestural vocabulary. The prizefight is a good example of an interview in which the participants send all their messages through changes in the positions of their arms, legs, body, and head, the fighters carefully watching each other telegraph their intentions via body language. Gifted mimes can communicate most of what they want to say without words. The sign language of the deaf, which is derived from the communication systems used in monastic orders pledged to silence, is evidence of the rich possibilities of the powerful language of nonverbal communication. However, the gestural language of the deaf, like Indian sign language, has a clearly established standard lexicon. Dictionaries of such gestures provide their definitions. This is not true for much of the nonverbal communication that the interviewer will want to decode.

Nonverbal communications are messages about the verbal communication. They are signals about signals. They tell us something about the validity of the message, its urgency, whether it is being sent humorously, seriously, or sarcastically. A hostile remark becomes softer if it is accompanied by a laugh. Laughter says something about the attitude toward the message of the person sending it, whether that person is concerned or indifferent or upset about the information in the message. Nonverbal communications say something about the speaker's relationship with the listener, whether the speaker feels inferior or superior, friendly or distant. Nonverbal messages help us interpret what we are hearing. Verbal communication is concerned with what we communicate; nonverbal communication is more concerned with how we communicate.

Such communication helps us to interpret verbal communications more accurately. What we see enables us to better understand what we are hearing. Think of a situation in which you cannot see the person you are talking to—as in telephone conversations. It is hard to determine what the other person really means, what that person is feeling about what is being said.

More accurately, communication is not verbal or nonverbal; it is a complex integration of both. Nonverbal communication means that we "listen" with our eyes as well as our ears. It is said that we "speak with our vocal organs and converse with our whole body" and that "man is a multisensorial being; occasionally he verbalizes."

Nonverbal behaviors are powerful communications that influence the judgments of interviewers and interviewees. Whereas verbal communication is a steady stream, nonverbal communication consists of a variety of discontinuous stimuli—gestural, paralinguistic, and proxemic. Nonverbal messages are vivid. They have particular salience at the beginning of the interview when both interviewer and interviewee are in a state of vigilant arousal, trying to get a handle on each other.

Nonverbal communication can be best understood if we know something of the context in which it is being displayed. The context of interest here is for the most part uniform—two people seated near one another in a small room, communicating in a formal manner.

In some respects nonverbal communication has advantages over verbal communication. We can transmit nonverbal messages over a number of different channels simultaneously. Verbal messages are more restricted to the one channel available for transmission. At the same time we can smile and gaze directly, vary the pitch and loudness of our voice, move closer to interviewees, touch their hand, and relax our posture. The message configuration is more complex and nuanced than any verbal procedure can achieve. Nonverbal messages can provide multiple meanings and perform multiple functions simultaneously.

Nonverbal messages have priority over verbal messages. Before you have said the first hello, you have already processed visual messages regarding the sex, age, race, physique, style of dress, and even income bracket of the interviewee. You are forming impressions that may determine the appropriateness or inappropriateness of some initial verbal communication. We are able to completely refrain from any verbal communication. We are never able to completely refrain from nonverbal communication. Nonverbal messages are omnipresent.

Nonverbal messages are more universal than verbal messages, which are tied to a language code. In the presence of a person whose language we cannot speak, we can still communicate joy and sadness and anger and friendliness.

Verbal messages are a digital yes-no. Nonverbal messages are analogous to the color spectrum, with gradual gradations in meaning. Thus nonverbal messages permit a subtlety in communication that is absent in verbal communication.

Sources of Nonverbal Communication

Researchers have identified a variety of sources of significant nonverbal data: chronomics, smell, touch, artifactual communication, paralinguistics, proxemics, and body language—kinesics.

Chronomics

In chapter 4 we discussed waiting time as it relates to the client's feelings at the start of an interview. Our discussion here is about time as a general nonverbal message, which is called "chronomic communication."

Managing time is an act of nonverbal communication. An old joke offers a pretty good definition of chronomic communication: if you come early for an appointment, you are anxious; if you come on time, you are compulsive; and if you come late, you are resistive. Time does talk.

Clients who must wait for an interviewer who is running late have lost a measure of control over their time. Lateness is an expression of the interview participants' difference in status. More often the lower status person is kept waiting by the higher status person. The higher status person has more access to the lower status person's time than the reverse. Lateness suggests to the waiting person that the party who is running late has something more important to do. Something or someone else is getting preference. Once the interview starts, the interviewer might take a phone call or speak "for a moment" to a colleague, again invading the client's time. Interruptions initiated by the interviewee are less likely.

Overscheduling appointments to make certain that the worker's time is fully used shows a greater respect for the worker's time than for the client's time. We tend to be generous with our time in talking to clients we like and enjoy, and we (perhaps unwittingly) reduce the time we spend with demanding or unappreciative clients. The power to control access to our time, as well as other people's time, provides the opportunity to make significant nonverbal statements.

Timing is an incremental metacommunication that can give the content of the message increased urgency. If a client calls a worker at 11 P.M., the timing suggests urgency, a special meaning.

Time is a valuable commodity. We spend time, we save time, we waste time, we buy time. How the interviewer manages time sends a message. The amount of time we are willing to "invest" in dealing with a situation or with a particular person says something about our evaluation of the significance of the situation or the person.

As interviewers we have a monochronomic sense of the use of time, that is, we expect to concentrate on one activity at a time. Other people may have a polychronomic sense of time—doing a number of things in the same time slot. This may present a problem in home interviews when the interviewee cooks or washes dishes or cleans the house while participating in an interview.

The culture communicates a great respect for time, time schedules, and promptness. Almost all of us wear watches and are constantly aware of the passage of time. We schedule interviews for a particular time, and we participate in the interview for a particular time period. Our supposition is that all interviewees have a similar attitude, but this may not be the case. Some individuals and some groups may have a more relaxed attitude toward time and its usage. Interviewees who are casual habitual latecomers or who never seem aware of the need to end an interview on time may be communicating a different perception of time.

Cultures differ in regard to time and time-related expectations. Interviewers take the expenditure of time seriously—they are bound by their schedule and their training to do so. Other orientations suggest a more relaxed attitude, what used to be called "street time." To Southeast Asians, such as Vietnamese and Cambodians, time is a flexible commodity and punctuality is not a great virtue.

Artifactual Communication

Artifactual communication is the language of objects. The channel is the visual, and the sources of information are the physical setting and personal adornments—clothes, hairstyles, makeup, jewelry, home decor, and the like.

Home visits provide a rich source of artifactual communication. People tend to express their interests and tastes in the objects they buy and display. In one home the book collection is prominent; in another home the sound system and CD collection are highly visible; in a third home plants are everywhere. The type of art on the walls, the magazines on the table, and the style of furniture communicate something about the people. Is the house open or closed to the outside world? Are curtains and shades drawn, or are the windows uncovered so that people can look out and in? Is the decor formal or loose and familiar, cluttered or uncluttered, bright or dull? Is the furniture arranged so that it encourages comfortable conversation? Does everyone have a bed and a place for privacy? Does the home have enough chairs to seat the whole family at one time, a table big enough for a family meal?

Office decor and arrangements are elements of artifactual communication. Comfortable lighting, room temperature, furnishings, and provisions for privacy communicate a measure of care and concern for the interviewee's comfort. We put diplomas on our walls to communicate expertise. The look of the interviewer's desktop says something about efficiency, neatness, and organization of work.

Clothing is another source of artifactual communication. Clothing identifies gender, age, socioeconomic status, and nationality. We expect people of different groups to dress differently. At the extremes the dress of a homeless person and a socialite permit clear identification. In the middle range drawing inferences may be difficult. Only a keen eye can distinguish the upper lower-income sales clerk from the upper middle-income mid-level manager.

We tend to associate certain dress with certain occupations; upon seeing it we draw inferences about the person. The most obvious examples are, of course, uniforms, such as the soldier's khaki, the priest's collar, and the nurse's uniform. The hospital uniforms distinguishing registered, practical, and student nurses require a practiced eye for accurate identification. But there is, further, a uniform implied in the designations "white-collar worker" and "blue-collar worker" and the stereotype of the tweed-wearing professor.

There are uniforms of group identification—the studded leather jacket and boots of the Hells Angels and the yarmulke of the Orthodox Jews.

Clothing is an extension of the body and is closely related to body image. It is therefore an expression of self and it conditions our self-image. Choice of clothing designed to make a short man look tall or a plump woman look slender, loose-fitting clothing to disguise corpulence, tight clothing to accentuate voluptuousness, or a scarf worn to conceal neck wrinkles tells us something about the interviewee's body image and response to this image. Clothes permit us to control access to information about ourselves. Some have described the selection of clothing to create a desired impression as "wardrobe engineering."

Our reliance on clothing to understand clients is most obvious when we are denied such information. The patient in the hospital and the prisoner in the institution wear the uniform of the setting. The interviewer is denied the information clothing might otherwise communicate.

In seeking additional artifactual information we can observe length of hair, whether the male interviewee is shaved or not, general level of cleanliness, the extent to which eyebrows are plucked and shaped, nails bitten or manicured. Choice of eyeglass style communicates a message as does hairstyle.

In *Hamlet* Shakespeare correctly notes that "the apparel oft proclaims the man." The problem lies in accurately deciphering the proclamation.

An older person wearing clothing identified with adolescents may suggest problems regarding attitudes toward aging.

The African American client wearing a dashiki may be making a political statement. "Such costumes are not only a reminder or a challenge to the outsider; they can also be a rebuke to other minority group members who are still walking around town in the garb of the majority" (Lurie 1981:93). Worn by a white middle-income client, a dashiki could be an expression of solidarity with the peoples of underdeveloped countries.

Wearing clothes that are outmoded may suggest an emotional attachment to the past, that the client has not been able to buy new more stylish clothing, or that the client has decided that the current fashions are ugly.

Subdued colors, restrained cut, and heavier fabrics tend to be associated with a conservative lifestyle. We can note the age and condition of clothing and how fashionable or how highly individualized it is. These say something about self-concept, concern for the image projected, level of narcissism, and attitude toward the interview; colors, cut, and fabrics may also reflect a concern with comfort in clothing or a concern with clothing as a means of decoration and self-expression.

High interest in dress does seem to suggest some dependence on others for stimulation and approval and more anxiety directed toward the environment of other people. Lower levels of interest in dress signal less dependence on the environment for stimulation and support. Because one motive that determines clothing choice is a desire to make a good impression on others, a careless disregard for dress suggests a disregard for the reactions of others. If this is not the result of rebelliousness against conventional society and the triviality of concern with dress, it may suggest a depressive withdrawal. Psychiatrists often chart improvements in psychotic patients in part by their appearance.

People also wear clothing for protection. The social worker in protective service, investigating cases of neglect, observes the child's clothing to determine whether it is adequate protection against cold, snow, or rain.

Jewelry is another unit of artifactual communication. Jewels as artifacts of conspicuous consumption say something about socioeconomic status. Elks pins, Phi Beta Kappa keys, and slogan buttons proclaim the subgroups with which the interviewee and interviewer are affiliated and feel identified. Wedding rings of course communicate marital status.

People consciously select clothing and jewelry, so these say something about personal preferences and lifestyle.

One caution is that, despite our best efforts and against our better judgment, we tend to make judgments when we first meet people on the basis of their attractiveness, clothes, hairstyle, and adornments. We are almost universally affected by what we see. Noting this tendency, Aristotle said, "Beauty is a better recommendation than any letter of introduction."

The interviewee also observes the clothing worn by the interviewer. If it is at variance with what is generally expected of a middle-income social worker, the worker communicates a disconcerting message.

Some workers may think they are making egalitarian efforts to establish rapport with lower-income clients by deliberately dressing informally. This may not have the effect intended. Casual dress may mean to the worker that "I feel comfortable, informal with you." The client might read this as "You don't give a damn and you didn't bother to dress for me." In a study of clients' reaction to workers' attire Hubble and Gelso found that "clients manifest the most desirable reactions to counselors who dress in a way that is one step or level more formal than the client's own dress level" (1978:584).

Whether explicitly defined or not, American culture has a loosely structured dress code to which both interviewee and interviewer respond. The client has some expectations of how a professional such as a social worker is to be dressed for a formal occasion such as an interview. Thus social workers need to give some reasonable regard to their dress.

Some interviewers who feel that self-disclosure is consistent with their participatory-humanistic orientation toward the interviewee use the office setting as a nonverbal channel for self-disclosure. They adorn these offices with family photographs and evidence of their hobbies, interests, and artistic proclivities.

Artifactual messages have the disadvantage of relative inflexibility. You can change your words with different clients. You cannot as conveniently change your attire or office arrangements.

Smell

The olfactory channel, a source of considerable communication for lower animals, is rarely, if ever, investigated or discussed as a useful source of human communication. Subtle changes in body odor can signal changes in emotional states. However, the cultural emphasis on cleanliness tends to mask all natural body odors. Also, our noses are not educated to detect changes in body odor, and such messages are rapidly attenuated over even the short distance that separates interview participants. Even if we do detect changes, we cannot make psychological sense of them because we have not studied them. We are aware of the heavily perfumed or the odoriferous interviewee and the smells of liquor and bad breath, and we draw some general conclusions from such data.

Some settings such as the hospital have a distinctive odor, and we use our noses in making some assessment in protective service situations—sniffing for smells of urine, mildew, garbage, and feces in cases of child neglect.

We may be aware in the interview of the smell that clings to the habitual marijuana smoker. Body odor tends to increase with anxiety and other kinds of tension. Without being aware of it we may increase our distance from the interviewee who projects a strong body odor. We may break eye contact more frequently with the interviewee who has bad breath or we turn our face, and nose, away.

The definition of a smell as pleasant or unpleasant is a result of cultural socialization. Because some ethnic groups may have a diet different from ours, we may react negatively to unfamiliar body odors without being fully aware of the basis of our reaction.

The widespread use of deodorants, soap, mouthwash, perfume, and the like is a testimonial to our recognition that smells do matter, that smells communicate messages. They attract or repel. We generally make some judgments about the interviewee based on what we smell. We make judgments about families based on the smells we detect as we come into a house on a home visit. We tend to associate unpleasant odors with undesirable personal habits and social characteristics.

Although we are aware of and react to smells, we are less explicitly conscious of our olfactory responses than we are of other sensory information. Olfactory sensations have a more direct pathway to the brain than sight, sound, or touch. Of all the senses olfaction seems to be the keenest for waking memories. Furthermore, olfactory memories are less influenced by the passage of time. Odors are memorable and evocative. We may, then, react more sharply than we know to certain odors associated with our experiences. A smell might be triggering feelings that stem from previous encounters rather than from this interviewee.

Confident of the relationship of certain odors and certain moods, commercial establishments have used odors to increase sales (O'Neill 1991:B1). Cypress and cinnamon are associated with calm and relaxation, lavender and peppermint with increased efficiency and a positive mood. Olfactory research might ultimately be applied to managing the odors of interviewing rooms in social agencies.

Touch

The interview rarely calls for use of our sense of touch. Touch is a powerful nonverbal method of communication. We use it as a sign of affection, as a message of understanding and empathy, as a show of comfort and support. We use it to request attention, regulate communication, and confirm solidarity.

Occasionally, in moments of great stress interviewers might reach over and briefly touch the interviewee in a gesture of comfort and sympathy, but workers use touching selectively. For the most part the normative cultural proscriptions tend to limit its use. We live in a culture that does not readily sanction touching.

Touching is formalized in the handshake that may begin and end the interview. Even when touching might be acceptable during an interview, our culture prescribes the zones of the body that might be touched.

If clients are crying and distraught, reaching across and touching their hand or holding their hand in a spontaneous gesture of sympathy and support might be acceptable. Putting a hand on the client's knee or upper arm might be less acceptable. Embracing or hugging between a female interviewee and a male interviewer would be eyebrow raising.

The gender of the participants, the nature of the interview, and the zones of the body are factors in the decision to touch or not to touch. Status is also involved. The interviewer's "entitlement" to touch the interviewee is greater than the interviewee's freedom to touch the interviewer. When interviewers decide to touch, they also must consider the nature of the gesture. We may brush, pat, stroke, squeeze, hold, or embrace. Each communicates a somewhat different message and the person touched receives each differently.

Touching is more socially acceptable when the interviewee is a child, but even here the worker needs to carefully consider whether to touch.

A 7-year-old child in a residential institution says he doesn't like himself, and nobody likes him, not even his mother who has "dumped" him and said he is a shit. He starts to cry inconsolably at that point. The worker says,

> I felt very tender toward John when I saw him crying so profusely. I wanted to hold him at the time but wasn't sure that my "gut level" response would be appreciated, for many disturbed children react hostilely to physical contact. John seemed ashamed that he was crying. I wanted to assure him that crying was not only acceptable but in this case helpful.

In the social work clinical context clients might regard touching as analogous to the touching by doctors and nurses when they are examining or treating a patient. This touching is an aspect of the professional function. When used appropriately in response to the client's needs, touching can help reduce tension, calm and comfort the client, stimulate self-disclosure, and enhance a sense of communion between worker and client (Lomranz and Shapiro 1974).

Responses from 231 psychotherapy patients regarding their reaction to touch in the interview found that most of them felt positive about the experience. They felt touch facilitated a feeling of bonding, was a sign that the interviewer really cared about them, that touch communicated acceptance and enhanced self-esteem. They also felt increased support, which enabled them to disclose threatening material (Horton et al. 1995).

The supposition of interviewers holding a humanistic orientation is that some forms of touching facilitate openness and sharing. Touching presumably communicates support, warmth, and caring.

Touching may make some people feel anxious. It imposes a greater measure of intimacy than they may be ready to concede. Others may feel that interviewers are taking advantage of their higher status. We interpret touching differently when interviewer and interviewee are of the same gender than when they are of opposite genders.

The available research suggests that the interviewer needs to carefully weigh the decision to touch for contextual appropriateness and the interviewee's receptivity. A touch can be helpful but it has its dangers. The effects of touch depend to some extent on the nature of the touch, the part of the body touched, the cultural background of the client, and the timing of the touch. The response to touch depends on the relationship to the toucher, the context in which touching takes place, and the intensity, duration, and frequency of the touching (Kertay and Reviere 1993).

Borenzweig (1983) conducted a questionnaire study of the clinical practice of social workers and found that they are positively oriented toward the judicious use of touch based on the needs of the client. Despite this attitude social workers are hesitant. The taboo against touching is strong and inhibits the use of this nonverbal gesture. The current increased concern about sexual activity between clients and therapists, general consciousness about sexual harassment, intensified legal restrictions regarding client-therapist sex, and publicity given to malpractice suits stemming from such activity have tended to increase circumspection about touching.

Touching is the most intimate form of nonverbal communication. It is the language of love and sexual arousal. We characterize sensitive matters as touchy subjects. Touching in the interview is touching in the context of a private encounter where touchy material is often discussed. Given these considerations, it is understandable, then, that touch is frequently monitored, regulated, and circumscribed. The difficulty in separating the clinical use of touching and its sensual affectional aspects leaves the intent of the gesture open to misinterpretation.

The unilateral prerogative of touching, reserved to the interviewer, expresses the power difference between interviewer and interviewee. Because touching so explicitly expresses this difference, the danger is that the client may resent being touched, however oriented the touch is to achieving the objectives of the interview. Touching is, after all, an invasion of the interviewee's privacy.

The interviewer has to be clear that the situation warrants touching, that the nature of the touch is appropriate, that its intent is nonerotic, and that it doesn't impose a greater degree of intimacy on the interviewee than the interviewee wants and can cope with. The gesture must be a response to genuine feeling and serve the needs of the interviewee. The interviewer has to decide whether a touch that is theoretically correct in terms of the needs of the interview is also ethically incorrect.

Despite the dangers and the care required in the use of touch, interviewers should not rule out its use. Given the great variations in the situations in which touch is appropriate and in which failure to touch might be regarded as unnatural, the answer must lie with the sensitivity of the interviewer to the moment.

Social workers do tend to do more touching than psychologists (Willison and Masson 1986:498). Ramsdell and Ramsdell (1994), studying both clients' and workers' perceptions of the effects of social workers' physical contact with clients, found that both groups feel that "shaking hands" and "client hugging counselor and counselor hugging client" when appropriate are therapeutically beneficial.

Paralinguistics

The principal channel of communication in the interview is of course the auditory channel, the transmission and reception of "noises" the participants make. Auditory interaction includes much more than the words. We can modify the meaning of our spoken words by the accompanying pitch, intensity, speed, stress, intonation, inflection, and articulation. These vocal but nonverbal communications are called "paralinguistic cues." They are the nonsemantic aspects of speech. These are the noises we make that shape the intonation and give color to the words we are speaking. The flat talk of robots in old space films gives us an idea of what is lost when paralinguistic cues are absent.

The same verbal communication can carry different messages, depending on the acoustical accompaniment. Vocal nonverbal communication tells us how the person speaks. These are the language sounds that accompany the words but are not a property of the words themselves. The paralinguistic cues are like aerial punctuation marks. *Paralinguistics* are sometimes defined as the "vocal sounds that are left after subtracting verbal content." If the words provide the cognitive aspect of the message's meaning, paralinguistics tend to provide the affective aspect. Through our manipulation of pitch, loudness, tempo, emphasis, and pauses, we give additional meaning and color to the words we articulate.

Pitch refers to differences in frequency, from low bass to high soprano. The *velocity* of speech refers to movement of the words as they issue from the mouth. Does one word follow another slowly or rapidly? Is the movement jerky or smooth? Is *articulation* precise to the point of being pedantic or slurred and mumbled? *Intensity* refers to volume of speech—so loud that it beats at you, so soft that you wonder whether the person wants to be heard. *Stress* refers to the pattern of increase and decrease in loudness within phrases or applied to different syllables within words. Stress is concerned with emphasis. We can say the same words matter-of-factly or in a mocking tone of voice. Voice quality refers to the pleasant or unpleasant characteristics of voice—raspiness, nasality, whining. *Inflection* refers to the change or lack of change in pitch. A flat inflection is monotonous or boring.

An often-cited dramatic illustration of the significance of paralinguistics in giving different meaning to the verbalization of the same words is the following:

> Woman, without her, man would be a savage.
> Woman, without her man, would be a savage.

Voice qualities often affect our perception of the interviewee because our response is dictated by cultural stereotypes. The man with the high-pitched voice is perceived as effeminate; the woman with the low-pitched voice is perceived as sexy.

Just as there are postural stereotypes associated with certain occupations—military bearing, a scholar's stoop—there are occupational voice stereotypes—a minister's voice, a teacher's voice, a drill sergeant's voice.

Dialects and accents are the paralinguistic music of the language, providing information about social status and regional and ethnic origins.

A voice can be emotional, so that it breaks, trembles, chokes, sighs, and reflects deep or rapid respiration. It can be flat, neutral, controlled. A voice can be full of energy or it can be thin. Smooth speech may show a lack of conflict or anxiety; it may also be evidence of a rehearsed speech, designed to deceive.

We spell out our emotions paralinguistically. We tend to express anger with a relatively fast rate of speech that is clipped and more than normally loud, with short durations and short pauses. High ratio of pauses and slowness of speech signal sadness; these are also characteristic of contempt, although the tone of voice differs. A relatively high pitch shows fear. A quavering voice may result from anxiety; a squeezed voice, depression. Dibner confirmed that repeating words and phrases, leaving sentences unfinished, making frequent changes in thought, shifting volume, and stuttering are related to level of anxiety (1956). Rate of speech and productivity increase with anxiety, and the silence quotient is low. Conversely, a low speech rate and a high silence quotient characterize depression. Vocal segregates such as "ah" and "er" express ambivalence or anxiety about what is being said.

To ensure continued control interviewees may speed up their speech and increase the volume in response to a perception that the interviewer wishes to interrupt. Interviewees may increase speed when talking about something embarrassing in order to get it over with and may decrease the volume at the same time, as if to hide the words.

Interviews are difficult events for the participants. Transcripts of actual interviews show that they usually are characterized by redundancies, rephrasings, hesitations, fractured sentences, mumbles and grumbles, and filled pauses such as "well," "see," "okay," "got me?," and "you know what I mean?"

Research has identified certain paralinguistic characteristics as being associated with interviewing. Differences in tone of voice communicate differences in warmth and differences in impressions of professional competence (Blanck et al. 1986). A moderate but lively rate of speech, variety in pitch, animated expressiveness, and little pausing evoke a positive response and enhance the interview's credibility. A clear robust voice also tends to evoke a positive image.

Because even our best friends hesitate to tell us, we do not realize that we often mumble or speak too rapidly. Good interviewing requires speaking clearly at moderate volume and moderate tempo, with few hesitancies, and no undue fidgeting, nervous laughter, or throat clearing.

Proxemics

Proxemics is the language of space and distance. It is the organization of space relationships between people—the study of space as nonverbal communication. Our culture has a normative distance that people interacting with each other maintain, generally a zone of four to seven feet; this is a comfortable social distance in American culture. Someone who moves closer than three feet invades our personal space, and the intruder is presuming an intimacy we may not be ready to grant. Increasing the distance to nine feet may be regarded as a rejection. Interviewer-interviewee distance is generally in the five- to eight-foot range, varying somewhat as participants lean forward to engage more fully, lean back to disengage.

Proxemics implies the existence of an invisible bubble that defines our personal territory; we perceive the invasion of this space as an invasion of the self.

The interviewer needs to be aware that interaction distance is a variable of some significance in the interview. Clients may perceive interviewers who remain beyond this space as cold and aloof; clients may see interviewers who come too close as inappropriately intimate and pushy.

The use of space is related to status. The interviewer may feel free about invading the personal space of the interviewee by moving closer. The interviewee is more likely to be hesitant about moving in on the interviewer.

Interviewers often have a tilt-chair on coasters, whereas the interviewee generally has a straight chair; this permits interviewers greater flexibility in modulating distance. They can tilt forward or back and slide the chair in or away from the interviewee. Interviewees have to deliberately and ostentatiously move their chair forward. They can lean forward some but cannot tilt away from the interviewer. The interviewee's leaning forward and back is a significant positive indication of a good relationship, signaling the client's more active involvement.

Proxemic shifts and posture changes are often associated with some transition in the interview. Participants physically change positions as they change topics or direction. Changing positions acts as a nonverbal message that a change is about to take place.

Proxemic preferences vary by culture. The normative distance for interaction among Mexican Americans is somewhat closer than is true for Anglos. Such clients may move closer to the interviewer with no intention of invading the interviewer's personal space; they are behaving normally.

The usual distance in conversational interaction among African Americans is greater than among whites. A white interviewer moving in close may be regarded by a black interviewee as an invader of intimate space.

Seating arrangements of interview participants are a proxemic nonverbal cue. Haase and DiMattia (1970) studied counselor and client preferences for interview seating arrangements by using four pictures of a male-female dyad talking to each other. In one photograph the participants' chairs were side by side at a forty-five-degree angle; in the second the chairs were opposite each other but on the same side of the desk; in the third the chairs were opposite each other with a desk between them; and in the fourth the chairs were at a forty-five-degree angle with only a corner of the desk between them. The researchers used a semantic differential scale in obtaining a statement of preference. The position most prefer, as stated by both counselor and client, is the one in which the participants interact over the corner of the desk. Although the counselors also show a high preference for two chairs facing each other with no desk between them, clients are decidedly more negative toward this arrangement. Apparently, the client does not feel sufficiently protected by the open position because it encourages openness of interaction. The researchers note that clients seem to prefer talking over the corner of a desk because the arrangement is somewhat open yet provides a partial barrier. "Conceivably such an arrangement might be preferred by the individual who enters counseling with trepidation about the experience, who is hopeful of help yet threatened by the therapeutic encounter. The 'protected sociopetal space' might serve the purpose of inviting a limited negotiation toward interaction yet offer the necessary security and safety required by most humans in a new and ambiguous situation" (1970:324).

The arrangement that counselors and clients like least is two chairs with a desk directly between. This format suggests that the participants are opposed to each other. A face-to-face position also forces each participant to look directly at the other or deliberately turn away, a gesture that hints at rudeness. An arrangement that puts the interviewee sideways to the desk or table and the interviewer across the corner permits the participants to let their gaze wander without seeming to avoid eye contact.

Although the desk corner position, representing a team interaction with the interviewer as leader, does result in more interaction than the other positions, some interviewers prefer the open (no desk) arrangement because it represents an orientation of mutuality and colleagiality.

Body Language—Kinesics

The study of body language, kinesics, is concerned with movements, gestures, posture, and facial expressions as an important form of nonverbal communication. Just as the paralinguistic cues depend on the sense of hearing, kinesics depends on sight.

The visual channel is a source of a great deal of information in the interview. Whether they explicitly recognize it or not, interviewers are constantly observing the great variety of motions the interviewee makes. As Hamilton (1946) says, we can observe without interviewing but we cannot interview without observing. Good interviewing requires that you be a good watcher as well as a good listener.

Visual sensations, like auditory ones, travel farther than olfactory or tactile sensations, although here too there are limits. Changes in the size of the pupils, tense neck muscles, contracted pelvic muscles, slight changes in skin coloration (blanching, blushing), and changes in respiration rate all require keen eyesight and are easily lost. At distances of five to eight feet these messages are extremely difficult to perceive. Being close to the interviewee may permit the worker to detect subtle movements, but the interviewer then may not be able to detect the more general changes because of lost perspective.

The frequency with which we use symbolic expressions to refer to the body demonstrates the importance of bodily communications. Schutz has collected a list of expressions in common use that describe behavior and feelings in bodily terms (1967:25–26). We talk of being tight-lipped to indicate secrecy, a stiff upper lip suggests fortitude, and when we are dejected we are down in the mouth

Our language brims with the translation of feelings into body language.

We tremble with rage, swallow our pride, jump with joy, feel our stomachs lurch in fear.

We put a hand over our mouth when we are embarrassed: we cover our eyes with our hands when we feel ashamed. Open-palm hand movements thrust what is being said in the interviewer's direction.

Posture is whole body communication. It might be the stiff posture of the society matron, the bent posture of the computer nerd, the loose casual posture of the lounge lizard. Posture can be open or closed—open, allowing access to the body; closed, denying access. Arms held across the chest or legs crossed high up, knee on knee, are posturally closed conditions.

Posture communicates strongly felt attitudes. A person who sits with a vigilant body, head erect, arms folded, and legs tightly crossed is likely to be nonverbally expressing disagreement with what the interviewer is saying. A slumping posture, head supported by the hand, legs straight out, might express boredom.

The body as an object of observation takes on particular importance today because of drugs. Needle marks on the arms and "tracks" (discoloration along the course of veins in the arms), accompanied by sniffling, flushing, drowsiness, and contracted pupils may give away the heroin addict. Shakiness, itching, tension, profuse perspiration, and body odor all suggest the use of amphetamines (speed). Use of marijuana is not likely to be observable because the effects wear off quickly and leave no evident signs. If seen shortly after inhaling a strong dose, the pot smoker may show reddening of the eyes and a cough from the irritating effects of the smoke. If interviewers know the characteristic odor of marijuana smoke, they may detect it.

The use of crack (rock cocaine) is more difficult to detect visually. Fast breathing and a runny nose are associated with the use of powdered cocaine.

The face The part of the body that offers the greatest number and variety of gestural cues is the face. The face is naked and thus open to observation. "You should have seen the look on his face" is testimonial to the expressiveness of facial gesturing. Courtesy and custom dictate that we look at the face of the person who is speaking, so it is legitimate to scrutinize the face for messages. The face is our window on the world. An old but valid saying is that the most important thing we wear is the expression on our face.

The organs we use to obtain sensory information—sight, sound, smell, taste—are located on our head, as are the entrances to our body for sustenance—air, food, and water. The face is the site of our speech production. Many stereotypes associated with facial features may suggest—often incorrectly—certain ideas about the person. We tend to think of people with thick lips as sexy, those with thin lips as determined and authoritative. A high forehead and glasses may connote intelligence and a fat face, jolliness whereas protruding eyes suggest an excitable person.

The face is the location of most of the automatic signals of tension—blushing, perspiration,dryness of the mouth and lips. We yawn in boredom and project the glazed look of indifference. We bite our lip in redirected aggression.

The muscles of the face are sufficiently complex to permit more than a thousand different expressions. The forehead wrinkles and furrows; eyebrows arch and knit; eyes shift and widen or narrow; eyelids close slowly or flutter rapidly; nostrils flare; and lips curl, tremble, turn up, turn down, open, and close and are moistened by the tongue; jaws clamp; and teeth grind. The head can nod or shake, be raised or lowered; the chin can be thrust forward or drawn in. Anger is expressed by a frown, tensed lips pushed forward, head and chin thrust forward, glowering eyes; a broad smile and lifting of the eyebrows show pleasant surprise.

The facial features are capable of considerable modulation in gesturing. The eyes offer a whole range of possibilities from closed to merely slitted to wide open. Just think of the variation between the slight smile and the loud laugh.

We all are experienced in arranging our faces so that they display the emotion that is socially appropriate for the occasion: sadness at a funeral, happiness at a graduation, disgust at an offensive action. We therefore suspect something is amiss when someone does not display an appropriate facial expression. Control over facial expressions furthers deception and management of the impression an individual wants to create for others. We control our displays of nonverbal behavior to influence the way others perceive us.

We learn display rules in the family—"Don't look so bored"; "Wipe that angry look off your face"; "Look happy when Grandma comes." Social work interviewers know such rules as the face they put on in meeting the client.

We may put on an expression that a social situation calls for but we do not honestly feel. In this case we may make only a partial display of the expression; some element may be missing. The false expression is also apt to be poorly timed—assumed a moment too late, turned off a moment too early.

Some smiles are tight, others frozen too long to convey sincerity; on-again off-again smiles belie the words of welcome accompanying them. Smiles with no depth remind us of a Chinese proverb: "Beware the man who laughs and his belly doesn't."

We laugh in happiness and we laugh in discomfort, confusion, and guilt. We smile in pleasure, embarrassment, appeasement, invitation, and ridicule. The same overt behavior results from a variety of different emotions. And just as there are many different kinds of smiles, there are different ways of crying.

We often can use the configuration of mouth, eyes, eyebrows, and forehead movements to identify facial expressions of sharply defined and clearly different feelings—fear, happiness, sadness, anger, surprise, disgust. But most often people blend their expressions so that the emotion displayed in the face is not so easy to read accurately.

Sometimes we abbreviate our facial displays. We may only widen our eyes rather than widen our eyes and raise an eyebrow to show surprise. Here we are activating only part of the face to express the emotion. We modulate the same expression to communicate questioning surprise, dazed surprise, puzzled surprise, or slight, moderate, or extreme surprise. To complicate matters we can also use a series of these complex expressions, each lasting a short period of time—sometimes as briefly as a fifth of a second. Different emotions expressed by different simultaneous facial expressions are termed *affect blends*.

We can hide our face behind our hands, as when we shield our eyes or mouth with our hands. We can also hide it behind sunglasses, which may block the eyes and part of the face, making them inaccessible. Removing our sunglasses may be a sign that we are ready to make ourselves more available. But a person who wears corrective glasses and removes them maybe temporarily withdrawing. Because this person sees less without the glasses, the world is masked.

Eyes "Don't look at me in that tone of voice" is a popular acknowledgment of the importance of the eyes in nonverbal communication. We see eye to eye when in agreement and receive an icy stare or our eyes shoot daggers when in disagreement. One look is come hither, another fishy, yet another sidelong. We control others with our eyes as reflected in the expression "She held him with her eyes." The eye is a powerful weapon— "the evil eye."

We speak of making eyes at someone and trying to catch a person's eye. Anybody who has tried to catch a server's eye in a restaurant knows that until you succeed, you are likely to be ignored. Eye contact obligates acknowledgment.

Looking, unlike listening, is pointed. We can fake listening; we cannot fake looking. Looking is not the same as eye contact. We can look at other people without necessarily looking into their eyes, which is implied in eye contact. Eye contact is an important component of attending behavior. The interviewer who looks at interviewees while they are talking is rated as more sincere and more involved. Eye contact reinforces mutual affiliation. A message delivered with eye contact has greater credibility. Eye contact affects the nature of the relationship and shows how the participants feel about each other. Interviewees tend to have more eye contact with an interviewer with whom they have a positive relationship. Eye contact achieves what physical proximity achieves—a sense of intimacy.

Eye contact may be an indication of liking. Or it may be perceived as a weapon—as a means of competitive dominance. Staring steadily at the interviewee has negative effects. It is a strain and may be embarrassing. Constant efforts to maintain eye contact often end in a power struggle—who will blink first? Constant eye contact suggests too great a desire for intimacy and not enough respect for the other person's privacy. Too little contact may suggest disinterest, deception, or dishonesty. A moderate amount of eye contact with intermittent breaks is the most desirable option.

We wonder about the meaning of nonverbal displays that last too long, an eye contact that becomes a stare, a prolonged handshake.

Interviewees use eye contact more frequently when they are discussing content that has a positive affect. They may avoid eye contact when discussing embarrassing material. Avoidance may signal shame or a desire to maintain a psychological distance. It may also represent a desire to reduce distraction from introspection, a wish to avoid being threatened by seeing the other person's reaction to the revelations, or a resentful withdrawal from the person who asks personal questions.

Thus a wise approach may be to avoid direct eye contact when asking highly personal questions or when the interviewee is sharing such content. Direct eye contact tends to accentuate feelings of guilt, shame, and fear.

Interviewers need to integrate various elements of attending behavior (see also chapter 6) so that a client does not perceive their total configuration as unduly intimate. Leaning closer to the client may call for a corresponding reduction of eye contact. As what the client is saying becomes more personal, interviewers need to reduce their attending behavior to maintain the equilibrium that contributes to a comfortable level of intimacy.

Eye contact has a clearly regulatory function in controlling the traffic of interviewer-interviewee discussion time. The person who is speaking looks at the listener from time to time to see whether that person is still paying attention and to obtain feedback. The speaker then looks away in order not to be distracted. The speaker can avoid being interrupted by avoiding eye contact. A person attempts eye contact more frequently when listening than when speaking.

Eye and hand gestures and body movements are regulators that tell the speaker to slow down, hurry up, continue, finish talking. When ready to yield the floor, the speaker looks directly at the listener and makes more prolonged eye contact. The speed of presentation slows down, gestures become relaxed, hands are lowered, the voice drops. All this communicates, "I am finished talking; I am ready to listen." Eye contact at the end of the comment obligates the listener to respond.

Women seek to maintain eye contact more consistently than men, an aspect of their greater orientation toward affectionate and inclusive relationships. Feminists have suggested that women use their eyes more consistently because as an oppressed social group they have to be more alert to the signals of others.

Researchers have found ethnic differences in the use of eye contact. African Americans and Hispanics tend to use eye contact less frequently than whites. As interviewees they have a greater tendency to avoid looking at the face of the interviewer. Native Americans and Asians tend to regard eye contact as disrespectful; restraint in the use of eye contact is a sign of deference. They make greater use of peripheral vision.

The extremities The hands, like the face, are naked but are easier to hide. By putting our hands in our pockets we can withhold them. We can put our hands in our lap if we are sitting behind a desk or table.

The fingers can make a fist or be extended. A palm held open, up, and extended toward the interviewer suggests supplication. We can interlace the fingers of both hands tightly or loosely, or we can make our fingertips meet to form a steeple. Hands held tightly locked suggest inhibited aggression.

We use our fingers to scratch or to pull our earlobes or rub our nose, knuckle our eyes, adjust our clothes. Touching the nose may suggest disdain or disgust. Scratching may suggest hostility turned inward. Finger play around the lips may suggest oral gratification. Picking, smoothing, and cleaning gestures may imply obsessive-compulsive traits.

We rub, clap, and wring our hands, drape them over the back of the chair, or clasp our knees with them. We rub our temples, slap a thigh or forehead, or snap a pencil during a stressful moment. When agitated, women make a rapid hand-to-neck movement, disguised as a hair-grooming gesture; men in similar situations may make an open palm-down sweep of the hair. A palm placed on the back of the neck is associated with a feeling of defensiveness. We pat our stomach to indicate hunger and press our hands to our heart to show sincerity.

Some hand gestures are self-comforting. We embrace ourselves by crossing our arms. We support our chin or stroke our face. We tend to gesticulate freely with our hands when we are talking fluently about comfortable contents. We shrug our shoulders and turn our palms up when we have difficulty verbalizing what we mean.

We use our hands to point at something, to draw a picture, or to indicate size: "It had a square shape and was about this big." We also use our hands as batons to punctuate what we are saying. When asked difficult questions and interviewees are not sure of the answers, they may have a tendency to touch their nose, pull at an ear lobe, and stroke their chin. Touching the nose and mouth-covering gestures sometimes suggest guilt.

Fidgeting and fiddling suggest anxiety. These are displacement activities, substitutes for action a person might like to take but cannot. Opening paper clips, playing with a pencil, opening and closing a bracelet, twirling hair, and jingling coins permit us to engage in motor activity while involved in the interview. The activity has a calming effect. Interviewers as well as interviewees engage in such nonverbal activity.

The feet and legs are less valuable sources of nonverbal communication. Generally, the lower part of the body is obscured by a desk or table. The feet are hidden in shoes, so that curling toes and arching insteps are difficult to detect. Even if the feet were open to view, gazing directly at them is generally considered impolite, particularly if the interviewer is a man and the interviewee a woman.

Feet and legs have a relatively limited repertoire of motions and the rearrangements cannot be executed rapidly. People can tap their feet and shuffle them by sliding them back and forth, and they cross their legs in a variety of ways. Women more frequently cross their legs with one knee over the other; men more frequently adopt an open leg cross, the ankle of one leg over the knee of the other. People swing their legs in a circular motion or kick back and forth.

We are more apt to sit in an open position that permits access to our body (no crossing of arms or legs) when we are communicating with someone we like.

Significance of Nonverbal Communication for Interviewing

What importance does nonverbal communication have for the interview? It tells us something about the nature of the relationship between the participants. Body movements toward or away from each other, changes in frequency of eye contact, and changes in positioning with reference to each other are telling. The nonverbal messages received by the eye help to confirm the validity of the spoken messages. Are the participants comfortable with each other, is there a sense of intimacy and understanding? Body language speaks to these considerations.

People who are interacting tend to synchronize much of their nonverbal behavior. They mimic and mirror each other's posturing. If one speaks loudly, the other tends to increase volume. If one speaks slowly, so does the other. Thus the interviewer, who is primarily responsible for the conduct of the interview, can consciously influence some of the nonverbal components. By manifesting a relaxed, interested, and open posture and speaking at a clearly understandable tempo and volume the interviewer can influence the client to respond in kind.

Nonverbal messages perform an impression-management function. By using a forward lean, relaxed open posture, eye contact, a smiling animated expression, direct body orientation, and judicious head nodding the interviewer consciously and deliberately sends nonverbal messages to create the impression of being interested, concerned, receptive, respectful, warm, likable, and trustworthy (Harrigan and Rosenthal 1986:46–49). Nonverbal messages perform interview management functions. Nonverbal messages are part of the ritualistic greetings and goodbyes of the interview. They help to signal that the interviewer is ready to start the interview and provide notice that the interview is coming to an end.

We use nonverbal signals in turn taking. To request a turn we lean forward and nod our head; we may raise a finger. In yielding a turn we face the listener, resume eye contact, drop our intonation, slow our tempo, decrease the volume, and increase the periods of unfilled silence. In refusing to yield a turn we continue to divert our gaze, raise our voice, gesture, and vocalize to fill pauses ("uh")

Nonverbal signals are also useful in managing transitions during the interview.

Nonverbal information helps to regulate communication. It provides some feedback that reveals whether the other person is listening, eager to say something, or is becoming bored and restive. Nonverbal messages help us to evaluate the client's emotional response to what we are saying. Is the client receiving the message with satisfaction or resentment, with hostility or indifference?

Nonverbal behavior may communicate what interviewees cannot bring themselves to say. Interviewees may not be able to put highly charged material into words, or they may not have sufficient verbal ability to express how they feel. Crying may communicate inexpressible grief; clients may communicate the shame they feel but do not want to acknowledge by hiding their eyes. Emotional expression by nonverbal response is the earliest means of communication available to us as children. In moments of stress we tend to revert to such "language." As Ruesch and Kees say, "There are certain things which cannot be said; they must be done" (1956:76).

Nonverbal communication provides information about feelings and attitudes of which interviewees have only dim awareness or of which they are unconscious. Nonverbal behavior "is less susceptible than verbal behavior to either conscious deception or unconscious censoring. . . . [Although people can hear what they are saying], most people do not know what they are doing with their bodies when they are talking and nobody tells them" (Ekman and Friesen 1968:181). Without such feedback it is difficult to control the body to transmit the message we would prefer to transmit. Thus nonverbal behavior tends to evade and frustrate efforts at self-censorship. Much nonverbal behavior is enacted below the level of conscious awareness. Blushing, twitching, or facial grimaces may erupt before the person can gain control.

Although every communication uses several channels,the degree to which we can consciously control the channels varies. There is a continuum. Tone of voice and body movement are less controllable than the face. Autonomic functions—blushing, sweating, trembling, and tensing—are not under our conscious control. These are channels that are likely to "leak" a deceptive communication.

When speech is difficult or the message would be too explicit if communicated directly, we tend to code it nonverbally. Then the message is indirect. We did not say it yet it was said. We are more capable of censoring what we actually say in words—only under considerable stress do we say things we had not intended to share. We have more difficulty controlling and censoring our nonverbal communication. Consequently, it is apt to be more genuine, more spontaneous, less deliberate, and more open to communication leakage, "saying" what we did not intend to communicate.

We rarely call explicit attention to the interviewee's gestures in the interview, nor do we ask, as we do for verbal material, "What do you mean by

that?" Clients are generally aware of what they have said. But they are usually unaware of their nonverbal comments, many of which are unintentional. All this suggests why it is easier for interviewees to use the nonverbal code to say what they do not fully intend to say and why the nonverbal
message might have importance for the interviewer.

Verbal messages are generally concerned with ideas, facts, or recital of
events. Nonverbal messages are more generally concerned with the affective aspects of interpersonal relationships. Nuances of feeling are easier to
communicate in nonverbal gestures, particularly of the face. The nonverbal channel then becomes the preferred channel of communication for
feelings.

Nonverbal messages may modify, refine, reinforce, clarify, elaborate, and
substitute for verbal messages. Nonverbal messages complement and supplement verbal messages. They create a frame of reference for interpreting
verbal messages.

Nonverbal communication also may amplify, emphasize, contradict,
accent, or anticipate the verbal message or part of it. All this information
helps us understand the verbal message, as in the examples that follow:

Amplification

She wants me to help with the shopping and watch the kids and clean the
house. Hell, I work hard enough on the job. I don't want any part of that crap
[*gestures with his right forearm, palm pushed out and away from his body, as
though he were pushing something away*].

Emphasis

Good, good, that's fine [*nodding head vigorously in a yes motion while smiling*].

And every goddamn time she [his wife] came to visit, you think she would
stay with me? No [*bangs desk*], not her! She had to see this doctor, or that
damn doctor [*bangs desk*]) or some damn social worker [*bangs desk*].

Anticipating

When Mrs. B. was speaking of her symptoms, with practically no mention
of her husband, she slid her wedding ring back and forth on her finger. Soon
she started to talk about her marital problems which were associatively linked
to her symptoms. Her wedding-ring play anticipated her verbalizations.
(Mahl 1968:322)

Accenting

You just can't make it on welfare. You're always behind. For God's sake, how
the hell would you like to live in this dump? [*As she said "you," she pointed a*

finger at the social worker; when she said "this dump," she swept her arm wide to
include the room and turned her head in half a circle, following her moving arm.]

CONTRADICTION

I'm not stupid, you know. I know it's wrong. Don't think I don't know that. I
am not proud of it, you know. [*Corners of mouth turn up in what seems a self-
satisfied smirk.*]

The interviewee, a bench hand and machinist's helper, deftly manipulated a
pencil through a motley of maneuvers extended over most of his interviews.
His skill failed him at only one point when he was defensively claiming that
his work efficiency was 100%. He lost control over his pencil and dropped it
on the floor.

(Mahl 1968:320)

The contradiction may fall anywhere between the verbal content and any
single channel of nonverbal communication. Mehrabian (1968) defines sarcasm as a message in which the information transmitted vocally contradicts
the message transmitted verbally. One nonverbal message can contradict
another. The body posture may be relaxed, but fingers drumming on the
table reveal tension. When people try to conceal something, whether feelings or facts, their nonverbal gestures may contradict rather than reinforce
each other. An interviewee who is lying may have a poker face and use eye
contact, which are belied by foot shuffling, crossing and uncrossing the feet,
and by hand movements.

Because the nonverbal messages are under less deliberate control the verbal message is often subordinate to the nonverbal message. If a discrepancy
exists, we tend to accord greater credence and authenticity to the nonverbal
message. We perceive a friendly statement in an unfriendly tone of voice as
unfriendly. But because this is not always the case we need to check out
each instance. The main meaning may lie with the verbal message, whereas
the nonverbal message is a modifier.

Because nonverbal messages are more ambiguous than verbal messages
we need to seek more feedback to confirm what we think we see when we
read nonverbal behavior.

You dropped your voice, you shifted in your seat and clasped your hands in
your lap when you said you might have to move to another city. What does
that mean?
I noted that you smiled and kind of clapped your hands when you told about
that. Am I right in thinking you were glad that it happened?

Although the interviewer should make a conscientious effort to observe nonverbal communication, we should also note that the usual rules of etiquette require that we sometimes avoid noticing such some communications. We may turn away from ear and nose picking much as we pretend not to hear stomach rumblings, belching, and farting. However, here the courageous interviewer may act on the supposition that the conventional rules of communication etiquette are suspended in the social work interview. Just as interviewers might "confront" interviewees with something they have implicitly said but are reluctant to acknowledge, so interviewers might call attention to persistent lip licking, for instance, and introduce explicit discussion of the gesture.

The interviewer is communicating nonverbal information as actively as the interviewee. The interviewer's behavior often is deliberate and consciously designed to elicit some kind of response from the client. Head nodding, smiles, body movements toward and away from the interviewee, and the like offer encouragement and support, emphasizing the verbal message of "Go on" or "Yes, I understand."

Interviewers, like the interviewee, have less conscious awareness of their nonverbal communication than of their words and so run the risk of saying what might best be left unsaid.

A 32-year-old woman on public assistance is talking about her children's vaccinations.

MRS. Y.: And I said, "Bill, when you were little, they put them in your butt."

WORKER: Mm-mmm.

The worker comments,

> There was more to this last "mm-mmm" than can be seen in the typescript. I have always had an aversion to the word "butt" and my distaste came out loud and clear in my inflection in this little "mm-mmm." It was clear that Mrs. Y. caught my attitude. A little later I noticed she used the word *thigh* rather than *butt* as we continued the discussion.

Interviewers need a level of self-awareness that involves not only what they are thinking, feeling, and saying but also the nonverbal behavior they are emitting and communicating.

To summarize the cautions that interviewers should consider in regard to nonverbal communication in using that information to maximize the interviewee's comfort and readiness to share and maximize your credibility and influence. The rooms that are conducive to interviewing are shielded from noise, provide privacy, adequate but not harsh lighting, a comfortable temperature, and a comfortable chair across the corner of a desk from the interviewer's chair; artifacts in the room convey a neutral message, and the room color is calming and relaxing. Interviewers are dressed casually or in business attire, wear no identifying insignia, and exude no perceptible odor. They make an effort to keep to schedule. Interviewers sit five to eight feet from the interviewee, make eye contact, smile, nod, lean forward, and gesture animatedly and appropriately. Interviewers' arms and legs are relaxed and in an open position, and they use their arms and hands in gesturing. Interviewers articulate clearly, speak fluently, and use a tempo that is animated but not too rapid. They vary their pitch, loudness, and emphasis appropriately.

Process Considerations

Nonverbal behavior at the start and end of the interview is likely to be especially significant. Interviewees' actions communicate their attitude toward the interview, the interviewer, and the agency. Do interviewees enter aggressively, with quiet confidence, or with apologetic diffidence? Do they knock timidly before entering or do they knock with assurance, asserting their right to the scheduled time? Do they interrupt an interview that has run past the time allotted or wait self-effacingly until called? Do they keep their coat on after they enter, protecting their escape route, or do they indicate that they are ready to remain? The family therapist should carefully observe the manner in which the family enters the room and the seating arrangements they choose—who sits next to whom.

During the interview nonverbal communication changes. If the interview is going well, interviewees most likely will begin to relax, and their stiff beginning posture should start to loosen, with precise diction giving way to some slurring, formal speech changing to more colloquial speech, and the clenched fist opening up. The interviewee will probably turn more directly toward the interviewer and lean more frequently in the worker's direction. If rapport has developed, the interviewee is likely to take more initiative in terminating silences.

Once interview rapport develops, interviewer and interviewee are more likely to mirror each other's postures—that is, if one rests the chin in one hand or is sitting sideways, soon the other will mimic the position without realizing what is happening. Similarly, they will mimic each other's specific nonverbal behavior, such as speech rate and foot wagging. Clients who speak rapidly because they are excited will, as rapport develops, begin to slow their speech and speak more calmly in synchrony with the interviewer.

Interviewers can use the tendency toward response matching to shape the interview behavior of the client.

At the end of the interview the participants' behavior again tends to show their attitudes toward each other and toward the interaction. Does the interviewer (or interviewee) keep looking at the clock? Does the interviewee leave hesitantly, trying to prolong the interview by a variety of actions—refusing to rise, don a coat, and move to the door—or does the client leave hastily, as though in flight?

Problems in Inferring Meanings

In general the study of nonverbal communication is much further along in describing and codifying behavior than in establishing its meanings. Detailed studies have identified many items in the nonverbal vocabulary, including five thousand distinctly different hand gestures and one thousand different steady body postures. Precise observation of nonverbal behavior is important, but it is only a first step. The interviewer still has to infer some valid meaning from the data. Accurate observation is necessary but insufficient for understanding the psychological relevance of the gesture.

How valid are the inferences we draw from our observations? Is it true that an uncluttered, neat, and clean home implies rigidity and anality? Are most women who use theatrical makeup narcissistic and flirtatious? What valid conclusion can we draw from fluttering eyelids? What exactly is a long-suffering look, a mocking smile, or a conspiratorial glance? Closing or screwing up the eyes *may* represent an effort to blot out the world—or an effort to see something in distance; wrinkling the nose *may* represent disgust—or an attempt to stifle a sneeze; swinging a foot in short arcs *may* represent annoyance—or a circulatory problem. What nonverbal manifestations differentiate the slow hesitant speech of the timid from the slow hesitant speech of the uninterested? Extreme and commonplace emotions are easier to read—depression, joy, and anger. But it is difficult to distinguish between anger and impatience or disgust, shame and embarrassment, hate and envy, fear and timidity.

A stiff posture may express a stiffness of character, but it may also result from military training—or arthritis. Crossing and uncrossing legs may be a protective nonverbal maneuver, but it may also be in response to poor circulation or pain in the feet.

In inferring meaning we do best if we respond not to the individual components of nonverbal communication but to the pattern formed by the total configuration. The facial expression of hostility is a firmly sealed mouth, level eyes, and steady staring;the body posture is erect and tense, oriented directly toward the interviewer; the arms are open and hands move firmly; voice is loud, steady, clipped, rapid, with even emphasis on each word.

The total picture presented by depression is different. Here the eyes narrow, the corners of the mouth turn down, body posture hangs forward—shoulders low, head down, body oriented away from interviewer, with loose arms and limp hand movements;the voice is slurred, low pitched, slow, and takes long pauses.

Scheflen rightly warns that attempts to ascribe meaning to nonverbal events should consider the context in which the events occur and the verbal accompaniments. Any interpretation that slights these considerations is on shaky ground. He notes by analogy that "a letter of the alphabet does not carry meaning until it is part of a word which is part of a sentence which is part of a discourse and a situation" (1964:324). The context gives meaning to the nonverbal communication. But in interpreting the meaning we also need to know the ethnic and socioeconomic setting in which the interviewee learned the gesture. The same nonverbal communication may be differently expressed by a white person and an African American person, differently expressed by a lower-income person of Scandinavian descent and a middle-income Italian American. Different "speech communities" assign greater or lesser importance to nonverbal aspects of communication and differ as well on the meaning assigned to specific gestures.

In addition, we have to assess the persistence and repetitiveness of the behavior. A single fleeting instance in which a father, during a family therapy session, turns his back on the rest of the family is quite different from frequent instances in which the father turns away and maintains this position for some time. It makes a difference too if he does this in a furtive, jerky, hesitant manner or if he does it in a deliberate open manner. The interviewer needs to consider the quality of the gesture.

Interviewers face yet another problem that those of us reading or writing a chapter on nonverbal communication are spared. Interviewers have the difficult task of receiving, sorting, understanding, and responding to the many messages being transmitted simultaneously and continuously on a variety of channels. And they have to do all this rapidly, even as they are bombarded by a continuous stream of multichannel messages.

In all this we infer more accurately on the basis of deviation. Because "there is no information in a steady state," only by establishing some baseline for the way the client talks, moves, dresses, and so on can we be aware that at this moment a gesture and/or speech is different. The very difference suggests that the client is communicating something. If an increase in the frequency of motions suggests anxiety, we need to know how much this interviewee tends to move around when at ease. If we say that people tend to express anger in a relatively fast rate of speech, we need to know how fast the interviewee tends to speak ordinarily. When the interviewee deviates from this baseline and speaks at a more rapid pace, we pay close attention to determine whether the client is in fact responding angrily.

We have learned nonverbal language as we have learned speech—as a consequence of daily practice, without explicit awareness of how we learned it or what we have learned. Because no standard lexicon of nonverbal language exists, we do not learn it as systematically as we learn speech; responses are apt to be highly individualized. Mahl and Kasl (1965) found that some people utter more "ahs" as they move into anxiety-provoking content. Others, however, become more studied in their speech.

Just as some stereotypes are associated with gender, ethnic group, and age, some stereotypes are associated with gestures, voice qualities, facial features, posture, and the like. And like sexist and racist stereotypes they tend to shape our picture of the interviewee without our being fully aware of the source of our judgments. We "know" the voice of a sexy female and of a homosexual; we "know" the rigid look of a determined person and the relaxed benign look of an avuncular person.

We unwittingly develop impressions and a mind-set toward the client on the basis of such cues. Thus we need to consciously examine the specifics that form our impressions. We are then in a better position to recognize our use of stereotypes and to correct or modify them in the individual instance.

There are problems then in deriving valid inferences from nonverbal communication. If, after so many years of talking to one another, we are still novices in the art of verbal communication, what permits us to presume a facility in the more difficult art of nonverbal communication? We must concede the validity of Edward Sapir's cogent summation. Despite the difficulties of conscious analysis, "we respond to gestures with an extreme alertness and, one might almost say, in accordance with an elaborate code that is written nowhere, known by none, and understood by all" (quoted in Birdwhistell 1970:182).

Summary: Chapter 11

Nonverbal communications are messages about verbal communication. Verbal communication is concerned with what we communicate; nonverbal communication is more concerned with how we communicate.

The management of time, or chronomics, is a nonverbal communication. Who waits for whom, the timing of messages, scheduling of appointments, and amount of time we are willing to invest in a person or situation all convey information. Cultural differences may exist with regard to time and time-related expectations.

Artifactual communication is the language of objects, and the source of communication is the physical setting and personal adornments—clothes, hairstyles, makeup, jewelry, and the like. Home visits provide a rich source of artifactual communication. Office decor and arrangements represent another source of artifactual communication. Clothing identifies age, socioeconomic status, and nationality. The interviewer who projects a neutral image with regard to clothing is least likely to offend clients.

Smell is another source of nonverbal communication in the interview. We generally make some judgment about the interviewee based on what we smell. We tend to associate unpleasant odors with undesirable personal habits and social circumstances.

Touch is a powerful nonverbal method of communication. For the most part the normative cultural proscriptions tend to limit its use in the interview. Interviewers may use touch with a client if the situation warrants touching, if the nature of the touch is appropriate, its intent nonerotic, and if it doesn't impose a greater degree of intimacy than the interviewee desires.

Paralinguistics refer to the nonsemantic aspects of speech and also are called paralinguistic cues. Through our manipulation of voice qualities of pitch, loudness, tempo, emphasis, and pauses we give additional meaning and color to the words we articulate.

Proxemics is the language of space and distance. The interviewer needs to be aware that distance is a variable of some significance in determining interview interaction. Cultures vary in regard to preferred distance between participants in an interaction.

Body language, kinesics, is concerned with movements, gestures, posture, and facial expressions. The face is the part of the body that offers the greatest number and variety of gestural cues. Eye contact has a clearly regulatory function in controlling the traffic of interviewer-interviewee interaction. Researchers have found ethnic differences in the use of eye contact. An open body posture is more generally used when in communication with a liked partner.

Nonverbal communication is significant because it conveys information about the nature of the relationship between the interview participants. Interviewers use nonverbal communication to maximize the interviewee's comfort and readiness to share and to bolster interviewers' credibility and influence.

Nonverbal communication is likely to be especially significant at the start and end of the interview. If the interview is going well, the postures of interviewer and interviewee will mirror each other.

The problem with nonverbal communication is inferring valid meaning from the data of our observations.

SUGGESTED READINGS

Michael Argyle. *Bodily Communication*, 2d ed. London: Routledge and Kegan Paul, 1988. (371 pp.)
A scholarly overview of the field of nonverbal communication.

Judee Burgoon et al. *Nonverbal Communication: The Unspoken Dialogue*. New York: Harper and Row, 1991. (432 pp.)
A useful comprehensive overview of some essentials of nonverbal communication.

Nancy M. Henley. *Body Politics: Power, Sex, and Nonverbal Communication*. New York: Touchstone, 1986.
Written from a strong feminist point of view the book spells out the implications of nonverbal communication in male-female interactions in a variety of contexts.

Mark L. Hickson and Don W. Stacks. *Nonverbal Communication: Studies and Applications*. Dubuque, Iowa: W. C. Brown, 1985. (259 pp.)
A systematic review of the varieties of nonverbal communication, followed by applications of the content to social situations and on the job.

Mark L. Knapp and Judith A. Hall. *Nonverbal Communication in Human Interaction*, 3d ed. New York: Holt, Rinehart, and Winston, 1992 (507 pp.).
A good comprehensive overview of the varieties of nonverbal behavior and their significance.

Alison Lurie. *The Language of Clothes*. New York: Random House, 1981. (273 pp.)
A witty and perceptive overview of the nonverbal significance of clothing. The book increases the reader's awareness of the meaning of the choices people make in the clothing they select and the messages they seek to transmit through clothing.

George S. Mahl, ed. *Explorations in Nonverbal and Vocal Behavior*. Hillsdale, N.J.: Lawrence Erlbaum, 1987. (411 pp.)
A more scholarly series of articles with some emphasis on speech disturbances as they relate to interpersonal problems. One detailed section of the book is "Gestures and Body Movements in Interviews."

Loretta A. Malandro and Larry Banker. *Nonverbal Communication*. Reading, Mass.: Addison-Wesley, 1983. (385 pp.)
A detailed overview with interesting graphics and cartoons.

Peter March, ed. *Eye-to-Eye: How People Interact*. Topsfield, Mass.: Salem House, 1988. (254 pp.)

Whereas the second half of the book is devoted to general social interaction, the first half presents the various aspects of nonverbal communication in a spritely manner supported by excellent graphics.

Desmond Morris. *Man Watching: A Field Guide to Human Behavior.* New York: Harry U. Abrams, 1977. (320 pp.)

A biologist discusses and shows, with a variety of photographs, people engaged in nonverbal behavior in many social situations.

Virginia P. Richmond, James C. McCroskey, and Steven K. Payne. *Nonverbal Behavior in Interpersonal Relations.* Englewood Cliffs, N.J.: Prentice-Hall, 1987. (305 pp.)

A review of the varieties of nonverbal behavior that is more systematic than most.

TWELVE

Cross-Cultural Interviewing

Problems frequently arise because the social work interviewer and the interviewee come from much different worlds. Socioeconomic group, race or ethnicity, gender, age, and sexual orientation are among the significant subcultural differences that may separate interviewer and interviewee, increase social distance, and limit understanding.

The statistically typical social worker is different from the statistically typical client in significant social characteristics. The statistically typical social worker is middle income, college trained, white, young, and female. The statistically typical client is likely to be a somewhat older lower-income female member of a minority group with less than high school education. The only significant social characteristic they hold in common is that they typically are both female (Gibelman and Schervish 1993).

We have a specific concern with only one aspect of these differences— the effect of such group membership on the interaction of the social work interview.

What explicit implications are there for the way in which the interviewer conducts the interview when the interviewer and interviewee are of different races? How do interviewers need to adapt their interviewing techniques if they are heterosexual and the interviewee is gay? If the interview needs to be modified to meet the cultural needs and/or perspectives of the interviewee, in what specific ways should the interviewer do that? A multicultural society embraces the diversity of values, lifestyles, and interests of its various subgroups. But many differences may not be significant in regard to how the interview is conducted.

The population of people likely to participate in a social work interview is increasing in diversity. Since the mid-1980s the literature that addresses the issue of cultural diversity has increased considerably. The 1965 edition of the *Encyclopedia of Social Work* devoted about five pages to cultural diversity. The 1995 edition contains about 130 pages on cultural differences. The *Journal of Multicultural Social Work* has many subscribers. Despite the proliferation of books and articles providing racial and ethnic information to social workers, they don't often discuss the explicit relevance of the information for conducting the interview.

Nonetheless recognition and appreciation of the effects of differences in age, socioeconomic group, ethnicity and race, and other factors on interview interaction are growing. These factors do tend to intrude in the interviewer-interviewee relationship.

There is, however, a need for balance in assessing the importance for the interview of these key identifying characteristics. An approach that ignores them and suggests that none makes a difference is as erroneous as the approach that holds that these attributes are determinant. One extreme denies the significance of vital shared group experiences; the other extreme denies the unique psychodynamics of an individual's responses.

The interviewer who is culturally neutral and color blind discounts the significance of cultural differences and gives priority to human similarities. Such a worker says, in effect, "He is black and I am white but we are both human." This worker gives priority to the similarities among people. The worker who gives priority to cultural differences says, "We are all human, but he is black and I am white." The culturally sensitive social worker is aware that we all have similarities and differences and that both deserve consideration in the conduct of the interview.

The problem for the interviewer, however, is to determine the significance of particular cultural differences for the conduct of the actual interview.

Selective Examples of Cross-Cultural Interviews

Space considerations again require that we be selective about what to include in this chapter. We define the term *cross-cultural* broadly. In addition to the four main ethnic categories usually included in the definition—African American, Latino/Hispanic, Asian American and Native American—we regard age, socioeconomic group, gender, and sexual orientation as differences between interviewer and interviewee that pose cross-cultural problems for interviewing. We have attempted to use the contexts of ethnicity and race, age, and sexual orientation as examples for identifying some essential and distinctive aspects of multicultural interviewing and the principal characteristics of the culturally sensitive interviewer.

Race

Racial differences between interviewer and interviewee are a potential source of problems in interviewing. Most often the interviewer is white and the interviewee is a person of color. Although this difference most frequently involves a white interviewer and an African American client, people of color include Hispanic, Asian American, and Native American interviewees. In some instances the interviewer is a person of color and the interviewee is white, posing special problems for interview interaction.

Interview participants of different races are keenly aware of the racial differences between them; nevertheless the racial factor is rarely discussed openly. It may be that race is not discussed because the participants regard it as truly irrelevant to the work at hand or that both participants conspire to ignore race because it is such a sensitive issue in American society.

If the interview is not concerned with matters that may call attention to race relations, the interaction is less likely to suffer from distortion. Although conscious of the racial differences between them, interviewer and interviewee can relate to each other within the neutral content of the interview. If, however, interview content has racial significance, participants may become uneasy. The difficulty is that today so much in the life of an interviewee of color may be regarded as implicitly related to racial problems.

To proclaim colorblindness is to deny the real differences that exist and need to be accepted.

White Interviewer, African American Interviewee

Because African Americans are by far the largest single nonwhite group and because most of the descriptive, clinical, and experimental literature concerning race as a factor in interview interaction focuses on the African American interviewee, much of our discussion concerns African American and white participants. Many statements are, however, relevant to other racial groups.

The African American interviewee often presents the interviewer with differences in socioeconomic background as well as differences in racial experience. Although the largest group of poor people in the United States is white, a disproportionate percentage of the African American population is poor. The median income of the African American family is substantially below the median income of the white family, and a large percentage of African Americans live on incomes below the poverty level. The material on interviews with the poor is thus applicable to many African American interviewees. But over and beyond the difference in socioeconomic background is the racial factor—the differences that stem from the experiences of living white and living black. This affects the interview with middle-income as well as lower-income African American clients.

If trust and openness between participants are necessary for a successful interview, how can we achieve them in the face of the long history in this country in which whites exploited, betrayed the confidence of, and violated the openness of black people? If African Americans feel paranoid in their mistrust of whites, this is not pathology but a healthy reaction to the reality they have long experienced. Persons of color have institutionalized "putting the white man on," a weapon necessary for survival but one that is antithetical to the requirements of an effective interview. Conditioned defensiveness in response to anticipation of prejudicial attitudes, based on expectations repeatedly confirmed in the past, may impede development of rapport between the white interviewer and African American interviewee. We need to accept and respect those African Americans who "play it cool," maintaining a cover and a reserve, in the presence of whites.

If empathy is crucial, how can the white interviewer imagine what it is like to live day after day in a society that only grudgingly and belatedly (if at all) accords people of color the dignity that is their right as a person? How can the white interviewer know what it is to live on intimate terms with rejection, discrimination, harassment, and exploitation?

If a feeling of comfortable untroubled interaction is necessary for a good interview, how can white interviewers achieve this in an atmosphere in which the African American interviewee feels accusatory and white interviewers feel uneasily guilty? In such a situation the African American interviewee may tend to resort to disguise and respond with discretion or accommodating behavior. African American clients' hesitance to share, is expressed by Langston Hughes in "Impasse":

> I could tell you,
> If I wanted to,
> What makes me
> What I am.
> But I don't
> Really want to—
> And you don't
> Give a damn.

> —*Langston Hughes,* The Tiger and the Lash
> *(New York: Alfred A. Knopf, 1967),*
> *reprinted with permission of the publisher.*

Whereas a white client may enter an interview with the presumption that the worker will be respectful and accepting, the African American client may enter the interview with just the opposite presumption. For the white client the white worker is innocent until proved guilty; the African American client presumes white workers are guilty until they prove themselves innocent. Experience in interacting with white people generally may shape clients' initial expectations.

The question is not whether cross-racial contact can be established but how it can be established.

What can be done to ease the real difficulties inherent in the white interviewer–African American interviewee interaction? On the most practical level white workers should observe with singular care all the formalities that are the overt signs of respect, interest, concern, and acceptance.

Discussion of racism has left many whites with the uneasy suspicion that, as children of their culture, they have imbibed prejudices in a thousand subtle ways in repeated small doses and that the symptoms of their racism, if masked to them, may be apparent to the African American interviewee. It may be necessary to accept such suspicions as true. The worker needs to acknowledge frankly the possibility of harboring racist attitudes and the obligation to make the effort to change. This suggests a paraphrase of a Chinese maxim. The prospective white interviewer who says, "Other white interviewers are fools for being prejudiced and when I am an interviewer I will not be such a fool" is already a fool.

A good interview requires that interviewers have some sense of security that they know their subject area. White interviewers certainly can make efforts to dispel their ignorance by reading about, and becoming familiar with, black language, African American history, culture, thinking, and feeling.

White workers may find it helpful to be explicitly aware of their reaction to racial difference in the interview. In making restitution for felt or suspected racism white workers may be overindulgent. They may tend to simplify the problems and attribute to race some behavior that they hesitate to ascribe to individual malfunctioning, although the difficulty truly is a dysfunction. When a client uses color as a rationalization, race is a weapon in the interview. The worker may be "too sympathetic to be of assistance; too guilty to be of help" (Heine 1950:375).

Some white liberal activists may be eager to validate their credentials as being nonracist or antiracist and might seek to achieve validation by using an oversolicitous approach. The danger lies in being paternalistic and overly compliant to the interviewee's demands and wishes.

Some workers feel a need to be visibly nonracist and increase their expression of liberal attitudes when the interviewee is of another race. Thus in one study white social workers evaluating an African American and a white client from the same background presenting the same problem in the same way tended to perceive the African American client in more positive terms. In an attempt to explain this finding the researchers note that "perhaps this can be seen as a kind of 'leaning over backwards' by predominantly white social workers in an effort to assume that their judgments were, at the least, fair" (Fischer and Miller 1973:108).

Interviewers who are least likely to be uncomfortable are those who have resolved their sense of racial identity, who do not need to deny racial differences but accept them and do not see them as threatening. These workers have no need to romanticize people who are racially, ethnically, or socially different, making others better than they are.

There is recognition that the African American worldview is different from the white middle-class Eurocentric worldview—more present oriented, less individualistic, more collectively oriented, more casual about time. Differences with regard to problem orientation and helping preferences are noted. African American interviewees are more likely to attribute problems to external factors rather than to intrapsychic considerations and prefer a structured guided interaction to a facilitative interaction (Leong, Wagner, and Tata 1995). Additionally, differences in nonverbal behavior may exist. Halberstadt (1985), in a review of the nonverbal behavior, notes that blacks and whites differ in terms of body orientation, frequency of gaze, and touch. The empirical research on differences is limited, and critics ask whether certain behaviors and attitudes ascribed to racial or ethnic status may not be more appropriately ascribed to socioeconomic group. Hanna notes that "the state of the art of nonverbal similarities and differences between Blacks and Whites is beset with little research and the interweaving of color with social class" (1984:403; see also Longres 1991; Atkinson and Lowe 1995:408).

African American Interviewer, White Interviewee

An interview by an African American interviewer with a white client poses its own problems. African American interviewers may be tense, fearing expressions of antipathy from the interviewee.

However, African American interviewers may have an advantage because their life experience has forced them to learn about the dominant white culture. Many white interviewers have never faced the same necessity of learning about African American culture.

Some white interviewees may be reluctant to concede to the African American interviewer a presumption of competence. The white interviewee, especially from the South, may be sensitive to the reversal in usual status positions. If interviewees bring a prejudicial attitude against African Americans into the interview, they are less likely to regard the interviewer as a source of influence and, hence, less likely to respond to the interviewer's efforts to socialize them to the interview situation or guide them in the interview. A prejudiced interviewee in such a situation is less responsive to overt and covert conditioning cues communicated by the interviewer. This is only one aspect of a general resistance to submit to any kind of influence from a negatively perceived interviewer. Prejudice produces a functional deafness, reducing receptivity to communication.

The Aged Client

Senior citizens are a group that everybody hopes to join eventually. But most social workers today are younger than many clients. Cultural aspects of age differences may operate as barriers to effective interviewing. The contact between younger and older people evokes the parent-child relationship, but here the positions of helper and helped are reversed. Both participants are apt to be somewhat edgy in response to this "unnatural" situation.

A generation gap is inevitable. The older client was socialized at a time when American problems, values, and mores were quite different. In effect the elderly grew up in a different country (Giles et al. 1992:292).

To impose on others, to take "charity," to be dependent, to express a concern for themselves and their needs was less acceptable in an earlier ethic to which many older interviewees subscribe. They also are less accepting of counseling and psychotherapy.

Educational differences between interviewer and interviewee are likely to compound age differences. By and large the educational attainment of older citizens is lower than that of the younger population.

Another component of the subcultural age gap derives from the differences in physiology between youth and old age. The abatement of instinctual needs, greater physical effort required for every activity, slower tempo, greater susceptibility to physical insult and injury, and the immediate awareness of the possibility and inevitability of death suggest that in a thousand major and minor details the world is a different place for the older person, beyond the easy imagining of a worker living in a 20- or 30-year-old body.

Studies have distinguished the young-old (60–80) and the old-old (older than 80). Both groups suffer some decline in physical and sensory capacity, but the decline is more precipitous among the old-old. Although the decline is not as great as and is more gradual than once thought, romanticizing aging as the "golden years," as a happy lark, does an injustice to the realities of decline.

It is not ageist to point to the objective reality of the inevitable, irreversible, progressive, incremental, and debilitating effects of aging, the gradual loss of strength and vigor and the attenuation of the sensitivity of our senses. Age is not youth with gray hair.

In moving from employment to retirement, which is the experience of most of the aged, older people suffer losses in role and status, isolation because of the severance of ties with the work family, and reduction of income. As friends and relatives die or become incapacitated, their circle of intimates becomes smaller still.

Ageism is an attitude toward the nature and the experience of old age that suggests a devaluation and disenfranchisement of the aged. A youthful society telegraphs messages, however subtle, that the aged are an unproductive surplus population, imposing an increasingly heavy burden on the community.

The language describes "old fogies" and "old geezers" as grumpy, crotchety, and cantankerous.

In many instances worried and/or overburdened relatives or concerned agencies refer the aged for service. The aged interviewee often is an involuntary applicant. Concerned about an actual growing dependence, aged people are reluctant to voluntarily seek help because doing so is an acknowledgment of dependence. These factors feed into the interview interaction, increasing the complexities the interviewer must deal with.

The need for communicating acceptance and respect, important everywhere, is of particular importance with this age group.

In the contact with the aged interviewers should maintain formality as far as names are concerned. Use first names with hesitance and only after asking permission.

Ageism is the stereotyping of all the aged as asexual, impaired psychologically, rigid, and incapable of changing. The stereotyping interviewer tends to be deficit oriented in approaching the aged client. This interviewer may also have a tendency to regard the aged as not fully capable of making decisions and to plan for or around them.

Even the interviewer who is oriented toward building on strengths rather than focusing on deficits needs to recognize the real losses inevitably and universally associated with aging. Encouragement may be desirable; challenging may be counterproductive.

Because of the greater likelihood that an interview will be fatiguing for the older interviewee, the interviewer needs to be sensitive to the need to schedule short but more frequent interviews. The pace of the interview needs to be slower than usual and set by the client. Stiffening joints and reduced kidney functioning make it difficult for some to sit in one place for a prolonged period. Shorter interviews with the possibility of taking a break are helpful.

The aged are susceptible to confusion about time periods, querulousness that stems from loneliness, and repetitive reminiscing, all of which interfere with efficient interviewing. Broad open-ended questions may tend to evoke long discursive answers; shorter more direct questions may be the better option.

A survey of about five hundred social workers working with the aged showed that they perceive differences in practice with this age group. Social workers perceive themselves as more active with the elderly, likely to show caring, and use reminiscence to help interviewees cope and be self-affirming (Tobin and Gustafson 1987).

Older interviewees tend to blur the focus of the interview by reminiscing. Rather than being random behavior of little purpose, reminiscing may contribute to the interview in important ways. Pincus points out that reminiscing has the "effect of bringing the older person mentally back through time to the same age or situation as that of the younger [interviewer], thereby in effect erasing the existing age difference" (1970:51; see also Sherman 1991). Older interviewee may use reminiscence if they regard the age difference as a threat to their status. Reminiscences about past accomplishments reassure interviewees that they once were more competent. Using such phrasing as "You're too young to understand this" or "This was before your time," the older client seeks to maintain status vis-à-vis the younger interviewer.

Interviewing in the home rather than the office may be necessary to spare the client the physical insult of a long tiring trip, often up and down stairs that are difficult to negotiate. However, because an office interview requires older people to leave their isolation for the world of other people, an office interview sometimes is the desirable choice.

Many of the old-old are living in institutions. Interviewing in such a setting generally involves working without privacy. Other residents' observations of the interviewer's behavior during the interview may affect interviews scheduled with other individuals at a later time.

Very often a third party—relatives or helpers—may be present at interviews with older clients. This may dilute the relationship between interviewer and client, inhibit the client from introducing intimate content, and reduce the participation of the older client when the third party answers questions directed toward the client (Greene et al. 1994).

Nonverbal information (discussed more fully in chapter 11) is of particular importance in interviewing the aged. Older people frequently have suffered a hearing loss, signs of which may be the forward lean, a tendency to turn one ear toward the speaker, or gazing intently at the interviewer's lips. Interviewers should be attentive to whether a client is wearing a hearing aid. A facial expression of strained listening and frequent requests to repeat a question suggest hearing difficulties. Interviewers with clients who have hearing problems may need to speak more briefly because the strain of listening is exhausting. The interviewer may also need to speak a little louder, more slowly, and more distinctly. Interviewers have to be careful to talk directly to the person with their face in a clear light to help the client who is lip reading. Interviewers should avoid covering their mouth while speaking. It is best to interview where background noise is minimal and lighting is adequate.

The aged client may present a greater difficulty than a younger client in being understood. Some older clients speak with a foreign accent; others have dental problems that affect the way they talk, or they slur their words. Strokes leave some older clients with impaired speech. Their voices may be weak and tremulous. Despite these considerations interviewers should avoid the tendency to overaccommodate through profuse head nodding, raising their voice, and talking down, all of which are patronizing.

One advantage of aging is the freedom to ignore the social niceties. An older person may be beyond caring about what others think. Such interviewees may be more outspoken, more insistent, more stubborn than the usual client and consequently more difficult for the interviewer to take in stride; the interviewer may need a greater measure of forbearance.

Interviewers may have special problems with their feelings when working with aged interviewees. The emotional reverberations initiated by contact with the older interviewee may create anxiety for the interviewer. The problems of illness and the constant reminder of the imminence of death haunt such interviews.

Working with the aged tends to intensify interviewers' fears of vocational loss, status devaluation, social disenfranchisement, and threats to bodily integrity. The older client is everyone's parent, and the problem of the young adult in relation to an aging parent is one that many interviewers face in their own lives.

Social workers may feel a sense of futility in response to what they regard as the limited resilience of the interviewee. Certainly, older clients have less of a future, and the interviewer may question the expenditure of effort in behalf of this age group. The interviewer may find the slow pace of interaction and change discouraging, particularly when these may be compounded by the confusions of incipient senility. Interviewers may feel drained by the demands made on them as human beings.

The world of many older clients is filling up with strangers. Faced with growing isolation, older interviewees may rank the expressive social functions of the interview interaction much higher than any instrumental rewards. Given their contracting social networks, more limited range of activities, and greater amount of free time, senior citizens may welcome an interview as a social event.

Because older interviewees are likely to be lonely as a result of losing a mate and their diminishing social circle, they are eager to talk to someone. The social work interviewer can play the role of confidant and companion to the older lonely interviewee. Such a relationship of social support contributes to mental health and morale (Greenberg 1990).

Because working with the aged frequently requires environmental modification the interviewer needs to be aware of the network of community resources available for older people. And because older clients may need a variety of services, the interviewer may have to assume the role of case manager in the interview.

Sexual Orientation

Sexual orientation is another consideration that may make for cross-cultural difficulty during the interview. Homosexuality, as a variation in sexual orientation, is expressed more openly than ever before. Although no valid census figures exist, estimates suggest that the sexual orientation of 10 percent of the population is homosexual, making this group one of the largest minorities in the country. With increasing frequency interviewers are in contact with clients who acknowledge that they are gay or lesbian. Much of what follows is true for both gay men and lesbians. Because of this, as well as space limitations, we are not pointing to the many differences between the two groups (Garnets and Kimmel 1993:25–28). Interviewers need to use care in applying the general material to gay men and lesbians of different ethnic and racial groups. Workers also need to recognize that despite what appears to be a label suggesting homogeneity, lesbians and gay men are differentiated by age, race, ethnicity, health, socioeconomic status, and many other factors. There are openly gay Republican as well as Democratic members of Congress.

Homophobia, fear and dislike of homosexuals, is pervasive in a hetero-sexual society. For many interviewers therapeutic neutrality and acceptance are difficult to achieve with lesbian and gay interviewees. We have all grown up in a culture that takes heterosexuality for granted and stigmatizes homo-sexuality as a deviation from which we need to defend. Not only does the general idea of homosexuality elicit anxiety and uneasiness, but the specific nature of sexual practices associated with homosexuality occasions even more discomfort. Interviewers who pride themselves for having a great measure of tolerance might want to ask themselves how they would feel if their child or spouse came out to them as lesbian or gay. A questionnaire study that included a homophobic scale found that many social workers hold homophobic attitudes (DeCrescenzo 1983–84; see also Wisniewski and Toomy 1987).

It is important for the interviewer to provide "an approach that frees the client to acknowledge his or her sexual orientation or affectional preference in the initial interview. . . . If the practitioner is assuming that the client is heterosexual and the client is assuming that the practitioner would be shocked or negatively biased against the client because he is gay, neither practitioner nor client can get on with the work that needs to be done" (National Association of Social Workers 1984:28).

The heterosexual interviewer may collude with the internalized homo-phobia of the gay interviewee to avoid open discussion of problems related to homosexuality (McHenry and Johnson 1993).

Perhaps the most common and difficult bias for interviewers to resolve is a pervasive and strong feeling that heterosexual relationships are "more natural" or "healthier" than other forms of sexual expression. This attitude is often manifested in subtle efforts to change or treat the gay or lesbian client's sexual orientation.

Homosexuals identity heterosexism as analogous to racism and sexism. Heterosexism is an attitude that suggests that heterosexuality is an intrin-sically superior sexual orientation. An affirmative point of view toward homosexuality perceives it as a nonpathological human condition that the interviewer needs to accept, value, and facilitate.

Heterosexuals tend to hold tenaciously the stereotypes of how gay men and lesbians look and behave because they have little experience with peo-ple who do not conform to the stereotype. Heterosexuals tend not to rec-ognize as gay those homosexual men and women who do not look and act according to stereotype. The stereotypes are thus self-validating. One worker was confident he could "spot" a homosexual:

Sometime during the third interview, he alluded to the fact that he was gay. I was really bowled over. I hope I did not show my surprise, but I really was. He didn't look or talk or gesture as I expected a gay would look and talk and act. I found I didn't know as much as I thought I knew.

In 1974–75, both the American Psychiatric Association and the American Psychological Associated voted that homosexuality no longer be classified as a mental disorder. In 1975 the American Psychological Association adopted a resolution to the effect that "homosexuality per se implies no impairment in judgment, reliability, or general social and vocational abilities" (Garnets et al. 1991:964).

Homosexuality is an alternative response to erotic and affectional needs, neither better or worse than heterosexuality but rather "a normal nonpathological form of human, sexual, and affectional expression" (Moses and Hawkins 1982:215).

The interviewer has to have some conviction that gay men and lesbians can and do lead satisfying, well-adjusted, productive lives, that many are in long-term stable relationships, and that their orientation is not a response to neurotic conflict and/or pathological development (Stein 1993:25).

The heterosexual interviewer needs to be familiar with the empirical research that confirms that differences in sexual orientation are not necessarily associated with pathology. Most gays and lesbians are generally well adjusted and free from personality disorders (Bell and Weinberg 1978; Gonsiorek 1982).

The interviewer whose sexual orientation is heterosexual may have some difficulty accepting the idea that for the client homosexuality is a "normal nonpathological form of human sexual and affectional expression" (Moses and Hawkins 1982, 2:215). The interviewer who is uncomfortable with gays and lesbians might be prompted to be reassuring—"It's just a stage"; "It happens to a lot of kids and they grow out of it"; or, as one interviewer said, "You're too pretty to be a lesbian."

Some researchers believe that the focus of erotic and affectional desire is biologically determined but that the particular manner in which people express such desires is shaped by the social environment (LeVay 1994). Furthermore, the likelihood of effecting change in this fundamental orientation is extremely limited (Haldeman 1991). Currently, the general approach is to help the interviewee enhance social and psychological functioning as a self-identified gay man or lesbian.

In this section our emphasis on the affectional as well as the erotic is to point out that genital acts do not define homosexuality. What is involved—and what is of greater importance—is that homosexuals and heterosexuals have the same needs: the need for comfort, support, acceptance, reassurance, and companionship in a relationship with a person they love. The response of the gay community in displays of care and concern for peers with AIDS demonstrates a capacity for love that the heterosexual community has not been ready to accord homosexuals—or heterosexuals with AIDS. Our vocabulary reflects this disparagement. Words like *marriage* are denied homosexuals, and the words left to them, such as *partner, friend, roommate, companion,* and *significant other,* suggest less commitment and greater transience (Martin 1982).

Because society generally does not regard homosexuality as a legitimate form of sexual expression, because society perceives it as a pathological adaptation rather than an acceptable variation, homosexuals suffer special stresses and problems in achieving a positive self-identification. They face community condemnation, ridicule, and misunderstanding. Homophobia, along with racism, sexism, and ageism, present members of minority groups with extra burdens in developing a healthy self-image and acceptable sense of self-worth.

Subjected to the same homophobic indoctrination in mass media, family, peer groups, schools, and other institutions, many lesbians and gay men face a problem of internalized homophobia.

Like ethnic minorities, gay men and lesbians live biculturally in the homosexual subculture and the mainstream culture. They sometimes have to balance and/or resolve conflicting demands and requirements imposed by the two cultures. They are seen, and may sense themselves, as marginal to the mainstream culture.

An interviewer needs to be sensitive to the process that gay men and lesbians live through in coming to a resolution of their orientation. The relevant literatures shows these sequential steps to be initial awareness of differences in sexual interests and activities from peers of the same gender, an early but ambivalent identification and labeling of such differences as homosexual, an integration of such an identification with the total personality, an acceptance of such an identification, and ultimately an affirmation of and commitment to such an identification (Troiden 1993).

The interviewer needs to be aware of the struggle about disclosing information that gay men and lesbians face, particularly as they reach resolution of their self-image. Should they share their perceptions with others—and with whom, when, how, and at what potential cost? Homophobia is alive and ubiquitous in the general culture. The fear and dislike of homosexuals is exemplified in the laws that limit their civil rights, deny them full social citizenship, permit job and housing discrimination and allow verbal harassment, physical abuse, and rejection from parents and peers. "Coming out" and openly revealing some essential but otherwise invisible aspect of life that invites stigmatization is a difficult and recurring problem. The stressful need to carefully manage information comes up almost daily in conversations about family, dating, marriage, children, living arrangements, and the like.

The interviewer has to be aware, however, that although same-sex erotic and affectional orientation is the defining characteristic of homosexuality, this is only one aspect, however consequential, of the total adjustment of the interviewee. Gay and lesbian interviewees face most of the general problems encountered by all people in addition to those unique problems associated with their sexual orientation. Interviewers should not assume that the problem the client brings is necessarily related to sexual orientation or give it inappropriate, exaggerated, and central importance.

Although some homosexuals may seek social work help in accepting their sexual orientation, many have done so and seek help with a variety of general problems that are affected by their sexual orientation.

Gays and lesbians have a set of problems that are unique; they have problems that are different from those faced by other minority groups. Although all face problems of discrimination and stigmatization, in the case of race or age their minority membership is visible. The homosexual's membership in a minority group based on sexual orientation is not visible. Group membership or group identification has an element of choice associated with it. Homosexuals have the problems of deciding whether or when to come out, of dealing with their self-accepting identification with a minority group, and of the anxiety associated with "discovery" by others.

Because sexual orientation is not obvious the client must disclose it. This poses a problem for the interviewer as well as the interviewee.

A medical social worker on a hospital cardiology service said,

I was asking about the patient's support system and who might be visiting. He said he wasn't married and when I asked if he lived alone, he said no somewhat hesitantly. After a pause, he said he had been living with somebody for some time. I asked if his friend would be likely to visit him. He said he wasn't sure he would be allowed visiting privileges. His friend was his family but not really family. In my mind, I thought he was implying that he was gay but I hesitated to ask about this. It was a kind of hazardous inference and a question or comment which suggested this might be resented. I opted for a kind of neutral response soliciting clarification. I said, "I am not sure what you mean by that." I guess (I hope) my demeanor communicated acceptance because after a long pause he said, "My friend is my lover." We then discussed visiting privileges, which in this hospital (unlike some other hospitals) homosexuals have family visiting privileges.

Although coming out may be psychologically healthier, and some clients may want the help of the interviewer in achieving this, some interviewees may want to remain undisclosed, and interviewers should respect this as well. Reluctance to come out is not necessarily evidence of self-hatred, internalized homophobia, or shame.

The problems, values, adaptations, lifestyle, and even language of homosexual clients are matters about which most interviewers are ignorant. The heterosexual interviewer has some responsibility to become acquainted with the voluminous literature available. *Sexual orientation* connotes much more than the specific nature of sexual interaction, "what people do in bed"; it includes lifestyle, political perspective, and a set of subcultural values and mores. The subculture of homosexual social groups and organizations, homosexual literature, national periodicals, and the like is a rich one. It is a subculture that provides mutual support and kinship.

Interviewers are likely to be able to conduct a more successful interview if they know something about the local gay and lesbian community and its resources—the bars and hotels that are open to homosexuals, medical services, hot lines, and discussion groups. However, because much of the subculture is not open to casual observation, as might be the cultures of more openly observable minority groups, heterosexual interviewers do not find it easy to gain a knowledge and appreciation of the gay subculture. The interviewer, perhaps more here than elsewhere, has to be receptive to learning from the interviewee. Many gay men and lesbian clients report that they spend a great deal of time and money educating their therapists regarding gay consciousness, lifestyles, and community issues (Rochlin 1982:27).

The incidence of AIDS in the gay community presents some special problems for understanding. The interviewer needs some detailed knowledge about how AIDS is spread, how its spread can be prevented, and about resources available in treating AIDS.

Individualizing the Cross-Cultural Client

Interviewers need to be careful about applying to an individual any of the broad generalizations we have discussed here regarding race, age, and sexual orientation. First, many of the generalizations have only limited empirical confirmation (Ho 1995). Second, the validity of some of generalizations becomes attenuated with changes in the social zeitgeist and in response to increasing acculturation of group members. Third, further difficulties result from the heterogeneity of interviewees identified by group labels—African American, Hispanic/Latino, gay, lesbian, and senior citizen.

African Americans include people whose forebears came to the United States as slaves centuries ago and those whose families emigrated more recently from Santo Domingo, Haiti, the West Indies, and African countries, to name but a few. African Americans include a sizable subgroup of people who are of mixed race heritage (Morganthau 1995:63–65). Examination of other major racial and ethnic groups suggests a similar array of subgroups that make it difficult for the interviewer to know what information is valid to apply in contact with the individual interviewee.

For instance, the Bureau of the Census has identified twenty different Asian subgroups, including Chinese, Japanese, Vietnamese, Korean, and Filipino Americans. The Native American subgroups include at least 263 tribes and bands. The Hispanic/Latino American subgroups include people of Mexican, Puerto Rican, Cuban, South American, Spanish, and Basque heritage.

And within each subgroup the individual interviewee is further differentiated in terms of socioeconomic status, gender, religion, level of group identification, degree of acculturation, personal attributes, and the like. All this calls for caution in applying cultural generalizations to an individual interviewee.

Should Interviewer and Interviewee Be Matched?

The problems inherent in interviewing across the barriers of socioeconomic group, race, age, and sexual orientation lead inevitably to the question of matching. Would it not be desirable to select an interviewer who resembles the interviewee in at least some crucial characteristics? Would this not reduce social distance and the constraints in interaction that derive from differences in group affiliation and related experiences and lifestyle?

A number of different theoretical preconceptions support the idea that cultural matching of the interviewer and interviewee facilitates communication and relationship development. The concept of *homophyly* suggests that people who share similar backgrounds are more likely to feel comfortable with each other, more likely to understand each other, and are more likely to disclose to each other. Homophyly as a factor in human interaction is basic to some agency programs and some agency policies.

The denominational agencies, agencies organized and staffed by people of color and programs such as Alcoholics Anonymous are predicated in part on homophyly. People who have shared the same significant experience are more likely to be culturally at home with each other.

Homophyly suggests that you are attracted to people whom you perceive as being like yourself because you assume that they hold similar beliefs and attitudes. Theories regarding social influence suggest that trust, attractiveness, liking, and expertise are related to increases in social influence. If people of similar cultural background are more inclined to trust and like each other, matching would increase the interviewer's degree of social influence. If a similarity in cultural experience increases the interviewer's knowledge of the client's situation, the implied enhancement of understanding adds to the perception of expertise, which increases the level of social influence. We see the people we perceive as being like ourselves as more trustworthy, credible, and competent because they have experienced and know a similar social reality. Matching implies ascribed trust, perception of competence, and credibility. The unmatched interviewer has to achieve trust, perception of competence, and credibility.

In chapter 5 we note the importance of the interviewer's empathic understanding as a condition for establishing a good relationship. A good relationship is evidence of compatibility of interview participants and reduces social distance. The worker's responses demonstrate that the client's life and feelings are not remote. Such empathic understanding is most easily achieved by the interviewer who shares the interviewee's world. "The quality of empathy expressed when a gay therapist tells a gay client 'I know how it feels' is of a different order than when a heterosexual therapist says 'I know how it must feel'" (Rochlin 1982:25).

Effective interviewing requires making some predictions about how the interviewee is likely to respond to our interventions. Increasing the accuracy of such predictions enables us to better control the interview and to avoid offending. Cultural similarity to the interviewee may be one way to increase predictive accuracy.

The facilitative conditions for good interviewing would suggest the desirability of pairing the interviewee with an interviewer who is similar. Trust and mutual liking may be greater under those conditions. The ability to paraphrase and accurately reflect is likely to be greater when the interviewer understands where the client is coming from and when they share language and an associated pattern of metacommunication. The readiness to disclose requires trust and confidence that the interviewer will receive the disclosures understandingly. Some claim that interviewers need more than shared humanity and an ability to empathize in order to be truly understanding. Understanding requires the actual experience of living as an

African American, senior citizen, or homosexual. Nothing can duplicate the intensity of learning achieved by the living experience.

Research on Matching

Despite the intuitive logic of matching that such preconceptions suggest, the empirical research available to date has not confirmed that matching is necessary for conducting a good interview. The research tends to validate only a tenuous relationship between cultural matching and various kinds of psychotherapy effects—use of therapy, dropout rates, number of sessions completed, and therapy outcomes. Since 1983 a series of reviews has looked at the relevant research (Atkinson 1983, 1985; Atkinson and Schein 1986; Sexton and Whiston 1994; Sue, Zane, and Young 1994; Atkinson and Lowe 1995). The general conclusion is that the effects of interviewer-interviewee ethnic similarity are equivocal.[*]

Reviewing the research regarding similarity effects, Atkinson and Schein conclude that the "current review found very little evidence to support a membership-group similarity effect. Across various categories of member-ship group similarity, evidence for similarity effect ranged from equivocal to none" (1986:338). Atkinson and Schein conclude their review by stating that "systematically matching counselors and clients on membership-group . . . is not warranted given the results of the current review" (p. 345).

Similarly, Jayaratne et al., reviewing a segment of the research, note that "overall, the available evidence does not support the contention that race matching results in better treatment. . . . Therefore, any programmatic effort to match clients and workers by race does not appear to be founded on research evidence" (1992:109).

A more recent review of the research by Sue, Zane, and Young states that there "is no clear evidence from studies of actual clients that ethnic match enhances outcome among African Americans" (1994:791). They reach sim-ilar conclusions regarding Native Americans (p. 796) and Latinos (p. 803). Matching is more important among Asians, but many in this group are recent immigrants who speak little English (p. 800).

In concluding a chapter concerned with a detailed review of the relevant research Davis and Proctor say that

> available evidence does not support the widespread assumption that work-ers cannot help racially dissimilar clients. Some studies in fact indicate that minority clients fare no worse than White clients when they are assigned to White workers. Moreover, there is some evidence to suggest that—if the

---

[*] The available research regarding matching is primarily concerned with race and ethnicity.

initial issues of familiarity and trust are satisfactorily resolved—experienced, skilled, and sensitive professionals can work effectively with racially dissimilar clients.

(1989:55).

Proctor and Davis reiterate this conclusion in a more recent review (1994:321).

A major national epidemiological survey conducted by the Veterans Administration in 1986–87, the National Vietnam Veterans Readjustment Study, provided data on the experience of African American veterans who were treated by white clinicians and African American veterans treated by African American clinicians. Whether treated by white or African American clinicians, African American veterans were more likely to have fewer treatment sessions, terminate early, and be less committed to treatment than white veterans. However, although African American veterans were likely to exhibit this pattern whether treated by a racially matched or racially unmatched clinician, they were more likely to exhibit this pattern when paired with a white clinician. If they stayed in treatment, however, treatment outcomes were the same for the unmatched pair group and the racially matched pair group. "These findings . . . suggest only a small effect of racial pairing on clinical outcome, an effect that is much weaker than for involvements in treatment" (Rosenheck, Fontana, and Cottrol 1995:562).

Such equivocal results are characteristic even of research regarding client preference for matching. A meta-analysis of seventeen research articles and four relevant dissertations related to the question of ethnic minority preference for ethnically similar counselors concludes that "although the results of the meta-analysis demonstrated that there seems to be a preference for ethnically similar counselors, the results are far from consistent" (Coleman, Wampold, and Casali 1995:62). "When individuals from various cultural groups were asked to nominate characteristics of a competent counselor, ethnic similarity was not a significant factor in their prototype" (p. 61).

A 1995 review of the relevant research by Atkinson and Lowe concludes that minority clients express a preference for ethnically similar counselors. However, they tend to give counselor competence, education, and similarity in attitude preference over ethnic similarity. Even the preference for an ethnically similar counselor varies according to the level of acculturation, cultural commitment, and development of racial identity in the interviewee (pp. 392–93). The available research does tend to support the idea that dropout rates and use of therapy are likely to be better for ethnically similar worker-client pairs than for unmatched pairs (p. 396).

Flaskerud and Liu (1991) studied the effect of language, ethnicity, and gender match for 1,746 Asian American clients. Although matching had a positive effect on number of sessions attended and the dropout rate, matching made little difference in the outcome of the contact for the group that remained. The authors note that "it is possible to place too much emphasis on client/therapist ethnicity and language match and thereby to overlook group ethnic difference in belief systems and communication styles. These can differ greatly within, as well as between, ethnic groups, and can effect outcome also" (p. 39).

Perhaps of some relevant interest is the research on the criteria used by therapists in choosing a therapist for themselves. In a study of more than five hundred psychologists, psychiatrists, and social workers who sought treatment no one mentioned matching on the basis of race, ethnicity, or gender as a criterion. They most often mentioned competence and clinical experiences criteria for selection. They also saw "warmth and caring" and "openness" as highly desirable characteristics in the therapists they selected (Norcross 1993:57, table 2).

Researchers using interviewing as the basic procedure in their research tend to support these conclusions. Weiss, who has conducted a number of large-scale sociological studies based on qualitative interviewing procedures, says,

> It seems like common sense that it would be better for the interviewer to be of the same race and if possible of the same ethnic background as the respondent. My own experience has been that here, common sense is mostly wrong. Racial and ethnic differences, insofar as the respondent can infer these, may play a role in the respondent's initial reaction to the interviewer, but my experience has been that once an interview takes hold, these differences have little effect on the quality of the interviewing partnership.
>
> (1994:139)

The National Opinion Research Center reached a similar conclusion after conducting a nationwide large-scale study of sexual practices in the United States in 1994 (Laumann et al. 1994). The center's researchers decided that gender and ethnic matching of interviewer and interviewee was not necessary. "The experience and belief among the National Opinion Research Center survey research professionals was that the quality of the interviewer was important, but not necessarily linked to gender or race. Quality is a complex product of personality, training, and experience" (Laumann et al. 1994:61).

It seems reasonable to suppose that culture does make a difference, but it is quite difficult to identify what difference it makes. Problems with the research are cited to explain the failure of most such studies to find consistent and significantly measurable effects of the matching variable, despite the intuitively attractive supposition of such effects. Few studies have control groups and rarely take in-group differences into account. Differences in levels of assimilation and acculturation, differences in racial self-identification (Ponterotto, Anderson, and Grieger 1986), and socioeconomic differences between members of the same racial, ethnic, or gender group rarely receive consideration. The impediments to and complexity of research regarding the effects of cultural differences between interviewer and interviewee defy the possibility of achieving unambiguous conclusions in which we can have reasonable confidence (Sue, Zane, and Young 1994:806–10).

The inherent complexity of the interview interaction adds to questions about research deficiencies for providing guidance to interviewers involved in cross-cultural interviews. The interview derives from multiple variables interacting in a complex idiosyncratic configuration. Any single variable, such as race, ethnicity, or gender, would have to be an unusually potent master variable to consistently determine the interview process. Common group membership may tell us little about the specific values, lifestyles, and behaviors of a particular interviewee and even less about how behavior is determined in the particular context of the interview. Extrapolating from ethnic or racial membership to the interview interaction is a long and perilous journey.

Part of the problem lies in the different components of "matching." What exactly do we match when we match?

Race or ethnicity, gender, age, sexual orientation, and other factors are broad indexes of compatibility. We assume that people who share these visible attributes share attitudes, values, beliefs, and interests. However, people simultaneously occupy a number of different statuses and roles, so that people matched on cultural background may be unmatched on education, class, occupation, and the like. Compatibility of attitudes, values, and beliefs may be more significant for relationship development and interview interaction than similarity in race or ethnic group. Similarities in other dimensions significant to a person's identity can compensate for racial, ethnic, or cultural dissimilarity. Reviewing the research, S. Sue notes that ethnicity per se (or gender, age, or sexual orientation)

> tells us very little about the attitudes, values, experiences, and behaviors of *individual* therapists or clients who interact in a therapy session. What is known is that although *groups* exhibit cultural differences, considerable individual differences may exist within groups. Ethnic matches may result in cultural mismatches if therapists and clients from the same ethnic group

show markedly different values (e.g., a highly acculturated Chinese American therapist who works with a Chinese immigrant holding traditional Chinese values). Conversely, ethnic matches do not necessarily imply cultural mismatches because therapists and clients from different ethnic groups may share similar values, lifestyles and experiences.

(1988:306).

The available research does not show that matching on the basis of race, ethnicity, or sexual orientation is necessary for conducting a successful interview.

Unmatched pairs frequently succeed in achieving the objectives of the interview. Apparently, culturally sensitive interviewers, observing some sensible precautions and using traditionally effective interview procedures, can and do transcend cultural differences in conducting an effective interview.

The generally effective approach gives visibility to cultural differences as one variable that interviewers need to consciously and explicitly consider in assessing the interviewee's situation and in formulating acceptable interview objectives. Furthermore, the approach involves a recognition that in many respects people have common needs, desires, hopes, and expectations that they may express in culturally different ways. An appreciation of such common human needs, coupled with an attitude that communicates respect, interest, concern, empathy, acceptance, and an effort to understand and individualize, can transcend cultural differences and enable the development of an effective interviewer-interviewee relationship. This suggests that culturally sensitive interviewers, basing their approach on universal elements in the interaction while recognizing the significance and effects of culture, can be effective interviewers in cross-cultural relationships (see box 12.1). Others concerned with the problem propose a similar approach to cross-cultural interviews (Patterson 1985; A. P. Lloyd 1987; Vontress 1988; Fukuyama 1990; Freeman 1993).

Box 12.1 Cross-Cultural Interviewing

The available research, however indefinite, suggests that workers can conduct a productive interview despite ethnic, racial, age, and sexual preference differences between interviewer and interviewee if interviewers observe some cardinal principles of good interviewing.

Interviewers must

- Be conscious of cultural factors that may intrude on the interview
- Acknowledge any stereotypical ideas they hold regarding the group the client represents
- Apply such stereotypes flexibly with a conscious effort to modify or

discard the generalization if it appears inappropriate for the particular interview
- Take the responsibility to learn about the culture of the interviewee so as to better understand any culturally derived behaviors the interviewee might manifest
- Respond to interviewees with respect, empathy, and acceptance, whatever their differences

Effective cross-cultural interviewing combines an acknowledgment of cultural differences with the general principles of good interviewing applicable to all groups of interviewees.

The crucial consideration may be interviewers' skill in developing and maintaining a productive relationship and the attitudes they bring to the interview. This includes willingness to learn about, credit, and accept differences. These factors, rather than consistent attempts at matching, which often are not feasible, may enable the interviewer to do the job required.

In distinguishing between research on initial preference for a matched interviewer and research on outcome of contact, we can have some greater measure of confidence in the results of studies regarding *initial* preference. If they have a choice, people of color tend to prefer a matched interviewer. This also seems to be true for gays and lesbians (Gambrill, Stein, and Brown 1984:64; McDermott, Tyndall, and Lichtenberg 1989:68; Lease, Cogdal, and Smith 1995:62). This would suggest that agencies have an obligation to develop a multicultural staff to increase the possibility of meeting a client's initial preference.

Cultural differences are most likely to be felt early in the interview when both interviewer and interviewee are guided by their stereotypes. African American interviewees, for example, initially carry into the interview perceptions derived from their experience with the white world; white interviewers react in terms of the generalizations they have developed about African Americans. Only gradually do the individuals emerge from these stereotypes as a relationship develops and the person replaces the stereotypical image. The research suggests that the effects of a good relationship can supersede the effects of cultural difference. People initially grant or withhold credibility on the basis of ascription, cultural similarity, or dissimilarity, but they confirm or discard this decision based on what takes place in the interview.. Credibility initially granted on the basis of cultural similarity may be revoked as the interviewer manifests incompetence. And credibility initially withheld because interviewee and interviewer are not culturally matched may be granted as the interviewer shows competence and understanding.

Defining the Culturally Sensitive Interviewer

Competence in multicultural interviewing is different from interviewing competence in general. General interviewing competence is a necessary but insufficient basis for effective multicultural interviewing.

The best interviewer, then, has cultural sensitivity and general competence in interviewing.

What does the culturally sensitive interviewer need to know and do to maximize the possibility of conducting a successful cross-cultural interview? What characteristics identify the culturally sensitive interviewer?

White interviewers need to recognize that they too have a culture—have been taught that certain ways of doing things are right and proper, to think in a certain way, perceive the world in a certain way, for example, as a white Christian middle-income female. Just as everyone else has an accent and we don't, we fail to recognize that we are products of our culture. We are like fishes who, never having experienced anything but water, are unaware of the water. White people generally tend not to clearly identify themselves as being racially white. They do not see themselves as a people of color, having a sense of racial identity and a distinct culture. Culturally sensitive interviewers are consciously aware of their culture and are explicitly knowledgeable of the stereotypes associated with it.

Culturally sensitive interviewers are aware of the stereotypes they hold in regard to others and test them flexibly against the reality of the individual client with a readiness and willingness to modify or discard the stereotype in the attempt to understand the individual.

In addition to being white, middle-income, female, and middle-aged the statistically typical professional social worker has been socialized to develop beliefs, attitudes, and behaviors that are congruent with the occupational role. This commitment is what is meant by becoming and acting like a professional social worker.

A study of the mental health values of professional therapists, which included 128 social workers among the 425 respondents, found that a high percentage endorse such values as "being open, genuine, and honest with others"; "assume responsibility for one's actions"; "find fulfillment in work"; "develop ability to give and receive affection"; "be committed to family needs and childrearing"; "apply self-discipline in use of alcohol, tobacco, and drugs"; and "increase one's capacity for self control" (Jensen and Bergin 1988:293, table 1).

Adherence to such values was seen as associated with positive mental health. The implication of the study is that values such as those that represent the professional social work culture give professional direction in selecting desirable interview objectives.

In developing an awareness of the values and attitudes that determine their interaction in the interview, interviewers have to make explicit not only the mainstream values and attitudes in which they were socialized but also the modification of such values and attitudes resulting from socialization to the professional social work culture. Adherence to social work values implies that, although cultural sensitivity requires respect for the interviewee's culture, it does not necessarily suggest invariable acceptance of all the interviewee's customs and traditions. We do not accept the definition of child discipline that involves the use of corporal punishment by immigrant groups "who think that hitting is the best way to teach children to be respectful" (Dugger 1996:A12). Nor do we accept traditional Hmong courtship practice, which involves bride abduction (Martell 1994). Admittedly, the limits of acceptance are ambiguous, except where custom and tradition are in conflict with the law.

The culturally sensitive interviewer attempts to conceptualize the problem situation so that it is compatible with the interviewee's belief system. The culturally sensitive interviewer attempts to formulate solutions that are compatible with the interviewee's culture.

The interviewer needs to be aware of cultural differences in formulating interview objectives. Seeking to help a Hispanic woman in a traditional marriage to develop greater assertiveness within the family is likely to be problematic. Encouraging an Asian American adolescent to express hostility toward his father runs counter to cultural prescriptions. Choice of objectives needs to pay respect to what is culturally compatible, appropriate, and acceptable.

The literature on culturally sensitive counseling speaks in broad generalities of the values, attributes, behaviors, and beliefs that characterize African Americans, Native Americans, Latino/Chicanos, Asian Americans, gays, lesbians, and senior citizens. The influence of culture on attitudes and behavior is subject to so many variables that the manner in which the individual interviewee interprets and expresses it is almost impossible to define. Consequently, we must, while being sensitive to the influence that culture may have, be open to learning from the individual interviewee the meaning of the culture to that client. This suggests the desirability of approaching the client with an attitude of ignorance and the necessity of individualizing the interviewee.

If solicitation of feedback from clients is a generally desirable approach to good interviewing, it is especially necessary with special populations of clients. Knowing less about the specifics of their culture, the interviewer needs to be more open to learning from the interviewee.

Because interviewers are less likely to have had the experience that permits empathic understanding of the culturally different interviewee, they need to be more ready to listen, less ready to come to conclusions, more open to guidance and correction of their presuppositions by the interviewee. The presumption of ignorance, needed in all interviews, is even more necessary here.

Box 12.2 lists the characteristics of the culturally sensitive interviewer.

Box 12.2 Desirable Characteristics of the Culturally Sensitive Interviewer

---

1. The culturally sensitive interviewer approaches all interviewees of whatever cultural background with respect, warmth, acceptance, concern, interest, empathy, and due regard for individuality and confidentiality.
2. The culturally sensitive interviewer exerts maximum effort in the early part of the interview when the interviewee's mistrust and suspicion are highest, when the interviewer is apt to be perceived as a stereotype rather than an individual, and in terms of the interviewer's status as a representative of the mainstream culture rather than as a person.
3. Culturally sensitive interviewers strive to develop an explicit awareness that they have a culture as a member of a particular racial or ethnic, gender, age, and occupational group and as such have been socialized to beliefs, attitudes, behaviors, stereotypes, biases, and prejudices that affect their behavior in the interview.
4. Having achieved such awareness, culturally sensitive interviewers are comfortably undefensive in their identity as a member of a cultural group.
5. Culturally sensitive interviewers are aware of the cultural factors in the interviewee's background that they need to recognize and accept as potential determinants of the interviewee's decision to come for help, the presentation and nature of the problem the client brings, and the choice of intervention.
6. The culturally sensitive interviewer is ready to acknowledge and undefensively and unapologetically raise for discussion cross-cultural factors affecting the interview.
7. Culturally sensitive interviewers recognize that the great variety of culturally distinct groups makes it impossible to have knowledge of all of them but accepts the obligation to study the cultural background of interviewees most frequently served by their agency.
8. Culturally sensitive interviewers are ready to acknowledge the limitations of their knowledge of an interviewee's cultural background and

are ready to undefensively solicit help from the interviewee in learning what they need to know.

9. The culturally sensitive interviewer communicates an attitude that cultural differences are not better or worse but rather legitimately diverse and respects such differences.

10. Culturally sensitive interviewers are aware of indigenous cultures' strengths, culturally based community resources that might be a source of help, and that some kinds of help may be culturally inappropriate.

11. Culturally sensitive interviewers are aware of the problems of disenfranchisement, discrimination, and stigmatization frequently associated with minority group status.

12. Although sensitive to cultural factors that might be related to clients' problems, the culturally sensitive interviewer is aware that such factors may be peripheral to the situation of a particular client, that personality factors may be of more significance than racial or ethnic cultural factors, and that culture does not adequately define the interviewee, who is unique.

At best the characteristics of the culturally sensitive interviewer are general guidelines that may be helpful if flexibly applied, with a listening ear and an understanding heart attuned to detect individual differences.

The Use of Interpreters

Language barriers are a significant problem in cross-cultural interviewing.

Language, the communication vehicle of any interview, is the most explicit manifestation of ethnic identity. All the effects of cultural difference between interviewer and interviewee are greater when they do not share a language.

For many clients English is a second language. Communication has to be clear, simple, and slow, with frequent solicitation of feedback. The interviewer may need to be more directive.

Even clients who seem fluent in English may do quite a bit of mental translating as they talk. This is demonstrated in studies that show that bilingual clients, when communicating in Spanish, show greater spontaneity, more active gesturing, and increased voice animation than when they communicate similar material in English. Nuances of feeling and communication of emotions require a richer vocabulary more likely to be available to clients in their primary language.

A basic problem in interviewing many Hispanic and Asian clients is the lack of fluency in a common language. Communication is difficult, if not impossible, between a client who speaks Spanish or Korean and an interviewer who speaks English.

One response is to hire bilingual staff members. However, this is a partial solution, given the number of different languages that clients speak. The alternative is to bring an interpreter into the interaction.

The interpreter must be acceptable to and respected by the client as well as the worker and agency. If clients are suspicious of the interpreter, they are likely to restrict what they say. Guarantees of confidentiality should specifically include interpreters, particularly if they are a member of the client's community.

The interpreter who focuses on exact literal translation may fail to communicate to the interviewer some subtle significant aspects of the interviewee's communication. This leads to correct translation but inadequate communication.

The best interpreter collaboratively participates in the interview under the direction of the interviewer and communicates not only the client's words but also the client's meanings. The best interpreter is a sensitive colleague of the interviewer, knowledgeable about the culture and lifestyle of the interviewee and neutrally communicating the sense of the client's verbal and nonverbal messages.

A competent interpret needs not only to be fluent in the language of the interviewee but also to know something about the social problem with which the client wants help.

Interpreters with whom a worker has developed a good working relationship are a valuable source of suggestions for more effectively interviewing members of the ethnic group. Interpreters can also help the worker to avoid culturally based errors in interviewing. In one instance a worker raised questions about finances with a client whose Southeast Asian background dictated sensitivity with regard to such information. The interpreter suggested that the worker hold such questions until a more intensive relationship developed (Baker 1981).

The interpreter should sit at the side of the interviewee, and the interviewer should face both of them. Even though clients may not be able to understand what the interviewer is saying, the interviewer should speak directly to the client. This is more desirable than speaking at the client through the interpreter. Asking the interpreter to ask the client about the problem depersonalizes the relationship. Cast the interpreter in the role of assistant rather than a principal informant on whom you are dependent.

Using an interpreter changes the relationship between interviewer and interviewee. As the interaction becomes triadic, it becomes more complex. The relationship between interviewer and interviewee may be attenuated. Some interviewers may be uncomfortable with an interpreter—they are sharing the interviewee with another person who is observing them. Further, the worker depends on the interpreter and loses some measure of control of the interview. The interpreter may compete with the interviewer for the client's approbation. The client might try to use the interpreter as either a pawn or an ally. One other danger in using interpreters is that an assertive interpreter may take over the interview.

Interpreters are colleagues but also members of the client's community. As such, they may be protective of that community. A Mexican woman, discussing her abusive marriage, seemed about to cry as she said, "Well, I'll tell you what's really happening." The interpreter became uncomfortable and defused the situation, saying, "You must have had some really hot chilies that night." Both laughed and the entire direction of the interview was broken (Putsen 1985:3346).

Because translation involves saying everything twice, the time allocated for the interviewer needs to be longer. It also is better to use short units of speech so that the interpreter can follow more easily.

Further, you need to decide whether you want a verbatim translation or a summary of what the client in saying. Another option is to allow for summary of some content and verbatim translation of other, more significant content.

The pace of an interpreted interview is necessarily slow. The worker needs to manifest patience. "The experience can be like watching a foreign film without subtitles" (Freed 1988:316).

Using children as interpreters for their parents is not desirable, although this is often necessary because of lack of an alternative. First, having a child translate reverses the usual relationship between parent and child. Second, parents may be hesitant about answering some questions because of reluctance to share this information with the child.

Being bilingual is a necessary but not sufficient qualification for an interpreter. Asking an agency clerk who speaks the language and happens to be available to interpret is not a good idea.

Interpreting for the Deaf

Interviewing a deaf person may require the use of a sign language interpreter. Communication in this instance is, of course, possible by writing notes. However, this is time consuming and cumbersome.

The hearing interpreter, in addition to being fluent in American Sign

Language, needs to be familiar and empathic with deaf culture. The caveats that apply to using a bilingual interpreter apply generally to those situations that require using an ASL interpreter in working with deaf clients (Roe and Roe 1991).

Federal legislation requires that interpreting be available free of charge to deaf clients by human service organizations that receive federal or government assistance in any form. Qualified ASL interpreters are listed with the National Registry of Interpreters for the Deaf in Silver Spring, Maryland.

Summary: Chapter 12

Problems in interviewing may result when socioeconomic status, color, ethnicity, age, or sexual orientation increase social distance between interviewer and interviewee and limit understanding.

When the interviewer is white and the interviewee is African American, they may face differences in socioeconomic background as well as in racial experience. The white interviewer, who may initially be regarded with suspicion by the black client, should observe with singular care all the formalities that are overt indications of respect for the client. Awareness of racist attitudes and efforts to change these attitudes, as well as familiarity with African-American culture, are tactics for establishing contact with the African American client. In making restitution for felt or suspected racism some social workers may compensate by viewing African American clients with an exaggeratedly positive bias. Acknowledging racial difference while avoiding a tendency to romanticize a client who is ethnically or racially different is important.

Because most social workers are younger than their clients, cultural aspects of age differences may also act as a barrier to effective interviewing. In working with elderly clients observing formalities is important, as are focusing on strengths while being realistic in acknowledging deficits, using direct questions, and shortening the interview. Reminiscing may serve an important function by helping the elderly client maintain self-esteem and a feeling of competence in relating to the interviewer. The social work interviewer can play the role of confidante and companion to the lonely elderly interviewee. The social worker may also function in the role of case manager.

Sexual orientation is another variable that may create cross-cultural difficulty between participants. Homophobia, fear, and dislike of homosexuals are pervasive in our heterosexually oriented society. The interviewer may find it difficult to resolve a strong feeling that heterosexual relationships are more "normal" than other forms of sexual expression.

Interviewers are more likely to conduct a successful interview if they are familiar with the gay community and its resources. The AIDS epidemic in the gay community poses some special problems for understanding the homosexual client.

The concept of homophyly suggests that people who share similar backgrounds are more likely to feel comfortable with, understand, and disclose to each other. The empirical research, however, has established only a tenuous relationship between cultural matching and positive outcomes in psychotherapy. The crucial consideration may be the interviewer's skills in developing and maintaining a productive relationship and the attitudes the interviewer brings to the interview.

Culturally competent interviewers are aware of the influence of their own culture and the stereotypes associated with it. They are also aware of the influence of the professional subculture of social work on interview interaction. Finally, culturally sensitive interviewers are aware of the influence of culture on how interviewees conceptualize their problem, the solution to the problem, and on their behavior and attitudes during the interview.

Interviewers can use interpreters if a language barrier is a significant problem in cross-cultural interviewing. Interviewing a deaf person may require the use of a sign language interpreter.

SUGGESTED READINGS

People of Color

Wynetta Devore and Elfriede G. Schlesinger. *Ethnic-Sensitive Social Work Practice*, 3d ed. New York: Macmillan 1991. (384 pp.)
Calls attention to ethnic factors relating to social work practice. The book's purpose is to raise the awareness of social workers in regard to ethnic variables that are relevant for worker-client interaction and the adaptations workers need to make to "ethnic reality."

Patricia L. Ewalt et al., eds., *Multicultural Issues in Social Work*. Washington, D.C.: National Association of Social Work Press 1996. (578 pp.)
Thirty-eight articles from social work journals on multicultural issues.

Dianne F. Harrison, John S. Wodarski, and Bruce Thayer. *Cultural Diversity and Social Work Practice*, 2d ed. Springfield, Ill.: C. C. Thomas 1996. (450 pp.)

Allen Ivey. *Intentional Interviewing and Counseling: Facilitating Client Development in a Multicultural Society*, 3d. ed. Belmont, Calif.: Wadsworth, 1994. (384 pp.)

Doman Lum. *Social Work Practice and People of Color: A Process Stage Approach*, 2d ed. Pacific Grove, Calif.: Brooks/Cole, 1992. (252 pp.)
This book focuses on the problem-solving process from inception to termination when working with people of color.

Freddy A. Paniagua. *Assessing and Treating Culturally Diverse Clients.* Thousand Oaks, Calif.: Sage, 1994. (139 pp.)

A concise review of the particularities of counseling members of several ethic minority groups.

Paul B. Pedersen et al., eds. *Counseling Across Culture,* 4th ed. Thousand Oaks, Calif.: Sage, 1995. (392 pp.)

Joseph G. Ponterotto et al., eds. *Handbook of Multicultural Counseling.* Thousand Oaks, Calif.: Sage, 1995. (679 pp.)

A series of articles that covers the knowledge skills that interviewers need when engaging in multicultural counseling.

D. W. Sue and D. Sue. *Counseling the Culturally Different: Theory and Practice.* New York: Wiley, 1990.

The Aged

Enid O. Cox and Ruth J. Parsons. *Empowerment-Oriented Social Work Practice with the Elderly.* Pacific Grove, Calif.: Brooks/Cole, 1994. (274 pp.)

Written by two social work professors, the book presents an attitudinal approach to the aged interviewee designed to empower the client.

Barbara B. Dreher. *Communication Skills for Working with the Elderly.* New York: Springer, 1987. (160 pp.)

Provides some practical suggestions for interviewing senior citizens.

Marion L. Beaver and Don A. Miller. *Clinical Social Work Practice with the Elderly: Primary, Secondary, and Tertiary Intervention,* 2d ed. Belmont, Calif.: Wadsworth, 1992. (432 pp.)

Sexual Orientation

Carlton, Carnett, ed. *Affirmative Dynamic Psychotherapy with Gay Men.* Northvale, N.J.: Janon Aronson, 1993. (264 pp.)

Oriented in terms of a psychodynamic approach, the readings provide useful suggestions for helping gay interviewees.

Khristine L. Falso, *Psychotherapy with Lesbian Clients* New York: Bruner/Mazel, 1991 (208 pp.)

John C. Gonsiorek. *A Guide to Psychotherapy with Gay and Lesbian Clients.* New York: Harrington Park Press, 1985. (212 pp.)

A variety of different approaches to helping gay and lesbian clients; explains some problems such clients face.

A. Elfin Moses and Robert O. Hawkins. *Counseling Lesbian Women and Gay Men: A Life Issues Approach.* St. Louis: C. V. Mosby, 1982. (263 pp.)

Written by a social worker and sexologist, the book is a good review of the problem faced by homosexuals in a heterosexual society. It provides a good analysis of what the interviewer might need to know and be aware of in counseling gay men and lesbian women.

Charles Silverstein, ed. *Gays, Lesbians, and Their Therapists: Studies in Psychotherapy.* New York: W. W. Norton, 1991 (275 pp.)

A collection of articles concerned with helping gay and lesbian clients. Despite unevenness in the hints they provide to interviewers, the articles are of enough interest to warrant citation.

Natalie J. Woodman and Harry R. Lenna. *Counseling with Gay Men and Women.* San Francisco: Jossey-Bass, 1980. (144 pp.)

Written by faculty members of a school of social work, the book helps to develop empathy with gay clients through clinical material illustrating counseling.

THIRTEEN

Some Problematic Interviews:
The Involuntary Adult Client and
the Sexually Abused Child

Cross-cultural interviews pose special problems in adapting the interview to cultural differences between participants. Some interviewees pose problems of adaptation because of special difficulties they bring to the interview situation. Physically or mentally handicapped clients and substance abuse clients are among those client groups that require modified interviewing.

Given the space limitations, we have selected two special interviewee groups for more elaborate discussion—the involuntary adult client and the sexually abused child. The involuntary client constitutes a fairly large interviewee subset. Interviewing children who may have been sexually abused is a task frequently assigned to social workers because the law often requires that other professionals—medical personnel, educators, and police—report any suspicions of abuse to social agencies.

Involuntary Interviewees

People come to an agency interview with various levels of commitment to the experience. Some make a completely voluntary decision to participate; others come involuntarily. The levels of voluntarism are in the nature of a continuum rather than a dichotomy, running from eager to get help to willing to tolerate service to ambivalence, reluctance, resistance, opposition, and hostility to use of the service.

Involuntary interviewees are those required by court order to seek agency help and those who have been pressured to use the service. These groups constitute a growing number of clients. It includes alcohol and drug abusers, those on probation or parole, and clients who have neglected or physically, emotionally, or sexually abused their children. Correctional programs, schools, mental institutions, substance abuse programs, child protection agencies, and spouse protection agencies refer these clients. Juvenile courts may refer adolescent offenders.

Such clients often make contact because not coming would result in the imposition of even more punitive conditions—activation of a suspended prison sentence, termination of parental rights, or return to a correctional facility. Another group of clients is coerced into coming as a condition of the restoration or preservation of a valued personal resource—return of a revoked driver's license, return of children placed in foster care—or as a condition of continued employment.

In other cases a spouse or an employer, a school administrator, or circumstances coerce clients to contact agencies. Coming to the interview in such instances is not in response to the interviewee's preference, but it is not legally mandated.

Coerced involuntary interviewees and mandated involuntary interviewees are different. Mandated clients are impelled by a legal decision requiring their participation. Coerced clients are propelled by social and emotional pressures from spouses, children, doctors, clergy, and school administrators who are recommending their participation.

Because the mandated client is an extreme instance of the involuntary client, much of what we say here is applicable to others in the coerced involuntary client group.

Our concern here is not with resistance as it is classically defined—namely, unconscious or preconscious defenses by the ego against communications that might create anxiety, guilt, shame, and the like. Resistance on the part of the mandated client is a defense against externally imposed threats. Resistance here means anything the interviewee does to impede the objectives of the interview. Our concern here is with conscious, deliberate, openly acknowledged efforts to oppose unwanted interactions or intrusions; to subvert the efforts of the worker to conduct an interview; and to reject the role of being a client of the agency. This kind of open opposition is similar to classical resistance in that both are concerned with maintaining the status quo.

The voluntary client comes to the interview having resolved any ambivalence about accepting the influence of the interviewer. The involuntary client comes resisting the interviewer's interventions. As Hutchison (1987) notes, the involuntary client is forced to recognize the formal authority of the interviewer as agency representative but has not accepted the interviewer's psychological authority. Mandated clients challenge professional authority and test its limits (Gitterman 1989).

Social work interviewers are uneasy about working with involuntary clients. They feel rejected and inadequate because their usually effective interviewing skills often fail to work. They resent having to expend time on those who refuse help when they might use the time to help those who would gratify them by responding positively.

Interviewers rarely encounter the kind of naked opposition that some mandated clients display, so they have little experience in dealing with it. It is easy to be intimidated by this kind of interviewee.

The seemingly incompatible demands of the community—that the agency be both helpful and controlling—become highly visible in an interview with the involuntary client.

The interviewer is faced with both an ethical and a pragmatic question. The ethical question involves the morality of acting as an agent of social control on behalf of the legal system, which has denied the client the right of self-determination in the decision to contact the agency. In cooperating with the legal system is the worker colluding in the unethical denial of the client's right to self-determination? The pragmatic question relates to whether the interviewer can be of use to a client who comes for help unwillingly. The two questions are concerned with the right to treat and the ability to treat.

Despite their uneasiness and skepticism, many social workers have resolved the dilemma of conflicting loyalties to the rights of the client and the rights of the community (Kenmore 1987). One factor is the ethical consideration that refusing to accept the mandated referral is a rejection of both the client's entitlement to and need for service, although the client does not recognize that need.

The answer to the pragmatic question reinforces the value of this approach. Can the worker be of any help in these instances? Workers' skepticism is based on the fact that, unlike some medical procedures, any kind of counseling requires active participation by the interviewee. Another prerequisite for effective helping is that the interviewee recognize that a problem exists. In the case of the involuntary client, this is often not the case. Other people are discomfited by the interviewee's behavior: the client is not. The interviewee attributes the problem to someone else. Involuntary clients are frequently in denial about the existence, significance, and/or consequences of their problem.

Despite these real concerns, the limited empirical evidence available suggests that the worker can in fact be helpful. Working with an interviewee who voluntarily seeks help is likely to be more effective than working with an oppositional interviewee who initially rejects help. But "less effective" does not mean ineffectual. A number of studies support the contention that, although coming involuntarily may not be the best condition for a successful interview, such a beginning is not inevitably ineffective (Margolis, Krystal, and Siegel 1964; Gallant et al. 1968; Brill and Lieberman 1969; Webb and Riley 1970; Wolfe et al. 1980; Dawson et al. 1986; Ben-Arie, Schwartz, and George 1986). Irueste-Montes and Montes observed the interaction of families mandated to go though a program of parent training as contrasted with those who voluntarily applied for such a program. They conclude that "court ordered treatment would seem to make even resistant and seriously deficient parents accessible to treatment" (1988:38) and equally successful in achieving treatment objections. Reviewing the relevant alcohol abuse literature, Larke concludes that the "predominant finding seems to be that there exists little or no differences between mandated or voluntary clients vis-à-vis success at modifying alcohol use" (1985:263).

Maletsky treated voluntary and court-referred sexually deviant clients using a desensitization procedure. Results "are striking for their lack of significant differences and do not lend support to the notion that court-referred patients are less compliant or have less satisfactory outcomes than self-referred patients, at least with the techniques employed here" (1980:313).

The California Child Sexual Abuse Treatment Program directed by Henry Giaretto has been copied throughout the country. Abuse perpetrators "are coerced into counseling by the judicial process" and asked to participate in this particular treatment program (Kroth 1979:22). Despite the initial involuntary nature of the counseling, the evaluation of the program shows it to be successful in effecting change in many abuse perpetrators (pp. 122–23).

Both Larke (1991:12–14) and Rooney (1994:80–82) reviewed studies relating to the possibility of successfully treating the involuntary client. Their general conclusion is that, although such clients present initially greater difficulty than voluntary clients, successful intervention is possible in many instances. Studying a group of court-ordered referred clients, O'Hare (1996) found that "over one-quarter (28.3%) of the court-ordered clients were either thinking about changing, actively engaged in doing something about the problem, or trying to maintain previous gains in dealing with the problem" (p. 420).

In summary Rooney notes that "a review of the effectiveness literature suggest(s) that legally mandated clients can have more successful results than we had earlier thought to be the case. However, these more positive results contain the caution that coerced intervention often produces time limited benefits that do not last beyond the use of external pressures" (1994:89).

Interviews with eleven "experienced social workers and psychologists" about their perception of the effects of court referral on treatment found that they do not believe court involvement interferes with the treatment (Gourse and Chescheir 1981). The clinicians believe that court referrals make some clients accessible to treatment who otherwise would not have come for help and that the use of authority to get some cooperation is not in violation of the client's right to self-determination.

The interviewer faces the problem of converting authority without power to influence into authority with freely granted power to influence. The worker has the authority—granted to the agency by the community and delegated by the agency to the worker—to schedule an interview with the client. However, initially the worker has no power to influence. In response to authority mandated clients are physically present. But in defiance these clients refuse to cooperate and block any effort by the worker to involve them in the interaction. Powerless to choose whether to be referred, powerless to choose their therapist, type of treatment, or date of termination of treatment, interviewees exert power in the only way they can—by refusing to participate (Schottenfeld 1989). Authority does not guarantee the worker the power to make interviewees do anything they choose not to do. Only as workers induce clients mitigate their opposition can interviewers attain any power to influence.

Engaging in some interaction with the interviewer initiates a process that can be helpful to the client. This then raises the question of how the interviewer can engage such a client to maximize the probability that the forced contact can be of help.

Opposition to becoming a client is understandable if we try to see it from the perspective of mandated interviewees.

The referring agency has robbed them of some measure of autonomy by requiring them to do something they would rather not. Like any mature adult, they react to such demeaning infringement on their freedom with anger and hostility.

What appears to be deviant, illogical, and self-damaging to others may be defined differently by interviewees. They do not have a problem, and others want the clients to change; even if clients' behavior is problematic to others, it's giving the clients some measure of satisfaction (hedonistic pleasure in drugs, release of aggression or sexual satisfaction in abuse, and so on), and they not sure they want to give this up. Even if these clients would like to change some of their behavior, they have no great confidence that the agency can help, and the psychic price and the dangers may be too high—they have to acknowledge failure and become involved in an unfamiliar process requiring a sacrifice of autonomy and a grant of some controls to others. They have to disclose much of their intimate life to others with no certainty as to how those people will use the information.

Even if they might want to change in the direction the agency wants them to change, these clients have anxiety about being able to (give up drugs, change their molesting impulses, and the like). To become involved with the agency may then mean another defeat. These clients may have had a previous experience in which therapy failed and that gives substance to their fears.

Involuntary interviewees may present themselves as blameless. They deny responsibility and give excuses—"I was drunk"; "I was sick"; "I was very upset"; "Nobody told me"; "They provoked me"; "My friends forced me." Rather than seeing themselves as needing help, coerced interviewees see themselves as a victim of other people's manipulations.

A correctional social worker says,

> When we interview guys in prison, our first job is to get them into prison. Now that sounds paradoxical, but while these guys are in prison physically, emotionally they are not. Many of them are convinced they shouldn't be there, they have been railroaded, it was these other guys, et cetera. So, our first job is to get them to accept that they are there for a reason and they are responsible for that reason.

Planning may not make much sense to clients who have learned that the future is unpredictable and who face the problem of meeting basic needs that require immediate satisfaction. Postponing present gratification that is assured for some future chancy gains is an unattractive cost-benefit equation for people who have little confidence that they can control events between the present and the future. A fatalistic passivity may be an adaptive learned response to the realities of a depriving environment beyond their control.

Their opposition is manifested by expressions of indifference—"It's no big deal"; "It really doesn't bother me."

Some involuntary interviewees may acknowledge fault and circumvent the purpose of the interview by ingratiating or supplication: "It was a one-time thing"; "I am sorry, I learned a lesson, it won't happen again." Visibly distressed and self-confessing, they have supposedly changed—the interview has no point.

Involuntary clients use a variety of evasive and diversionary tactics to avoid serious discussion of their problems. The overtalkative rambling interviewee's resistance may be equally effective but less apparent than that of the openly taciturn interviewee. Interventions by the interviewer are met with vague uncommunicative responses, brief uninformative answers, evasive comments, inattention, irrelevant diversions, and persistent silence. Verbosity and small talk are oppositional behaviors, frustrating productive interviewing. Although some clients openly acknowledge that they "wouldn't have come if I hadn't been told I had to" or "I didn't ask to come or want to come," others are covert resisters. They go through the motions—they are overly compliant or excessively agreeable, defensively avoidant or uncooperatively taciturn.

All this suggests not that these interviewees are unmotivated but that they are differently motivated. The problem is to influence interviewees to change their motivation to some degree from opposition to acceptance of the interview, the role of interviewee, and obligation to participate in the tasks that the role requires. The effort is to have interviewees accept responsibility for the situation and acknowledge that they have a problem that they need to address.

Mandated clients often have a strong motive for cooperating in the interview. For some cooperation may result in the end of probation, return of a driver's license, or regaining custody of their children. Interviewers can use such motives to obtain interviewees' active participation.

INTERVIEWEE: It's hell being without a driver's license. It's more than inconvenient; it's embarrassing.

INTERVIEWER: What would you like to do to get it back?

INTERVIEWEE: Well, you tell me. I think I might be ready to listen.

INTERVIEWER: That's very good. Let's talk about that.

In responding to the interviewee's oppositional behavior the interviewer manifests all the facilitating attitudes that counter the attitudes that fuel such behavior. Being accepting, empathic, respectful, interested, individualizing, maximizing, to the extent possible, the interviewee's entitlement to autonomy, makes it difficult for the interviewee to maintain a negative stance. It is hard to fight with someone who does not want to fight with you, who listens acceptingly to what you want to say, who does not challenge or threaten you.

The facilitating approach demonstrates to interviewees how they will be treated if they decide to become involved with the agency. The interviewer disarms the client's motivation to continue to be negative, enhancing the client's motivation to cooperate. Faced with persistent negativity, the interviewer might wedge the door open by asking neutral questions about the interviewee's life and general situation that have nothing to do with the substance of the referral.

The interviewer needs to be alert to any intimation, however slight or oblique, that some aspect of opposition is moderating and encourage it.

Initially, the worker needs to deal directly and explicitly with the resentment of the coerced client. The worker does this by openly recognizing the circumstances that brought the interviewee to the interview and the negative feelings this likely has evoked and by expressing empathy with the feelings:

> I know that you have been required by the court to meet with me. I can understand that since this is something you yourself did not freely decide to do, you might have some strong feelings about this. People don't like to be told what to do and I can't blame them. I am interested in learning from you how you feel about this.

Rather than countering the opposition directly, the interviewer goes with it, joining the interviewee by affirming the interviewee's entitlement to opposition. Acceptance of and empathy with the interviewee's oppositional statements tend to defuse them. Working with the opposition rather than adversarily rejecting it allies the interviewer with the interviewee. To start with attention to the interviewee's opposition is truly to start where the client is.

Interviewees who come because they are forced to are highly likely to have negative feelings about coming. Consequently, the risk is low in suggesting the interviewee share any feelings of anger: "Since everyone is different, I don't know for sure that you feel this way, but I can imagine that you might be angry about having to meet with me."

Trying to understand what prompts the interviewee's anger, depersonalizing it, recognizing, and validating it help to defuse the anger.

There are ways to respond to anger in a constructive manner without demeaning or challenging the interviewee. The social worker in a family agency was discussing arrears in child support payments by a father of schoolaged children. The divorce had been a bitter one; the father was resistant to paying anything and was ordered to meet with the worker to discuss this. When the worker pointed out that the children were suffering, Mr. L. said bitterly and vehemently,

Tell that to that goddamned bitch. She has more money than she knows what to do with. Fuck her and fuck you. You're just taking her side against me. I'll piss on your grave before I give her a dime.

The interviewer said,

I don't appreciate that kind of language in any case, and I especially don't appreciate it when it's directed at me in an interview. I feel trapped because I cannot respond to the way I feel—angry, sore, insulted. So I took a deep breath and sat on myself. I felt that any response from me in kind, triggered by my anger, and Mr. L. would hit the roof. I finally managed to say, with surprising calm, I might add, that I could see he was angry, coming from his position, but I wanted him to know that saying what he did gave me cause for being angry too. But having said that, I didn't think our getting sore helped the situation any. The problem still needed to be dealt with and rather than getting sore with each other, we needed to get on with that. I think he was a little disappointed at my not responding angrily to his provocation. In any case he settled down a bit and we got on with the interview.

Interviewers encounter considerable stress in exercising control and communicating acceptance in response to a client's hostility and rejection. To react with anger, defensiveness, or withdrawal, eminently human and socially acceptable reactions, would be a violation of professional norms. Such a response would then evoke guilt and a feeling of professional failure.

If things do get heated, interviewers can increase the physical distance between themselves and the interviewee and decrease eye contact. Aggressive people tend to need more space between themselves and others and feel intruded upon by eye contact (Davies 1988).

Interviewers have been threatened, harassed, verbally abused, and physically assaulted (Guy, Brown, and Poelstra 1992). If they have reason to anticipate such incidents, interviewers take the precaution of interviewing with the office door open, formulate contingency plans for summoning help, and avoid working alone in the office.

Although accepting and responding empathically to hostile, even insulting, responses from an interviewee who feels imposed on, the worker does not apologize because the interviewee has been required to come. The worker is explicit in making the conditions of the contact clear:

It's very clear that you are really angry about this. And I can imagine that if I were in your shoes I would feel the same way. But the court has made contact with us a condition of your continuing in the community. And we work along with the court in implementing the requirement. If you fail to maintain contact, we would have to notify the court and you would have to serve your prison time.

We can depersonalize the issues by referring to the court order and agency rules that constrain the behavior of the interviewer as well as the interviewee:

> I can understand that, given where you are coming from, the requirement that you meet with me may seem like an oppressive imposition. But both you and I are stuck with that. Now given the reality that we have to meet, how do you want to use the time? Is there anything you would like to talk about? Anything with which you think we can be of some help? It's your choice. It's up to you. I can only help you if you help me to help you.

The social worker should describe the terms of the mandate to the client, including the client's behavior under question, the sources of the sanction for the agency's involvement, what happens if the client ducks participation, and the threshold at which coercive action will be undertaken. The interviewer should present this information in a straightforward unthreatening way (Hutchison 1987:594).

Interviewers are genuine in accepting that they have authority vis-à-vis the interviewee. Workers can express this authority in the contact with the involuntary client in such a way that the client perceives it as an expression of caring. Interviewers can merely point out that their authority in this instance is designed to help the involuntary client to refrain from engaging in self-damaging behavior. The interviewer acts in the guise of a surrogate supportive superego.

Aware that the interviewee probably is identifying the interviewer with the punitive court, the worker is clear and explicit that the agency is not the court, that the interviewer is not an employee of the court, and that agency treatment is not punishment.

Involuntary clients often use silence as an impregnable defense in opposing the interview and as an aggression against the interviewer. The interviewer needs to respond.

Jane is a 16-year-old delinquent, a high-school dropout ordered by the juvenile court to see a social worker. Jane enters the interview room, does not acknowledge the social worker's greeting, and sits down with her face averted.

INTERVIEWER: I know you are seeing me because the court ordered you to, and I can imagine you're not too happy about the whole thing.

JANE: [*Silence.*]

INTERVIEWER: Could you tell me how you feel about this?

JANE: [*Silence.*]

INTERVIEWER: Could you tell me what you're thinking about now? I'd very much like to hear.

JANE: Nothing.

INTERVIEWER: Is there anything you would like to talk about?

JANE: [*Silence.*]

INTERVIEWER: I would like to help you in any way I can, and I think I can be of some help. But you would have to tell me what you might want me to help you to change.

JANE: [*Silence.*]

Saying something like "Sometimes I guess you feel like talking, but other times, like now, I guess you don't" tends to suggest that the interviewee's resistant behavior is not a fixed personality attribute but a response to this situation.

Interviewers who disclose that they have reacted similarly on occasion sometimes find that doing so helps to dissolve some of the resistance: "Your silence reminds me of the times I felt forced to go to confession but did not want to confess anything to anybody."

Rooney (1988) notes that confrontation can be effective with involuntary child-abusing clients if interviewers are careful in formulating the confrontation. The worker says, "I hear your frustration that your child does not obey you the way you feel he should *and* striking your child with a belt and raising a welt is not a legal way to get him to obey you." Rooney says that the "linguistic sequence affirms the validity of both the emphatic statement and the confrontation and does not suggest that the two statements contradict each other" (p. 136). Conflict between the two statements is more explicit if the worker uses the conjunction *but* instead of *and*.

After attending to the matter that brought the person to the agency, the worker next should find a problem for which the interviewee accepts some ownership. The basis for this is finding something about which the interviewee wants help. The worker then explores with the interviewee what aspect of the client's life, however limited, causes dissatisfaction.

We presume that interviewees will be motivated to reduce their opposition and increase their participation if an interviewer can convince them that the personal gains from cooperation are worth the pain, embarrassment, and losses incurred. The interviewer then has to increase the personally satisfying outcomes that the client can anticipate and reduce the penalties.

Assuming that clients might want help with some aspect of their life is not an act of arrogance on the part of the worker. When the legal system refers interviewees, they are likely to want to change something, if only to get the legal system off their back. Alcoholics, drug addicts, criminals, abusers, and neglectful parents are sufficiently attuned to their environment to know that their behavior carries a stigma. People like to live in harmony with others and experience pleasure rather than pain in marriage, parenthood, and on the job.

Interviewees are aware of the personal negative consequences of their behavior. Some component of interviewees' ambivalence about their situation does press for change. Interviewers ally themselves with this positive component.

In tipping the balance the interviewer may have to intensify the discomfort for interviewees now. Calling attention to—or, better still, helping the interviewee make explicit—the negative aspects of their living arrangements and behavior increases the likelihood that they will feel that they do have a problem.

Throughout the interview the worker tries to maximize the interviewee's scope of self-determination. By mandating the contact the court has limited the interviewee's right in one respect—the client's right to refuse contact with the agency. Within the limits of the agency contact the worker has discretion to provide a variety of options. In consultation with interviewees and in response to their preferences, interviewers determine what part of the general situation the client wants to deal with, the specifics of scheduling, how the interviewer chooses to deal with the subproblem they have selected for consideration, and the like. We can also suggest autonomy by asking interviewees how they would like to be addressed.

Interviewees have the autonomous right to refuse contact with the agency and accept the consequences that result from such a refusal. We are all familiar with the concept of informed consent. Similarly, we need to help the interviewee with a decision of informed opposition. Do interviewees clearly know and understand what will happen if they choose to continue to reject contact with the agency? The worker has to be clear about the consequences of this.

Because another agency that has mandated the intervention may have referred the interviewee to your agency, you need to be clear about your relationship with and obligations to the referring agency. What conditions imposed on the interviewee by the referring agency must the interviewer be aware of? Under what conditions is the interviewee in violation of the requirement? What reports are you required to provide to the referring agency that might limit the interviewee's right of confidentiality?

The worker has to be knowledgeable of these issues in order to be able to clearly communicate to the interviewee what elements of the situation are fixed and what elements are negotiable, within the limits of the worker's discretion.

Rooney (1994) has presented the most detailed analysis of what is involved in helping the involuntary client and the social work interventions that show some promise of effectiveness. We have included many of his suggestions in our discussion.

Box 13.1 provides several suggestions for interviewing the involuntary client.

Box 13.1 Suggestions for Interviewing the Involuntary Client

1. Be aware of your attitudes toward this group of interviewees.
2. Understand your relationship with and obligations to the referring agency.
3. Know the requirements and limits of the mandate imposed on the interviewee by the referring agency.
4. As in all interviews, but of particular importance here, manifest the basic attitudes and approaches that make for establishing a positive relationship.
5. Warmth and respect communicate an empathic understanding of the negative, oppositional, and resentful feelings that such interviewees generally bring to the interview—roll with the resistance.
6. Make it clear to the client that you must act in accordance with the limitations and consequences of the mandate imposed on the inter- viewer-interviewee relationship.
7. Seek to respect and extend the negotiable freedoms of choice available to the interviewee within the limitations of the mandate.
8. Actively explore with interviewees what help they might be interested in accepting from the agency in working on any problem of concern to them—make a deal.
9. Attempt throughout to act not as an adversary but as an ally seeking to formulate a service the agency can provide and the interviewee is inter- ested in accepting.
10. Communicate a sense of hope that, although the initial contact is imposed, such relationships can effect positive change.

Interviewing in Intrafamily Child Sexual Abuse

Interviewing child victims of intrafamily sexual abuse is a specialized task and a treacherous minefield. Social workers frequently undertake this assignment because laws require other professionals to report suspicions of abuse to social agencies. The investigative interviews conducted by social workers in such cases are of prime importance because, unlike other types of physical abuse, objectively discoverable evidence and witnesses seldom exist. "In most child sexual abuse cases, there will be little or no physical evidence and few if any physical findings to support the allegation" (Sgroi Porter, and Blick 1982:48).

Sexually transmitted diseases and/or pregnancy resulting from sexual abuse are rare. Vaginal or anal injury as a result of penile or digital penetration is somewhat more frequent but still absent in most cases. Validation of a report of sexual abuse rests primarily on the information provided by the child victim and obtained by the social worker in the interview.

False allegations of sexual abuse, although highly visible and dramatic, constitute a limited number of cases. Furthermore, such cases tend to cluster around contested issues of custody and visitation among divorced couples (Benedek and Schetkey 1986; Goodman and Helgeson 1986).

Mikkelsen, Gutheil, and Emens (1992) reviewed the studies analyzing false allegations of sexual abuse. False reports average 8 percent or less of all referrals to child abuse clinics. A considerably higher percentage of false reports occurs in cases of divorce and custody disputes. Adolescents generate more false allegations than young children (see also Everson and Boat 1989).

However, when false accusations occur, they create disproportionate problems for social workers. In ruling on a number of highly publicized cases of child sexual abuse involving a large number of children, the courts have blamed biased social work interviewing as the basis of dubious allegations by children. Among the most notorious of such cases are the McMartin nursery school case in California (Reinhold 1990), the sexual abuse "ring" in Jordan, Minnesota ("Minnesota" 1985), and the case of Margaret Kelly Michaels in Newark, New Jersey (Nieves 1994).

A 1995 article in the *New York Times Magazine* noted that "appeals courts are dismantling many of the mass molestation cases that seemed epidemic in the mid 1980's. Since 1990, when the McMartin preschool case in California was finally dismissed, more than a dozen cases have been overturned" (Hess 1995:38).

Although these cases represent a fraction of the sexual abuse cases for which social workers are responsible, they can have a disproportionate effect, both on the willingness of prosecutors to build cases based on information elicited by social workers and on the public perceptions of the profession's credibility and the state of its knowledge. Consequently, although a relatively small percentage of cases involve fallacious reports, attention must be paid.

Myers, who edited a book on the child abuse backlash, notes that "poor interviewing, particularly excessive use of leading questions, contributes significantly to skepticism about professional competence and children's credibility" (1993:26).

Suggestions about how to conduct an interview of alleged victims of child sexual abuse are a frequent item in the child sexual abuse literature (MacFarlane and Krebs 1986; Myers 1987; Haugaard and Reppucci 1988; Jones 1992; Yuille et al. 1993; Morgan 1995; Ceci and Bruck 1995; Wood 1996).

Basic Attitudinal Approach to the Interview

Faller categorically states that "children do not make up stories asserting they have been sexually molested. It is not in their interest to do so. Young children do not have the sexual knowledge necessary to fabricate an allegation. Clinicians and researchers in the field of sexual abuse are in agreement that false allegations by children are extremely rare" (1984:475). The tendency is to see children as innocents who have no cause to lie.

Lying implies a conscious and willful attempt to deceive with a preconceived objective in mind and an awareness of the falsity of the communication. If this generally accepted definition is applied to the sexual abuse situation, Faller's statement, which social workers accept as a truism, is probably accurate. However, sometimes children who are not lying are not necessarily telling the truth.

Younger children may misinterpret a complex confusing situation. They are somewhat more likely than adults to confuse what did happen with what they think happened, failing to clearly distinguish fantasy from reality. As Myers notes, "While children rarely fabricate incidents on their own, they may succumb to suggestive coaching and questioning by adults with preconceived notions of what happened" (1987:503). In a review of the literature Melton notes that "young children's immaturity of moral and social reasoning may make them more vulnerable to adult suggestion" (1985:63).

Children can be honestly mistaken and can "truthfully" misperceive and/or misinterpret what has happened. If the social worker approaches the interview with a predisposition to think the reports of abuse are invariably valid and that children never lie, the worker's approach is likely to be oriented around helping the child resolve any ambiguities or inconsistencies in the child's account of the experience.

This worker's questions are likely to be suggestive and the interviewer's verbal and nonverbal reactions are likely to reinforce approval of any statement that confirms the report in any way.

The worker who comes to the interview with the attitude that children don't lie, that abuse has taken place, may feel a responsibility to obtain details that confirm abuse. If the child provides disconfirming content that raises doubts about abuse, the worker sees the child as being in denial. This worker sees the child who is reluctant to disclose details as responding to embarrassment, guilt, and/or fear. The worker's objective is to obtain validation of the allegation, and the worker selects interviewing procedures that achieve this outcome. The worker may believe that leading and probing questions are necessary. There is a difference between facilitating the disclosure of information and extracting such information.

In response to a conviction that the child has actually been abused but has been intimidated by the perpetrator to keep the secret, the worker might feel justified in using a more directive style of questioning. The worker might believe that this strategy will counter feelings of fear, guilt, and embarrassment that might intensify the child's hesitance to disclose.

Such an approach is more potent with children than adults because young children are generally more susceptible to direction and suggestion from adults. More specifically, adults in positions of authority, such as the interviewer in these situations, have undue influence over the child.

Children may not lie, but they are ready to acquiesce in directive questions to please powerful adults. If such agreement elicits a response of "Right," "That's good," "Fine," or a pleased smile from the interviewer, the response reinforces the child's tendency to go along with the interviewer's suggestion, however oblique or subtle. The line between "helping" the child to remember and the danger of suggesting what the child should recall is a tenuous one.

The interviewer who, however subtly, presses the child to reveal what the child is resisting revealing or induces the child to "remember" what never happened out of the interviewer's conviction that it did happen is courting subsequent retraction of the child's statements. Professional credibility suffers once again. Furthermore, prosecutors might be reluctant to use information obtained in such an interview, resulting in a decision not to prosecute a truly guilty abuser.

When the interviewer's intention, whether recognized consciously or not, is to help the child to confirm abuse, the probability of suggestive direction increases. The problem is made more difficult because social workers interviewing the child are torn between meeting the evidentiary needs of the court and the therapeutic orientation toward meeting the needs of the child. The traditional social work role is supportive concern with the child's subjective reality, which the worker may give priority over the concern for a critical evaluation of objective reality. However, the interviewer's task is to determine as objectively as possible what actually took place. The principal guideline for such an interview is facilitation without contamination.

Interviewing in child sexual abuse situations is inextricably intertwined with the legal system because such abuse is criminal. The interview content and procedures may be subject to legal review. Such interviews are examples of forensic casework and may be subject to rigorous challenge.

The most desirable approach that the interviewer can take is one of open-minded neutrality, not certain about what did or did not happen and ready and willing to give the child the optimum opportunity to tell the story without pressure in any direction. As Everson and Boat state, "Neither excessive skepticism nor unexamined acceptance of every allegation is a defensible position" (1989:235). The neutral attitude does conflict with the usual requirement that the social worker protect the child by being an advocate for the child. The need to protect seems antithetical to a scrupulous concern with neutrality in a situation in which the child might be at risk.

The research supports the desirability of a neutral attitude. Detailing the results of an experiment involving children's recall of a dramatic incident they had witnessed, Dent notes that the "most counter-productive interviewing occurred when the interviewer formed a strong pre-conceived impression about what had happened" and that "the rapport and interaction between the child and the interviewer are the most important factors determining the quality of the recall" (1982:288, 289). Research on children's recall finds that "regardless of an interviewer's experience with children, the least accurate reports were obtained from child witnesses when the interviewer held preconceived notions about what had happened" (Myers 1987:505).

Ceci and Bruck (1995) note that they "believe that suggestive techniques exert their greatest toll on testimonial accuracy when they are used by interviewers with a *confirmatory bias*" (emphasis in original, p. 296). Warning signals are most applicable when suggestive techniques are allied with the attitude that the allegation of abuse is in fact valid.

Extensive review of the relevant research by Ceci and Bruck (1993, 1995) finds that young children are susceptible to suggestions and direction from an interviewer. The limitations of children's language and the level of cognitive development limits their ability to encode details for later retrieval. The lack of life experience means further that the child has fewer schema and scripts in memory that help assimilate and organize information for later retrieval.

However, some children are capable of declining adults' suggestions, refusing to participate in attempts at soliciting confirmation of the interviewer's hypotheses (R. M. Lloyd 1992:121; Ornstein, Gordon, and Larus 1992).

As Ceci, Ross, and Toglia note, "Very young children's memories *can* be distorted through post event suggestion, not that they inevitably *will* be" (emphasis in original, 1987:47).

While maintaining neutrality, the interviewer needs to entertain the possibility that sexual abuse did occur. Interviewers have been accused of not hearing the child because of the belief "that these things don't happen."

This rather lengthy introduction to the sexual child abuse interview is meant to highlight the caution that should characterize the general attitudinal approach to such interviews.

The worker has to maintain an attitude of neutrality about the validity of the report. This may be a sexual abuse situation; it may not be. Children do not lie, but they may be confused, misinterpret what happened, or unable to fully dissociate reality from fantasy.

General Guidelines

The interview should be held in a neutral and psychologically comfortable place. Workers should avoid interviewing suspected abuse victims at home, where the abuse might have occurred, because it is associated with the perpetrator and the hurt.

The interview should be private, but if the child appears uncomfortable being alone with a stranger and wants a parent present, this should be permitted. Obviously, the parent permitted in the interview should not be the suspected perpetrator, and the worker must instruct the parent sitting in to be unobtrusive. Children are not comfortable maintaining eye contact or sitting still and talking, and they do not have long attention spans. The interviewing room should be large enough to permit the child to move around.

Interviewing children requires some appreciation and understanding of the changing nature of the child's communicative skills, reasoning capacity, social skills, memory encoding, and retrieval skills. A developmentally sensitive interviewer approaches a 5-year-old with a different orientation and expectations than a child of 10.

The interviewer works with some sensitivity to the child's level of discomfort in being asked to recount the details of an emotionally upsetting experience. Where appropriate, workers can use dolls, drawing, and play activity to have children clarify and demonstrate what they are saying and what children are not able to verbalize.

As much as possible, allow children some control over the content of the discussion, the pace of the presentation, and the method of disclosure (doll play, drawing, games, puppets, and so on).

Obtaining details about the events requires recognition that children have a limited understanding of time. Instead of asking about when things happened, ask whether it was light or dark at the time, whether it was a school day or a weekend, and so on. Children also find it difficult to be precise about time. In trying to determine *when* something happened, you need to associate it with some event—"about the time you went on a trip," "about the time your brother was born," "about the time your mother went to the hospital."

Interviewing is an unfamiliar experience for most children. Therefore your approach should mirror the informal conversation with which the child is familiar. As in every interview, the worker has to show a readiness to listen, be supportive, be understanding, and to protect the child from overwhelming feelings.

Workers should explicitly instruct children that they do not have to answer questions, that they should feel free to answer questions in any way they want, and that they may disagree with or correct the interviewer's reflections or summaries of what the child is saying.

Because sexual child abuse has legal implications, in some situations police and social workers interview the child together. These interviews may be tape recorded or, even better, videotaped. This may obviate the necessity of subjecting the child to multiple interviews and makes available a record to confirm that the interview was neutrally nondirective.

Audio or videotapes capture the details of the child's account without the distractions occasioned by note taking. The record they provide can reduce the number of times the child must be subjected to anxiety-provoking interviews. The disadvantage of tapes is that they provide evidence of any errors in directivity and suggestibility that the interviewer might have made. On the other hand, a taped interview can be to counter any subsequent attempt by the child to retract the statements because of pressure by the perpetrator.

Because of the legal implications of sexual child abuse the interviewer needs to be honest with the child about the limits of confidentiality. The worker also will have to share information with the court and the parents that validates the report obtained from the child.

As for any interview, the interviewer should prepare by reviewing any material already available—age and gender of the child, who reported what to the agency, composition of the family, relationship to the child of the reported perpetrator, and so on.

Interviewing in a location that provides privacy and minimizes external influences and distractions, interviewers identify themselves, establish some general understanding with the child about what brings them together, and discuss what they will be doing together.

As in every interview the interviewer must establish a relationship of trust, comfort, and support. But here it is somewhat more difficult. The child, having been victimized by an adult, is likely to be uneasy about being interviewed by an adult.

The secrecy and conspiratorial nature of the sexual abuse experience has suggested to the child that something is unacceptable and unmentionable about it, making the child shy about openly discussing it.

Interviewers face additional difficulty in freeing the child to talk because the perpetrator often has threatened the child about the consequences of telling—for the child, the perpetrator, and the family—and because the child may feel some guilt at having been involved in the abuse.

In cases of intrafamily sexual abuse the child most often has an ambivalent relationship with the perpetrator—father, stepfather, grandfather, brother, mother's boyfriend, mother. The child needs much love and support to counter the hurt, which further inhibits the child from freely sharing details of experiences that might make trouble for the perpetrator.

In attenuating the effects of some of these feelings interviewers should clearly communicate their readiness and ability to protect children from repercussions and assure children that they are not guilty or at fault. The interviewer communicates safety, permission, and absolution.

In allaying the child's fears and resolving feelings of blame, shame, or guilt the interviewer might say, "It's not bad to tell what happened"; "You won't get into trouble if you tell"; "We won't let anybody hurt you if you tell"; "What happened is not your fault"; "You are not to blame."

Because the child may make revelations about the event with considerable hesitance the interviewer has to adapt the pace of the interview to the child's slowly developing feelings of comfort. The interviewer needs to carefully monitor the child's reactions and be ready to back off if approaches to highly affective material seem more than the child can deal with. The child's needs, not administrative pressures from the agency or the legal system, should determine the pace of the interview.

Begin by asking children questions to which they know the answer. Name, age, gender, and address are neutral questions that put children at ease and give them a sense of confidence. Encourage children to talk about general aspects of their life—family, friends, activities of interest, and the like. The object here is not only to establish a relationship but to get some baseline data on the child's communication skills, cognitive capacity, and language proficiency.

At the outset interviewers should state that they have had experience in interviewing children who might have been sexually abused:

> I'd like you to know that we have talked with many children who have gone through what might have happened to you. I know that it is hard to talk about these things. Take your time, tell me whatever it is you want to tell me. The more you tell me, the more I can be of help to you.

This tells the child not only that the interviewer is competent but also that the child is not alone in having experienced sexual abuse.

In defining their role interviewers might say,

> My job is to talk to children about the things that might be troubling them, bothering them, things that make them feel unhappy or upset. I want to try to be of help to you. To do this I need your help. You can help me to help you by talking to me about anything that is bothering you.

The child also needs some clear explanation of how it came about that you are talking with her. You need to make clear your position and the relevance to the child's situation of what you are planning to do: "I understand that some things might have happened to you to make you upset or sad. I am here to try to help you feel better."

Such interviews require more patience and tact than interviews with children involving less sensitive concerns with no legal implications. The worker must need to wait for the child to focus on sexual abuse directly before asking for details. Asking children general questions about things that are troubling them or that make them unhappy, general questions about their relationship with members of their family, the interviewer has to listen for any implication of sexual abuse. This permits a legitimate non-suggestive entry to what the child might say about abuse.

At this point the interviewer begins to focus on the sexual abuse allegations in a gentle unthreatening way—"I know from talking to other children that they have some things happen to them that upset them, that bother them. Has anything like that happened to you?" The series of questions and interventions that follow are open ended and reflective, letting children speak freely and spontaneously at their own pace without interruption, challenge, or correction. The interviewer's responses at this point are neutral—they encourage, accept, request elaboration or clarification of what the child offers, but they do not add to it.

After it appears that the child is not likely to be able to provide additional information in response to open-ended interventions, the interviewer may legitimately use probing, cuing, and direct closed questions to stimulate the child's recall.

In 1993 an international group of child sexual abuse experts met with a mandate to evaluate what we know about the ways in which we can investigate child abuse allegations most productively. Here is what the group decided:

> The most reliable and accurate information is obtained from children who are responding to open-ended questions designed to elicit free narrative accounts of the events they may have experienced. Most children are capable of providing such accounts of their experiences, but younger children (especially those under five) are unlikely to provide lengthy narratives and as much information as older children. Direct or focusing questions are usually needed to access firmer information.
>
> (Lamb 1994:155).

Interventions such as open-ended questions encourage free association memories. The child needs no direct prompting but communicates content retrieved from memory on spontaneous recall.

In general spontaneous recall is more accurate than cued recognition recall but is less detailed in young children. Obtaining children's detailed testimony solely by relying on free spontaneous recall is not likely to be satisfactory.

Interviewers may have to use leading questions not only to cue the retrieval of detailed information but to counter the child's reluctance or resistance to disclosure. As MacFarlane states, "Interviewers who remain neutral, non-probing, and detached rarely succeed in breaking through to small frightened children" (quoted in Jacobson 1991:15).

After reaching what appear to be the limits of free association or spontaneous recall to obtain the details, the worker needs to consider facilitating the child's communication through greater structure, more probing, increased directivity, cuing, and prompting. Although the worker may have to use this approach to obtain the detail needed, such directiveness runs the risk of eliciting inaccurate, suggested, and contaminated information.

The interviewer's responsibility is to cue the child "just enough to stimulate recognition, but not enough to contaminate the child's recall" (Wehrspann, Steinhauer, and Klajner-Diamond 1987:616).

As with interviews generally, this interviewer should attempt to follow a funnel procedure, using broad open-ended questions followed by detached probing questions. However, many younger children find it difficult to answer general questions and are better in responding to specifics. The interview might then follow an inverted funnel format, beginning with some specific questions and followed by general questions. "Tell me what happened" is too general for some children.

The interviewer exploits all five senses in obtaining information. What did you see? What did you hear? What did you smell? How did the touch feel? What did it taste like?

Going to bed, bathing, using the toilet, and dressing and undressing are the events most closely associated with child sexual abuse. Asking the child specifics regarding these events—Who puts you to bed? Who bathes you? How do they go about washing you? Is anybody in the tub with you? Who undresses you?—can provide the details of abuse events.

Colby and Colby (1987) offer a list of questions that interviewers might ask in covering essential content in sexual abuse interviews (see also Faller 1988).

The progression of questions around sensitive content proceeds, here as elsewhere, from the impersonal to the more personal. "Sometimes people touch children between their legs or in other places. Do you know of any children who had that happen to them?" Then, "Has this ever happened to you?"

The focus on sexual abuse has a progressive specificity:

Is there anything you feel uncomfortable about that you would like to talk about?

[Then]

Has anyone touched you or your body in ways that made you feel uncomfortable?

[Then]

I talk to a lot of children and sometimes to kids who have been touched on private parts of their bodies. It can help to talk about such things. Has anything like that ever happened to you? (Jones and McQuiston 1986:20–21)

The worker can introduce the relevant subjects indirectly by asking about neutral analogous experiences. General questions about secrets—"Do you know any secrets?"; "Did anybody tell you any secrets?"—and general questions about touching—"When you play with others do you touch anybody? Where?"—provide indirect lead-ins to more relevant questions about abuse without influencing the report.

Formulations such as "Isn't it true that . . ." and "Didn't you . . ." are obviously suggestive. But more subtly the use of the definite article *the* can be suggestive. "Was the person in bed with you?" is more suggestive than "Was a person in bed with you?" "Did he touch you down there?" is more suggestive and yield a more ambiguous answer than "Where did he touch you?"

Double positives also are suggestive: "I think you said he showed you his pee-pee. Isn't that true?"

So are double negatives: "You did not want him to do that, did you?" Children can subtly reinterpret words, converting uncertainty and ambiguity to confirmation of the allegation.

> INTERVIEWER: What did you two do?
>
> CHILD: We played in the bedroom.
>
> INTERVIEWER: So he touched you in the bedroom. Who was it, Bob or Harry?
>
> CHILD: I don't know.
>
> INTERVIEWER: Which one of the two was with you in the bedroom, Harry or Bob?
>
> CHILD: I think it was Harry.
>
> INTERVIEWER: So it was Harry that touched you in the bedroom. What else did he do?

Here the child's term, "play," becomes "touch," and the child's "think it was Harry" becomes "so it was Harry." The reinterpreted material reaches the status of probable truth.

Because of scripts in the interviewer's mind the interviewer might introduce information that is not in the child's account:

> When you were in the bedroom together and he got in bed with you, what happened?

The child had said that they were in the bedroom together but had not said that the alleged perpetrator had gotten in bed with the child.

Interviewers need some awareness that children's knowledge, use, and interpretation of words may be different from that of adult usage. What we intend to ask of children may not be the same as what they think we have asked. Further, children are not likely to share with us their understanding of what we asked (Walker and Warren 1995).

The interviewer who has established a warm positive relationship with the child needs to be aware that this represents a hazard to suggestibility. Because the child likes the interviewer, the child may feel a greater eagerness to be acquiescent, striving to please the interviewer.

Asking a question demands an answer from a child. Children feel obligated to respond to questions not only because they have been taught to obey adults and want the approval of the adults but also because children feel that adults would not be asking if they did not think children could answer. Not answering risks disappointing the adult authority and eliciting disapproval or rejection. In not answering the child is performing inadequately and risks humiliation and loss of self-esteem.

But when children decide to respond, they may lack certainty in formulating a response because of encoding and memory retrieval deficiencies, which are more pronounced in young children. When this happens, young children may be uncertain about what they remember.

When children are uncertain about what they know while in contact with an adult whom they trust and whose praise they seek, they are highly suggestible. Answering with some hesitance, children monitor the interviewer's reaction to their response. Is the answer satisfactory? Does the interviewer seem pleased, disappointed, dubious, competent? Most children are eager to get it right, because this is likely to please the adult and the child is rewarded by the adult's approbation.

Different nonverbal responses to what the child says can reinforce answers that confirm the interviewer's presuppositions. In addition to an unsuppressed "Good" or "That's fine" when the child presents material confirming sexual abuse, the interviewer might lean forward with increased interest and even pat the child. Disconfirming statements may elicit no such rewarding comments or nonverbal responses.

The interviewer has to be comfortable in using the words the child might use in describing the event. Some are the words of the child's world, *wee-wee, poo-poo, pee-pee.* Some are the words of the street—*prick* and *cock* for penis, *pussy* and *cunt* for vagina.

Interviewers also need to be comfortable with the deeds—cunnilingus, fellatio, rectal or vaginal intercourse, ejaculation, mutual masturbation—if they are to ask about these without communicating embarrassment.

The meanings of words are not always obvious and may need to be further explored. If a child says, "Daddy," does that mean father, mother's boyfriend, stepfather, or grandfather? "We had sex" may mean anything from kissing to fondling to masturbation to intercourse. What does the child mean by saying, "We had sex"?

Does the term *private parts* mean the same to the child as it does to the interviewer who uses it in a question?

What is the child referring to exactly when speaking of daddy's "thing" or "ding-dong"? Can the interviewer assume what the child means or should the worker ask more questions?

Children may misconstrue essentially innocent or ambiguous conduct. *Touching* is an ambiguous word and relates to many highly personal things that parents do with young children in bathing, toilet training, undressing, and caressing in normal and affectionate ways; all can be misconstrued (Rosenfeld, Siegel, and Bailey 1987).

Here is an example of neutral probing questioning that gives the child options for response without leading:

CHILD: He started rubbing his wiener and that stuff came out.

INTERVIEWER: What stuff?

CHILD: I don't know, I don't remember.

INTERVIEWER: I'll help you. What color was it?

CHILD: I don't remember.

INTERVIEWER: Was it yellow, or white, or red?

CHILD: White, it was white.

INTERVIEWER: How much was there?

CHILD: I don't remember.

INTERVIEWER: Just one drop, or two or three drops, or a whole lot?

CHILD: A whole lot.

INTERVIEWER: How do you know?

CHILD: Because I remember, it came shooting all over the place.

INTERVIEWER: If you touched it, was it thin like water, or sticky like glue, or solid like chocolate pudding?

CHILD: Sticky, like glue.

INTERVIEWER: How do you know?

CHILD: Because I got some of it all over my face.

INTERVIEWER: Can you show me, using the dolls?

(Wehrspann, Steinhauer, and Klajner-Diamond 1987:616)

The availability of anatomically correct dolls with a detachable penis, pubic hairs, a mouth, rectum, and vagina that can be opened to reenact insertion has enabled children to demonstrate experiences they might find otherwise difficult to verbalize (Shamroy 1987; Boat and Everson 1988). Such dolls communicate permission to discuss sexual matters and enable the child to identify the words the child is using for genitalia. About ten different companies now make anatomically correct dolls. They are available in black, white, and tan colors, some with Asian features.

We can provide a long list of studies regarding the advantages and disadvantages, the value and dangers of the use of anatomical dolls as an aid in child sexual abuse interviewing. Perhaps the most expeditious way to deal with the controversy here is to cite a recent review of the research and the conclusions that seem to have some consensual support (Everson and Boat 1994). The dolls are useful as a demonstration aid in "helping the child 'show' rather than 'tell' what happened. This is especially important when limited skills or emotional issues . . . interfere with direct verbal description." (p. 117). The use of the dolls as a validation tool is less defensible. Deciding on the basis of the way the child plays with the dolls that the child has been abused is open to question, given the lack of definitive information regarding the way children generally respond to the dolls.

Some behaviors in the interview might alert the interviewer to the possibility of fabrication. The child who reports details of abuse without much hesitance or anxiety, in adult language, might have been coached or rehearsed. One child spoke of having "oral sex—whatever that is."

Detailed, spontaneous, undefensive sharing of highly charged material early in the interview could suggest experiences that did not happen. If the parent who is not a suspect is present during the interview and the child seems to be checking the parent's responses or seeking the approval of the parent when answering, this might suggest a coached report.

If the child makes no allusions to any events that suggest sexual abuse, interviewers cannot assume that the child is in denial or not ready to disclose. In fact, the child may not have been abused.

In terminating, the interviewer, as always, needs to help the child understand the next steps in the procedure. And because these interviews are generally upsetting for the child, the interviewer should commend the child for having participated in the interview.

Box 13.2 is a list of basic do's and don'ts for sexual child abuse interviewing.

Box 13.2 The Basic Do's and Don'ts of Interviewing

Do's
- Be objective and nonjudgmental.
- Review all existing information before interviewing the child.
- Try to find out what the child knows about you and your purpose in speaking to the child.
- Interview the child as soon after disclosure as possible. The younger the child, the more critical this becomes.
- Interview the child alone whenever possible. Explain to the parent or caregiver what you will be doing and the reason for interviewing the child alone. Do this before interviewing the child.
- Choose a neutral, quiet, and comfortable setting.
- Try to ensure that the alleged perpetrator is nowhere in the vicinity.
- Learn about the child's developmental level and communication skills before the interview.
- Spend time building rapport and making sure that you can communicate with the child by playing or talking about neutral subjects.
- Choose an interview time according to the child's schedule, not yours.
- Explain your role to the child.
- Encourage the child to tell what happened in his or her own words.
- Give appropriate interview instructions to the child.
- Attempt to learn what concerns the child may have that could prevent or hinder disclosure.
- Use the funnel interview technique.
- Whenever possible, obtain disclosure (assuming there is one to obtain) before using dolls, diagrams, or other tools.
- Use the phrase "show me" (cautiously) for clarification with younger children.
- Use the child's words. Use age-appropriate language. Understand the child's sense of time.
- Use maps, diagrams, pictures, videos, television shows, and the like to

establish anchors that orient the child in time, place, relationships, and/or events.

- Explain the need for additional interviews and end the interview on a positive note, thanking the child for working hard.

DON'TS

- Do not interview the child in the presence of anyone who may influence the interview one way or the other. This includes siblings who may also have been victims.
- Do not touch the child or invade the child's space unless the child invites you to do so.
- Do not begin the sensitive part of the interview unless you are reasonably sure you are able to communicate and have developed rapport with the child.
- Do not interview the child for a period of time longer than the child's attention span. Take breaks.
- Do not rush the interview.
- Do not ask leading and suggestive questions unless and until you have exhausted all other options. Remember, if you use leading and/or suggestive questioning, you may or may not be able to rely on the information you obtain. Assess the reliability of the information you obtain in light of other evidence that corroborates or contradicts what the child told you.
- Avoid repeating a question without explaining why you are doing so.
- Avoid "why" questions. They have a tendency to infer guilt or responsibility. Also, answering a why question may require skills the child does not have.
- Do not react to a child's disclosure of abuse except perhaps to show interest.
- Avoid prompts and reinforcements such as "Good job" or "I'm so happy that you told me about this."
- Do not bribe a child with food, toys, or other improper rewards for a disclosure.
- Do not make promises you cannot keep.
- Do not allow the child to feel "in trouble" or at fault.
- Never ask the child to remove clothing to explain or demonstrate the abuse.
- Do not "gang-interview" the child. A police officer and a child protective services worker are sufficient.

Source: Compiled and edited from various sources by Thomas J. Fallon, assistant attorney general, Wisconsin Department of Justice, Madison.

Summary: Chapter 13

This chapter discusses two special interviewee groups—involuntary clients and sexually abused children—that pose unique problems for the interviewer.

Clients who are socially or legally mandated to have contact with a social worker may be resistant. The first problem the interviewer must solve in working with the involuntary client is how to engage the client in order to maximize the probability that the forced contact can be of some help. In responding to the interviewee's oppositional behavior the interviewer manifests all the facilitating attitudes that counter the attitudes that fuel such behavior. Rather than countering the opposition directly, the interviewer goes with it, joining the interviewee by affirming the interviewee's right to be opposed to the requirement. At the same time the worker should be explicit in making the conditions of the contact clear. Throughout the contact the interviewer attempts to maximize the scope of the client's self-determination.

Interviewing child victims of intrafamily sexual abuse is a difficult and specialized task. Although false allegations of sexual abuse are rare, when they occur they pose serious problems for the profession. Several highly publicized cases of child sexual abuse, later found to be without merit, have indicted biased social work interviewing as the basis for the dubious allegations.

In approaching the interview with the child in cases of alleged sexual abuse workers must keep in mind that children can be honestly mistaken and can truthfully misperceive and/or misinterpret what happened. Workers who come to the interview with the attitude that children don't lie may believe that abuse has taken place and may feel a responsibility to obtain details that confirm abuse. However, the most desirable approach for an interviewer is one of open-minded neutrality, uncertain about what did or did not happen, and ready and willing to give the child the optimum opportunity to tell the story without pressure.

The interview of the child should occur in a neutral and psychologically comfortable setting. Because of the emotionally upsetting nature of the interview the worker should give the child control of the content selected for discussion, the pace of the discussion, and the method of disclosure (doll play, drawing, games, and such).

Interviewers should begin by asking children questions to which they know the answer—name, age, gender, and address. Interviewers should state that they have had experience interviewing children who might have been sexually abused to convey that they are competent and that the child is not alone is having experienced abuse. Asking children general questions about things that are troubling them or that make them unhappy permits a nonsuggestive entree to inquiring about the alleged abuse.

Using open-ended questions encourages the child to free associate and retrieve memories. However, it may be necessary to use leading questions not only to cue the retrieval of detailed information but to counter the child's reluctance or resistance to disclosing information. Although this approach may be necessary to obtain details, such directiveness may elicit inaccurate, suggested, and contaminated information.

Interviewers must be comfortable using words that describe sexual acts and genitalia so that they can communicate without embarrassment. The use of anatomically correct dolls is advantageous as an interviewing aid in allowing the child to show rather than tell what happened. The interviewer should be alert to a pattern of behavior that suggests the possibility of fabrication.

Suggested Readings

The Involuntary Client

Ronald H. Rooney. *Strategies for Work with Involuntary Clients.* New York: Columbia University Press, 1994. (405 pp.)
    Written by a professor of social work, the book is a detailed analysis of the process of offering help to such clients.
George A. Harris and David Watkins. *Counseling the Involuntary and Resistant Client.* Laurel, Md.: American Correctional Association, 1987. (110 pp.)
    A good brief overview of the essentials necessary for working with this group of interviewees.

The Sexually Abused Child

Stephan A. Ceci and Maggie Bruck. *Jeopardy in the Courtroom: A Scientific Analysis of Children's Testimony.* Washington, D.C.: American Psychological Association, 1995. (336 pp.)
    The latest suggestions for sexual child abuse interviewing derived from the research.
Kathleen C. Faller. *Evaluating Children Suspected of Having Been Sexually Abused.* Thousand Oaks, Calif.: Sage, 1995. (128 pp.)
    Published in cooperation with the American Professional Society on the Abuse of Children, this is a comprehensive critical review of research and practice about how to interview children who may have been sexually abused.
Gail S. Goodman and Bette L. Bottoms, eds. *Child Victims, Child Witnesses: Understanding and Improving Testimony.* New York: Guilford Press, 1993. (333 pp.)
    One of the better compilations of articles, many of which pertain to the responsibilities of sexual child abuse interviewing.

PART FOUR

The Essence of the Good Interview

FOURTEEN

The Competent Interviewer

This chapter summarizes the attributes of the competent interviewer and recapitulates the differences between more competent and less competent interviewers.

Personality Attributes

Research that attempts to factor out personality characteristics associated with competence in interviewing yields a rather confused picture. The confusion may result because interviews conducted for different purposes may ideally require different kinds of interviewing personalities.

The warm accepting qualities necessary for interviews whose primary purpose is therapeutic are not those required for the interview whose primary purpose is assessment. In an assessment interview the therapeutic interviewer may fail to probe inconsistencies or may make compassionate allowance for an interviewee's reluctance to discuss essential but difficult areas. The interview whose primary purpose is diagnostic assessment may require a reserved outward-focused person; the therapeutic interview may require a warmer more spontaneous person. The interviewer engaged in advocacy may need a more aggressive directive approach to the interview.

Although a clearly structured directive style may be best for obtaining the detailed factual material required for understanding the client's situation, it may not be the best style for eliciting emotional reactions to the situation. Here a less structured and more reflective approach that is responsive to emotional cues and encourages the expression of feelings is the more desirable option (Cox, Rutter, and Holbrook 1981).

Different interviewers may be more or less competent with different kinds of interviewees. For instance, some interviewers are uncomfortable unless they are in a higher status position than the interviewee. Consequently, although they may be competent in interviews with lower-income clients seeking agency help, they would be uncomfortable in interviews with the director of an agency whose influence they are trying to enlist on their clients' behalf. Because different kinds of interviews require different kinds of approaches, because different kinds of interviewees require different interview styles, the good interviewer has to be flexibly capable of using different approaches and different styles.

Studies show an association between intelligence and good interview performance, although intelligence is not a guarantee of good performance. The findings generally agree that interviewers should have a variety of interests and a wide range of experiences. These interviewers have the capacity to empathize with a greater range of people, because their experience may parallel those of clients. These interviewers also have a broader base for communication.

The studies of the behavior of experienced interviewers provide somewhat clearer results. The supposition is that the more experienced interviewer is the more competent. Studies show that experienced interviewers are apt to be less controlling, less active, and less inclined to offer advice than inexperienced interviewers. Inexperienced interviewers are apt to talk more and to take more responsibility for the conduct of the interview. The difference may reflect the greater anxiety of the beginning interviewer rather than technical inexperience. Experienced interviewers are not passive, however. They tend to be more discriminating and modulate their activity. They say only what needs to be said, when it needs to be said; thus experienced interviewers are more efficient, making every comment count.

Training for psychotherapeutic interviewing may also affect the differences between experienced and inexperienced interviewers. As a result of such training interviewers become more reluctant to initiate interaction, giving the interviewee greater opportunity to take the lead, and are less inclined to interrupt the client.

In one study interviewers were shown a film of an actual interview. The researchers stopped the interview at various points and asked the participating interviewers how they might have responded at these points. Inexperienced interviewers tended to ask questions; experienced interviewers tended to make statements. Inexperienced interviewers tended to respond to discrete ideas, to specific words or phrases; experienced interviewers tended to respond to the gestalt of the client's presentation (Ornston et al. 1968).

Studying differences between most effective and least effective therapists, Strupp and Najavits found that the more effective therapists "displayed more warmth and friendliness and more affirmation and understanding" (1994:119). Such therapists had high scores on measures of the helping alliance.

Experienced interviewers tend to make fewer directly manipulative responses, instead using responses that are more communicative, conveying a thought or feeling. For example, a client begins to pace the floor in an interview. The inexperienced therapist is more likely to make a statement designed to elicit a desired response, such as "If you don't sit down, I'm afraid I won't be able to help you." A communicative response of the more experienced interviewer might be "I have a feeling that you are trying to impress me with how upset you are" (Ornston, Cicchetti, and Towbin 1970:10).

The most judicious conclusion to be drawn from the variety of studies available is that no clear pattern of personality traits distinguishes the good from the poor interviewer. Good interviewing is the result of the complex interplay of the interviewer, interviewee, purpose of the interview, and setting in which it is conducted. The research findings generally suggest that more successful interviewers are likely to be warm, accepting, and psychologically open but in flexible control of themselves and the interview situation.

Need for Knowledge

A thorough knowledge of the subject matter of the interview is a mark of the competent interviewer. Medical social work interviewers must have at their command a detailed specialized knowledge of the social antecedents, concomitants, and consequences of physical illness; psychiatric social workers, of mental and emotional illness; gerontological social workers, of old age.

Such a knowledge base enables workers to make sense of what they are hearing, to see relationships that would escape someone ignorant of the subject matter. Knowledge alerts interviewers to areas of significance that the client has not discussed; informed interviewers use their observations to formulate appropriate questions. Knowledge provides the basis for evaluating the validity of the information obtained. Because knowledge is the basis of more interpretive associations it helps interviewers remember what has occurred during the interview. Chance favors a prepared mind. Some statements by the interviewee that have no meaning for an interviewer with scant knowledge will suggest a series of fruitful questions to the interviewer who knows what the remarks imply.

Assessment interviews require a knowledge of normative expectations. If the child is toilet trained at 20 months, is that late or early? If a child first started talking at 15 months, does this represent a developmental lag or normal development? What parental behavior suggests overprotection, and what kinds of separation behavior are normal for a hospitalized schoolage child? To recognize what is atypical the worker needs to know the typical.

Interviewers whose purpose is advocacy, and whose interview orientation is to convince, need considerable knowledge of the rights and entitlements of their clients; advocates need good command of the regulations and procedures of the agency. Without such information they cannot challenge with assurance any decision that denies their client aid. Advocates must understand the agency's structure so that they can appeal, or threaten to appeal, an adverse decision.

Furthermore, knowledge of potential solutions, available resources, and therapeutic procedures is necessary because that information guides interviewers in determining which aspect of the client's situation might be most productive to explore.

Knowledge increases security and lessens anxiety. If workers go into the interview with an expert knowledge of the literature and practice wisdom of the field, not only with regard to the etiology of problems but also to how they might help, they are more apt to feel confident in their ability to conduct the interview successfully. This alone increases the probability that workers will conduct a successful interview. Lack of precise knowledge makes interviewers uncomfortable and unsure of themselves in handling the interview.

An applicant who is applying to become a Big Brother asks the interviewing social worker whether the agency's insurance covers Big Brothers in the event of an accident while on a trip or during swimming. The worker, not really familiar with the policy, says,

> This is something the YMCA is looking into right now. I know that our insurance covers group activities that are a function of the Y, and as far as we know we are checking into ones specifically if it goes as far as Big Brother and Little Brother pair activities. It seems like it should cover but, ah, to tell you the truth, I don't know.

Commenting on his response, the interviewer says,

> Mr. M. asked a good question that I was not prepared to answer. Because I felt on the spot, I hedged, feeling uncomfortable. The more I fumbled the more Mr. M. seemed to be turning off. That's when I decided to level with

him and admit I didn't know. I should have said at this point that I would try
to find out. I didn't say this till later in the interview.

Thus interviewers must have two different areas of expertise. One is
expert knowledge regarding the conduct of the interview. The second is
knowledge about the subject matter of the social problem—its nature, ori-
gin, and approaches that may ameliorate it. The social work interviewer is
both a specialist in interviewing and a specialist in the social aspects of
mental deficiency, old age, child neglect, or marital conflict, to name but a
few, and the stresses encountered by people facing such problems and the
variety of ways people cope with such stresses.

Clients are not competent to assess the expertise of the interviewer in
regard to interviewing, although clients know in a general way when an
interview is competently or poorly conducted. Clients are, however, competent to assess the social worker's knowledge of the subject matter because
they are living the problem. Senseless irrelevant questions or comments that
clearly demonstrate that the social worker knows little about the situation
encourage disrespect for the worker and erode the client's confidence. A
thorough understanding of the subject area enhances the client's confidence. Detailed knowledge of the problem area reduces social distance by
showing that interviewer and interviewee share some familiarity with the
problem. If clients perceive the interviewer as knowledgeable and realize
that the interviewer is likely to meet any fanciful deceptive responses with
skepticism, interviewees are more likely to be straightforward.

Kinsey, Pomeroy, and Martin found knowledge of the subject matter to
be an important component in rapport. "The background of knowledge
which the interviewer has is of greater importance in establishing rapport
with his subjects. The importance of this cannot be over-emphasized. An
[interviewee] is inevitably hesitant to discuss things which seem to be both
outside of the experience of the interviewer and beyond his knowledge"
(1948:60).

We emphasize the importance of knowledge because an anti-intellectual
derogation of its importance seems to be prevalent among social workers.
The profession has emphasized feeling and doing rather than knowing and
thinking. But good interviewing is impossible without a considerable
amount of knowing and thinking. In public opinion interviewing or in
research interviewing the staff has thoroughly analyzed the relevant knowledge and has formulated a series of relevant questions and probes to be used
by the interviewer, who consequently does not need to be a subject matter
expert. Social work interviewers, however, have to be their own staff person,

formulating appropriate questions and responses as the interview unfolds. They translate their hypothesis into an interview outline and specific questions. Knowledge provides each interviewer with a cognitive map of the area to be covered.

As we read typescripts, listen to, and watch tapes of interviews, and observe live interviews, both role-played and real, we are impressed by the frequency with which an interviewer fails for lack of knowledge rather than lack of proper attitude. Interviewers frequently manifest the proper attitude—basic decency, compassion, acceptance, and respect. But interviewers often do not know enough about the particular subject of the interview to ask perceptive questions, to make sense of what they are hearing, to know what facets of the problem to explore, the normative stresses the problem situation creates, and the recurrent adaptations people have developed in responding to such stresses. Interviewers also often do not know enough to answer the client's implicit or explicit request for information or advice.

Resolving Antithetical Demands

The role of the social work interviewer requires the difficult balancing of antithetical demands. Prescriptions for effective interviewing suggest that the interviewer do contradictory things simultaneously. We ask that interviewers be spontaneous while being deliberate in selecting their responses. We also ask that interviewers be authentic, genuine, and consciously controlled. Interviewers must be objective, maintaining some emotional distance from the client, while being empathetic, figuratively putting themselves in the client's situation.

Workers must see and treat the client as an individual. At the same time workers often must label the client for diagnostic reimbursement and administrative purposes. Labeling inevitably involves some stereotyping.

Workers are asked to respect clients as people but reject their dysfunctional behavior. Workers are asked to accept clients as they are and are expected to help clients to change because their behavior is not acceptable. In these ways workers must balance the antithetical attitudes of acceptance and expectations of change.

Workers need to maintain a balance between support and expectation, helping the client to feel psychologically comfortable in the interview yet communicating expectations that the client will attend to the work of the interview.

Interviewers have to establish a sense of closeness so that the interviewee can feel free in confiding in them. At the same time workers have to maintain a sense of distance so as not to overwhelm the client. Workers must maintain a disciplined objectivity while communicating a spontaneous subjectivity—they must be involved with the interviewee yet not overinvolved.

Stress is associated with the antithetical pressures of being a professional in a worker-client relationship and upholding social work's humanistic tradition. The professional relationship implies inequality in knowledge and power; the humanistic tradition strives for equality and colleagiality. As professionals we are "better," in the specific sense of our expertise, than the clients. The therapy relationship is inherently a relationship of unequals. We are helpers, and clients need our help. But this inequality offends us, and we feel a sense of stress from the dissonance between reality and our egalitarian orientation (Klienman 1981).

The activities the worker should perform in establishing a good relationship contain antithetical elements. If the interviewer, in being a patient unhurried listener, has to wait while the interviewee speaks of concerns that are not relevant to the agency's services, the next interviewee is likely to have to wait. What makes for a good relationship with one interviewee makes for a bad relationship with the person waiting.

Interviewees' Perceptions of the Good Interviewer

Studies have found that interviewees have an image of the ideal interviewer: someone who does not engage in behavior that signals a lack of respect for clients, such as being "aloof, insincere, in a hurry, interrupting, yawning, lacking warmth, being late for the interview; [clients] said they would not like the [interviewer] to do most of the talking but stated significantly more annoyance at the idea of her doing little of it" (Pohlman and Robinson 1960:550). Clients prefer interviewers whose "actions suggest that they can help them *do* something about their problems" (Pfouts and Rader 1962:552). Clients perceive the interviewer's "warmth" as self-assurance, sensitivity, and competence.

Interviewees may focus primarily on the interviewer's capacity to help them. Yet they are gratified when the social worker acts in a manner that shows personal interest and respect and when the worker takes the trouble to personalize even interviews that have a restricted purpose.

A client discussing her experience with a public welfare social worker says,

> She's supposed to ask, "How are you doing? What do you need? What can I do for you?" My investigator—she is always in a rush. There's only two things she ever asks—"Where is your light bill?" and "Where is your rent receipt?" Then she rushes out.

An investigator like that has no appearance. There are a few good ones. Like a friend of mine, she has an investigator when he sees her on the street he stops and says, "Hello!" He says, "How are you? When did you see your mother last? How is your sister?" Now that's mighty fine of him. An investigator like that makes you feel good. It can't help making you feel good when someone talks to you like that.

Like, I had an investigator once—a man. If he came in and there were people around, he'd say, "Is there someplace where we can talk?" And then he'd go into another room with you and ask you how you were doing. But most of them, they come in and tell you what to do. They treat you like a child; no, worse than that, they treat you like a doll, like a nothing. You have to beg and whine and it makes you feel—well, terrible.

Another client describes his picture of the "good" social worker:

[One] who in your first acquaintance lets you know by his or her expression that he's in your home to be of service to you if possible, and to show trust because most people are trustworthy if one shows trust in them; to be able to understand reasonably well problems concerning the family as a whole; not to criticize but to analyze why a person or a family is in unfavorable circumstances; to give helpful advice in a way that isn't demanding but that lets a person feel that it's his own idea; one who has a sincere desire to help people, feeling that it might have been her as well as they but for the grace of God; one who encourages you to go above the capabilities that you thought you possess; one who guides you and makes the way possible but insists that you do for yourself what you're capable of doing.

(Overton 1959:12)

Repeated interview reports from a group of clients in psychotherapy showed that they experience the most satisfactory interview when the interviewer is "actively collaborative, genuinely warm, affectively expressive," and humanly involved, rather than when the therapist displays an impassive, detached, studied neutrality (Orlinsky and Howard 1967; see also Strupp, Fox, and Lessler 1969). Clients also prefer interviewers who share their own experiences when doing so is pertinent.

As might be expected, clients' preferred characteristics for interviewers tend to vary with the kinds of problems clients bring. Grater (1964) found that interviewees with personal social problems regard the interviewer's affective characteristics (warmth, friendliness, kindness) as more important than cognitive skills (logic, knowledge, efficiency). Interviewees with primarily educational or vocational problems are more likely to prefer interviewers who demonstrate cognitive skills. Although no research is available on this, clients whose problems are primarily related to a deprived social environment probably would show initial preference for interviewers with strong political power who command access to jobs, housing, and an increase in income.

Clients' preferences are also related to the personality characteristics of the interviewee. Egalitarian interviewees prefer a client-centered nondirective interviewer; the more authoritarian interviewees prefer a more directive, more structured interview approach.

Interviewees' Contribution to Interviewer Competence

A good interviewer also needs a good interviewee in order to conduct a good interview. Because interviewing is an interactional and transactional experience, to focus on the interviewer while ignoring the interviewee is analogous to saying that my brother is an only child.

The interviewer is only half of the dyad and only partially determines the success or failure of the interview. The willingness and capacity of the interviewee to perform competently is also an important determinant. Although the interviewer takes responsibility for providing the psychological atmosphere in which a good relationship can be initiated, the interviewee has to have the capacity to engage in a relationship. Clients have to have some capacity for communicating, some ability to translate feeling and thinking into words, and some ability to organize their communication.

Nothing the interviewer does, however skillfully, can ensure success. Success requires the skillful contribution of the interviewee as well. Unless the interviewee is committed to collaboration, capable of enacting the responsibilities of the role of interviewee, and accepts the objectives of the interview, the client can frustrate the best efforts of the interviewer. "No interview can succeed unless it has the active engagement and interactive collaboration of an interviewee who has some basic communicative skills competence" (Orlinsky, Grawe, and Parks 1994:361).

Research confirms the significance and importance of the client's contribution. Lambert and Bergin note that studies "rating the therapeutic alliance contain a heavy emphasis on *patient* variables, mainly the client's ability to participate productively and collaboratively in therapy" (emphasis in original; 1994:165).

A study of 253 research findings regarding the association between a positive therapeutic bond and outcome shows that the patient's contribution to the therapeutic bond is as significant as the therapist's contribution in accounting for a successful outcome (Orlinsky, Grawe, and Parks 1994:34; 318–19, table 8.33;320, table 8.34). We might say that just as good children make it easy to be a good parent and good students make it easier to be a good teacher, good interviewees make it easier for an interviewer to be a competent performer.

Distinguishing More and Less Competent Interviewers

At various points throughout the text we have referred to attitudes, skills, and behaviors that distinguish the more competent interviewer from the less competent interviewer. The table that follows recapitulates distinctions in performance between the two. The table moves through the interview process from beginning to termination.

THE MORE COMPETENT INTERVIEWER	THE LESS COMPETENT INTERVIEWER
Observes the usual social amenities in a relaxed way. Makes clear the identity of participants, purpose of the interview, and interviewer's agency affiliation.	Evidences strain, as though from some difficulty in distinguishing the difference between social and professional interaction. Sometimes neglects to identify themselves, their affiliation, and the purpose of the interview.
Communicates unobtrusively and with assurance the conditions of a good interview—respect, caring, warmth, empathic understanding, acceptance, genuineness—thus reducing the interviewee's anxiety, defensiveness, and resistance, increasing the client's willingness to share and openness, and motivating the client to participate.	Attempts to communicate the facilitative conditions but the feelings as expressed appear mechanical or contrived. Appears to be playing a role, displaying an element of phoniness and an occasional manifestation of moralistic, punitive, rejecting, disrespectful, and unprofessional behavior, all of which increase interviewees' resistance and anxiety and reduce their motivation to participate.
Demonstrates some preparation for the interview, knows and uses whatever limited information is available on the interviewee, has the interview folder and other necessary materials available, arranges for privacy, proper lighting, and the like.	Gives no sign of having prepared for this particular interview.
Is sensitive to the problems of interviewees in fulfilling their role and	Is not aware of the problems or confusions of the interviewee in enacting

seeks to help them with this—
clarifying, explaining, deliberately
showing how people act in an interview situation.

Appears to keep the interviewee as
the exclusive focus of attention and
concern, responding to the interviewee's needs and the interviewer's
feelings. Gives primary priority to
the needs of the interviewee and the
purposes of the interview.

Controls the progress of the interview but in a flexible adaptable
manner. Is self-assured, which
permits the interviewee to share control when appropriate.

Has a clear idea of the purpose of
the interview and structures the
interview to achieve the purpose.
Moves to achieve purpose of the
interview in a flexible and adaptable
manner that permits modification
if necessary.

Appears to have direction and logic
in formulating questions, which are
based on an awareness of where the
interview should go and how to
get there.

Asks questions, formulated effectively, that are

1. Appropriate and well timed.

2. Concise, well-phrased, and
   unambiguous.

3. Tactfully phrased.

the role of interviewee. Makes little
effort to help with this.

Appears to alternate between a focus
on the interviewee and a focus on the
interviewer, and between the interviewee's frame of reference and the
interviewer's; occasionally gives
interviewer's needs priority.

Loses control of the interview, permitting unproductive, prolonged
digressions or role reversal so that
interviewer is being interviewed.
When in control, keeps the interview
inflexibly on course, permitting the
interviewee little freedom.

Is not entirely clear about the
purpose of the interview so that
structure is loose and focus wanders.
When clear about the purpose,
rigidly adheres to it, giving client
little freedom to modify the purpose.

Is uncertain about the direction of
the interview or how to get there.
Asks questions that appear to have
no direction, logic, or predictable
sequence. Interview seems somewhat
chaotic, confused, and confusing.

Asks questions that often are not
formulated effectively, that are

1. Inappropriate or poorly timed in
   terms of what the client is saying.
2. Often wordy, garbled, ambiguous,
   apt to include meaningless verbal-
   isms such as "you know" and "see
   what I mean."
3. Tactlessly phrased.

4. Asked one at a time.

5. Not suggesting an answer.

6. Sometimes appropriately answerable by yes or no.

7. Designed more to obtain answers to "what" and "how" than "why," "when," or "where."

8. Mostly open ended, with fewer closed or leading questions, all of which are used appropriately.

Shows through the wording of questions sensitivity to the client's vocabulary level; communicates in ways that consider age, race, income level, and ethnic differences between interviewer and interviewee.

Uses nonverbal behavior (eye contact, a forward lean, distance) to reinforce verbal interventions and to demonstrate careful attention to and following the interviewee.

Uses congruent verbal and nonverbal communications—supplementing, supporting, clarifying to communicate an unambiguous message.

Rarely interrupts, or overrides interviewee or finishes the client's sentences. Is sensitive to client's rights to autonomy and has no need to exert power or assert control.

Conducts the interview so that the ratio of talk time clearly favors the interviewee.

Uses silence effectively and comfortably, is sensitive to the different kinds of silences, and makes appropriate differential interventions.

4. Double questions.

5. Telegraphing the answers the interviewer expects.

6. Easy to answer with only a yes or no.

7. Designed to obtain answers to "why," "when," or "where" more frequently than "what" and "how."

8. Asks closed and leading questions more frequently than open questions.

Words questions beyond the vocabulary level or habitual usage of interviewee. Inappropriately uses professional jargon. Does not vary the communication pattern to accommodate differences in age, race, and ethnicity.

Uses nonverbal behavior that sometimes suggests inattentiveness; uses verbal interventions that are inappropriate to or a digression from what the interviewee has been saying.

Displays verbal and nonverbal behavior that often is incongruent and contradictory, sending a double or confused message.

Frequently interrupts clients, overrides them, and ends sentences for them. Clients perceive this as a violation of their autonomy and a manifestation of the interviewer's power and control.

Talks more than the interviewee.

Is apt to be unnerved by silence; is not sensitive to different meanings of silence; timing in ending or prolonging silence is inappropriate.

Knows when to end and when to permit silence to continue.

Has a relaxed unhurried pace. Allows a pause between the client's statement and the worker's response.	Uses a pace that appears hurried and tense. Seldom delays a response to a client's statement.
Has the courage to risk being impolite, interrupting interviewees and redirecting their communication if interviewees have lost their way.	Is hesitant about redirecting even an interviewee who clearly is engaged in an unproductive digression.
Comfortably explores the client's situation, covering relevant intimate details. Facilitates the client's self-disclosure in the context of their relationship and encourages disclosure. Communicates assurance about being entitled to the information, conviction of the need for the information, and willingness and ability to deal with emotionally charged material without anxiety.	Is awkward, hesitant, ineffectual, and without assurance in exploring the client's situation. Is embarrassed or anxious when dealing with emotionally charged content, does not feel entitled to intimate information about client, fails to communicate conviction in the need for the information.
Sharply focuses exploration of the client's situation based on experience and knowledge of what information is pertinent so the worker can be of help. Has expert knowledge of the social problem raised, human growth, and the social environment. Efficiently and quickly obtains most information necessary to understand the client's situation.	Is diffuse and protracted in exploring client's situation. Is not clear about what data are most significant for understanding of the client's situation because of limited knowledge of the social problem, human growth, and the social environment. Despite greater expenditure of time and effort, obtains less significant useful information.
Is comfortable with emotional contact and thus can help the interviewee explore in depth, where appropriate, areas of function that have potential significance for achieving the purpose of the interview. Is able to explore both range and depth of these emotions. Refrains from solving problems too soon and from prematurely engaging in highly affective content.	Is uncomfortable with emotional and intimate personal details, so tends not to explore in depth. Moves rapidly over a range of topics of potential significance but does little exploration in depth. Has a tendency to move too quickly toward problem solving and becomes involved too early in heavy emotional content.

Makes smooth transitions from one topic to another with appropriate explanation. Selects transitions that demonstrate attentiveness to what the client has been saying, thus preserving continuity in content and mood.

Tends to hold conclusions and inferences lightly and tentatively, seeking feedback about tentatively held hypothesis.

Uses interventions that seem to suggest the interviewer is open minded and attempts to individualize the interviewee.

Uses reflection, confrontation, and summarizing appropriately in timing, dosage, formulation, and phrasing.

Uses a variety of interventions flexibly and selectively or in combination, rather than tending to use one kind of intervention repetitively. Is equally competent and confident in using a variety of procedures.

Tends to be minimally directive in problem solving, offering advice, and proposing solutions. Maximizes the interviewee's involvement in finding a solution.

Reassures only when facts seem to justify doing so.

Uses transitions that are abrupt, not explained, and often irrelevant and unrelated to what the client has been talking about. Interview seems to be fragmented and discontinuous.

Tends to come to closure on conclusions too early, assuming more than the client has disclosed; does not seek confirmation or disconfirmation of conclusions.

Uses interventions that seem to suggest stereotypical thinking and categorizing of the interviewee in terms of predetermined assumptions.

Uses reflection, interpretation, confrontation, and summarizing that are often not relevant to the objective of the interview, are poorly timed or inappropriate in view of the manifest and latent content of the client's preceding statements, and are phrased in ways that heighten rather than dissipate resistance.

Tends not to be selective in using a variety of intervention procedures.

Tends to be more active and directive in offering advice and proposing solutions. Tends to do for the client in implementing problem solutions.

Offers reassurance despite little apparent basis for making reassuring statements.

Takes notes unobtrusively without breaking continuity of the interviewing or intruding on the progress of the interview.

Note taking tends to interfere with the continuity of the interview and its primary purposes.

Always uses role-appropriate behavior, making a clear distinction between social and professional relationships.

Inappropriately makes highly personal references, unprofessional irrelevant interventions, or permits prolonged small talk.

Explores the client's situation or uses interventions designed to help the client change with an attitude of being helpful rather than popular.

Focuses on interviewer's needs, which means the choice of action is determined by a desire to be consistently popular rather than invariably helpful, to please the client or at least not to offend, rather than to do what is needed to help the client.

Plans the end of the interview consciously and deliberately, basing it on achievement of interview objectives. Prepares clients for interview termination, controlling the level of affect. Summarizes, recapitulates, and ties this interview to the next contact.

Ends the interview in a ragged, often sudden, and abrupt manner that is not in line with where participants are in the interview at that point. Does not prepare interviewee for ending; neglects to summarize, recapitulate, and tie this interview to their next contact.

Summary: Chapter 14

Research that attempts to factor out the personality characteristics associated with competence in interviewing yields a rather confused picture. That may be because interviews conducted for different purposes may ideally require different kinds of interviewing personalities. Although no clear pattern of personality traits distinguishes the good from the poor interviewer, the general direction of the research suggests that the more successful interviewers are likely to be warm, accepting, psychologically open but in flexible control of themselves and the interview situation.

A thorough knowledge of the subject matter of the interview is one mark of the competent interviewer. Interviewers must be experts in conducting the interview, and they must have expertise in the subject matter of the social problem under consideration. Many interviews fail for lack of knowledge rather than lack of proper attitude.

The role of the social work interviewer requires the difficult balancing of antithetical demands; the competent interviewer seeks to resolve them. Prescriptions for effective interviewing suggest that the interviewer do contradictory things simultaneously.

Interviewees prefer interviewers who are respectful, competent, interested, warm, actively collaborative, and affectively expressive. Clients also prefer interviewers who share their experiences when these are pertinent. However, the client's ability to participate productively and collaboratively in therapy is also an important determinant of whether the interview is successful.

L'ENVOI—

It's been a long journey, from the beginning of the book to the end of the book; from the beginning of the course to the end of the course.

We have attempted much—and hope we have achieved it. We started by distinguishing an interview from a conversation and the social work interview from other types of interviews. Because the interview is a particular kind of communication, we included a discussion of some essential elements of the communication process.

And because people establish a relationship whenever they communicate in whatever context for whatever reason, we discussed the characteristics of a good relationship. We reviewed attitudes identified as associated with a positive, facilitative, helping relationship—acceptance, empathic understanding, self-determination, authenticity, and confidentiality.

We then returned to the social work interview, our principal concern, to introduce the participants—the social work interviewer and the social work interviewee. We tried to delineate what each of the participants brings to the interview, the tasks each is required to perform, and the problems they encounter.

The largest segment of the book is concerned with the interview process, the series of steps that interviewer and interviewee jointly engage in to move the interview toward achievement of its purpose. We discussed the beginning of the process, the routes interviewees take in coming to the agency, their reception and introduction to the interviewer, and the beginning of the interaction. We explained the activities the worker performs in extending the range and depth of the interview—attending, reflecting, paraphrasing, making transitions, summarizing, questioning, and probing. We followed interviewers as they engage the interviewee in clarifying, confronting, and interpreting, in the efforts to help interviewees solve the problems that brought them to the agency. Once they accomplish the purpose of the interview, as it is hoped, their interaction moves toward termination of the interview. We discussed the procedure for termination and noted the postinterview obligations for evaluation and recording.

Some significant aspects of the interaction did not fit neatly into the discussion of the interview process. We reviewed these in chapters devoted to problems of feedback, self-disclosure, immediacy, and such activities as listening, silence, and humor.

We recognize that all general discussions of the interview do an injustice to the individuality of the interviewee. The great variety of interviewees from different cultures and different backgrounds demands that social workers pay some attention to the heterogeneity of interviewees. We used as examples the material about the adaptation required of the interviewer in contacts with African Americans, the aged, and homosexuals.

And because people communicate nonverbally as well as verbally and sometimes more nonverbally than verbally, we included a chapter on nonverbal communication—proxemics, kinesics, paralinguistics, artifactual communication, touch, and smell. We discussed general problems in interviewing encountered by the interviewer and the particular problems associated with interviewing the involuntary client and the child suspected of having been sexually abused.

We warned the reader at the start of our association that ultimately interviewing can only be learned experientially. We still think this is true. But we are equally confident that social workers can learn much from a book that systematically presents information about interviewing. It was—and is—our feeling that such learning, such content, helps add competence to commitment. Only the reader knows whether this is purely a matter of faith and hope or whether this has some basis in the reality of the reader's experience.

Transcribed Interview and Critique

Throughout the book we have used excerpts to illustrate various aspects of interviewing. Aware that this gives a disjointed picture, we are presenting in this appendix a full interview. This presents the sweep of the interview process from beginning to termination and includes interview techniques in context.*

Interview and Critique

Record and critique of a tape-recorded discharge planning interview at _____ Hospital, Chicago, November 1994. The client consented to the taping. The interviewer is a white, 32-year-old, social worker with a master's degree. The interviewee is a white, widowed, 72-year-old female homemaker and retired checkout worker who formerly worked part time at K-mart.

Preinterview Preparation and Preliminaries

I was asked by Dr. _____ to see Mrs. R., who he said would be medically ready for discharge later in the week. She had been in the hospital for ten days, having suffered a stroke.

Before arranging to see Mrs. R., I read her chart and face sheet and spoke to the attending nurse. The stroke had left her [Mrs. R.] with some

---

* While this interview follows the process characteristic of social work interviews generally, the particular context of this interview is the hospital social work discharge planning interview (Kadushine and Kulys 1993).

residual impairment in the use of her right arm and fingers. Prior to her hospitalization, Mrs. R. suffered from inflammatory arthritis, which made walking painful. As a result of the arthritis and the stroke Mrs. R. could not walk without the aid of a walker.

Mrs. R.'s physician felt that she could regain much of the functioning on her right side through a program of physical therapy. Physical therapy was started at the hospital with a plan to continue the therapy after discharge.

The review of the chart, face sheet information, and discussion with the nurse was designed to give me some idea of the client's demography, physical problems, hospitalization experience, and current situation. Before actually attempting to see Mrs. R. I checked with the nurse to find out if she was awake, without visitors, in a condition for an interview, and that no procedures were scheduled for the next hour so we could meet without interruption. I knocked on the door and asked if I might come in before entering, as a general courtesy in respect to her privacy.

On being invited in I saw Mrs. R. sitting up in bed, the back of which was raised at about a forty-five-degree angle. Mrs. R. looked older than the age [72] noted on the chart. Her face was heavily lined and jowly. Her hair was thinning and all gray. She seemed, from the drape of the bedcovers, to be slight of build. Her eyes, however, were bright and alert, and her voice was vigorously loud. I learned from the first exchanges that her hearing did not seem to be impaired. I was somewhat surprised to see few cards or flowers on display despite the fact that she had been in the hospital for more than a week. Apparently, she had received few visitors.

Mrs. R. had been watching TV and turned it off as I came in.

Mr. R. gave me a pleasant smile, apparently glad to see a visitor. I walked over to the right side foot of the bed, asked if I could sit down, and talked with her for a half or three quarters of an hour. In choosing to sit down rather than stand and talk at her bedside put me on her level so that she did not have to look up at me. Sitting was also more physically comfortable, less tiring for me. Choosing to sit at the side and foot of the bed enabled Mrs. R. to talk to me without turning her head. The distance did not permit me, however, to be close enough to hold her hand or give her a comforting pat if the interview were to become very emotional for her.

I reviewed the general focus of a discharge planning interview in my mind in preparation. It was designed to help the client make plans for post-hospital care that was acceptable to the client and was at the same time safe and suitable for return to good health and the highest level of self-management possible. In implementing whatever plan was acceptable to the client, I would help facilitate access to the necessary services, resources, and equipment. Those responsibilities established some general parameters for the interview.

The interview was somewhat atypical in that the interviewer initiated the interview with a purpose in mind. The purpose was not the result of a collaborative consensual decision, as might be true in other interviews. In fact, the institution rather than the interviewer determined the focus here due to the influence of the DRG (diagnostic related group) on hospital procedures. As a result of the Medicare prospective payment system it is generally required that a plan be made for discharge when the patient was medically ready.

As I thought about this in preparation for the interview, I planned to leave some time, if possible, once a discharge plan had been formulated, to give the client an opportunity to discuss any health or hospital experience problems with which she might want help.

The Interview Starts—
First Phase: Establishing Purpose,
Defining Roles, Establishing Relationship

1.

INTERVIEWER: Mrs. R., first let me tell you who I am and why I am here. My name is _____. I am a social worker assigned to the social work department at the hospital and was asked by Dr. _____ to see you.

MRS. R.: Oh yes. I remember Dr. _____ said that he would ask a social worker to see me.

1.

Although I identified myself and my affiliation and told Mrs. R. how I came to be there, I did not at first tell her why I was seeing her. I wanted to learn if she had been told the reasons for the interview by Dr. _____ to determine what her expectations and anticipations might be.

2.

INTERVIEWER: What did Dr. _____ say about why he wanted a social worker to see you?

MRS. R.: Actually, he didn't say and I didn't ask him.

2.

An open-ended question.

3.

INTERVIEWER: Well, as you might know the doctor thinks you made enough progress so that you can leave the hospital shortly. I was asked

3.

Since she had not apparently been told anything about my reasons for seeing her, I couched the purpose of the interview in very general terms.

to see you to discuss with you what happens after you leave the hospital.

MRS. R.: Well, I think that's simple. I just go back to my home and do like I did before.

In saying "leave the hospital shortly" I was somewhat indefinite about the discharge date. To have stated a definite time would raise expectations which might result in a disappointment if discharge was delayed for medical reasons or because a safe plan for her care after discharge had not been formulated.

4.

INTERVIEWER: Did like you did before. Could you tell me what it was like before?

MRS. R.: Well I live on my own in _____ (a lower middle-income suburb of Chicago). I've been living there with my husband and children since about 1955. I don't have to go to a nursing home or anything like that because I can go home and live on my own as I have before.

4.

Reflecting and soliciting clarification through an open-ended question.

5.

INTERVIEWER: So that your plan is to leave the hospital and go back to living independently in your own home.

MRS. R.: Right; right.

5.

A paraphrase of Mrs. R.'s statement. It was clear that Mrs. R. had her own discharge plan, which she expressed with considerable vigor and conviction. I noted the stress on independence and the converse antipathy to a nursing home and "anything like that."

Data Gathering— Problem Exploration Phase

6.

INTERVIEWER: Who can you count on to help you at home when you leave the hospital?

MRS. R.: Well, my husband and children did live with me previously, but they can't help now.

6.

At this point I am beginning a second phase in the interview—a data-gathering phase. I need to get some specific information about support systems available, the nature of the home, physical set-up in relation to her physical situation, et cetera. I need to know this to be able to make some assessment of the feasibility of Mrs. R.'s preferred plan and what we might need to do to help make it more feasible. The data-gathering phase begins with an open-ended question soliciting information.

7.

INTERVIEWER: How's that?

MRS. R.: Well, my husband is dead. He died about five years ago after retiring. He was an automobile repair mechanic in a small shop. I just continued on in the house after he died.

7.

Open-ended question soliciting information.

8.

INTERVIEWER: [*Silent for about four seconds.*]: And the children?
MRS. R.: [*After a two- to three- second pause after the question. A sigh.*]: Well, I have two children. The older girl Mary, twenty-seven, is divorced. The young one, Lib, twenty-five, is married. Mary lives in Seattle; Lib lives in San Jose, California. So neither one lives close by in Illinois. They have both been out of the house on their own for sometime now, living their own lives, both have young children, and both are living on a small income. I really can't look to them for any help.

8.

I kept silent because I thought she might go on to explain about the availability of the children, but she seemed reluctant to discuss this without some encouragement so I broke the silence to ask a question designed to encourage Mrs. R. to disclose further.

While she started to talk with some hesitancy, once she got started she seemed comfortable in sharing family information with me. The initial uneasiness that is characteristic of any relationship between strangers was beginning to dissipate, and I began to feel a sense of comfortableness between us beginning to develop.

9.

INTERVIEWER: You really can't look to them for help.

MRS. R.: Well, no. Both of them have jobs where they live—not that it pays very much and they really can't leave the kids and move back home.

9.

In interviewer nine I merely reflected what she had said to encourage further sharing.

Mrs. R.'s response to interviewer nine was said with some vehemence as though she were trying to convince herself as well as me.

10.

INTERVIEWER: How would you feel if one or both of them would volunteer to do that?

MRS. R.: Well, I don't think I can accept that. I always took care of myself, and I don't want to be a burden on them even if they said they would do it. But mostly I don't think it would be fair to the kids. They have young children who need looking after. That's what they should be doing, taking care of the kinds, not taking care of me. [*Pause.*] Besides, I don't think they would volunteer to help in any way. [*Said in a low key, sadly.*]

10.

Given that interviewer nine seems a little confrontational, somewhat challenging, coming back to Illinois would seem like the most drastic option. I think I was trying to find out what were limits of what help we might expect from her children.

11.

INTERVIEWER: You don't think they would?

MRS. R.: Well, we are not on the best of terms. Aside from Christmas cards and an occasional phone call, we haven't been in touch much in the last few years.

They know I had a stroke, and they know I have been in the hospital and they called a couple of times, but they never visited.

11.

Some guilt; some anxiety about being dependent; some concern for the children. Didn't seem promising. And the last sentence seemed to suggest resignation to the situation. Interviewer eleven was a reflection that encouraged continuation and implied request for an explanation.

12.

INTERVIEWER: That must have hurt.

MRS. R.: Well, it did some, sure.

12.

Ruptured parent-child relationships are always sad. Mrs R. expressed some of this in what she said and the way she said it. My response was designed to be supportively empathetic. Mrs. R.'s response acknowledged this, but she wasn't ready to give in out of pride.

13.

INTERVIEWER: Yes, I think it would. [*Pause.*] But then from what you are telling me, there does not seem to be anybody in your immediate family who would be available to provide you with any help you might need once you got home. Isn't that so?

MRS. R.: I guess so.

13.

At this point I had a decision to make as to how to proceed. I recognized and acknowledged the concern she felt around a difficult and hurtful parent-child problem. But opening this up for discussion, possibly counseling, would have been a digression from my purpose. The questions about her husband and family were raised for the purpose of determining how much they could provide as a support system contribution to - planning for discharge, what support system would be available to her at home. At this point that was my necessary purpose so I eased away from parent-child problems and refocused on support through the use of a summary. The summary ended with a closed-ended question that almost forced assent on her part. It would have been softer and less authoritative to have asked, "How does that sound to you?" As it was, the question that was asked got a tentative grudging agreement: "I guess."

14.

INTERVIEWER: What about other people who might be available to help—relatives, friends?

MRS. R.: Well, my only relative in the state is my husband's brother, but he's worse off than I am. He has Parkinson's.

15.

INTERVIEWER: And friends?
MRS. R.: Well, I used to be close to a group of women from my church. But after my husband died and my arthritis made it more difficult, I

14, 15.

Sticking with possible support system alternatives. It might have been better for the purpose of clarity to have asked this using two questions—the first focusing on relatives; the second on friends—which I finally did.

kinda stopped going regularly and we gradually lost contact with each other. There is really only one woman—a widow a little older than myself with whom I am still close. We keep in contact, but she has her own physical problems—a big smoker. She has lung trouble. But I would imagine she could stop in and see me once in a while. But I don't think you could count on her to help out.

16.

INTERVIEWER: It would seem to me, then, from what you are saying that essentially no one from immediate family, relatives, and friends that you could readily count on to help you if you needed someone to help you in the home.

MRS. R.: But that's nothing new. That's the way it has been for the last two or three years. But I was still able to keep going and take care of myself and the home. So the situation is the same as before I went to the hospital.

17.

INTERVIEWER: I hear you value your independence very highly and I respect you for this, and in any plans that we make together, we will keep this in mind. But let me ask you, is everything really the same as it was before?

MRS. R.: I don't get you. What do you mean?

16.

Summarizing the last few interchanges and making explicit a problem posed by her plan to return home.

17.

I felt at this point that I needed to confront Mrs. R. with the reality of her currently more limited physical capabilities. The confrontation was a direct challenge to her effort to maintain her perception of herself as being as capable as she was before the stroke and hip fracture. Because of the threat implied in the challenge, I used a lead-in which was supportive and reassured her that we would make plans "together" with her preference in mind. In raising the confrontational question, the use of "really" suggests there is only one answer that is valid so that it restricts the response.

18.

INTERVIEWER: Well, since the time *before* , you have suffered a stroke. As a consequence the things you used to do *before* are likely to be much more difficult to do now. Because of these physical changes, despite your best intentions, do you think you can do now what you did before in regard to taking care of yourself at home?

MRS. R.: Are you saying that I am not as able physically as I was before?

18.

I think I was feeling some impatience with Mrs. R.'s refusal to see what seemed obvious—that the situation for adequate self-manage-ment and self-care was not what it was before; that the nature of the changed reality situation needed to be factored in when formulating the discharge plan. Consequently, my closed-ended question was struc-tured to elicit the answer I wanted to hear from Mrs. R. Rather than have me say the answer for her, I should have permitted her to come to this answer on her own.

19.

INTERVIEWER: Well, are you? What do you think? [I raised the question then shut up. There was a long pause during which Mrs. R. turned her face away from me and seemed to be struggling with this. For a moment she seemed to be crying softly and then seemed to catch herself and stop. She turned back to me and said]

MRS. R.: I hate to come to this. All my life I prided myself on being independent. I had to be. I hate to think of having to be dependent on others who will do things for me. Things I used to do for myself.

19.

Despite my heavy handedness with this last question, Mrs. R. continues to elude me. "Well, are you?" in interviewer 19 is unnecessary. The simple second question, "What do you think?," was sufficient in itself and more desirable.

20.

INTERVIEWER: Having been so independent in the past must make it doubly difficult for you to think of living in a different way than you

20.

With great difficulty Mrs. R. begins to accept the reality of her situation. She accepts the situation but with considerable regret and, I hypothe-

have in the past. It is tough. [*Pause.*] But where is the blame for this in your mind?

MRS. R.: Well, maybe I should have been more careful or taken better care. I don't smoke now, but I used to so maybe what happened wouldn't have happened. [*Pause.*] Oh, I don't know. Strokes happen and the thing with the hop was an accident, and now I can barely use my left hand and walking is difficult even with the walker.

sized, with some self-blame. I could have offered her some trite bromides in reassurance, i.e., "We all get old and more dependent"; "People your age frequently suffer from strokes and accidents over which they have no control"; et cetera, but I wanted to throw the question back to her and help her resolve feelings of inadequacy, self-blame, guilt.

This is important for discharge planning because if we were to make arrangements for providing support and help and she continued to be resistant, then she could easily, without being openly aware of this, defeat the plan through noncompliance.

21.

INTERVIEWER: You're so right. You cannot blame yourself for what happened. But for whatever reason you are not the same woman coming out of the hospital as when you came in—before the stroke. Does that seems a fair statement to you?

MRS. R.: Well, I guess so.

21.

Support and reassurance embedded in the summary. But once again I end up with a closed-ended question that is not really a question but a suggested answer. Not so good.

22.

INTERVIEWER: And from what you told me before, there is no one available to help when you go home, as you prefer. I respect your decision. But I need to plan with you so that your home situation is safe, that you are provided with the help you need, and to improve your physical condition. [*Pause.*] Let me ask you a number of questions that would help in planning—okay?

MRS. R.: Okay.

22.

Once again a kind of grudging, not committed, agreement. I still need to get some specific information about the set-up in the home—information we need for a good assessment of Mrs. R.'s situation. I am still at the data-gathering stage of the interview process.

The question at the end of interviewer twenty-two is a preparation for a transition—letting her know I am going on to something different.

23.

INTERVIEWER: For one thing, is the home a ranch-style home, everything is on one floor?

MRS. R.: No, it's a duplex—upstairs and downstairs.

24.

INTERVIEWER: Is the bedroom upstairs?

MRS. R.: Yes.

25.

INTERVIEWER: Is there a bathroom on the lower floor?

MRS. R.: No. Only one bathroom—upstairs.

25.

INTERVIEWER: Is the stove in the kitchen—which, I take it, is downstairs—gas or electric?

MRS. R.: Gas.

26.

INTERVIEWER: How's your sense of smell? I ask because you would need to be able to detect gas leaks.

MRS. R.: Well, I really don't know, but I think I would be able to smell gas.

27.

INTERVIEWER: And your furnace—is it gas or oil? And is it in good working condition?

MRS. R.: It's gas and it's pretty new. We replaced it shortly before my husband died.

23, 24, 25, 26, 27.

Are closed-ended, clarifying, probe questions, which are intended to provide us with the specific information we need to know in order to provide us with the specific information we need to know in order to provide the resources and equipment that Mrs. R. would need to have to make a return-home plan feasible and safe.

Question twenty-six needed an explanation because the reason for the question is not immediately obvious—and because the question seems personally intrusive.

Assessment and Problem-Solving Developmental Phase

After these series of questions I think I have a good assessment of the situation so that I could go ahead with planning some intervention with confidence. In my mind I am putting the information together at the assessment stage of the process. Mrs. R. has some serious physical impairments which, while they make a return-home plan possible, would require that she have some help. She was very independent, reluctant to see herself as needing help, but was also pretty realistic about her situation. Mrs. R. had no support group of her own, so we would need to provide the help she would need. I had a picture of the home set-up which suggested the kind of help and equipment she would need.

28.

INTERVIEWER: Now I would like to suggest some things that would enable you to go home from here, in line with your preference, but with assurance of a safe situation and assurance of support to meet your personal needs. Please let me know if you have any questions or objections to any I will suggest. [*Pause.*] For one thing, your bedroom is upstairs, which means a hazardous difficult climb up and down. I would suggest that you move the bed downstairs for a time. Is there anyone you know, a friend, a handyman, a neighbor who could do this for you?

MRS. R.: Well, I am not sure I like to do that, but it seems sensible and we have the room for a bed downstairs. Yes, I think I know someone who could do this for me.

29.

INTERVIEWER: Second, I would suggest that we could provide you with a commode for personal needs so you would not have to go up and down stairs to the bathroom. We can provide a homemaker for cleaning, bed-

28, 29

The beginning of [section] twenty-eight is, once again, preparation for a transition. The offer of services was couched as suggestions with encouragement on her part to reject them if she was not accepting. We outlined the services and equipment I thought would be needed if the discharge plan to her own home had a chance for success.

making, meal preparation four hours a day, three days a week, and we can also provide Meals-on-Wheels on the days when the homemaker is not there. Dr._____ has ordered a physical therapist who will visit you in the home after you leave the hospital. You will need a walker as well, which we can provide.

MRS. R.: Well, that seems like a lot. And the more you suggest, the more uneasy I get.

30.
INTERVIEWER: Could you tell me what makes you feel uneasy?

MRS. R.: Well, who's going to pay for all this? It sounds like a lot and I am living on a small Social Security income.

30.
The request for clarification, using her words, for the way she felt "uneasy."

31.
INTERVIEWER: I know this is a personal question, but I need to know for planning purposes exactly what your income is.

MRS. R.: Well, I get a check for four hundred seventy dollars a month.

31.
Asking about income is generally regarded as a personal intrusive question, so I think my question required an explanation.

32.
INTERVIEWER: Well, your income makes you eligible for assistance from the Illinois Department of Aging who will provide the home-maker and Meals-on-Wheels. Your Medicare insurance makes you eligible for things like the commode, the walker, and the physical therapist's visits.

MRS. R.: That help from what—the Department of Aging—isn't that welfare?

32.
Providing specific information as to the sources for the help Mrs. R. would need.

33.

INTERVIEWER: Yes, it is a program of assistance to people with limited income to meet health care needs.

MRS. R.: I don't know. I came from a generation which lived at a time when asking for welfare was a matter of shame. There was a stigma associated with it. No self-respecting person took welfare and I guess I still feel that way somewhat.

33.

An informational statement in response. While the answer to her question is accurate, I fudged in answering. I did not say directly, "Yes, it is a welfare program," which is really what Mrs. R. is asking. I think I sensed that "welfare" had negative connotations for Mrs. R.—which it had.

34.

INTERVIEWER: Yes. Although I grew up at a different time, I think I can understand how you feel. My parents felt the way you do. But when my father's Alzheimer's condition got worse, my parents were forced to apply for assistance in order to provide the nursing home care he needed. They had no choice and they came to recognize that they were entitled to the help. They, like you and your husband, paid for these programs with your tax dollars while you were working.

MRS. R. [*Pause.*]: Okay. I can see that Alzheimer is very serious and you would need that help maybe. But my situation is not that serious. I am not sure I would like to take welfare.

34.

I felt for Mrs. R.'s struggle about this. I used self-disclosure to help her begin to move toward a resolution of her feelings. It brought us closer together. If "nice" people like ourselves could use assistance, maybe she could also.

35.

INTERVIEWER: I can appreciate your hesitance. It seems to me that you are saying that you can go home and manage without the kinds of supports that welfare can make available.

MRS. R.: Well, it's very hard for me to see myself in that situation. It's hard to think that you might need to . . .

35.

This is an interpretation of what is implied in her objection to welfare. The validity of the interpretation, it seemed to me, is based not only on what she had just said but her earlier expressions of her struggle with dependency. Welfare people were dependent people from Mrs. R.'s point of view.

36.

INTERVIEWER: It *is* hard to think that you might need to—[*Pause.*]

MRS. R.: It is. It is.

36.

A reflection in which I affirm Mrs. R.'s struggle with her feelings. It is interesting that in the last statement Mrs. R. said "you might need to" rather than "I might need to," which is more immediate.

37.

INTERVIEWER: I know it is. [*Pause.*] But try for a moment to picture the situation. You go home. You have limited use of your right arm, leg, and fingers. You have difficulty walking, climbing stairs because of your stroke and arthritis. Picture yourself in the home, cooking, bathing, toileting, washing clothes, getting to bed without help. [*Pause.*]

MRS. R.: It doesn't look so good does it [said with a slight smile, like she was admitting but not admitting it. Then the smile broadened and she laughed]. I just had a picture of myself peeing on the stairs while trying to get up to the bathroom. Doesn't do the carpets any good, does it?

37.

Having acknowledged that it is difficult, I try to confront Mrs. R. directly with the reality of her situation.

38.

INTERVIEWER: It sure doesn't. [We both laugh together. After a pause, we savor the positive effects of the laugh together.]

38.

The necessity of accepting dependency was a painful one. The humor made the inevitable easier to accept. I was a little surprised at her imagery because it seemed out of character, but since she initiated the humor, I felt free to join in. As a result of this humorous interchange, the mood of the interview lightened perceptively. The question at the end of interviewer thirty-seven is a reversional transition. In a way this interchange was a wrap-up. She knew she needed help, we could provide the kind of help she needed, and she was beginning to accept it.

Termination

39.

INTERVIEWER: Well, just let me quickly go over what we covered. You will be leaving the hospital shortly—and, incidentally, we will arrange transportation—and returning to your own home. Because it appears that there is little likelihood of your being able to count on immediate family, relatives, or friends for support, we plan to arrange for a homemaker, Meals on Wheels, periodic visits from a physical therapist. We will arrange for a walker and a commode. [*Pause.*] Is there anything I missed? Anything you would like to add?

MRS. R.: No. I think that's it. I can't think of anything else.

39.

In interviewer thirty-nine I am moving to the final step in the interview process—termination. In doing so I summarize what I think we have covered and solicit an opportunity for Mrs. R.'s corrections or amendments.

As I made this last statement, I slowly got up, approached the head of the bed, and gave her my card. Mrs. R. had to reach across her body with her left hand to take the card, and we briefly made physical contact.

Before I actually left the room I asked Mrs. R. a series of questions (Are you comfortable? Should I lower the bed? Do you want me to ask the nurse to see you about anything?) all of which Mrs. R. answered negatively. We were moving out of the interview context as I said in parting, "It was nice talking to you. Take care."

40.

INTERVIEWER: Well, that's it for the immediate future. I will tell you when the homemaker will start and when you can expect to get the commode. I will also give you the schedule of the physical therapist. The physical therapy department at the hospital will furnish you with the walker. Finally, I will give you information for the Department of Aging contact.

40.

Termination left something to be desired in that I never gave Mrs. R. a chance to raise with me any questions that she might have had about her health and/or hospitalization. She may have had her own purpose for the contact which she did not have the opportunity to discuss.

Evaluation

I think I accomplished the purpose of the interview. We had a feasible discharge plan formulated with plans for the resources and equipment that would make the plan feasible, safe, and contribute to the rehabilitation.

The main intervention focus was around environmental modification— providing the social support that would make safe return home possible. However, there were clinical components that made the plan acceptable to Mrs. R. and would contribute to its implementation—i.e., involving her in decision making to resolve her ambivalence about accepting help and the arrangements to finance it.

I am aware that this ambivalence may still create problems for implementing the plan, and I may have to arrange counseling sessions with Mrs. R. to help with this. I am also aware that there is a problem of the conflict between Mrs. R. and her children. While I did not involve myself with this on the grounds that it was peripherally relevant to our concerns, Mrs. R. may want help with this in the future, and I will, if we continue to have contact, make a referral to a family service agency in her area.

At some points in the interview I feel I was exerting some pressure on Mrs. R. to agree to the planning. In extenuation I might note that we are obligated to make plans to get patients out of the hospital once they are medically ready.

I was assisted by Mrs. R. in accomplishing the purpose of the interview. She was an articulate interviewee, aware of her feelings and ready to express them. While defensive of her position, she was at the same time realistic and, despite reluctance and regret, ready to recognize the reality of her situation.

References

Abramson, Marcia. 1985. "The Autonomy-Paternalism Dilemma in Social Work Practice." *Social Casework* 66 (September): 387–93.

——. 1989. "Autonomy Versus Paternalistic Beneficence: Practice Strategies." *Social Casework* 70 (February): 101–105.

American Psychiatric Association. 1994. *Diagnostic and Statistical Manual of Mental Disorders, DSM-IV.* Washington, D.C.: American Psychiatric Association.

Anderson, Sandra C. and Deborah L. Mandall. 1989. "The Use of Self-Disclosure by Professional Social Workers." *Social Casework* 70 (May): 259–67.

Angier, Natalie. 1995. "Scientists Mull Role of Empathy in Man and Beast." *New York Times,* May 7, pp. C1, C6.

Atkinson, Donald R. 1983. "Ethnic Similarity in Counseling Psychology: A Review of the Research." *Counseling Psychologist* 11, no. 3: 79–92.

——. 1985. "A Metareview of Research on Cross-Cultural Counseling and Psychotherapy." *Journal of Multicultural Counseling and Development* 13, no. 4: 138–53.

Atkinson, Donald R. and Susan M. Lowe. 1995. "The Role of Ethnicity, Cultural Knowledge, and Conventional Techniques in Counseling and Psychotherapy." In Joseph G. Ponterotto et al., eds., *Handbook of Multicultural Counseling,* pp. 387–414. Thousand Oaks, Calif.: Sage.

Atkinson, Donald R. and Sandra Schein. 1986. "Similarity in Counseling." *Counseling Psychologist* 14, no. 2: 319–54.

Baird, K. A. and P. A. Rupert. 1987. "Clinical Management of Confidentiality: A Survey of Psychologists in Seven States." *Professional Psychology: Research and Practice* 18, no. 4: 347–52.

Baker, Nicholas G. 1981. "Social Work Through an Interpreter." *Social Work* 26 (September): 391–97.

Baldock, John and David Prior. 1981. "Social Workers Talking to Clients: A Study of Verbal Behavior." *British Journal of Social Work* 11, no. 1: 19–38.

Barker, Robert L. 1991. *The Social Work Dictionary,* 2d ed. Silver Spring, Md: National Association of Social Workers.

Beck, Dorothy F. and Mary A. Jones. 1973. *Progress on Family Problems: A Nationwide Study of Clients' and Counselors' Views on Family Agency Services.* New York: Family Service Association of America.

Bell, A. and M. Weinberg. 1978. *Homosexualities: A Study of Diversity Among Men and Women.* New York: Simon and Schuster.

Ben-Arie, O., L. Schwartz, and G. C. W. George. 1986. "The Compulsory Treatment of Alcoholic Drunken Drivers Referred by the Courts: A Seven- to Nine-Year Outcome Study." *International Journal of Law and Psychiatry* 8, no. 2: 229–35.

Benedek, Elissa and Diane Schetkey. 1986. "Allegations of Sexual Abuse in Child Custody and Visitation Disputes." In D. Schetkey and E. Benedek, eds., *Emerging Issues in Child Psychiatry and the Law,* pp. 145–56. New York: Brunner-Mazel.

Bergin, Allen E. and Sol L. Garfield, eds. 1994. *Handbook of Psychotherapy and Behavior Change,* 4th ed. New York: Wiley.

Beutler, L. E., M. Crago, and T. G. Arizmendi. 1986. "Therapist Variables in Psychotherapy Process and Outcome." In S. Garfield and A. Bergin, eds., *Handbook of Psychotherapy and Behavior Change,* pp. 257–310. New York: McGraw-Hill.

Beutler, Larry E., Paulo P. Machado, and Susan A. Neufeldt. 1994. "Therapist Variables." In Allen E. Bergin and Sol L. Garfield, eds., *Handbook of Psychotherapy and Behavior Change,* 4th ed., pp. 229–69. New York: Wiley.

Biestek, Felix P. 1951. *The Principle of Client Self-Determination in Social Casework.* Washington, D.C.: Catholic University of America Press.

——. 1957. *The Casework Relationship.* Chicago: Loyola University Press.

Biestek, Felix P. and Clyde C. Gehrig. 1978. *Client Self-Determination in Social Work: A Fifty-Year History.* Chicago: Loyola University Press.

Billingsly, Andrew. 1964. *The Role of the Social Worker in a Child Protective Agency: A Comparative Analysis.* Boston: Massachusetts Society for the Prevention of Cruelty to Children.

Birdwhistell, Ray L. 1970. *Kinetics and Context: Essays on Body Motion Communication.* Philadelphia: University of Pennsylvania Press.

Blanck, Peter D. et al. 1986. "Therapists' Tone of Voice: Descriptive Psychometric Interactional and Competence Analysis." *Journal of Social and Clinical Psychology* 4, no. 2: 154–78.

Blau, Peter M. 1955. *The Dynamics of Bureaucracy.* Chicago: University of Chicago Press.

Boat, Barbara and Mark D. Everson. 1988. "Interviewing Young Women with Anatomical Dolls." *Child Welfare* 67 (July–August): 337–52.

Borenzweig, Herman. 1981. "The Self-Disclosure of Clinical Social Workers." *Journal of Sociology and Social Welfare* 7 (July): 432–58.

——. 1983. "Touching in Clinical Social Work." *Social Casework* 64 (April): 238–42.

Bradburn, Norman and Seymour Sudman. 1979. *Improving Interview Methods and Questionnaire Design.* San Francisco: Jossey-Bass.

Bradmiller, Linda. 1978. "Self-Disclosure in the Helping Relationship." *Social Work Research and Abstracts* 14 (summer): 28–35.

Brill, L. and L. Lieherman. 1969. *Authority and Addiction.* Boston: Little, Brown.

Brody, Jane E. 1988. "Personal Health." *New York Times,* April 7, sec. II, p. 8.

Buller, Mary K. and David B. Buller. 1987. "Physicians' Communication Style and Patient Satisfaction." *Journal of Health and Social Behavior* 28, no. 4: 375–88.

Cannell, Charles F., Floyd J. Fowler, and Kent H. Marquis. 1968. *The Influence of Interviewer and Respondent: Psychological and Behavioral Variables on the Reporting in Household Interviews.* Public Health Service Publication, series 2, no. 26. Washington, D.C.: U.S. Government Printing Office.

Cantril, H. 1956. "Perception and Interpersonal Relations." *American Journal of Psychiatry* 114 (August): 119–26.

Ceci, Stephan J. and Maggie Bruck. 1993. "Suggestibility of the Child Witness: A Historical Review and Synthesis." *Psychological Bulletin* 113, no. 3: 403–39.

——. 1995. *Jeopardy in the Courtroom: A Scientific Analysis of Children's Testimony.* Washington, D.C.: American Psychological Association.

Ceci, Stephan J., D. F. Ross, and M. P. Toglia. 1987. "Suggestibility of Children's Memories: Psychological Implications." *Journal of Experimental Psychology* 116: 38–49.

Chelune, Gordon J. and Associates. 1979. *Self-Disclosure: Origins, Patterns, and Implications of Openness in Interpersonal Relationships.* San Francisco: Jossey-Bass.

Cirello, Leonard and Cathleen Crider. 1995. "Distinctive Therapeutic Uses of Metaphor." *Psychotherapy* 4, no. 39: 511–19.

Claiborne, C. D., S. R. Ward, and S. R. Strong. 1981. "Effects of Congruence Between Counselors' Interpretation and Client Beliefs." *Journal of Counseling Psychology* 28, no. 2: 101–9.

Coady, Nick F. 1993. "The Worker-Client Relationship Revisited." *Families in Society: Journal of Contemporary Human Services.* 74, no. 5: 291–300.

Cohen, Pauline and Merton S. Krause. 1971. *Casework with Wives of Alcoholics.* New York: Family Service Association of America.

Colby, Ira and Deborah Colby. 1987. "Videotaping the Child Sexual Abuse Victim." *Social Casework* 68 (September): 117–21.

Coleman, Hardin L. K., Bruce F. Wampold, and Sherry L. Casali. 1995. "Ethnic Minorities' Ratings of Ethnically Similar and European American Counselors." *Journal of Counseling Psychology* 42, no. 1: 55–64.

Collins, Glenn. 1988. "How Punch Lines Bolster the Bottom Line." *New York Times,* April 30, sec. I, p. 37.

Converse, Jean M. and Howard Schuman. 1974. *Conversations at Random: Survey Research as Interviewers See it.* New York: Wiley.

Cook, M. 1982. "Perceiving Others: The Psychology of Interpersonal Perception." In D. M. Davey and M. Harris, eds., *Judging People*. London: McGraw-Hill.

Corrigan, J. D. et al. 1989. "Counseling as a Social Influence Process: A Review. *Journal of Counseling Psychology Monographs* 27, no. 4: 395–441.

Cousins, Norman. 1979. *Anatomy of an Illness*. New York: W. W. Norton.

Cox, A., M. Rutter, and D. Holbrook. 1981. "Psychiatric Interview Techniques. A Second Experimental Study: Eliciting Feelings." *British Journal of Psychiatry* 139 (July): 144–52.

Dallas, Mecedes and Robert S. Baron. 1985. "Do Psychotherapists Use a Confirmatory Strategy During Interviewing?" *Journal of Social and Clinical Psychology* 3, no. 1: 106–22.

Davies, William. 1988. "How Not to Get Hit." *Psychologist* 5 (May): 175–76.

Davis, Larry E. and Enola K. Proctor. 1989. *Race, Gender, and Class: Guidelines for Practice with Individuals, Families, and Groups*. Englewood Cliffs, N.J.: Prentice-Hall.

Dawson, B. et al. 1986. "Cognitive Problem Solving Training to Improve the Child Care Judgment of Child Neglectful Parents." *Journal of Family Violence* 1, no. 3: 209–21.

Day, Peter R. 1985. "An Interview: Constructing Reality." *British Journal of Social Work* 15, no. 5: 487–99.

DeCrescenzo, Teresa A. 1983–84. "Homophobia: A Study of the Attitudes of Mental Health Professionals Toward Homosexuality." *Journal of Social Work and Human Sexuality* 2, no. 2–3: 115–31.

Dent, Helen R. 1982. "The Effects of Interviewing Strategies on the Results of Interviews with Child Witnesses." In A. Tronkwell, ed., *Reconstructing the Past*, pp. 279–97. Devanter, The Netherlands: Kluwer.

DePaulo, Bella et al. 1987. "Accuracy of Person Perception: Do People Know the Kinds of Impressions They Convey?" *Journal of Personality and Social Psychology* 52, no. 2: 303–15.

DePaulo, Bella M., Julie I. Stone, and G. D. Lassiter. 1985. "Deceiving and Detecting Deceit." In B. R. Schlenker, ed., *The Self and Social Life*, pp. 323–70. New York: McGraw-Hill.

Deutscher, Irwin. 1966. "Words and Deeds: Social Science and Social Policy." *Social Problems* 13, no. 3: 235–54.

Dewayne, Claudia. 1978. "Humor in Therapy." *Social Work* 23 (November): 508–10.

Dexter, Lewis A. 1970. *Elite and Specialized Interviewing*. Evanston, Ill.: Northwestern University Press.

Dibner, Andrew. 1956. "Cue Counting: A Measure of Anxiety in Interviews." *Journal of Consulting Psychology* 20:475–78.

Dickson, David and David Bramford. 1995. "Improving the Interpersonal Skills of Social Work Students: The Problem of Transfer of Training and What To Do About It." *British Journal of Social Work* 25, no. 1: 85–104.

Dillon, J. T. 1990. *The Practice of Questioning*. New York: Routledge.

Dohrenwend, Barbara S. 1965. "Some Effects of Open and Closed Questions." *Human Organization* 24: 175–84.

——. 1970. "An Experimental Study of Directive Interviewing." *Public Opinion Quarterly* 34 (spring): 117–25.

Dugger, Celia W. 1996. "Immigrant Cultures Raising Issues of Child Punishment." *New York Times*, February 29, p. 1 and p. 12.

Edwards, Carla E. and Nancy L. Murdock. 1994. "Characteristics of Therapist Self-Disclosure in the Counseling Process." *Journal of Counseling and Development* 72 (March–April): 384–89.

Egan, Gerard. 1986. *The Skilled Helper: A Model for Systematic Helping and Interpersonal Relating.* Monterey, Calif.: Brooks/Cole.

Ekman, Paul. 1986. *Telling Lies.* New York: Berkeley.

——. 1989. *Why Kids Lie.* New York: Penguin.

——. 1992. *Telling Lies: Clues to Deceit in the Marketplace, Politics, and Marriage.* New York: W. W. Norton.

Ekman, Paul and Wallace V. Friesen. 1968. "Nonverbal Behavior in Psychotherapy Research." In John M. Shlien, ed., *Research in Psychotherapy: Proceedings of the Third Conference*, pp. 179–216. Washington, D.C.: American Psychological Association.

Epstein, Laura. 1985. *Talking and Listening: A Guide to the Helping Interview.* St. Louis: Times Mirror/Mosby.

Erickson, Frederick and Jeffery Schultz. 1982. *The Counselor as Gatekeeper: Social Interaction in Interviews.* New York: Academic Press.

Everson, Mark D. and Barbara W. Boat. 1989. "False Allegations of Sexual Abuse by Children and Adolescents." *Journal of the American Academy of Child and Adolescent Psychiatry* 28, no. 2: 230–35.

——. 1994. "Putting the Anatomical Doll Controversy in Perspective: An Examination of the Major Uses and Criticisms of the Dolls in Sexual Abuse Evaluations." *Child Abuse and Neglect* 18, no. 2: 113–28.

Ewalt, Patricia and Janice Kutz. 1976. "An Examination of Advice Giving as a Therapeutic Intervention." *Smith College Studies in Social Work* 47 (November): 3–19.

Falk, Dana R. and Clara E. Hill. 1992. "Counselor Interventions Preceding Client Laughter in Brief Therapy." *Journal of Counseling Psychology* 39, no. 1: 39–45.

Faller, Kathleen C. 1984. "Is the Child Victim of Sexual Abuse Telling the Truth?" *Child Abuse and Neglect* 8, no. 4: 473–82.

——. 1988. *Child Sexual Abuse: An Interdisciplinary Manual for Diagnosis, Case Management, and Treatment.* New York: Columbia University Press.

Fanshel, David and William Labov. 1977. *Therapeutic Discourse: Psychotherapy as Conversation.* New York: Academic Press.

Farrelly, Frank and Jeff Brandsma. 1974. *Provocative Therapy.* Fort Collins, Colo.: Shields.

Farrelly, Frank and Michael Lynch. 1987. "Humor in Provocative Therapy." In William

F. Fry and Waleed A. Salameh, eds., *Handbook of Humor and Psychotherapy: Advances in the Clinical Use of Humor*, pp. 81–106. Sarasota, Fla: Professional Resource Exchange.

Farrelly, Frank and S. Matthews. 1981. "Provocative Therapy." In R. J. Corsini, ed., *Handbook of Innovative Psychotherapies*, pp. 678–93. New York: Wiley.

Ferriter, Michael. 1993. "Computer-Aided Interviewing in Psychiatric Social Work." *Computers in Human Services* 9, no. 1–2: 59–68.

Fischer, J. and H. Miller. 1973. "The Effect of Client Race and Social Class on Clinical Judgment." *Clinical Social Work Journal* 1, no. 2: 100–109.

Flaskerud, Jacquelyn and P. Y. Liu, 1991. "Effect of an Asian Client-Therapist Language Ethnicity and Gender Match on Utilization and Outcome of Therapy." *Community Mental Health Journal* 37, no. 1: 31–41.

Foran, Robert and Royston Bailey. 1968. *Authority in Social Casework*. London: Pergamon.

Fortune, Anne E. 1979. "Communication in Task-Centered Treatment." *Social Work* 24 (September): 390–96.

———. 1981. "Communication Processes in Social Work Practice." *Social Services Review* 55 (March): 93–128.

Freed, Anne O. 1988. "Interviewing Through an Interpreter." *Social Work* 33 (July–August): 315–18.

Freedberg, Sharon. 1989. "Self-Determination: Historical Perspectives and Effects on Current Practice." *Social Work* 39 (January): 33–38.

Freeman, Suzanne C. 1993. "Client-Centered Therapy with Diverse Populations: The Universal Within the Specific." *Journal of Multicultural Counseling and Development* 21, no. 4: 248–54.

Fremont, Suzanne and Wayne Anderson. 1986. "What Behavior Made Counselors Angry? An Explanatory Study." *Journal of Counseling and Development* 65 (October): 67–70.

———. 1988. "Investigation of Factors Involved in Therapists' Annoyance with Clients." *Professional Psychology: Research and Practice* 19, no. 3: 330–35.

Freud, Sigmund. 1959. "Fragments of an Analysis of a Case of Hysteria (1905)." *Collected Papers*, vol. 3. New York: Basic Books.

Fry, W. F. 1994. "The Biology of Humor." *Humor: International Journal of Humor Research* 7, no. 2: 111–26.

Fry, W. F. and W. A. Salameh, eds. 1987. *Handbook of Humor and Psychotherapy: Advances in the Clinical Use of Humor*. Sarasota, Fla.: Professional Resource Exchange.

Fukuyama, Mary. 1990. "Toward a Universal Approach to Multicultural Counseling." *Counselor Education and Supervision* 30 (September): 6–17.

Gallant, D. M. et al. 1968. "Enforced Clinic Treatment of Paroled Criminal Alcoholics." *Quarterly Journal of Studies in Alcoholism* 29:77–83.

Gambrill, E. D., T. J. Stein, and C. E. Brown. 1984. "Social Service Use and Need

Among Gay/Lesbian Residents in San Francisco Bay Area." *Journal of Social Work and Human Sexuality* 3, no. 1: 51–69.

Garnets, Linda D. and Douglas C. Kimmel. 1993. "Lesbian and Gay Male Dimensions in the Psychological Study of Human Diversity." In L. D. Garnets and D. C. Kimmel, eds., *Psychological Perspectives on Lesbian and Gay Male Experiences*, pp. 1–51. New York: Columbia University Press.

Gaston, L. 1990. "The Concept of the Alliance and Its Role in Psychotherapy: Theoretical and Empirical Considerations." *Psychotherapy: Theory, Research, and Practice* 27, no. 2: 143–14.

Gelso, Charles S. and Jean A. Carter. 1985. "The Relationship in Counseling and Psychotherapy: Components, Consequences, and Theoretical Antecedents." *Counseling Psychologist* 13, no. 2: 155–243.

Gibelman, Margaret and Phillip H Schervish. 1993. *Who We Are*. Washington, D.C.: National Association of Social Workers.

Giles, Howard et al. 1992. "Intergenerational Talk and Communication with Older People." *International Journal of Aging and Human Development* 34, no. 4: 271–97.

Gitterman, Alex. 1989. "Testing Professional Authority and Boundaries." *Social Casework* 70 (March): 165–71.

Golan, Naomi. 1969. "How Caseworkers Decide: A Study of the Association of Selected Applicant Factors with Workers' Decisions in Admission Services." *Social Service Review* 43 (September): 286–96.

Gonsiorek, J. 1982. "Results of Psychological Testing on Homosexual Populations." *American Behavioral Scientist* 25 (March–April): 385–96.

Goodman, Gail S. and Vicki S. Helgeson. 1986. "Child Sexual Assault: Children's Memory and the Law." In L. E. Walker, ed., *Handbook on Sexual Abuse of Children*, pp. 109–36. New York: Springer.

Goodman, J. 1983. "How to Get More Mileage Out of Your Life." In P. McGhee and J. H. Goldstein, eds., *Handbook of Humor Research*, pp. 1–21. New York: Springer-Verlag.

Gourse, Judith E. and Martha W. Chescheir. 1981. "Authority Issues in Treating Resistant Families." *Social Casework* 62 (February): 67–73.

Grater, Harry A. 1964. "Client Preferences for Affective or Cognitive Counselor Characteristics and First Interview Behavior." *Journal of Counseling Psychology* 11, no. 3: 248–50.

Greenberg, Leslie S., Robert K. Elliott, and Germain Lietaer. 1994. "Research on Experiential Psychotherapies." In Allen E. Bergin and Sol L. Garfield, eds., *Handbook of Psychotherapy and Behavior Change*, 4th ed., pp. 509–39. New York: Wiley.

Greenberg, Lisa. 1990. "Self-Disclosure in Psychotherapy: Working with Older Adults." In B. Stricker and M. Fisher, eds., *Self-Disclosure in the Therapeutic Relationship*, pp. 175–189. New York: Plenum.

Greene, Michele G. et el. 1994. "The Effects of the Presence of a Third Person on the Physician—Older Patient Medical Interview." *Journal of the American Geriatric Society* 42:413–19.

Greenhouse, Linda. 1996. "Justices Uphold Psychotherapy Privacy Rights." *New York Times,* June 14, pp. 1A, 13A.

Grinnel, Richard and Nancy S. Kyte. 1975. "Environmental Modification." *Social Work* 20 (July): 313–16.

Gurman, Alan S. 1977. "The Patient's Perception of the Therapeutic Relationship." In A. S. Gurman and A. M. Razim, eds., *Effective Psychotherapy: A Handbook of Research,* pp. 503–43. New York: Pergamon.

Guy, James D., Catherine K. Brown, and Paul L Poelstra. 1992. "Safety Concerns and Protective Measures Used by Psychotherapists." *Professional Psychology: Research and Practice* 23, no. 5: 421–23.

Haase, Richard F. and Dominic J. DiMattia. 1970. "Proxemic Behavior: Counselor, Administrator, and Client Preference for Seating Arrangement in Dyadic Interaction." *Journal of Counseling Psychology* 17, no. 4: 319–25.

Hackney, Harold L., Allen E. Ivey, and Eugene R. Oetting. 1970. "Attending Island and Hiatus Behavior: A Process Conception of Counselor and Client Interaction." *Journal of Counseling Psychology* 17, no. 4: 342–46.

Halberstadt, A. G. 1985. "Race, Socioeconomic Status, and Nonverbal Behavior." In A. W. Seigman and S. Feldstein, eds., *Multichannel Integration of Nonverbal Behavior,* pp. 227–66. Hillsdale, N.J.: Erlbaum.

Haldeman, Donald C. 1991. "Sexual Orientation Conversion for Gay Men and Lesbians: A Scientific Examination." In J. C. Gonsiorek and S. D. Weinrich, eds., *Homosexuality: Research Implications for Public Policy,* pp. 149–76. Newbury Park, Calif.: Sage.

Hall, Anthony. 1974. *The Point of Entry: A Study of Client Reception in the Social Services.* London: Allen and Unwin.

Hall, Judith A. and Michael C. Dorman. 1988. "What Patients Like About Their Medical Care and How Often They Are Asked: A Meta-Analysis of the Satisfaction Literature." *Social Science and Medicine* 27, no. 9: 935–39.

Halmos, Paul. 1966. *The Faith of the Counselors.* New York: Schocken.

Hamilton, Gordon. 1946. *Principles of Social Case Recording.* New York: Columbia University Press.

Hancock, Betsey L. and Leroy Pelton. 1989. "Home Visits: History and Function." *Social Casework* 70 (January): 21–28.

Hanna, J. 1984. "Black/White Nonverbal Preferences: Dance and Dissonance: Implication for Desegregation." In *Nonverbal Behavior Prospects, Applications, and Intercultural Insights,* pp. 373–409. Lewiston, N.Y.: Hogreje.

Harrigan, Jinni A. and Robert Rosenthal. 1986. "Nonverbal Aspects of Empathy and Rapport with Physician-Patient Interaction." In P. D. Blank, R. Buck, and R.

Rosenthal, eds., *Nonverbal Communication in the Clinical Context,* pp. 36–73. University Park: Pennsylvania State University Press.

Harrigan, Jinni A., Thomas E. Oxman, and Robert Rosenthal. 1985. "Rapport Expressed Through Nonverbal Behavior." *Journal of Nonverbal Behavior* 9 (summer): 95–109.

Haugaard, Jeffrey and N. Dickon Reppucci, 1988. *The Sexual Abuse of Children: A Comprehensive Guide to Current Knowledge and Intervention Strategies.* San Francisco: Jossey-Bass.

Hein, Eleanor, C. 1973. *Communication in Nursing Practice.* Boston: Little, Brown.

Heine, R. W. 1950. "The Negro Patient in Psychotherapy." *Journal of Clinical Psychology* 6 (October): 373–76.

Heppner, P. P. and C. D. Claiborn. 1989. "Social Influence Research in Counseling: A Review and a Critique." *Journal of Counseling Psychology Monographs* 36, no. 3: 365–87.

Heppner, P. P. and P. A. Frazier. 1993. "Social Psychological Processes in Psychotherapy: Extrapolating Basic Research to Counseling Psychology." In S. D. Brown and R. W. Lent, eds., *Handbook of Counseling Psychology,* 2d ed., pp. 161–75. New York: Wiley.

Herlihy, Barbara and Vernon L. Sheeley. 1987. "Privileged Communication in Selected Helping Professions: A Comparison Among Statutes." *Journal of Counseling and Development* 65 (May): 479–83.

Hess, Mary. 1995. "Kelly Michaels Wants Her Innocence Back." *New York Times Magazine,* September 10, pp. 37–41.

Ho, David Y. F. 1995. "Internalized Culture, Culturocentrism, and Transcendence," *Counseling Psychologist* 23, no. 1: 4–24.

Hochschild, Arlie R. 1983. *The Managed Heart: Commercialization of Human Feeling.* Berkeley: University of California Press.

Hodges, Kay. 1993. "Structured Interviews for Assessing Children." *Journal of Child Psychology and Psychiatry* 34, no. 1: 49–68.

Hollis, Florence. 1967. "Explorations in the Development of a Typology of Casework Treatment." *Social Casework* 48 (June): 338–49.

Horton, Judith A. et al. 1995. "Touch in Psychotherapy: A Survey of Patients' Experiences." *Psychotherapy: Theory, Research, and Practice* 32, no. 3: 443–57.

Horvath, A. O. and L. S. Greenberg. 1994. *The Working Alliance: Theory, Research, and Practice.* New York: Wiley.

Horvath, A. O. and L. Luborsky. 1993. "The Role of the Therapeutic Alliance in Psychotherapy." *Journal of Counseling Psychology* 61, no. 4: 561–73.

Horvath, A. O. and B. D. Symonds. 1991. "Relation Between Working Alliance and Outcome in Psychotherapy: A Meta-Analysis." *Journal of Counseling Psychology* 38, no. 2: 139–49.

Hubble, M. A. and C. J. Gelso. 1978. "Effect of Counselor Attire on an Initial Interview." *Journal of Counseling Psychology* 25, no. 6: 581–84.

Hutchison, Elizabeth D. 1987. "Use of Authority in Direct Social Work Practice with Mandated Clients." *Social Service Review* 61 (December): 581–98.

Hyman, Herbert H. 1954. *Interviewing in Social Research.* Chicago: University of Chicago Press.

Irueste-Montes, Ana M. and Francisco Montes. 1988. "Court-Ordered Versus Voluntary Treatment of Abusive and Neglectful Parents." *Child Abuse and Neglect* 12, no. 1: 33–39.

Jacobson, Wendy E. 1991. "Child Abuse and the Courts: Is McMartin the Best We Can Do?" *Social Thought* 17, no. 1: 12–21.

Janis, Irving L. 1983. *Short-Term Counseling: Guidelines Based on Recent Research.* New Haven, Conn.: Yale University Press.

Jayaratne, S. et al. 1992. "Workers' Perceptions of Effectiveness and Minority-Relevant Education as a Function of Worker and Client Ethnicity." *Journal of Teaching in Social Work* 6, no. 1: 93–116.

Jensen, Jay P. and Allen E. Bergin. 1988. "Mental Health Values of Professional Therapists: A National Interdisciplinary Survey." *Professional Psychology: Research and Practice* 19, no. 3: 290–97.

Johnston, Norman. 1956. "Sources of Distortion and Deception in Prison Interviewing." *Federal Probation* 20, no. 1: 43–48.

Jones, David P. H. 1992. *Interviewing the Sexually Abused Child.* London: Gaskel.

Jones, David P. H. and Mary McQuiston. 1986. *Interviewing the Sexually Abused Child,* 2d ed. Denver, Colo.: C. Henry Kempe National Center for the Prevention and Treatment of Child Abuse and Neglect.

Jones, Mary, Renee Neuman, and Ann W. Shyne. 1976. *A Second Chance for Families: Evaluation of a Program to Reduce Foster Care.* New York: Child Welfare League of America.

Kadushin, A. and Judith Martin. 1988. *Child Welfare Services.* New York: Macmillan.

Kadushin, Goldie and Kulys, Regina. 1993. "Discharge Planning Revisited: What Do Social Workers Actually Do in Discharge Planning? *Social Work* 38 (November): 713–26.

Kagle, Jill D. 1984. *Social Work Records.* Homewood, Ill.: Dorsey.

——. 1987. "Recording in Direct Practice." In Anne Minahan et al., eds., *Encyclopedia of Social Work,* 18th ed., pp. 463–87. Silver Spring, Md.: National Association of Social Workers.

——. 1993. "Record-Keeping Directions for the 1990s." *Social Work* 38 (March): 190–96.

——. 1995. "Recording." In R. L. Edwards, ed., *Encyclopedia of Social Work*, 19th ed., pp. 2027–33. Washington, D.C.: National Association of Social Workers Press.

Kagle, Jill D. and Sandra Kopels. 1994. "Confidentiality After *Tarasoff.*" *Health and Social Work* 9, no. 3: 217–22.

Kahn, Alfred J. et al. 1966. *Neighborhood Information Centers: A Study and Some Proposals.* New York: Columbia University School of Social Work.

Kassell, Suzanne D. and Rosalie A. Kane. 1980. "Self-Determination Dissected." *Clinical Social Work Journal* 8, no. 3: 161–78.

Kenmore, Thomas K. 1987. "Negotiating with Clients: A Study of Clinical Practice Preference." *Social Service Review* 61 (March): 132–43.

Kertay, Les and Susan L. Reviere. 1993. "The Use of Touch in Psychotherapy: Theoretical and Ethical Considerations." *Psychotherapy* 30, no. 1: 32–40.

Kinsey, Alfred, Wardell Pomeroy, and Clyde Martin. 1948. *Sexual Behavior in the Human Male.* Philadelphia: Saunders.

Klienman, Sherryl. 1981. "Making Professionals into Persons: Discrepancies Between Traditional and Humanistic Expectations of Professional Identity." *Sociology of Work and Occupations* 8, no. 1: 61–87.

Knapp, Mark L. 1973. "The Rhetoric of Goodbye: Verbal and Nonverbal Correlates of Human Leave Taking." *Speech Monographs* 40 (August): 182–98.

Koeske, Gary F. 1993. "The Effect of the Professional Identification of the Therapist on the Perceived Recovery of the Client." *Journal of Social Services Research* 17, no. 1–2: 119–33.

Komarovsky, Mirra. 1967. *Blue Collar Marriage.* New York: Random House.

Kopels, S. and J. Kagle. 1993. "Do Social Workers Have a Duty to Warn?" *Social Service Review* 67 (March): 101–26.

Krause, Robert M. 1987. "The Role of the Listener: Addressee Influences on Message Formulation." *Journal of Language and Social Psychology* 6, no. 2: 81–98.

Kroth, Jerome A. 1979. *Child Sexual Abuse: Analysis of a Family Therapy Approach.* Springfield, Ill.: C. C. Thomas.

Kubie, Lawrence. 1971. "The Destructive Potential of Humor in Psychotherapy." *American Journal of Psychiatry* 127, no. 1 : 861–86.

Lamb, Michael E. 1994. "The Investigation of Child Sexual Abuse: An International Interdisciplinary Consensus Statement." *Family Law Quarterly* 28, no. 1: 151–61.

Lambert, Michael J. and Allen E. Bergin. 1994. "The Effectiveness of Psychotherapy." In Allen E. Bergin and Sol L. Garfield, eds., *Handbook of Psychotherapy and Behavior Change,* 4th ed., pp. 143–89. New York: Wiley.

Larke, Jerry. 1985. "Compulsory Treatment: Some Practical Methods of Treating the Mandated Client." *Psychotherapy: Theory, Research, and Practice* 22, no. 2: 262–67.

——. 1991. "Some Practical Methods of Treating the Mandated Client." In George A. Harris, ed., *Tough Customers: Counseling the Unwilling Client,* pp. 12–24. Laurel, Md.: American Correctional Association.

Laumann, Edward O. et al. 1994. *The Social Organization of Sexuality: Sexual Practices in the United States.* Chicago: University of Chicago Press.

Lease, Suzanne H., Pamela A. Cogdal, and Davis Smith. 1995. "Counseling Expectancies Related to Counselors' Sexual Orientation and Clients' Internalized Homophobia." *Journal of Gay and Lesbian Psychotherapy* 2, no. 3: 51–65.

Leong, Frederick, Nicole S. Wagner, and Shiraz P. Tata. 1995. "Racial and Ethnic

Variations in Help-Seeking Attitudes." In Joseph G. Ponterotto et al., eds., *Handbook of Multicultural Counseling*, pp. 415–38. Thousand Oaks, Calif.: Sage.

LeVay, Simon. 1994. *The Sexual Brain*. Cambridge, Mass.: MIT Press.

Levine, Jacob. 1977. "Humor as a Form of Therapy." In Anthony J. Chapman and Hugh C. Foot, eds., *It's a Funny Thing, Humor: International Conference on Humor and Laughter*, pp. 127–39. New York: Pergamon.

Lewin, Tamar. 1996. "Question of Privacy Roils Arena of Psychotherapy." *New York Times*, May 22, pp. 1, A8.

Lindenthal, Jacob L. 1988. "Social Workers' Management of Confidentiality." *Social Work* 33 (March–April): 157–58.

Lloyd, Arthur P. 1987. "Multicultural Counseling? Does It Belong in a Counselor Education Program?" *Counselor Education and Supervision* 26 (March): 164–67.

Lloyd, Robin M. 1992. "Negotiating Child Sexual Abuse: The Interactional Character of Investigative Practices." *Social Problems* 39, no. 2: 109–24.

Lomranz, J. and A. Shapiro. 1974. "Communication Patterns of Self-Disclosure and Touching Behavior." *Journal of Psychology* 88, no. 2: 223–27.

Longres, John F. 1991. "Toward a Status Model of Ethnic Sensitive Practice." *Journal of Multicultural Social Work* 1, no. 1: 41–56.

Luborsky, L. 1994. "Therapeutic Alliance as Predictors of Psychotherapy Outcomes: Factors Explaining Predictive Success." In A. O. Horvath and L. S. Greenberg, eds., *The Working Alliance: Theory, Research, Practice*, pp. 38–50. New York: Wiley.

Luborsky, L. et al. 1985. "Therapist Success and Its Determinants." *Archives of General Psychiatry* 42 (June):603–10.

Luborsky, L. and A. H. Auerbach. 1985. "The Therapeutic Relationship in Psychodynamic Psychotherapy: The Research Evidence and Its Meaning for Practice." In R. E. Hales and A. S. Francis, eds., *Psychiatry Update: American Psychiatric Association Annual Review*, vol. 4, pp. 550–61. Washington, D.C.: American Psychiatric Press.

Lurie, Alison. 1981. *The Language of Clothes*. New York: Random House.

MacFarlane, Kee and Sandy Krebs. 1986. "Technique for Interviewing and Evidence Gathering." In K. MacFarlane and J. Waterman, eds., *Sexual Abuse of Young Children*, pp. 67–100. New York: Guilford.

Mahl, George F. 1968. "Gestures and Body Movements in Interviews." In John M. Shlien, ed., *Research in Psychotherapy: Proceedings of the Third Conference*, pp. 295–346. Washington, D.C.: American Psychological Association.

Mahl, George F. and S. V. Kasl. 1965. "The Relationship of Disturbances and Hesitations in Spontaneous Speech to Anxiety." *Journal of Personality and Social Psychology* 1:425–33.

Mahoney, M. J. and K. Patterson. 1993. "Changing Theories of Change: Recent Developments in Counseling." In S. D. Brown and R. W. Lent, eds., *Handbook of Counseling Psychology*, 2d ed., pp. 673–89. New York: Wiley,

Maletsky, Barry M. 1980. "Self-Referred Versus Court Referred Sexually Deviant Patients: Success with Assisted Covert Sensitization." *Behavior Therapy* 2 (June): 306–14.

Maluccio, Anthony N. 1979. *Learning from Clients: Interpersonal Helping as Viewed by Clients and Social Workers.* New York: Free Press.

Margolis, Marvin, Henry Krystal, and S. Siegel. 1964. "Psychotherapy with Alcoholic Offenders." *Quarterly Journal of Studies on Alcoholism* 25:85–99.

Martell, Chris. 1994. "A Bond of Love Rediscovered." *Wisconsin State Journal,* May 13, DayBreak sec., p. 1E.

Martin, April. 1982. "Some Issues in the Treatment of Gay and Lesbian Patients." *Psychotherapy: Theory, Research, and Practice.* 19, no. 3: 341–48.

Martin, R. A. and J. P. Dobbin. 1988. "Sense of Humor, Hassles, and Immunoglobulin: Evidence of Stress-Moderating Effects of Humor." *International Journal of Psychiatry and Medicine* 18, no. 2: 93–105.

Marziali, E. and L. Alexander. 1991. "The Power of the Therapeutic Relationship." *American Journal of Orthopsychiatry* 61, no. 3: 383–91.

Mattinson, Janet. 1975. *The Reflection Process in Casework Supervision.* London: Tavistock Institute of Human Relations.

Mayer, John E. and Noel Timms. 1969. "Clash in Perspective Between Worker and Client." *Social Casework* 50 (January): 32–40.

Maynard, Douglas M. 1991. "Bearing Bad News in Clinical Settings." In B. Dervin and M. S. Voigt, eds., *Progress in Communication Sciences,* pp. 143–72. Norwood, N.J.: Ablex.

McDermott, D., L. Tyndall, and J. W. Lichtenberg. 1989. "Factors Related to Counsel of Preference Among Gays and Lesbians." *Journal of Counseling and Development* 68 (September–October): 31–35.

McGuire, John M., Phillip Toal, and Buron Blau. 1985. "The Adult Client's Conception of Confidentiality in the Therapeutic Relationship." *Professional Psychology: Research and Practice* 16, no. 3: 375–84.

McHenry, S. and J. W. Johnson (1993). "Homophobia in the Therapist and Gay or Lesbian Client: Conscious or Unconscious Collusions in Self-Hate." *Psychotherapy: Theory, Research, and Practice* 30, no. 1: 141–51.

Megdell, Jacob I. 1984. "Relationship Between Counselor-Initiated Humor and Client's Self-Perceived Attraction in the Counseling Interview." *Psychotherapy: Theory, Research, and Practice* 21, no. 4: 517–23.

Mehrabian, Albert. 1968. "Communication Without Words." *Psychology Today,* September, pp. 52–55.

Melton, Gary B. 1985. "Sexually Abused Children and the Legal System: Some Recommendations." *American Journal of Family Theory* 13, no. 1: 61–67.

Menninger, K. A. and P. S. Holzman. 1973. *Theory of Psychoanalytic Technique,* 2d ed. New York: Basic Books.

Merton, Robert K., Marjorie Fiske, and Patricia Kendall. 1956. *The Focused Interview.* Glencoe, Ill.: Free Press.

Mikkelsen, Edwin J., Thomas G. Gutheil, and Margaret Emens. 1992. "False Sexual Abuse Allegations by Children and Adolescents: Contextual Factors and Clinical Subtypes." *American Journal of Psychotherapy* 46, no. 4: 556–70.

Miller, David J. and Frank H. Thelen. 1987. "Confidentiality in Psychotherapy: History, Issues, and Research." *Psychotherapy* 24, no. 4: 704–11.

Miller, David J. and M. M. Thelen. 1986. "Knowledge and Beliefs About Confidentiality in Psychotherapy." *Professional Psychology: Research and Practice* 17, no. 1: 15–19.

Millstein, Susan G. 1987. "Acceptability and Reliability of Sensitive Information Collected via Computer Interviews." *Educational and Psychological Measurements* 47 (summer): 523–33.

Mindess, Harvey. 1976. "The Use and Abuse of Humor in Psychotherapy." In A. J. Chapman and H. C. Foot, eds., *Humor and Laughter: Theory, Research, and Applications,* pp. 331–41. New York: Wiley.

"Minnesota Says Abuse Case Was Improperly Conducted." *New York Times,* February 13, 1985, sec. I, p. 16.

Morgan, Marcia. 1995. *How to Interview Sexual Abuse Victims: Including the Use of Anatomical Dolls.* Thousand Oaks, Calif.: Sage.

Morganthau, Tom. 1995. "What Color Is Black?" *Newsweek,* February 13, pp. 63–72.

Morton, Thomas D. and Elizabeth W. Lindsey. 1986. "Toward a Model for Interpersonal Helping Skills: Use and Training in Public Welfare Practice." *Journal of Continuing Social Work Education* 4, no. 1: 18–24.

Moses, A. Elfin and Robert D. Hawkins. 1982. *Counseling Lesbian Women and Gay Men: A Life-Issues Approach.* St. Louis: Mosby.

Mullen, Edward S. 1969. "Differences in Worker Style in Casework." *Social Casework* 50 (June): 347–53.

Murphy, P. M., D. Cramer, and F. J. Lillie, 1984. "The Relationship Between Curative Factors Perceived by Patients in Their Psychotherapy and Treatment Outcome: An Exploratory Study." *British Journal of Medical Psychology* 57 (June):187–92.

Myers, John E. R. 1987. *Child Witness Law and Practice.* New York: Wiley.

Myers, John E. R., ed. 1993. *The Backlash: Child Protection Under Fire.* Thousand Oaks, Calif.: Sage.

National Association of Social Workers. 1967. "Model Statute Social Workers' Licensing Act." *National Association of Social Workers News.*

Nelsen, Judith. 1975. "Dealing with Resistance in Social Work Practice." *Social Casework* 56 (December): 587–92.

——. 1980. "Support a Necessary Condition for Change." *Social Work* 25 (September): 388–92.

Nelson-Jones, R. 1988. *Practical Counseling and Helping Skills,* 2d ed. New York: Holt, Rinehart, and Winston.

Nicholi, A. M. 1988. "The Therapist-Patient Relationship." In A. M. Nichol, ed., *The New Harvard Guide to Psychiatry,* pp. 7–28. Cambridge, Mass: Belnap-Harvard Press.

Nieves, Evelyn. 1994. "New Jersey Sex Abuse Case Ends with Charges Dropped." *New York Times,* December 3, sec. I, p. 25.

Norcross, John C. 1993. "Tailoring Relationship Stances to Client Needs: An Introduction." *Psychotherapy: Theory, Research, and Practice* 30, no. 3: 402–403.

Norris-Shortle, Carole and Ruth Cohen. 1987. "Home Visits Revisited." *Social Casework* 68 (January): 54–58.

Nugent, William R. 1992. "The Affective Impact of a Clinical Social Worker's Interviewing Styles: A Series of Single-Case Experiments." *Research on Social Work Practice* 2, no. 1: 6–27.

Nunnally, Elam and Carl Moy. 1989. *Communication Basics for Human Service Professionals.* Newbury Park, Calif.: Sage.

O'Hare, Thomas. 1996. "Court-Ordered Versus Voluntary Clients: Problem Differences and Readiness for Change." *Social Work* 4 (July): 417–22.

O'Neill, Molly. 1991. "Taming the Frontier of the Senses Using Aroma to Manipulate Moods." *New York Times,* November 27, pp. B1, B5.

Oldfield, R. C. 1951. *The Psychology of the Interview.* London: Methuen.

Orfanidis, Monica. 1972. "Children's Use of Humor in Psychotherapy." *Social Casework* 53 (March): 147–55.

Orlinsky, David E. and Kenneth I. Howard. 1967. "The Good Therapy Hour: Experimental Correlates of Patients' and Therapists' Evaluation of Therapy Session." *Archives of General Psychiatry* 16 (May): 621–32.

——. 1986. "Process and Outcome in Psychotherapy." In S. L. Garfield and A. E. Bergin, eds., *Handbook of Psychotherapy and Behavior Change,* 3rd ed., pp. 311–84. New York: Wiley.

Orlinsky, David E., Klaus Grawe, and Barbara K. Parks. 1994. "Process and Outcome in Psychotherapy—Noch Einmal." In Allen E. Bergin and Sol L. Garfield, eds., *Handbook of Psychotherapy and Behavior Change,* 4th ed., pp. 270–378. New York: Wiley.

Ornstein, Peter A., Betty N. Gordon, Deanna M. Larus. 1992. "Children's Memory for a Personally Experienced Event: Implications for Testimony." *Applied Cognitive Psychology* 6, no. 1: 49–60.

Ornston, Patricia et al. 1968. "Some Parameters of Verbal Behavior That Reliably Differentiate Novice from Experienced Psychotherapists." *Journal of Abnormal Psychology* 73, no. 3: 240–44.

Ornston, Patricia S., Domenic Cicchetti, and Alan P. Towbin. 1970. "Reliable Changes in Psychotherapy Behavior Among First-Year Psychiatric Residents." *Journal of Abnormal Psychology* 75, no. 1: 7–11.

Overton, Alice. 1959. *Clients' Observations of Social Work.* Mimeo. St. Paul, Minn.: Greater St. Paul Community Chest and Councils, Inc., Family-Centered Project.

Overton, Alice and Katherine Tinker. 1959. *Casework Notebook.* Mimeo. St. Paul, Minn.:, Greater St. Paul Community Chest and Councils, Inc., Family-Centered Project.

Parker, William. 1987. "Flexibility: A Primer for Multicultural Counseling." *Counselor Education and Supervision* 26 (March): 176–80.

Patterson, C. H. 1985. *The Therapeutic Relationship: Foundations for an Eclectic Psychotherapy.* Monterey, Calif.: Brooks/Cole.

Perlman, Helen H. 1979. *Relationship: The Art of Helping People.* Chicago: University of Chicago Press.

Pfouts, Jane H. and Gordon E. Rader. 1962. "The Influence of Interviewer Characteristics on the Initial Interview." *Social Casework* 43 (December): 548–52.

Pilsecker, Carleton. 1978. "Values: A Problem for Everyone." *Social Work* 23 (January): 54–57.

Pincus, Allen. 1970. "Reminiscence in Aging and Its Implications for Social Work Practice." *Social Work* 15 (July): 47–53.

Pithouse, Andrew. 1987. *Social Work: The Social Organization of an Invisible Trade.* Brookfield, Vt.: Gower.

Pohlman, Edward and Francis Robinson. 1960. "Client Reaction to Some Aspects of the Counseling Situation." *Personnel and Guidance Journal* 38 (March): 546–51.

Pollio, David E. 1995. "Use of Humor in Crises Intervention." *Families in Society: Journal of Contemporary Human Services* 76, no. 6: 376–84.

Ponterotto, Joseph G., William H. Anderson, and Ingrid Z. Grieger. 1986. "Black Students' Attitudes Toward Counseling as a Function of Racial Identity." *Journal of Multicultural Counseling and Development* 14, no. 2: 50–59.

Pope, Kenneth and Barbara Tabachnick. 1993. "Therapists' Anger, Hate, and Fear and Sexual Feelings: National Survey of Therapist Responses, Client Characteristics, Critical Events for Complaints and Training." *Professional Psychology: Research and Practice* 24, no. 2: 142–52.

Proctor, Enola K. and Larry E. Davis. 1994. "The Challenge of Racial Difference: Skills for Clinical Practice." *Social Work* 39 (May): 314–23.

Putsen, Robert W. 1985. "Cross-Cultural Communication: The Special Case of Interpreters in Healthcare." *Journal of the American Medical Association* 254, no. 23: 3344–48.

Ramsdell, Penny S. and Earl R. Ramsdell. 1994. "Counselor and Client Perceptions of the Effect of Social and Physical Contact on the Therapeutic Process." *Clinical Social Work Journal* 22, no. 1: 91–104.

Reamer, Frederic G. 1987. "Informed Consent in Social Work." *Social Work* 32 (September–October): 425–29.

———. 1995. *Social Work Values and Ethics.* New York: Columbia University Press.

Rees, Stuart and Allison Wallace. 1982. *Verdicts on Social Work.* London: Edward Arnold.

Reid, William S. 1978. *The Task-Centered System.* New York: Columbia University Press.

Reid, William S. and Barbara Shapiro. 1969. "Client Reaction to Advice." *Social Service Review* 43 (June): 165–73.

Reid, William S. and Ann Shyne. 1969. *Brief and Extended Casework.* New York: Columbia University Press.

Reinhold, R. 1990. "McMartin Case: Swept Away by Panic About Molestation." *New York Times,* January 24, pp. A1, A18.

Rhodes, M. D. 1992. "Social Work Challenges: The Boundaries of Ethics." *Families in Society: Journal of Contemporary Human Services.* 73, no. 1: 40–44.

Rhodes, Sonya L. 1978. "Communication and Interaction in the Worker-Client Dyad." *Social Service Review* 52 (March): 112–31.

Robitschek, C. G. and P. R. McCarthy (1991). "Prevalence of Counselor Self-Reference in the Therapeutic Dyad." *Journal of Counseling and Development* 69 (January–February): 218–21.

Rochlin, Martin. 1982. "Sexual Orientation of the Therapist and Therapeutic Effectiveness with Gay Clients." In John Gonsiorek, ed., *Homosexuality and Psychotherapy: Practitioners' Handbook of Affirmative Models,* pp. 21–31. New York: Haworth Press.

Roe, Donald L. and Connie E. Roe. 1991. "The Third Party: Using Interpreters for the Deaf in Counseling Situations." *Journal of Mental Health Counseling* 13, no. 1: 91–105.

Rogers, C. R. 1957. "The Necessary and Sufficient Conditions of Therapeutic Personality Change." *Journal of Consulting Psychology* 21, no. 2: 95–103.

Rooney, Ronald H. 1988. "Socialization Strategies for Involuntary Clients." *Social Casework* 69 (March): 131–40.

——. 1994. *Strategies for Work with Involuntary Clients.* New York City: Columbia University Press.

Rosen, Aaron and Elizabeth Mutschler. 1982. "Correspondence Between the Planned and Subsequent Use of Interventions in Treatment." *Social Work Research and Abstracts* 18 (summer): 28–34.

Rosenfeld, Alvin, B. Siegel, and R. Bailey. 1987. "Familial Bathing Patterns: Implications for Cases of Alleged Molestation and Pediatric Practice." *Pediatrics* 79 (February): 224–29.

Rosenheck, Robert, Alan Fontana, and Cheryl Cottrol. 1995. "Effect of Clinician-Veteran Racial Pairing in the Treatment of Posttraumatic Stress Disorder." *American Journal of Psychiatry* 152, no. 4: 555–63.

Rosenheim, Eliyahu and Gabriel Golan. 1986. "Patient's Reaction to Humorous Interventions in Psychotherapy." *American Journal of Psychiatry* 50, no. 2: 110–24.

Rothman, Jack et al. 1996. "Client Self-Determination and Professional Intervention: Striking a Balance." *Social Work* 4 (July): 396–406.

Ruesch, Jurgen and Weldon Kees. 1956. *Nonverbal Communication: Notes on the Visual Perception of Human Relations.* Berkeley: University of California Press.

Ryan, Mary S. 1966. *Clothing: A Study in Human Behavior.* New York: Holt, Rinehart, and Winston.

Saarni, C. and M. Lewis. 1993. "Deceit and Illusion in Human Affairs." In M. Lewis and C. Saarni, eds., *Lying and Deception in Everyday Life*, pp. 1–29. New York: Guilford.

Sainsbury, Eric. 1975. *Social Work with Families*. London: Routledge and Kegan Paul.

Scheflen, Albert F. 1964. "The Significance of Posture in Communication Systems." *Psychiatry* 27 (May): 316–31.

Schlesinger, Herbert J. 1994. "How the Analyst Listens: The Presages of Interpretation." *International Journal of Psychoanalysis* 75 (February): 31–37.

Schottenfeld, Richard S. 1989. "Involuntary Treatment of Substance Abuse Disorders: Impediments to Success." *Psychiatry* 52 (May): 197–209.

Schulman, Eveline D. 1974. *Intervention in Human Services*. St. Louis: Mosby.

Schutz, William C. 1967. *Joy*. New York: Grove Press.

Schwartz, A. Y., E. W. Gottesman, F. D. Perlmutter. 1988. "Blackwell: A Case Study in Feminist Administration." *Administration in Social Work* 12, no. 2: 5–15.

Segal, Daniel L., Michael Hersen, and Vincent B. Van Hesselt. 1994. "Reliability of the Structured Clinical Interview for DSM III-R: An Evaluative Review." *Comprehensive Psychiatry* 35, no. 4: 316–27.

Senger, Harry. 1984. "First Name or Last? Addressing the Patient in Psychotherapy." *Comprehensive Psychiatry* 25, no. 1: 38–43

Sexton, Thomas L. and Susan C. Whiston. 1994. "The Status of the Counseling Relationship: An Empirical Review, Theoretic Implications, and Research Directions." *Counseling Psychologist* 22, no. 1: 6–77.

Sgroi, Suzanne, Frances S. Porter, and Linda C. Blick. 1982. "Validation of Child Sexual Abuse." In S. Sgroi, eds., *Handbook of Clinical Intervention in Child Sexual Abuse*, pp. 39–79. Lexington, Mass.: Lexington Books.

Shamroy, Jerilyn A. 1987. "Interviewing the Sexually Abused Child with Anatomically Correct Dolls." *Social Work* 32 (March–April): 165–66.

Shaugnessy, Michael and T. M. Wadsworth. 1992. "Humor in Counseling and Psychotherapy: A Twenty-Year Retrospective." *Psychological Reports* 70 (June): 755–62.

Shepard, Marin and Margerie Lee. 1970. *Games Analysts Play*. New York: Putnam.

Sherman, Edmund. 1991. *Reminiscence and the Self in Old Age*. New York: Springer.

Sherman, Edmund et al. 1973. *Services to Children in Their Own Home: Its Nature and Outcome*. New York: Child Welfare League of America.

Shulman, Lawrence. 1977. *A Study of the Helping Process*. Vancouver, Canada: University of British Columbia.

——. 1991. *Interactional Social Work Practice*. Itasca, Ill.: Peacock Press.

Shulman, Rena. 1954. "Treatment of the Disturbed Child in Placement." *Jewish Social Service Quarterly* 30, no. 3: 315–22.

Simon, Judith. 1988. "Criteria for Therapist Self-Disclosure." *American Journal of Psychotherapy* 42, no. 3: 404–15.

——. 1990. "Criteria for Therapist Self-Disclosure." In G. Stricker and M. Fisher, eds., *Self-Disclosure in the Therapeutic Relationship*, pp. 207–24. New York: Plenum.

Siporin, Max. 1984. "Have You Heard the One About Social Work Humor?" *Social Casework* 65 (October): 459–64.

Socor, B. J. 1989. "Listening for Historical Truth: A Relative Discussion." *Clinical Social Work Journal* 17, no. 2: 103–15.

Stein, Terry. 1993. "Overview of Developments in Understanding Homosexuality." In Jim Oldham, M. B. Riba, and A. Tasman, eds., *Review of Psychiatry*, vol. 12, pp. 9–40. Washington, D.C.: American Psychiatric Press.

Stiles, W. B., D. Shapiro, and R. Elliot. 1986. "Are All Psychotherapies Equivalent?" *American Psychologist* 4, no. 2: 165–80.

Stone, George C. 1979. "Patient Compliance and the Role of the Expert." *Journal of Social Issues* 35, no. 1: 34–59.

Strupp, Hans H. and Lisa M. Najavits. 1994. "Difference in Effectiveness of Psychodynamic Therapists: A Process Outcome Study." *Psychotherapy: Theory, Research, and Practice* 31, no. 1: 114–23.

Strupp, Hans H., Ronald Fox, and Ken Lessler. 1969. *Patients View Their Psychotherapy.* Baltimore: Johns Hopkins University Press.

Sue, Stanley. 1988. "Psychotherapy Services for Ethnic Minorities: Two Decades of Research Findings." *American Psychologist* 43, no. 4: 301–308.

Sue, Stanley, Nolan Zane, and Kathleen Young. 1994. "Psychotherapy with Culturally Diverse Populations." In Allen E. Bergin and Sol L. Garfield, eds., *Handbook of Psychotherapy and Behavior Change*, 4th ed., pp. 783–812. New York: Wiley.

Sullivan, Harry Stack. 1954. *The Psychiatric Interview.* New York: W. W. Norton.

Tannen, Deborah. 1990. *You Just Don't Understand: Women and Men in Conversation.* New York: Appleton-Century-Croft.

Tobin, Sheldon and Joseph D. Gustafson. 1987. "What Do We Do Differently with Elderly Clients?" *Journal of Gerontological Social Work* 10, no. 34: 107–21.

Troiden, Richard. 1993. "The Formation of Homosexual Identities." In L. D. Garnets and D. C. Kimmel, eds., *Psychological Perspectives on Lesbian and Gay Male Experiences*, pp. 191–217. New York: Columbia University Press.

United Nations. Department of Economic and Social Affairs. 1963 *Report on the World Social Situation.* New York: United Nations.

Urdang, Esther. 1979. "In Defense of Process Recording." *Smith College Studies in Social Work* 50 (November): 1–15.

Videka-Sherman, Lynn, 1988. "Meta-Analysis of Research on Social Work Practice in Mental Health." *Social Work* 33 (July–August): 325–38.

Vontress, Clemmont E. 1988. "The Existential Approach to Cross-Cultural Counseling." *Journal of Multicultural Counseling and Development* 16, no. 2: 73–82.

Walden, Theodore, Greta Singer, and Winifred Thomat. 1974. "Students as Clients: The Other Side of the Desk." *Clinical Social Work Journal* 2, no. 4: 279–96.

Walker, Ann G. and Amye R. Warren. 1995. "The Language of the Child Abuse Interview: Asking the Questions, Understanding the Answers." In Tara Ney, ed.,

True and False Allegations of Child Sexual Abuse, pp. 153–62. New York: Brunner/ Mazel.

Watkins, S. A. 1989. "Confidentiality and Privileged Communications: Legal Dilemma for Family Therapists." *Social Work* 34 (March): 133–36.

Webb, Allen P. and Patrick V. Riley. 1970. "Effectiveness of Casework with Young Female Probationers." *Social Casework* 51 (November): 566–72.

Wehrspann, William H., Paul D. Steinhauer, and Halina Klajner-Diamond. 1987. "Criteria and Methodology for Assessing Sexual Abuse Allegations." *Canadian Journal of Psychiatry* 32 (October): 615–23.

Weiner, Myron F. 1978. *Therapist Disclosure: The Use of Self in Psychotherapy.* Boston: Butterworths.

Weiss, Robert S. 1994. *Learning from Strangers: The Art and Method of Qualitative Interview Studies.* New York: Free Press.

Weiss, Y. and N. Elad. 1993. "Teaching Bedside Interviewing Skills in a Social Work Training Program." *Social Work in Health Care* 18, no. 3–4: 201–207.

Weller, Leonard and Elmer Luchterhand. 1969. "Comparing Interviews and Observations on Family Functioning." *Journal of Marriage and the Family* 31 (February): 115–22.

Wells, Tricia. 1994. "Therapist Self-Disclosure: Its Effects on Clients and the Treatment Relationships." *Smith College Studies in Social Work* 65 (November): 23–41.

Wharton, A. S. 1993. "The Affective Consequences of Service Work: Managing Emotion on the Job." *Work and Occupations* 20, no. 2: 205–32.

Whitley, Bernard E. 1979. "Sex Roles and Psychotherapy: A Current Appraisal." *Psychological Bulletin* 86, no. 6: 1309–21.

Williams, Rosemary A. 1982. "Client Self-Determination in Social Casework: Fact or Fancy? An Exploratory Study." *Australian Social Work* 35 (September): 27–34.

Willison, Beverly G. and Robert L. Masson. 1986. "The Role of Touch in Therapy: An Adjunct to Communication." *Journal of Counseling and Development* 64 (April): 497–500.

Wisniewski, J. J. and B. G. Toomey, 1987. "Are Social Workers Homophobic?" *Social Work* 32 (September–October): 454–55.

Wolberg, Lewis. 1954. *Techniques of Psychotherapy.* New York: Grune and Stratton.

Wolfe, D. et al. 1980. "The Importance of Adjudication in the Treatment of Child Abusers: Some Preliminary Findings." *Child Abuse and Neglect* 4, no. 2: 127–35.

Wood, Barbara. 1996. "Semistructured Child Sexual Abuse Interviews: Interview and Child Characteristics Related to Credibility of Disclosure." *Child Abuse and Neglect* 20, no. 1: 81–91.

Woods, Leonard. 1988. "Home-Based Family Therapy." *Social Work* 33 (May–June): 211–14.

Woods, Mary E. and Florence Hollis. 1990. *Casework: A Psychosocial Theory,* 4th ed. New York: McGraw-Hill.

Yarrow, Marian R., John D. Campbell, and Roger V. Burton. 1964. "Reliability of Maternal Retrospection: A Preliminary Report." *Family Process* 3, no. 1: 207–18.

Young, J. Gerald et al. 1987. "Research on the Clinical Interview." *Journal of the American Academy of Child and Adolescent Psychiatry* 26, no. 5: 613–20.

Yuille, John C. et al. 1993. "Interviewing Children in Sexual Abuse Cases." In Gail S. Goodman and Bette L. Bottoms, eds., *Child Victims, Child Witnesses: Understanding and Improving Testimony,* pp. 95–115. New York: Guilford.

Zadik, Y. 1993. "Breaking Confidentiality Survey." *Medicine and Law* 12, no. 35: 257–62.

Index

Abrupt transition, 156

Abstraction level, questions and, 243

Abuse of child, *see* Child sexual abuse interview

Accenting, nonverbal communication for, 312

Acceptance, in client-worker relationship, 104–8

Accountability, of interviewer, 9; confidentiality and, 121; recording for, 282–83

Address, forms of, 89–90; with aged clients, 328

Adoption interview, 13

Advice: guidelines in offering, 212–13; as intervention, 208–13, 230, 231

Advocacy interview, 389, 392

Affect blends, 305

African American client: African American interviewer and, 323–26; white interviewer and, 323–26

Aged client, 327–31

Ageism, 328

Agency, 80; advantages of, 81; areas covered by, 14; assessment interview required by, 16; client's attitude toward, 71–72; client's decision to contact, 69; content of interview defined by, 12; interviewer behavior and, 67; location of, 71–72; physical accessibility of, 71; physical appearance of, 71–72; receptionist of, 73–74; referral to, 229; selecting and locating, 69–71; waiting room of, 74

AIDS, 334, 336

Alcoholic Anonymous, 337–38

Alternative questions, 263–64

American Sign Language (ASL), 350–51

Amphetamines (speed), signs of use of, 303

Amplification, nonverbal communication for, 311

Anatopolsky, C., 105

Anger, of mandated client, 362–63

Antecedents, questions classified by, 244

Anticipating, nonverbal communication for, 311

Appraisal interview, *see* Assessment interview

Aristotle, 293

Articulation, of speech, 299

Artifactual communication, 291–94

Assessment interview, 13, 15, 16, 137, 389, 392; example of, 418–21

Attending behavior, 137–39; eye contact and, 306–7; listening and, 6–7, 51–52

Attitude, with questions, 261

Authenticity: in client-worker relationship, 111–13; interviewer self-disclosure and, 190, 192

Authority, *see* Power

Back-channel responses, 36

Background: of client, 66–67; of interviewer, 67–69

Bad news interview, 202–3

Beginning interview, *see* Client-worker relationship

Bias: artifactual communication and, 293; questions and, 250–51; *see also* Stereotypes

Body language, 302–9; for attending behavior, 137–38; extremities and, 307–9; face and, 303–5; interviewer noting, 88–89; listening indicated by, 52; reflecting feelings and, 147; *see also* Eye contact; Nonverbal communication

Borge, Victor, 225

California Child Sexual Abuse Treatment Program, 358

Casework, 13

Catharsis: humor and, 219; interviewer self-disclosure provoking in client, 193

Change, effecting, 230

Child-abusing clients, confrontation with, 365; *see also* Child sexual abuse interview

Child as client, touching during interview and, 296; *see also* Child-abusing client; Child sexual abuse interview

Children of client, playroom for, 76

Child sexual abuse interview, 368–83; attitudinal approaches for, 369–72; coaching of children and, 369–70, 372; confidentiality and, 120, 121, 373–74; dolls used in, 381; false allegations and, 368–69, 381; funnel procedure for, 377; guidelines for, 372–83; home interview for, 83; honesty of children and, 369–70, 372; intrafamily sexual abuse and, 374; legal issues and, 370–71, 373–74, 375; neutrality in, 371, 372, 376, 380–81; nonverbal communication in, 379; open-ended questions for, 376, 377; setting for, 372, 374; suggestive questions for, 370–72, 373, 375, 376, 378–79; tapes for, 373; termination of, 382

Chronomics, nonverbal communication and, 289–91

Clarification, 173–75; humor and, 223; probes seeking, 246–47; reflection of feeling and, 149

Clarity probes, 246–47

Client: aged, 327–31; background of, 66–67; behavior of interviewer perceived by, 128–32; clothing of, 291–94; contribution of to competent interviewer, 397–98; decision to contact agency and, 69; decoding by, 31–32; encoding by, 33–34; image of interview of, 79–80, 395–97; individuality of, 122–24; inducting in role of interviewee, 95–96; interviewer addressing, 89–90; interviewer stereotyping, 123–24; interview preparation and, 71–72; knowledge of interviewer and, 393; listening difficulties and, 51; nonverbal communication by, 309–15; role of in client-worker relationship, 5–6, 127–28; self-determination of, 113–18; silence and, 214–15; as violent, 76; *see also* Child-abusing client; Child as client; Child sexual abuse interview; Involuntary client; Self-disclosure, client

Client-worker relationship, 18, 96, 99–134; acceptance in, 104–8; behavior versus feelings of interviewer in, 128–32; client factors in, 127–28; client self-determination in, 113–18; communication and, 34, 36; confidentiality in, 118–22; definition of, 99–100; developing positive, 103–27; empathy in, 108–11; example of establishing, 409–10; feelings in, 6; forms of address and, 89–90; genuineness and authenticity in, 111–13, 129; humor in, 224–25; individualizing client in, 122–24; as interactional event, 127–28; interest in, 124–26; interviewer characteristics and, 103; as nonreciprocal, 6; outcome and, 101–3, 132–33; respect in, 126; significance of positive, 100–3; transference in, 127; trust and, 127; warmth in, 126

Closed questions, 237–38, 239, 241–43, 252–53

Clothing, artifactual communication and, 291–94

Cocaine, signs of use of, 303

Coerced clients, *see* Involuntary client

Cognitive dissonance, behavior and attitude and, 132

Coming out, homosexuals and, 335, 336

Communication, 27–47; artifactual, 291–94; barriers to, 31, 32, 33–35, 39–42; chronomic, 289–91; client-worker

relationship and, 36; content in, 29, 44–45; decoding in, 28, 29, 31–32; defense mechanisms and, 32, 33; definition of, 27–29; encoding in, 28, 29, 30–31, 33–34; feedback in, 43–45; feelings in, 29, 30; immediacy and concreteness in, 41–42; jargon in, 40–41; latent content in, 44–45; manifest content in, 44–45; metacommunication and, 29–30; noise in, 31; nonverbal information regulating, 310; paralinguistics and, 298–300; patterns of, 9; phatic, 90; positive client-worker relationship and, 101; relationship in, 29; selective perception and, 32; setting and, 35–36; transmission in, 31, 36; understanding in, 36–38; words and meanings and, 39–40; *see also* Listening; Nonverbal communication; Paraphrasing

Completion probes, 245–46

Computers: recording and, 283; use of in interviews, 21–22

Concreteness, reflection of feelings and, 149

Confidence, sharing and, 34

Confidentiality, 8; child sexual abuse interview and, 120, 121, 373–74; in client-worker relationship, 118–22; interview setting and, 75, 76; receptionist violating, 73

Confirmatory strategy, questions and, 268

Confrontation, 183–90, 230; guidelines for, 190; humorous, 221, 222; with involuntary clients, 365

Content of interview, 4–5; reflection of, 144–45; *see also* Latent content; Manifest content

Contiguity, confrontation and, 186

Contradiction, nonverbal communication for, 312

Conversation: in beginning and end of
interview, 90–92; interview versus, 4–11
Court referral, *see* Involuntary client
Cousins, Norman, 218
Crack, signs of use of, 303
Cross-cultural interviewing, 321–54;
African American interviewer with
white client and, 326–27; aged client,
327–31; culturally sensitive interviewer
needed for, 322, 343, 345–48; with the
deaf, 350–51; individualizing in,
336–37; interpreters used in, 348–51;
interviewer/client matching and,
337–45; racial differences and, 323–27;
sexual orientation differences and,
331–36; white interviewer with African
American client and, 323–26
Cued transition, 155
Cultural diversity, *see* Cross-cultural
interviewing; Multiculturalism
Culturally sensitive social worker, 322,
343, 345–48
Curiosity, interest versus, 126

Data assessment, *see* Assessment
Data gathering, 137; example of, 410–17;
see also Techniques
Deaf person, interviewing, 350–51
Decision-making interview, *see*
Assessment interview
Decoding, in communication, 28, 29,
31–32
Defense mechanisms, as communication
barrier, 32, 33
Depth of interview, 163; reflection of
feeling and, 145; sensitivity to and
labeling of latent content and, 167
Developmental phase, *see* Problem-
solving interventions; Questions
Diagnostic and Statistical Manual of
Mental Disorders (DSM), 21, 22

Differentiated focus, questions classified
by, 243–44
Direct questions, 243, 262
Disclosure, *see* Self-disclosure,
interviewer
Displacement, as communication
barrier, 32
Dissonance theory, 132
Distance: for attending behavior, 138;
proxemics and, 300–2
Diversity, *see* Cross-cultural interviewing;
Multiculturalism
Dolls, child sexual abuse interview
using, 381
Double question, 254–55
Dress, *see* Clothing
Drug abuse, signs as evidence of, 303

Elderly, interviewing, 327–31
Emotions, *see* Feelings
Empathy: in client-worker relationship,
108–11; in cross-cultural interviewing,
347; in interviewers' preparation, 79;
with mandated client, 363–64;
matching client and interviewer and,
338; reflection of feelings and, 148
Emphasis, nonverbal communication
for, 311
Encoding, in communication, 28, 29,
30–31, 33–34
Encouragements, minimal, 139–41, 146,
245
Environmental modification, 228–29;
aged client and, 331
Ethics: dissimulation of feelings by
therapist and, 130–31; Social Work
Code of Ethics, 67, 118–19; *see also*
Confidentiality
Ethnic differences, *see* Cross-cultural
interviewing; Multiculturalism
Ethnic humor, 225

Etiquette: confrontation violating, 189; inhibition of thoughts violating, 33; interview suspending, 8–9; nonverbal communication and, 313; silence and, 213

Euphemisms, feelings and, 167

Evaluation, 279–80; example of, 423; *see also* Assessment interview

Expectations, listening and, 59–60

Exploration, 136, 230; *see also* Attending behavior; Techniques

Extremities, gesture cues from, 307–9

Eye contact, 305–7; for attending behavior, 138; interview termination signaled by, 273; with mandated client, 363

Face, gesture cues from, 303–5

Facilitating approach, with mandated clients, 361–62

Family conflict, home visit encountering, 84–85

Feedback: in communication, 43–45; in cross-cultural interviewing, 346–47; listening and, 51

Feelings: behavior of interviewer versus, 128–32; in client-worker relationship, 6; in communication, 29, 30; discouraging expression of, 168–69; euphemisms and, 167; facial gesturing showing, 303–5; identifying and calling attention to, 163–65; indirection and, 167; interviewing aged clients and, 330–31; nonverbal communication indicating, 310, 311; paralinguistics and, 299–300; reaching for, 163–69; reassurance and support and, 207; reflection of, 145–49; sanctioning, 165–67; self-disclosure and, 194

Feet, body language from, 308–9

Figures of speech, as intervention, 228

Fingers, body language from, 307–8

Food, offers of in home visit, 84

Freud, Sigmund, 219–20, 287

Freudian slips, 33

Fromm-Reichmann, Frieda, 179

Funnel procedure, for child sexual abuse interview, 377

Furniture, in interview room, 76

Garbled question, 255–56

Gay men, interviewing, 331–36

Gender: agency selection and, 70; touching during interview and, 296, 297

Gender differences: in eye contact, 307; in language, 40

Genuineness: in client-worker relationship, 111–13, 129; interviewer self-disclosure and, 112–13, 190, 197

Gerontological social worker, 17; aged client and, 327–31

Greeting, in interview, 90

Group membership: clothing and, 292; humor and, 225

Halo effect, 124

Hands, body language from, 307–8

Handshake, 90, 296

Head nodding, 141

Health maintenance organizations, confidentiality and, 121

Hearing, listening versus, 49–50

Hearing interpreter, for interviewing deaf person, 350–51

Hedge questions, 260

Heroin, signs of use of, 303

Heterosexism, 332

"Hmm-hmms," minimal encouragement from, 139–40

Home-based family treatment program, 82

Home interview, 80–85; for aged clients, 329; artifactual communication and, 291

Homework, interviewer assigning at interview termination, 278

Homophobia, 332, 334

Homophyly, matching of client and interviewer and, 7, 337–38

Homosexuality, as interview consideration, 331–36

"Horns effect," 124

Hospital, interview in, 86–87, 88

Hughes, Langston, 324

Humor, as intervention, 218–28

Huxley, Aldous, 104

Hypothetical probes, 263

Immediacy: confrontation and, 186; reflection of feelings and, 149

"Impasse" (Hughes), 324

Impression-management function, of nonverbal messages, 309

Indirection, feelings and, 167

Indirect projective questions, 263

Indirect questions, 243, 262

Individuality of client: cross-cultural client and, 336–37; interviewer respecting, 122–24

Inference, in interpretation, 178

Inflection, in speech, 299

Information-gathering interview, see Social study interview

Information sharing, 200–3, 308; humor in, 224; informed consent and, 120; with questions, 262

Informed consent, information sharing and, 120

Informed opposition, involuntary client and, 366

In-service training, interviewer behavior and, 68

Insight, humor and, 223

Institutions, interview in, 85–88; aged clients and, 329

Insurance companies, confidentiality and, 121

Intensity, of speech, 299

Interest, in client-worker relationship, 124–26

Interpretation, 175–82, 230; confrontation versus, 183–84; guidelines for, 182; humor for, 222

Interpreters, in cross-cultural interviewing, 348–51

Interruptions, transitional, 156–57

Interventions, 8; interviewer selecting, 6; listening and, 51; see also Problem-solving interventions; Questions; Techniques

Interview, 3–26; adoption, 13; advocacy, 389, 392; bad news, 202–3; common features of, 18–19; computers and, 21–22; content of, 4–5; conversation at beginning and end of, 90–92; conversation versus, 4–11; critique of complete, 407–23; definition of, 11–14; as diffuse, 14; interviewer preparing for, 76–77; length of, 52, 273; life space, 86; limitations of, 19–20; listening related to, 51–52; nonreciprocal relationship in, 5–6; parties involved in, 10–11; preinterview amenities, 88–92; preparation for, 71–72; professional norms in, 7–9; reciprocity and, 5–6, 397–98; series of, 18–19; small talk in, 90–92; social study, 13, 14, 15; start of, 88–96; structured, 7, 20–21, 230; therapeutic, 14–15, 16–17, 389; transition from opening phase to body of, 132–33; unique instance as concern of, 13; universal aspects of, 17–18; unstructured, 20, 21; waiting for,

74–75; *see also* Assessment interview;
Cross-cultural interviewing; Latent
content; Manifest content; Purpose of
interview; Setting of interview;
Termination phase
Interviewee, *see* Client
Interviewer, 14; accountability of, 9, 121,
282–83; addressing client, 89–90;
antithetical demands on, 394–95;
behavior versus feelings of, 128–32;
client addressing, 89; client's attitude
toward, 71; clients' contribution to
competence of, 397–98; client's image
of, 79–80, 395–97; clothing worn by,
293–94; competent, 389–405;
confidentiality issue and, 118–22;
content of interview selected by, 4–5;
culturally sensitive, 322, 343, 345–48;
etiquette suspended by, 8–9;
experienced versus inexperienced,
390–91; flexibility of, 390; genuineness
and authenticity of, 111–13, 129, 190,
192, 197; influence potential of, 101;
intelligence of, 390; interest shown by,
124–26; knowledge needed by, 391–94;
nonjudgmental attitude of, 104–8;
personality attributes of, 389–91;
preparation for interview by, 76–77;
professionalism and, 9, 67–68, 130;
respect shown by, 126; role of, 5–6,
79–80; stereotyping clients and,
123–24; stress of, 395; task of, 5; *see also*
Power of interviewer; Self-disclosure,
interviewer
Interview listening, social listening
versus, 52–56
Interview management functions, of
nonverbal messages, 309
Interview outline, 77–79
Intimacy, interviewer self-disclosure
and, 199

Involuntary client, 70, 355–67; aged
interviewee as, 328; anger of, 362–63;
confrontation with, 184, 365;
cooperation of, 365–66; definition of,
355–56; facilitating approach with,
361–62; helpfulness of interviewer for,
357–59; informed opposition and, 366;
mandated, 355–56; power with, 359,
364; referral of, 366–67; resistance and,
356; right versus ability to treat and,
357; self-determination of, 366; silence
and, 364–65; suggestions for
interviewing, 367; violence with, 363

James, William, 223
Jargon, miscommunication and, 40–41
Jewelry, artifactual communication, 293
Jordan, Minnesota sexual abuse "ring,"
368

Kinesics, *see* Body language
Knowledge: interviewer needing, 391–94;
value of for listening, 56–57

Lange, James, 132
Language barriers, in cross-cultural
interviewing, 348–51
Language, socioeconomic differences in,
39; *see also* Communication
La Rochefoucauld, 112, 219
Lateness, as nonverbal communication,
290
Latent content: in communication,
44–45; sensitivity to and labeling of,
167
Leading (suggestive) questions, 248–53
Leading (suggestive) questions: for child
sexual abuse interviews, 370–72, 373,
375, 376, 378–79
Lead-ins, with questions, 260–61
Legal issues: child sexual abuse interview

and, 370–71, 373–74, 375;
confidentiality, 119, 120–21; touching
during interview and, 297
Legs, body language from, 308–9
Lesbians, interviewing, 331–36
Life space interview, 86
Listening, 49–61; attending behavior for,
6–7, 51–52; conditions for good, 50–51;
distractions from, 53–56; errors in, 60;
expectations and, 59–60; guidelines
for, 57–60; hearing versus, 49–50;
interview and, 51–52; knowledge and,
56–57; social versus interview, 52–56;
stereotypes and, 58–59

McMartin nursery school case, 368
Mandated client, *see* Involuntary client
Manifest content, in communication,
44–45
Marijuana, signs of use of, 303
Matching, of client with interviewer,
337–45
Medical social worker, 17, 33
Metacommunication, 29–30; *see also*
Nonverbal communication
Metaphor, 228
Michaels, Margaret Kelly, 368
Minimal encouragements, 139–41, 146, 245
Modeling: as advice, 208; interviewer
self-disclosure and, 192
Model Statute Workers' Licensing Act, 11
Multiculturalism: agency selection and,
70; culturally sensitive social worker
and, 322, 343, 345–48; eye contact and,
307; humor and, 225; nonverbal
communication meaning and, 316;
proxemics and, 301; smell and, 295;
time concepts and, 290–91; touching
and, 295–96; voice qualities and, 299;
word meanings and, 39–40; *see also*
Cross-cultural interviewing

Mutational transition, 156

Names, *see* Address, forms of
Negative feelings, reflection of feeling
and, 149
Neutral settings, for interview, 81
Noise, in communication, 31
Nonjudgmental attitude, by interviewer,
104–8
Nonverbal communication, 30, 287–320,
330; advantages of, 289; from
artifactual communication, 291–94;
in child sexual abuse interview, 379;
from chronomics, 289–91; by client,
309–15; definition, 288; by interviewer,
313–15; interview room allowing for, 76;
interview termination signaled by, 273;
listening indicated by, 51–52; office
light and, 75; from paralinguistics,
298–300; problems in inferring
meanings from, 315–17; from
proxemics, 300–2; racial differences in,
326; significance of for interviewing,
309–15; from smell, 294–95; as support
intervention, 206, 207; from touch,
295–98; *see also* Body language
Note taking: after termination, 282–83;
during interview, 280–82
Nudging probes, *see* Completion probes

Observation, 19–20
Office: artifactual communication and,
291; self-disclosure via, 294
Office interviews, *see* Agency
Open-ended questions, 237–41, 242–43,
245, 247, 248; for child sexual abuse
interview, 376, 377
Opening question, of interview, 92–93
Outcome, client-worker relationship and,
101–3, 132–33
Outreach programs, 70

Overscheduling, 290

Paralinguistics, 298–300
Paraphrasing, 30, 137, 141–43, 149, 245;
    listening indicated by, 52; matching
    client and interviewer and, 338;
    reflecting and, 143, 144, 145–46, 148
Paternalism, client self-determination
    versus, 116–18
Pauses, silences versus, 213–14
Permanency planning movement, 82
Pets, home visit and, 83
Phatic communications, 90
Physical distance, with mandated client,
    363
Pitch, of speech, 298
Postinterview conversation, at
    termination phase, 276–78
Postinterview interview, 33
Posture, as whole body communication,
    303
Power of interviewer: advice-giving and,
    209; client self-disclosure and, 196;
    client-worker relationship and, 34;
    humor and, 226; involuntary clients
    and, 359, 364; lateness of interviewer
    and, 290; proxemics and, 301;
    questioning and, 252; silence and,
    214–15; touching during interview
    and, 296, 297
Praise, as support intervention, 206
Prefaces, with questions, 260–61
Preparation for interview: example of,
    407–9; homework by interviewer,
    76–77; interview outline for, 77–79;
    role image of interviewer and, 79–80
Primary groups, of client, 66
Prison, interview in, 85–87
Privacy, see Confidentiality
Privileged communication, social workers
    and, 121

Probing questions, 244–48, 262–63
Problem exploration phase, see
    Techniques
Problem-solving interventions, 173–234;
    advice, 208–13, 230, 231; changes in
    during sequence of interventions,
    231–32; empirical studies of, 229–32;
    environmental modification, 228–29,
    331; example of, 418–21; figures of
    speech, 228; humor, 218–28; see also
    Clarification; Confrontation;
    Information sharing; Interpretation;
    Self-disclosure, interviewer; Silence;
    Support
Problem-solving process, 136; see also
    Techniques
Professionalism, interviewer behavior
    and, 9, 67–68, 130
Projection, as communication barrier, 32
Projective questions, 263–64
Provocative therapy, humor and, 223–24
Proxemics, 300–2
Ptah-Hotep, Vizier, 132
Public assistance interview, 13
Purpose of interview, 4, 14–18; assessment
    interview, 16; content of, 11–12;
    example of establishing, 409–10;
    initial phase of interview clarifying,
    93–95; interview outline and, 77–79;
    for listening, 57; social study interview,
    15; therapeutic interview, 16–17

Qualifiers, with questions, 260
Questions, 136, 235–69; abstraction level
    and, 243; as advice, 209; with aged
    clients, 329; alternative, 263–64;
    antecedents and, 243; attitude used
    with, 261; biased, 250–51; for child
    sexual abuse interviews, 376; clarity
    probes, 246–47; closed, 237–38, 239,
    241–43, 252–53; completion probes,

245–46; confirmatory strategy and, 267; differential focus and, 243–44; direct, 243, 262; double, 254–55; formulation, 248–68; garbled, 255–56; hedge, 260; hypothetical probes, 263; indirect, 243, 262; indirect projective, 263; information offered with, 262; lead-ins with, 260–61; open-ended, 237–41, 242–43, 245, 247, 248, 376, 377; opening, 92–93; prefaces with, 260–61; preparation for asking, 265–68; probing, 244–48, 262–63; projective, 262–63; purpose of, 235–37; reaction probes, 247; responsibility and, 243; risks involved with, 260–61; selecting, 259; "why," 256–58; "yes or no," 253–54; *see also* Leading (suggestive) questions

Racial differences, between interviewer and interviewee, 323–27; *see also* Cross-cultural interviewing; Multiculturalism
Range of interview, 163
Rapport: confrontation and, 189; knowledge of interviewer and, 393; positive client-worker relationship and, 101
Reaction formation, as communication barrier, 32
Reaction probes, 247
Reassurance, 205–7, 230; *see also* Support
Receptionist, of agency, 73–74
Reciprocity effect, interviewer self-disclosure and, 192
Recovery, Inc., 337–38
Reference group: of client, 66; of interviewer, 67
Referral: agency selection and, 70; for environmental modification, 229; *see also* Involuntary client
Reflection, 137, 144–49, 230, 245; of

content, 144–45; of feeling, 145–49; paraphrasing and, 143, 144, 145–46, 148
Relationship, in communication, 29
Reminiscing, in interview with aged clients, 329
Repression, as communication barrier, 33
Resistance: as communication barrier, 33; involuntary client and, 356
Respect, in client-worker relationship, 126
Responsibility, questions and, 243
Reversional transition, 156
Review, after termination, 279–80
Role image, interview preparation and, 79–80

Sapir, Edward, 317
Sarcasm, 312
Scheduling interview, 72–73; for aged clients, 329; location of agency and, 71; negative attitude from, 70; overscheduling, 290; at termination phase, 275
School social worker, 17
Seating arrangements, proxemics and, 301–2
Selective perception, 32
Self-awareness, inappropriate feelings controlled by, 130
Self-censorship, 33
Self-determination of client: interviewer maximizing, 113–18; of involuntary client, 366
Self-direction, *see* Self-determination of client
Self-disclosure, client: confidentiality and, 119–20; interviewer self-disclosure encouraging, 192–93, 194–95; matching client and interviewer and, 338; power of interviewer and, 196
Self-disclosure, interviewer, 190–200; as

advice, 209; authenticity and, 112–13, 190, 192; dangers and disadvantages of, 194–200; feelings avoided in, 130; guidelines for, 198; matching client and interviewer and, 338; negative feelings and, 130; objectives of, 192–94; office for, 294

Setting of interview, 5, 10–11, 35–36, 75–76; of child sexual abuse interview, 372, 374; home interview, 80–85; hospitals, 80, 86–87, 88; institutions, 80, 85–88; life space interview, 86; neutral, 81; nonagency, 80–88; prison, 85–87; see also Agency

Sexually abused child, see Child sexual abuse interview

Sexual orientation, as interview consideration, 331–36

Shakespeare, William, 111, 292

Sign language interpreter, for interviewing deaf person, 350–51

Silence, as intervention, 213–18, 245; involuntary clients using, 364–65

Simile, 228

Skills, 136; see also Techniques

Small talk: in interview, 90–92; at termination phase, 277–78

Smell, nonverbal communication from, 294–95

Smooth transitions, 155

Social listening, interview listening versus, 52–56

Social service, definition of, 11

Social study interview, 13, 14, 15

Social work, definition of, 11–12

Social Work Code of Ethics, 67, 118–19

Social worker, see Interviewer

Social work interview, see Interview

Socioeconomic differences, see Cross-cultural interviewing; Multiculturalism

SOLER behavior, for attending behavior, 138

Speech, see Communication; Paralinguistics

Status, see Power of interviewer

Steering, referring versus, 229

Steering messages, as transitions, 155

Stereotypes: ageism and, 328; clients' stereotypes of interviewers and, 71; of culturally sensitive interviewers, 345; on homosexuality, 332–33; individualizing client versus, 123–24; listening and, 58–59; with nonverbal communication, 317; in voice qualities, 299; see also Bias

Stress, of interviewers, 395

Stress, in speech, 299

Structured Clinical Interview, for DSM III, 21

Structured interview, 7, 20–21, 230

Suggestions, as intervention, 208

Suggestive (leading) questions, 248–52; in child sexual abuse interview, 370–72, 373, 375, 376, 378–79

Sullivan, Harry Stack, 157, 267

Summarizing, 150–52; guidelines for, 152; interpretation and, 181–82; listening indicated by, 52; in termination phase, 276

Support, 205–7, 230; aged client and, 331; humor providing, 224; from touching during interview, 296

Supreme Court, on confidentiality of psychotherapy, 119

Tarasoff v. Board of Regents of the University of California, 120

Team approach, information sharing and, 120

Techniques, 135–71; definition of, 135; example of use of, 410–17; minimal encouragements, 139–41, 146, 245; *see also* Attending behavior; Feelings; Paraphrasing; Problem-solving interventions; Questions; Reflection; Summarizing; Transitions

Termination phase, 6, 271–84; of child sexual abuse interview, 382; example of, 422; guidelines for, 279; preparation for, 271; recording after, 282–83; reluctance of client and, 273–74; review and evaluation after, 279–80; summary and postinterview conversation at, 276–78; techniques for, 272–76

Therapeutic interview, 14–15, 16–17, 389

Therapeutic relationship, *see* Client-worker relationship

Third party, in attendance at interview with aged clients, 329–30

Time, chronomic communication and, 289–91

Time orientation, child sexual abuse interview and, 373

Timing of interview, 7, 232

Touch, 76, 295–98; handshake and, 90, 296

Transference: in client-worker relationship, 127; self-disclosure and, 200

Transitional interruptions, 156–57

Transitions, 152–53; cued (smooth), 155; guidelines for, 163; interviewee-initiated, 160–63; making, 155–56; mutational (abrupt), 156; nonverbal

signals for, 309; preparation for, 157–60; proxemics and, 301; reversional, 156; steering messages and, 155; transitional interruptions, 156–57

Transmission, in communication, 31, 36

Trust, in client-worker relationship, 126–27

Turn taking, nonverbal signals for, 309

Twain, Mark, 79

"Uh-huhs," minimal encouragement from, 139–40

Unstructured interview, 20, 21

Velocity, of speech, 298–99

Verbal following, for attending behavior, 138–39

Verbal reports, limitations of, 20

Violence, of client, 76

Visual sensations, *see* Body language

Vocalization, 30; *see also* Communication

Voice, *see* Communication; Paralinguistics

Waiting for interview, 74–75

Waiting room, 74

Warmth, in client-worker relationship, 126

Whitehead, Alfred North, 28

"Why" question, 256–58

Whyte, William F., 43

"Yes or no" question, 253–54